The Early History And Antiquities Of Wycombe In Buckinghamshire

John Parker

Alpha Editions

This Edition Published in 2020

ISBN: 9789354306266

Design and Setting By
Alpha Editions
www.alphaedis.com
Email - info@alphaedis.com

TO

THE RIGHT HONOURABLE

CHARLES ROBERT, BARON CARINGTON,

WHOSE INTEREST IN THE WELFARE AND PROSPERITY

OF WYCOMBE IS WELL KNOWN,

This Volume

IS

(WITH KIND PERMISSION)

DEDICATED

BY

THE AUTHOR,

WITH EVERY EXPRESSION OF RESPECT AND ATTACHMENT.

PREFACE.

ALTHOUGH Wycombe occupies the proud position of ranking amongst the most ancient of the Incorporated Towns in England, yet it is remarkable that no Chronicler has been raised up to record, at length, its early history and antiquities. The Reverend Thomas Langley* in 1797 published "The History and Antiquities of the Hundred of Desborough;" a work of considerable merit, and justly deserving great commendation. In 1847 Dr. Lipscombe published "The History and Antiquities of the County of Buckingham." And this was followed, in 1848, by Mr. H. Kingston's History of Wycombe, with recollections of his native Town. These works contain but brief and imperfect sketches of the early History of Wycombe. And the Author feels it due to himself to state, that, without detracting from the làbours of Dr. Lipscombe and Mr. Kingston, much of the reliable information found in the two latter works relating to Wycombe was furnished by himself, when he held the Office of Town Clerk to the Corporation.

These histories, while affording much valuable information, contain inaccuracies, which the Author has corrected ; and important omissions are supplied in the following work, which he trusts may prove not

---

* He was Rector of Whiston, Northamptonshire, and died July 28, 1801.

altogether uninteresting to the Antiquary, the Topographer, and the general reader. The sources from whence he has derived his information are chiefly, the muniments deposited in the Archives of the Wycombe Municipal Charity Trustees, the National Record Office, the British Museum, and the Bodleian Library.

It may be added, that the muniments of the Corporation, which were formerly deposited in the Church chest, were some years since examined, and a schedule of them made by the Author; and their investigation has considerably facilitated his researches and simplified his labours.

The Author has not deemed it expedient to encumber his pages with elaborate details, but simply to give a faithful, unvarnished, and concise History of Wycombe in the olden times. He is very sensible of the many imperfections of the Work, but trusts that it will meet with the indulgence and approval of the candid reader.

The Charters and Grants relating to the Borough, long since out of print, are introduced as an Appendix, including in it translations, not before published, of an Agreement in the Court of Westminster, the 10th of Henry III., between the Burgesses of Wycombe and Alan Basset. Also of a Charter of Confirmation, of Queen Mary; and an Office Copy of a Charter of Confirmation of King Charles II., granted "to the Forrens of Chiping Wickham and other places."

The Author very gratefully acknowledges his special obligations to his friend Edward J. Payne, Esquire, M.A., of Lincoln's Inn, Barrister-at-Law, and Fellow of University College, Oxford, for the valuable assistance rendered by him in the compilation of the Work.

WYCOMBE GUILDHALL AND HIGH STREET. 1772.

J. O. Griffits, Esq., Q.C., Recorder of Reading. 3 Copies.

Lieut.-Col. Creaton, 7, Sydney Place, Onslow Square, Brompton.

The Rev. Charles Lowndes, M.A., Hartwell Rectory, Aylesbury.

The Rev. Robert Chilton, M.A., Vicar of Wycombe. 2 Copies.

W. Lowndes, Esq., J.P., The Bury, Chesham.

A. Gilbey, Esq., J.P., Wooburn Park.

William Rose, Esq., J.P., Wycombe.

Arthur Vernon, Esq., J.P., Wycombe.

Thomas Wheeler, Esq. 3 Copies.

The Rev. James Poulter, M.A. 3 Copies.

Miss Wheeler, Wycombe. 3 Copies.

Edward Wheeler, Esq.

Mrs. Wheeler, Wycombe.

Henry S. Wheeler, Esq., Wycombe.

George Wheeler, Esq., Wycombe.

Mrs. Henry Wheeler, Beech Wood, Wycombe. 2 Copies.

Francis Wheeler, Esq., Wycombe. 2 Copies.

Miss Emma Wheeler.

T. B. Grove, Esq., Water Croft, Penn.

Matthew Harpley, Esq., Royal Horse Guards.

Owen Peel Wethered, Esq., Marlow.

Joseph A. Piggot, Esq., The Elms, Bedford.

A. H. C. Brown, Esq., J.P., Kingston, Tetsworth.

The Rev. H. T. Young, M.A., Mallard's Court, Stokenchurch.

James Watson, Esq., J.P., Langley House, near Slough.

H. M. Musgrave, Esq., 45, Holland Park, Kensington.

The Society of Antiquaries, Burlington House, Piccadilly. W. C. Knight Watson, Esq.

The Rev. John Hayden, Fairwood, Weybridge.

John Turner, Esq., Wycombe.

T. J. Reynolds, Esq., Wycombe.

Mrs. Lias.

D. Clarke, Esq., Town Clerk, Wycombe.

W. V. Baines, Esq., Wycombe.

W. Parker, Esq., Solicitor, Thame, Oxon.

Thos. Lucas, Esq., Wycombe. 3 Copies.

B. Lucas, Esq., Wycombe. 2 Copies.

Thos. Marshall, Esq., Solicitor, Wycombe.

Thomas Griffits, Esq., Wycombe.

Mr. Taunt, Wycombe.

J. M. Davenport, Esq., Solicitor, Oxford.

Mr. C. Pierce, Wycombe.

Mrs. Meres, Brunswick Villa, Kew Road, Kew Gardens.

Alfred Leadbetter, Esq., Wycombe.

Miss M. E. Carter, Allan Bank, Great Malvern.

H. J. Jenour, Esq., 23, Belsize Square, Holloway, London.

Mr. Tottle, Wycombe.

Mrs. Field, Fir Grove, Weybridge.

Thos. Essex, Esq., Eastbourne.

Mr. Edmund Pierce, Wycombe.

John Letts, Esq., 8, Bartlett's Buildings, Holborn, London.

John Letts, Jun., Esq., 8 Bartlett's Buildings, Holborn, London.

The Rev. W. J. Burgess, M.A., Lacey Green, near Risborough.

Mr. Walter Skull, Wycombe.

F. Benham, Esq., 11, Gloucester Terrace, Regent's Park.

Joseph Albright, Esq., Wychwood House, Charlbury.

James Tatem, Esq., Reading.

A. Gaviller, Esq., Spring Hill, Upper Clapton.

William Terry, Esq., Peterborough House, Fulham.

Henry Rose, Esq., 8, Porchester Square, London.

William Wildes, Esq., The Moor, Wooburn.

Richard Rotton, Esq., 3, The Boltons, West Brompton.

The Rev. J. W. Buckley, M.A., St. Mary's Rectory, Paddington.

Richard Smith, Esq., Solicitor, 7, New Square, Lincoln's Inn.

W. H. Hayden, Esq., Wycombe.

The Rev. T. H. Browne, F.G.S., Wycombe.

Mr. Mawer, Wycombe.

Mr. Gardner, Wycombe.

John Thomas, Esq., Wooburn, Bucks.

Edward Baxter, Esq., 16, Cockspur Street, Pall Mall, London.

J. E. Prestage, Esq., Solicitor, Manchester.

R. J. Coltman, Esq., The Prebendal, Thame.

Mr. John Kibbles, Wycombe.

Charles Hall, Esq., Twickenham.

Miss Loader, Thame.

Mr. Abbott, Draper, Thame.

Joseph Eedes, Esq., 2, George Street, Euston Road, London.

Mrs. Edwards, Castle Hill, Wycombe.

Mrs. Hooper, 6, Cecil Road, Clifton, Bristol.

Mr. John Smith, Oxford Road, Wycombe.

H. C. Rooke, Esq., 12, Bruce Grove, Tottenham.

Mrs. Fowler, Great Marlow.

B. North, Esq., Princes Risborough.

Mr. Alfred Wright, Wycombe.

Mr. T. Glenister, Wycombe.

Samuel Lacey, Esq., The Willows, Thame.

Philip D. Tuckett, Esq., 10, Old Broad Street, London.

Walter L. Vernon, Esq., 4, Trinity Street, Hastings.

Mrs. Prosser, The Elms, Thame.

Messrs. Franklin, Ascott, Wallingford.

H. B. Downing, Esq., Apna Villa, Boxmoor, Hemel Hempstead.

Mr. R. Collins, Jun., Wycombe.

Mr. R. Vernon, Wycombe.

Mrs. Edelman, No. 8, Montpellier Crescent, Brighton.

Mrs. D'Urban, 13, Beacon, Exmouth, Devon.

W. H. Charsley, Esq., Charsley's Hall, Oxford.

L. W. Pearson, Esq., Warwick House, Cheltenham.

Mr. Dracott, Wycombe.

Mr. J. P. Gegg, Cressex Farm, Wycombe.

The Rev. Oliver J. Grace, M.A., Saunderton Rectory.

John Hussey, Esq., Custom House, Liverpool.

Edward J. Payne, Esq., M.A., 23, Old Square, Lincoln's Inn.

Mrs. Rooke, 12, Finsbury Park Villas, Green Lanes.

Edward Griffin, Esq., Manor House, Towersey, Bucks.

A. Barron, Esq., St. John's Lodge, St. Ann's Road, Stamford Hill, N.

William Weller, Esq., Springfield, near High Wycombe.

The Rev. George Venables, M.A., Vicar of Great Yarmouth.

J. M. Dean, Esq., Southampton Lodge, Lordship Road, Stoke Newington, N.

R. S. Besant, Esq., Kingston Crescent, Portsmouth.

Mr. Thos. Field, Aylesbury.

Mr. John Bowler, Wycombe.

S. Jones, Esq., 67, Peckham Grove, Camberwell, Surrey.

Mr. R. T. Jones, Easton Street, Wycombe.

Mr. W. A. Redington, London Road, Wycombe.

Mr. Edwin Saunders, Slough.

Mr. Joseph Child, White Hart Street, Wycombe.

The Rev. R. Barlow Simpson, M.A., The Terrace, Spalding, Lincolnshire.

George D. Heatley, Esq., Hazlemere Lodge, Wycombe.

F. Charsley, Esq., The Lodge, Iver, Uxbridge.

Mr. Amos Abbott, Wycombe Marsh.

James Medwin, Esq., Elm Lodge, Denmark Hill.

Henry Fryer, Esq., Solicitor, 1, Gray's Inn Place, Gray's Inn.

Mr. John Smith, Builder, Great Marlow.

The Rev. J. F. Coslett-Williams, M.A., Senior Curate of High Wycombe.

J. G. Wrigley, Esq., Mus. Bac. Oxon, F.C.O.

THE

Early History and Antiquities of Wycombe,

IN

BUCKINGHAMSHIRE.

———◆———

WYCOMBE is a town of great antiquity; it formed part of the territory of the Cassii, and was occupied by a tribe called by Ptolemy the "Catyeuchlani," and by others "Catuvillani."

Brewer, in his learned introduction to the "Beauties of England and Wales," mentions Wycombe as having been a Roman Station or camp; but it is not enumerated in the list of stations given in the Itinerary of Richard of Cirencester. It is situated about eight miles distant from the Ikening or Icknield Street, or Road of the Iceni, which was first constructed by the aborigines, and improved by the Romans. This road skirts the Chiltern Hills and runs by Wendover, Ellesborough, Little and Great Kimble, the Risboroughs, and Bledlow. Wycombe is situated on the very ancient road forming a short cut between the Thames at Hedsor and the Icknield Way, and this accounts for the presence of the Roman remains, which will now be described.

In the year 1724, in a mead called Great Penns Mead, a Roman tesselated pavement was discovered, of which the following record is contained in the third volume of the "Journals of the Wycombe Municipal Charity Trustees":—

"Burgus de Chepping Wycombe in Com. Bucks.
"Primo die Jullii Anno Dni 1724°.
"MEMORAND: That then was found in a Mead called great Penns Mead, belonging to the Right Honourable the Earle of Shelburne, about a quarter of a mile from the said Burrough,

B

an old Roman Pavement set in curious figures, as circles, squares, diamond squares, eight s·juares, hearts, and many other curious figures, with a Beast in the center, in a circle, like a dog standing sideways by a tree, all set with stones in red, black, yellow, and white, about a quarter of an inch square ; the whole pavement was about ffourteen foot square ; the ffine work in the middle was ten ffoot long, and eight ffoot broad, the rest was filled up with Roman brick about an inch and a halfe square."

The following is an extract from Delafield's MSS., Gough Collection, Bib. Bodl., Oxon. Small vol. of miscellaneous memoranda, which refers to the above pavement :—

" Mr. John Bates, Draper of this place [Wycombe,] (a Gentleman of a good understanding and of a public spirit) ordered a copy of it after the original to be taken, which he had painted on a canvas footcloth, and which for many years served as an occasional carpet for his Parlour. I have seen it many a time, and as far as I can remember, it was diversified into a great variety of work in small squares, and the middle set off with the form of a perfect wild beast."

In the year 1862 Great Penns Mead was identified by means of a lease granted in the reign of Henry VIII. of the Lady Mead, which is described as being situate at the east end of the Rye, and abutting south upon the meadow called Penn Mead. The late Lord Carington kindly granted permission, and provided labourers, to explore the meadow with a view of discovering the pavement thus recorded, when the remains of a Roman villa were uncovered, consisting of the foundations of a portico, the floors of several apartments, and an atrium or hall, consisting of a square flanked by two oblongs, the whole being enclosed by bands of double and single guilloche. The oblong compartments contain a series of sea monsters with twisted tails. The square is again resolved into a smaller central square (the design of which is lost), with four still smaller squares at the angles, which are occupied by female busts, representing the Horæ, or god-desses of the seasons. The one that remains perfect appears to represent Spring. All the mosaics are executed with very fine tesserulæ of black, blue, red, yellow, and white, on a solid basis of flints and rubble. Another compartment also contained mosaic pavement with a margin of common red tesseræ. This pavement is totally destroyed, but the tesserulæ found, many of which were no larger than peas, show it to have been of singularly fine and minute workmanship. The pavement on the right of this was also destroyed, showing the hypocaust. Three of the pilæ remained perfect on the floor. The site of the pavement discovered in 1724, was at the entrance to the villa, and no doubt was the well known Cave Canem, recorded as having been found; the whole was destroyed, but most of the tesserulæ found on the spot were of the finest and most minute character. The entire central building lay only from twelve to eighteen inches below the surface. Leaving the central building, we proceed through the court of the villa to the eastern fortification walls. At the north end, near the brook which runs close by, are the foundations of inner and outer walls; in the latter are the remains of two turrets, eighteen feet apart; between these was an entrance to the villa, traces of which still remain in the wall. The turrets project five feet from the wall, and are paved with common red tesseræ, each having a seat of the same pavement. Southward from these turrets are the most remarkable remains brought to light, composing a distinct set of apartments of much larger dimensions than those in the central building. The largest apartment had a hypocaust, and the ruins of the pilæ were found mixed with pieces of guilloche pavement of superior workmanship, and rubbed to a fine surface. Nearly adjoining the larger apartment, at a depth of about four feet, was found, what without doubt was the bath, having pavement composed of white tesseræ, each about half an inch square, the margin and other parts being laid in red. The sides were plastered, and decorated in fresco; a part of a fish resembling a roach was painted on one of them, with the colours in a good state of preservation. The bath projects from the wall to correspond with the turret. The following relics were found, i.e., an arrow-head, two bone hair-pins, and a statera or miniature steelyard in bronze, similarly engraved to one found at Cirencester, and which is considered one of the most rare and valuable of Roman remains. Many broken pieces of pottery were also found, but without any potter's mark. It is remarkable that none of the remains lately discovered appear to have been known to the antiquaries of 1724.

Nearly adjoining to Great Penns Mead, and which was only separated by the Windsor Way, or Loakes Lane, is the ancient British camp, with its inner and outer entrenchments, called Keep Hill. In 1826 eleven ancient British gold coins, in fine preservation, were found deposited in the hollow of a stone on this hill, five of which were purchased by the late John Norris, Esquire, of Hughenden House; three of them were presented by him to the British Museum, and one to the Antiquarian

loose chalk which obstructed the further exploration of what would seem to have been the remains of the old castle. The ancient well on the lawn, in front of the present House, was no doubt an appurtenance to the castle. In the year 1863, an excavation was made in the Wycombe Cemetery, which forms part of Malmer's Well, and which, as we have observed, was in the immediate neighbourhood of the above two ancient camps; when a pit was discovered, which may be described as a nearly circular chamber, seven feet deep, eight feet in diameter at the top, and slightly tapering to a diameter of six feet at the bottom. These limits were well defined, the chalk having been sharply cut away all round and at the bottom. The chamber occupied the whole of the grave spaces numbered 329 to 332, and portions of those numbered 386 to 388 of the division of children's graves marked D on the Cemetery Plan on the unconsecrated side. The chamber was filled up with layers of different substances; a little less than three feet of the bottom consisted principally of charred wood, evidently the remains of a cremation. Three feet above this was a mass of bones, unburnt pottery in fragments, and chalk rubbish. The pottery was partly red, partly black, partly unbaked, and of Celtic manufacture; several pieces of the black pottery were put together, and formed the principal portion of a small urn. Among the bones were the jaw-bone of a boar, and the teeth of horses, etc. Besides these, there was a fragment of iron, and some roughly-shaped flint implements. These relics were covered with a stratum, twelve inches thick, of large squared flints, which come up to within a few inches of the surface; other remains have since been discovered, of which no record has been preserved. Langley, in his history, mentions that many years since, part of a Roman vessel was found, when a cellar was dug in a house in the High Street, now belonging to Mr. Herbert Simmonds. Roman coins have also been found in the neighbourhood, of the Emperors Nerva, Antoninus Pius, and Marcus Aurelius; and a few years since, in the garden in front of the house in Allhallows Lane, adjoining the house formerly called Wellysbourne House,* but lately The Priory, on the west, was discovered a Roman well, which is the sure sign of the proximity of a Roman station. On the same premises, tesselated pavements of an early type were at the

---

* This house was for several years the residence of the Wellysbourne family, from which it took its name.

same time found; and when digging the foundation for Wesley Chapel, in the immediate vicinity, a portion of ancient walling was uncovered, which most probably formed part of the station.

The name Wycombe is variously spelt in early records. The earliest spelling is Wycumb, or Wicumbe, after which, in the fourteenth century, we have Wycombe, as the name is now spelt, and not until the end of the fifteenth century was the prefix of Chipping or Chepping introduced. In the sixteenth century we have the spellings, Wyckham, and Wickham, which were commonly used for above a hundred years. From the fifteenth century downwards, the town is sometimes called East Wycombe, Much Wycombe, and Great Wycombe (Wycombe Magna); of late years the prefix High, which dates from the time of Charles I., has been chiefly in use. Camden, in giving the derivation of the name Wicombe, says, " Wi, (Saxon) Holy; Wic, Wich, comes from the Saxon pic, which, according to the different nature and condition of places, hath a threefold signification, implying either a village, or bay made by the winding banks of a river, or a castle." Dr. Johnson says, Comb in the end and Comp in the beginning of the names, seems to be derived from the British Kum, which signifies a valley, and had the same meaning anciently in the French tongue. Chip, Cheap, Chipping, in the names of places imply a market, from the Saxon Cæpan, to buy. The name of Wycombe is really compounded of two Celtic elements Wy, one of many forms of the common element, meaning water, and Cum, a valley. It is thus, like Penn in the immediate vicinity, a genuine ancient British name, of an antiquity far exceeding most of the names in the neighbourhood. There is an ancient tradition, that the stream made the mills, the mills the market, and the market the town, and the Celtic word is thus of some significance.

The first historical record connected with Wycombe occurs about the year 800, when, says Lambarde in his Topographical Dictionary, page 438 : " Earl Ethelmund departed from Wycombe in Buckinghamshire, to fight against Weolstan at Cumberford. Weolstan having knowledge, met him forthwith with his men of Wiltshyre, and gave him a great Batteil, wherein bothe the Capitaines weare slayne, but the Wilteshyre men kept the field."

Fabius Ethelwerd, in his Chronicle of King Egbert's Conquests, gives a rather different version of this battle. He says, "that on the very same day as Egbert was raised to the kingdom of the West Saxons, Ethelmund was passing through a farm, Wiecum, intending to go to a ford called Kempsford, Duke Woxstan met him there with the centuries of the inhabitants of the province of Wiltshyre. Both of them fell in the battle, but the men of Wilts remained the victors." It is not certain that Wycombe is the place here referred to, but it is clear that Wycombe was, in Saxon times, an important settlement, from the great extent of common fields, divided by the ancient lynchits, already referred to.

William of Malmesbury, in his Life and Miracles of St. Wulstan, who was the last of the Saxon Bishops, and presided over the Diocese of Worcester from A.D. 1062 to 1067, records two miracles which the Bishop is said to have performed at a town called Wicumbe, the identity of which place is established by its then being situated in the Diocese of Lincoln, and on the high road from Worcester and Oxford to London. The account of these miracles is obviously taken from the work of Coleman, who was chaplain and biographer of the saint, as we find in the Harleian MS., No. 322: " As St. Wulstan was journeying to the court at London, he lodged at a town called Wicumbe, in an old house, whose ruinous appearance threatened a speedy fall. And in the morning, when he was about to recommence the journey, the building began to crack, and the rafters and beams to give way downwards. All the servants jumped out of doors in a fright, so panic-struck as to forget altogether that their master was alone within ; but once safely out of doors, they remembered him, and shouted loudly to him to come out before the whole building fell down together; but none was brave enough to go in and rescue him. But he, fortified with the buckler of faith, stood calm and immovable; and by virtue of his sanctity, the impending destruction was suspended, until the horses and baggage were safely got out and loaded ready for departure. Then the holy man went forth from the building, and immediately the whole house was violently shaken, and fell with a terrible crash, walls and roof, into a chaotic heap of ruins."

Here Coleman records the second miracle which the Bishop wrought in the same town (Wycombe), though six years after that just described: "Spording, of abundant fortune, and a well known admirer of the saint, had built a church there at his own costs, which he resolved should be consecrated by no other than Wulstan, but that could not be done without the permission of the Bishop of the Diocese; so he obtained license to that effect from Bishop Remigius of Lincoln. On the appointed day, the Bishop came and consecrated the church, taking especial pains in preaching to the people, and confirmation of children. After which he goes to Spording's house to dine. Now the wife of Spording had a maidservant who was afflicted with a grievous disease; her head was horribly swollen, and her tongue was enlarged to the size of an ox's, and protruded from her mouth. She took no food, except a little meat already masticated for her, or drink poured down her throat with a spoon. The matron feared to enter into conversation with the Bishop, but told the circumstance to Coleman, who acquainted the Bishop with the case. The Bishop had a piece of gold, which had been pierced with the head of the Holy Lance; this he took and dipped in the water which he had previously blessed in the consecration of the church, and gave it the girl to drink. This healing draught was speedily followed by a complete cure, as the matron and other witnesses declared on oath to Coleman some days afterwards." For an account of the discovery of the head of the Holy Lance, see Gibbon's "Decline and Fall," vol. vi., quarto edition, page 51. At this early period the people of Wycombe were attached to Pagan superstitions, which Hugh, Bishop of Lincoln,* a century after, had some difficulty in persuading them to relinquish. "Northampton laid aside the worship of a robber (*i.e.*, some Teutonic hero-deity), and Berkhampstead and Wycombe gave up the worship of springs, through Hugh's vigorous exertions." Probably the powerful spring called the Round Basin, is the spring alluded to, which rises at the east end of the Rye, close to the remains of the Roman villa in Great Penns Mead, and the Roman fortification in Holywell Mead. These remote historical records must, however, be accepted with some reserve, as they are not unfrequently of a legendary character, and are not to be relied upon for their veracity with implicit confidence. We shall have occasion hereafter to refer to the church and its consecration, and to correct some errors relating thereto in the statements made by Langley.

Wycombe is not only a town of great antiquity, but it is recognized in the charters of successive sovereigns as a prescriptive borough; but when it was incorporated, does not appear from our municipal muniments. It is, however, remarkable, that it is not so described in Domesday Book; and at the period of its compilation, Brady, in his History of Boroughs,

---

* See Life of St. Hugh.

after remarking that it is curious that Wycombe is not ranked in Domesday Book as a borough, says, "Wycombe formed part of the Terra Episcopi Wintoniensis; and, as appears in Domesday Book, the manor was allotted to the Monks of Winchester for their diet." Brady here makes an error. It was the manor of West Wycombe that was so allotted: but the two Wycombes are not distinguished from each other by any prefix in Domesday Book. The omission to designate Wycombe a borough in Domesday Book does not militate against the possibility that it may have been at that time a prescriptive borough.

The following extracts are taken from the Missenden Cartulary, deposited in the archives of the British Museum, and relate to properties of Missenden Abbey in Wycombe; the muniments referred to are rendered remarkable for their great antiquity, the earlier of which belongs to the 12th century, and dates of this period are everywhere rarely to be met with.

"In the temp. of Henry 1ˢᵗ.

"Mabel, Sawards dauʳ. of Wycombe, grants to the Canons of Missenden, Teñts once held by Hervey Merchant, Robᵗ. of Berkhampstead, Ernald Sprot, Adam Fitz Robert, Robert del Brook, Martin Cultier [Cutler], Gilbert Fitz Brickman, and that now held by Gumdwin." Witnesses, Thoˢ., Chaplain of Godstow, Adam, Chaplain of Wycombe, Godfrey, Clerk, Allan Tanner, Geoff. Fitz Baldwin, and orˢ., (these names have been transcribed as a specimen; all the documents have numerous witnesses, sometimes with names of interest).

Wm. Fitz Hervey.—"Two shops towards the west from his great messuage towards the Market Place of Wyc." "Rent charge of 8d. per year to the Church of Wycombe."

"Godfrey, Clerk of Wyc., gives his house and land in Wyc. after the death of his wife." [Qy. to the Church of Wycombe.]

The above muniments are probably of a date not much later than the foundation of the abbey at Missenden in 1133.

"Elias Gwynant gives to the abbey, his mill in the fee of Wycombe, called Gwynant's Mill with the appˢ·ₜ viz., "as the water divideth Frienett, from the corner of the Upper Mill Croft, down to the bridge below the said mill, and on the other side next my house, as meres [qy. metes] and bounds show," etc. "Also, all between the mill-head and the water which divides Frienett, except the new garden. "Also the whole meadow of Bulleswell, and 1½ acre of his meadow, i.e., that 1½ acre in West Wycombe Mead, etc. (i.e., Upper King's Mead)." "Also land in East Field, West Field, and Middlefield," and "that heved's acre in Figel furlong, and 3 acres in Rube furlong, and all East grove," which lies under "Rainers-grove." . . . "The Canons are also to have by view of his bailiff, all necessary timber out of his woods for the repair of sᵈ· Mill. Rent charge payable to Gwynant's mother."

This is clearly the mill at Wycombe Marsh, belonging to Henry Wheeler, Esq.

"S⁴ Elias Gwynant gives half of his mead in Wycombe, five marks coñson."

This deed is remarkable as being the first with a date. It is dated "the year in which King Richard came back from Germany, *i.e.*, 1194."

Robert of Rouen.—" All his land between Cerasarii and Hurt-pleie, and half of the head-lands around same."

(Elias Gwynant is a witness.) Cerasarii "the cherry orchards "(?) Wycombe having at a very early period been famous for its cherries.

S⁴ Elias Gwynant—a long deed, mentions "the Seye" [qy. Reye or Rye] as a common field, or pasture. Also a shop next to Fitzhervey's "Curia" or farm yard, in Wycombe.

Walter de Rouen, "land between Bull's Croft and 'Sinker's Dell' in the fee of Wycombe."

Ralph Fitz Isabel, "all his Ten⁴ in Wycombe." (Geoffrey of Oakridge and Matthew of West Wycombe, are witnesses.)

Do. "Messuage late Gladwin the Smith "—" save a rent of four horse-shoes, which was payable to Geoffrey Fitz Angod."

Agnes Cole of Wyc., Spinster.—" All her heritage from her father William Cole, ' *within and without the borough.*'" This is the earliest notice, so far as is known, of the borough boundaries.

This document is of the thirteenth century, as it mentions Thomas Walder, whose will is dated A.D. 1291.

Avice, daughter of William Rufus (Redhead or Russell) of Wyc.—" Messe and appts. in Wycombe. Rent chge. of 1*d.* to the light of the Ch. of Wycombe."

" Indres. of Fine, 22nd of Henry III., 6 acres of arable, 1 of meadow, 1 mess and 2 mills in Wycombe."

Do. "In the King's Court at Wycombe, 30th of Henry III., before Rog. de Tharkeby, Gilbert Preston, Simon de Winton and John Cobham, Justices in eyre—Abbey of Missenden v. Rich⁴ Fitz Geoffrey, Deforciant."

Do. "At Dunstable (3rd Henry III.) in wcʰ Matthew Brand seeks agᵗ Elias Gwynant, Deforciant, the 5th part of a Knight's fee with the appᵗˢ in Wycombe."

Do. "At Aylesbury (20th Henry III.) W. Fitz Hervey rents in Wycombe."

THE MANOR

was, at the Conquest, holden by Robert de Oily, or D'Oyley, who had his fee in right of his wife, taxed at ten hides. There were thirty carucates [about 1,000 acres] of land. In the demesne, four hides and three carucates. There were forty villeins, with eight bordars [peasants or cottagers] having twenty-seven carucates : eight servants and four bordars ; and six mills, worth seventy-five shillings per annum; pasture, three carucates, and for the horses of the Lord's Court, and the carts for the villeins. Woods for five hundred hogs. In the whole valued at £26, as also when surveyed; when Robert first had it, £10, and in King Edward's time, £12. This manor belonged, before the Conquest, to Brictric, who held under Queen Edith (see Bawdwen's Domesday Book—Bucks, page 49).

The great and independent possessions which belonged to Robert D'Oyley, in right of his wife, were derived by her from that powerful Saxon Thane, her father, Wigod de Wallingford.

We have abundant evidence of the early confederation of our ancestors and predecessors, to protect themselves against the insolence and aggressions of the marauding barons of those ancient times. It has justly been remarked by Dr. Robertson, that "the institution of Municipal Boroughs has conduced more than any other circumstance to the emancipation of Europe from the thraldom of the feudal system; and contributed more, perhaps, than any other cause to introduce regular government, police, and arts. Their establishment was the effect of that spirit of liberty which has gone abroad. They became wealthy associations. Their traffic not only brought them riches, but gave them power. Their increasing wealth and commerce established among them burgher watch and ward, and voluntary associations for the protection of property." The question whether Wycombe was a borough town at the Conquest may be answered in the affirmative. In the Charter of the 21st of Henry III, we find the burgesses pleading the liberties they had of the ancestors of the Lord the King, which would carry us back to Henry I., to whom the incorporation of the borough is, on all hands, ascribed; but his charter was most probably only confirmatory of liberties and privileges long previously enjoyed by the burgesses, and which were also confirmed by Magna Charta, cap. ix. About the time of the Conquest," says Camden (vol. i., page 327), "Wigod de Wallingford was Lord of the Borough of Wycombe, and of the out village (*i.e.*, parish) belonging to it (as an old Inquisition expresses it), after whose death Henry I. appropriated it to the Crown."

In the 9th of Edward I., this borough again reverted to the Crown, and was a second time annexed to the Honour of Wallingford; and accordingly the steward, or bailiff of that liberty, received the profits of the Manor of Wycombe; and upon demand of burgesses for this town, executed the return of them during the reigns of Edward the First and Second, and in the beginning of that of Edward the Third.

The burgesses, ever distinguished for their loyalty, were amongst the very few from the boroughs who at first, in obedience to the Royal Precept, returned members to represent them in Parliament.

There is no doubt that the Borough of Wycombe was originally the property of the Crown, and was, in all probability, granted to farm to the burgesses at a certain fixed rent.

Maddox, in his "Firma Burgi," says, "there are numerous instances of boroughs granted to farm to the burgesses in fee, or for term of years, or at the king's pleasure. The burgesses must have been incorporated to a certain degree, at least; for the payment of the rents reserved on these grants was made long before there are any traces of charters of municipal incorporation." In further confirmation of the antiquity of the borough of Wycombe, we find in the Pleas of the Crown, Hilary Term, 3rd Edward I., an ancient custom in this borough "to sell land and serve on juries at twelve years of age," was recorded. In the year 1825 the records then deposited in the Tower of London were searched, in the hope of finding Henry the First's Charter granted to Wycombe, when it was ascertained that none of his charters were extant; but from a very interesting article in the *Standard* newspaper of January, 1873, on the Public Records, it is stated that no charters of Henry the First were extant prior to the 18th year of his reign; yet we find, according to Brady, in his History of Boroughs, that Henry the First granted large immunities to boroughs. In consequence of Brady's assertion, a further search was made at the Public Record Office for this charter, but without success. As, however, the ancient court called the Aula Regia then existed, and which followed the king and his household in all his progresses and expeditions through his dominions, accompanied by the Chief Justiciar or Capitalis Justiciarius totius Anglicæ, who had the custody of the public records, and which were conveyed from place to place by strong pack-horses, the religious houses being under requisition to provide these horses for the purpose, free of expense; it cannot be considered surprising that, from such a precarious mode of transport, a great deficiency of these early records exists, and which was the subject of complaint, even in the reign of Henry II.

The rent reserved in the case of this borough, with certain manorial rights, was, from time to time, granted by the Crown to the more powerful barons, and ultimately to (one of their number) Alan Basset,* of Wycombe, as appears by the charter of the fifth of John. Alan Basset was present at the signing of Magna Charta. It is very evident, as will presently appear, that Alan Basset was guilty of acts of aggression towards the burgesses of Wycombe. The late Dr. Lipscombe, in the course of the Author's correspondence with him on the Topographical History of Wycombe, kindly sent him a manuscript copy of the agreement made in the Court at Westminster, in the 10th year of the reign of King Henry III., between the burgesses of Wycombe and Alan Basset; and which is recited in the charter of confirmation of the 21st of the same King's reign; a translation of which agreement, with some explanatory notes by the learned doctor, is as follows :—

From the Fine Rolls.
Bucks, 10 Hen. 3. No. 125.

" Between the burgesses of Wycombe Querents and Alan Basset, of certain damages and injuries which the said Alan had done to the said burgesses, as they aver, contrary to the liberties which the same burgesses say that they hold of the ancestors of the Lord the King.

"Alan granted to the said burgesses the whole borough and town of Wycombe, with the rents, markets, and fairs, and with all other things to a free Burgh appertaining, etc.; and with the edifices of † *Knavesthorn* and the rents, etc., excepting the demesnes of the said Alan, and his lands in the foreigns, and the mills there reserved in a fine passed between the aforesaid Alan Basset, and the Abbess of Godestowe [Co. Oxon], so as that the rents and customs which the men of the said Abbess were wont to render to the said Alan, may remain to the said Burgesses and their heirs in aid of the aforesaid fee farm to be paid according to the former fine passed between the said Alan and the aforesaid Abbess. Saving always to the said Alan and his heirs all reasonable aids, when the Lord the King and his heirs shall make talliage of the

---

* Arms of Basset : Barry nebule of six argent and azure.

† This singular expression (says Dr. Lipscombe), "is probably intended to mean the Knavestorn, that is the Prison House, or place for custody of thieves, and transgressors against the laws. A Knaves' Hall, or hall for strangers, was not an unusual appendage to old mansions, not even of the higher orders, but in old houses about Queen Elizabeth's time, and I remember one in the house of my father which was not inappropriately converted into a pantry."

With every respect for the judgment of the learned doctor as a distinguished etymologist, we are compelled to repudiate his opinion as to the probable true rendering of the word " Knavesthorn," as it is beyond reasonable doubt " cnihtenthorn " [Saxon] which means " Court of Burgesses," the buildings in question being simply the guild- or mote-hall. Sheriffs-torn is the common word in Domesday Book for the County Court, and " Cniht " [Saxon], or " Knight " the common english for a burgess in a city. See Stubb's " Constitutional History," vol. i.

domain lands throughout England. And be it known that the aforesaid Alan and his heirs acquit and release to the aforesaid Burgesses, etc., as against the said Lord the King and his heirs, the fee farm of twenty pounds which the said Alan was thereupon indebted to the Lord the King, and in like manner of the service of one Knight's fee which the aforesaid Alan was accustomed to pay as his service, which the aforesaid Alan held of the grant of King John. Be it known likewise, that the favis de averiis,[*] annually on the lands of the said Alan shall be and remain as they have been accustomed, saving to the said Burgesses and their heirs the customs thence issuant. And the said Alan and his heirs shall have all fairs holden in the streets of Wycombe, etc. And let it be known that many Burgesses named and acknowledged in the Town there, shall be in peace, agreeable to the same."

These fairs, with the lands on which they were held, were by fine released and transferred by Alan Basset to the burgesses of Wycombe.

In 1212-13, Alan Basset gave King John £133 6s. 8d. and an excellent palfrey, that his daughter might marry William Lord de Lanvallei.

King John divided the out village of Wycombe between Alan Basset and Robert de Vipont, who was also a powerful baron[†] and was present at the signing of Magna Charta. And by the charter of the 5th John (as already referred to), the whole of the manor of Wycombe was granted to Alan Basset, except what Vipont held, on payment of £20 per annum, and doing the service of one knight's fee. Alan Basset died in the 17th year of Henry III., 1232, leaving issue, Gilbert, who married Isabel, daughter of William de Ferrers; he died 25th Henry III., 1240, and his only son soon after, in consequence of which, Wycombe came to Foulke Basset, Dean of York, afterward Bishop of London, and he paid the rent for it, 30th Henry III., 1245; but, being a clergyman, his estate devolved to Philip Basset. He married Hawise, daughter of John Grey of Eaton, and left issue a daughter and heiress, Alice, wife of Hugh le Despenser, Lord Chief Justice, who was killed at the battle of Evesham, August 6th, 1264. This Alice or Olivia married, secondly, Roger le Bigod, Earl Marshal, who in right of his wife, together with the Knights Templars, claimed the right of frank pledge, assize of bread, etc., in suburbio de Wycomb, 4th Edward I. She died 9th Edward I., 1280, leaving issue Hugh le Despenser, her heir, on whose attainder, 1326, this manor reverted to the Crown.

"Escaet. 9 Edward I. 9. Elen Lady le Despenser died, seised of Wycombe. The manor house and herbage was returned to be worth 2ˢ per annum, 260 acres of arable land worth 2ᵈ per

---

[*] Averii (equi jugales) that is a yoke of oxen.   [†] Arms of Vipont: Or, six amulets, gules.

acre, and five mills worth . . . and the Jurors likewise declared Hugh le Despenser her heir."

In 1326 the manor reverted to the Crown by attainder.

In 1332–6 and 7, Edward III., the king, for the good service rendered him, granted the manor to William de Bohun, who was afterwards, viz., 1337, created Earl of Northampton, K.G., and on a partition of the estates of that noble family in 1421, the manor again became vested in the Crown.

In 1479, 18th Edward IV., the Queen, the Archbishop of York, and others being seized to the use of the King, and his heirs and successors, of the manor of Wycombe called Bassetsbury, the fee farm of the town of Great Wycombe, etc., they, on the special command of the king, demised and granted the premises, with the appurtenances, to the Custos or Dean and Canons of Windsor and their successors, until the king, his heirs or successors, should grant them other land of the same value. (See Ashmole's Garter, p. 170.)

The manor has, since this date, been in the possession of the Dean and Canons of Windsor, who have leased it to successive lords and ladies. The family of Raunce were lessees of the manor for many years prior to 1574 ; and John Raunce rebuilt the manor house in the reign of James the First.

The following is a list of the names of the earlier lessees of Bassetsbury Manor.

1574.   Edward Lord Windsor.
1657.   Thomas Gower, Esq.
1666.   Roger Rea, Esq.
1670.   Edward Atkins, Esq.
1679.   John Loggan, Esq.
1682.   Althea, Mary, and Elizabeth Loggan.
1683.   Mary Loggan.
1691.   Sir Orlando Gee, Knt.
1717.   Sir Francis Dashwood, Bart.

The manor is now vested in the Ecclesiastical Commissioners, and is held on lease by the representatives of the late Sir George H. Dashwood, Bart.

The rent charge of £30 13s. 4d. was, by an indenture dated the 24th March in the 15th of Henry the Seventh's reign, reduced to £26.

The other manors, included in the grant of king John to Robert de

Vipont, are called Temple Wycombe, Loakes, and Windsor or Chapel Fee. Robert de Vipont demised and granted these manors to the Knights Templars, to whom he was a great friend and benefactor, and who enjoyed them till the dissolution of their Order, by Edward II. in 1324, when it is supposed Temple Wycombe was granted to the Knights of St. John of Jerusalem. In the 22nd of Edward IV. Robert Bardsey died, seized of the manor of Loakes, which was held as of the Honour of Wallingford by fealty.

From a rent roll preserved, it appears that the manors of Temple Wycombe, Loakes, and Windsor or Chapel Fee, were in the Crown in the 4th of Henry VIII. King Edward the Sixth, in the 7th year of his reign (1552) granted the manor of Temple Wycombe, with all its appurtenances formerly belonging to the Knights of St. John of Jerusalem, to John Cock.

The court rolls of the manors of Temple Wycombe, Loakes, and Windsor or Chapel Fee.

The court rolls begin 1st Richard II., 1377, from which the following extracts are taken :

2 Henry IV.	"Item; they present that John Dryvere doth not set up a cross upon his house."
4 Henry IV.	"Lord grants to R^d Pymme and John Ravenynge his Fulling Mill, called Gosenham Mulne in the fee of the Temple."
12 Henry IV.	"Item; they present that R^d Sperlyng hath cut down the wood of the lord at Castel Grene."
	"That John Frenschemon hath committed trespass on the Castel Grene."
7 Henry V.	"At this Court was granted to William Ker a certain 'hegge rowe' near le Old Castell, by Ralph Astley in conson of 20^s to be paid to the Lord."
3 Henry VII.	"Decr 15, Russell, a baker, presented for keeping a scolding Harlot in his house."
22 Henry VII.	"They present that Wm Pavear hath committed an assault upon Andrew Loxborough with one 'Aleboll' of the value of a ½^d "
	"Item; that Geoffrey Welshman hath committed an assault on Andrew Loxborough with one weapon called a 'dager,' of the value of 2^d and drew blood, contrary to the peace."
	"Item; that the s^d Geoffrey Welshman committed an assault on Wm Mapulton with his fist, contrary to the peace."
	"That Nich^s Baker hath sold fish before they were seen and tasted by Thos Grene the taster of meat and fish, and hath also sold fish to make to himself excessive profit."
	"Wm Russell and Wm Pavear presented for harbouring vagabonds and divers other suspicious foreigners, and for allowing misrule and unlawful games, namely, 'disyng and cardying,' contrary to the form of the statute."
	"That the ditch by Temple Slowe is obstructed to the hurt, etc. Also the watercourse at the 'Mershe' near the Mill called 'Gowes Myll.'"
20 Henry VIII	"April 14th George Sawyer's Wife presented for keeping ill government in her Inn. Bailiff ordered to remove her."

March 12. "A presentment against the Inhabitants of Wycomb, because they have not bowes and arrows according to the Statute in that case provided" [viz. 22 Edw. IV., cap. 4].

In 1604, 3rd James the First, June the 22nd, John Raunce conveyed Loakes to Richard Archdale, Esq.; and afterwards, August 28th, 1628, he conveyed Temple Wycombe, and Windsor or Chapel Fee manors (which last he had purchased of Thomas Wells, Esq., in 1609) to the said Richard Archdale.

In 1700, Thomas Archdale, Esq., conveyed the above manors to Henry Petty, Lord Shelburne, who was second son of the famous Sir William Petty (remarkable for his literary and scientific attainments) by Elizabeth, daughter of Sir Hardress Waller, Knt., of Castletown, Co. Limerick. In 1699 he was created Baron Shelburne, and in 1709, Viscount Dunkerron and Earl of Shelburne. His Lordship having survived all his children, died in 1751, after devising his estates to John Fitzmaurice, second son of his sister, Anne, Countess of Kerry; which John was, on the 7th October, 1751, created Viscount Fitzmaurice and Baron Dunkerron; and on the 26th June, 1753, Earl of Shelburne; he was made a Peer of England on the 17th May, 1760, as Baron Wycombe; and dying 14th May following, was succeeded by his eldest son William, who was created Viscount Calne and Calnston, Earl of Wycombe, and first Marquess of Lansdowne, on the 30th Nov., 1784, and K.G. He married first, 5th February, 1765, Sophia, daughter of John Earl Granville, by whom he had John Henry (afterwards Marquess of Lansdowne); another son, William, who died young; and secondly, Louisa, sister of the Earl of Upper Ossory, who died 7th August, 1789, and by whom he had Lord Henry Petty, born in 1780, upon whom, after the issueless death of his elder brother, devolved the Marquisate, with this estate.

Lord Shelburne, having served in important offices of State under the Bute, Grenville, and Chatham Ministries, and also under the Rockingham Ministry of 1782, became Prime Minister of England, in 1783. He died the 7th May, 1805, and was buried in the family vault in the north aisle of the chancel; but it is most surprising that there is no inscription in the Church to perpetuate the memory of this eminent statesman.

We may here add some particulars from the life of his Lordship, by his grandson, Lord Edmund Fitzmaurice, which may be interesting to the reader.

Extract from the Lady Shelburne's Diary.

"Wycombe, Saturday, 28th January, 1768. . . . At four o'clock, Lord Shelburne came [to Loakes] and brought Lord Clare with him; in the evening we had a party; and at half an hour after six, our company began to assemble. Amongst our Ladies was a very pretty bride, the wife of the Mayor (Mr. Rose *). Lord Clare divided his compliments between her, and Miss Kitty Shrimpton.† We sup'd at eleven, in the India Paper Room, that we might not encroach upon Sunday morning. And the whole was over at twelve o'clock, and nobody the worse for this sober recreation."

"November 6th. Lord Shelburne and Colonel Barré came and sat with me and renewed a conversation they had with Lord Chatham, till Mr. Price [Vicar of Wycombe] whom we had sent for to christen our little boy,‡ arrived from Wycombe, who sup'd with us."

"Lord Camden rated Lord Shelburne's oratorical powers above those of any peer of his time, Lord Chatham alone excepted. Lord Thurlow complimented him on the correctness and minuteness of his information, and even Walpole does not deny him a high place amongst the debaters of his time."

Boswell, in his "Life of Johnson," mentions that "Johnson was at a certain period of his life a good deal with the Earl of Shelburne, as he doubtless could not but have a due value for that nobleman's activity of mind, and uncommon acquisitions of important knowledge, however much he might disapprove of other parts of his Lordship's character, which were widely different from his own. Johnson was a frequent guest at Loakes House."

From the Memoirs of the Abbé Morellét, as quoted in the Life of Shelburne, we make the following extracts relative to his visit to Wycombe.

[A translation from the French.]

"Arriving in London, I found Lord Shelburne absent, but he had left orders to receive me; indeed, he had done more, and having forewarned his brother Fitzmaurice, then member for Wycombe, of my arrival, he (whilst waiting the return of my Lord) brought me to Wycombe, a place situated about seven or eight leagues from London, and the first title in the peerdom of Lord Shelburne, which is now his son's. He carried off also Col. Barré, Doctor Hawkesworth, director of the first voyage of Banks round the world, and Garrick, and Franklin, two men whom it is sufficient to name. We passed, or spent five or six days at Wycombe, and as you may see in sufficiently good company. Franklin, who already showed to England as the

---

* Grandfather of William Rose, Esq., J. P.   † A maternal ancestor of the author.
‡ The Honourable William Petty, who died 27th January, 1778.

politician and statesman, that she had soon to fear, was then much more known in Europe by his grand discovery of the identity of electric fire with that of thunder; and by his beautiful theory of electricity; but public economy and government matters occupied me more than philosophy, and the conversation naturally returned to these subjects. We discussed much the general question of the liberty or freedom of trade, and the two great questions, which hang on that, the freedom of commerce in India and the freedom of commerce in corn; ideas upon population in general, and upon that of America in particular; upon the relation of Colonies with the Capitals; upon the progress of English America, and of those one ought to foresee, had their turn in our conversation. We spoke also of music, for he loved it; and philosophy, and morals, but in few words, and at long intervals, for nobody practised better the maxim of Fontaine,

'The wise man is sparing of time and words.'

I saw him make there the experiment of calming the waves with oil, that one has looked upon as a fable in Aristotle and Pliny. It is true that they were not the waves of the sea, but those of a little river which flowed in the park of Wycombe. It was ruffled by rather a fresh wind. He ran back about two hundred steps from the place where we were, and making some magical gestures, he shook three times over the stream a flask which he had in his hand; a moment after the little waves weakened themselves or calmed down by degrees, and the surface of the water became smooth as glass. In the explanation which he gave us of this phenomenon, he told us that the oil contained in his flask, spreading very much as soon as it was thrown in, and making the surface of the water smoother, prevented the wind from having a hold on it, and principally over the part of the river which received the first impulse of it, and that the agitation of the inferior parts began to calm of itself, and not being renewed from the part above, nor communicated to from below, calm spread itself everywhere."

We find in the journal of the venerable John Wesley, that in one of his visits to Wycombe, viz., Oct. 11th, 1775, he makes the following entry relative to Loakes.

"I took a walk to Lord Shelburne's house; what variety in so small a compass! a beautiful grove divided by a serpentine walk, conceals the house from the town; at the side of this, runs a transparent river with a smooth walk on each bank. Beyond this a level lawn, then the house with sloping gardens behind it; above these is a lofty hill, near the top of which is a lovely wood, having a grassy walk running along just within the skirts of it. But can the owner rejoice in this paradise? No, for his wife is snatched away in the bloom of youth." [Lady Shelburne died January 5th, 1771.]

"It may not be amiss" (remarks Lord Shelburne in a very striking passage which brings to light the unenviable position of the owner of a close borough), "to say a few words upon the subject of boroughs."

"Family boroughs, (by which I mean boroughs which lie naturally within the reach of cultivation of any house or property), are supposed to cost nothing; but I am sure from my own experience and observation, that if examined into, they will be found to cost as much as the purchase of any burgage tenure whatever, by means of what I call insensible perspiration. Like public taxes, the amount is not perceived for a great while, and by some people not at all ; but it consists in paying always a little, and most commonly a great deal too much, on every article ; and in every transaction you are confined to a particular set of tradesmen, and often to their connections in town, and can never control their charges. The rents of houses and lands must be governed by the moderation of voters. You must be forthcoming on every occasion, not only of distress, but of fancy ; to subscribe too largely to roads, as well as every other project which may be started by the idlest of the people ; add to this, livings, favours of all sorts from Govern-ment, and stewardships, if there is an intriguing attorney in the town, who, under the name of your agent, will deprive you of all manner of free agency upon your own property, and some-times of the property itself, if it is a small one; without mentioning the charges and domestic disorder attending a great deal of obscure hospitality, and a never ceasing management of men and things. And after all, when the crisis comes, you are liable to be outbid by any nabob or adventurer ; and you must expect all that you have done to go for nothing, and the most you can look for is a preference. What can you say to a blacksmith who has seven children, or to a common labouring man who is offered £700 for his vote ; or to two misers who are offered £2,000, which are instances distinctly upon record at Wycombe, since Mr. Dashwood's election."

The manor house of Loakes was enlarged and much improved by William, Earl of Shelburne. The Marquess of Lansdowne disposed of all his estate at Wycombe (except the advowson of the vicarage) in August, 1798, to The Right Honourable Robert Lord Carrington, formerly Robert Smith, the friend and confidential adviser of the younger Pitt, who often retired to Loakes from the cares of State. The manor house, now called Wycombe Abbey, was very considerably enlarged and greatly improved by his lordship, from designs, and under the direction, of the celebrated architect, James Wyatt. His lordship died the 18th September, 1838, and was suc-ceeded in his title and estates by his son, The Honourable Robert John Smith ; he was born January 16th, 1796, was elected Member of Parliament for Wendover, and subsequently for the county of Bucks, in 1820; and in 1831 he was returned, with Sir Thomas Baring, Bart., as member for the borough of Wycombe. His lordship succeeded His Grace the Duke of Buckingham as Lord Lieutenant and Custos Rotulorum of Buckingham-shire, and Colonel of the Royal Bucks King's Own Militia. He was a F.R.S. He took the surname of Carington by royal license, 26th August, 1839. In 1822 he married the Honourable Elizabeth Katherine Forester, second daughter of Cecil Weld, 1st Baron Forester; she died in 1832, leaving issue, Mary Isabella, b. 1824, d. 1840; Cecilia Katherine Mary, b. 1826, m. 1853, Charles John Colville of Culross, P. C., 11th Baron in the Peerage of Scotland. His second marriage was on August 2nd, 1840, with the Honourable Charlotte Augusta Annabella Drummond Willoughby,

WYCOMBE ABBEY

Ireland, and gave half to the said Symon, as he acknowledged to many persons."   Records of Bucks, 11–271.

The "Pleas de quo warranto Bucks, Rot. 1, Edw. I., 1286," afford us an amusing story of a proceeding by ejectment.   Gilbert de Thornton, King's Attorney at the assizes at Wycombe * in this year, claimed against the Abbot of Missenden, a messuage in Wycombe, as the King's escheat, as the property of a Norman born, Nicholas le Vinetur, who died seized of it.   The abbot came in person and declared that Nicholas passed the house to him, by a fine, and held it afterwards of him for life only, but that now it ought to revert to him as the right of the Church of Missenden. To this Gilbert replied, that this was not the case, but that all the abbot's right consisted of actions of intrusion after the death of Nicholas.   And that he should prove that the said Nicholas continued his possession by himself, his wife, and his servants, and never changed his estate.   And so issue was joined.

Then the sheriff was enjoined to form a jury of twelve men residing near the Town of Wycombe, and twelve men of the town itself, none of whom were connected with the Abbot, to try the cause; but hereupon came the Mayor and bailiffs of Wycombe, and declared that they had such liberty in their town of Wycombe, that all enquiries of assize and law concerning houses and property in Wycombe, ought to be made before burgesses of the town and not by foreigners; and they demanded that this liberty should be in no respect infringed.   They also declared that the Abbot had calumniated and injured the commonalty of the town in other respects.   Now this was clearly the worst thing they could have done, and prevented their obtaining their demand.   Ultimately the jury was

---

* We gather from the Annals of Tewkesbury (1248), pa. 137, that Wycombe was an Assize Town in the earlier part of the 13th century.

"1. Richard, Earl of Gloucester, sued us (the monks of Tewkesbury) for advowsons of Churches, to wit, of Hambledone, of Merlawe [Marlow], of the Church of All Hallows, London, by the King's Writ before the Justices in Eyre at Wycomb, and obtained judgment with one cheerful assent."

"2. In the same year, on the 8th day after St. Hilary, the Justices in Eyre held the assizes for the County of Bucks at Newport, and after finishing the business for (the north) part of the county there, adjourned for the remainder of the Court to Wyckumbe, on the 8th day of the following Easter."   The assizes were also held here eleven times between the years 1684 and 1711.   Gough's MSS.

formed of seven burgesses and five foreigners; "thus saving," says the Record, " to the said burgesses, their liberty aforesaid." Then the jury gave their verdict, which will be given in the words of the Record.

"And William de Saunderton, Robert Fitzwalter of Daventre, Richard le Wydington, Reginald de Beauchamp, Thomas le Talyer—Foreigners. Roger le Cordewaner, William le Orfeure, Roger le Hynton, Richard le Saundwell, Robert le Poor, Matheu le Folur, and Geoffrey le Clerk, Burgesses of Wycombe, declare that the said Nicholas was a Norman and born in Normandy; and purchased that house of one Alice la Peynture, to hold to the said Nicholas and his heirs; and afterwards the said Nicholas sojourned in the Abbey of Missenden, where he had a certain pension of meat and drink (corrodium) and there by a certain sickness was detained; and then, in that sickness the said Nicholas made to the said abbot and convent the aforesaid grant; and a certain letter directed to one Gilbert le Mercer his servant, who took care of his taverne (tabernam) at Wycumb, concerning putting them (*i.e.*, the Abbot and convent) in possession; thereupon, which grant and letter, one Reginald de Chovel, Canon of Missenden, carrying with him to that house, entered that house; and thereupon Gilbert gave him possession according to the aforesaid letter. But they declare that the said Reginald found in that house the wife, the family, the household goods, and other chattels of the said Nicholas. And the same Reginald considering these things, asked the wife of the said Nicholas, that she should go out into the street to buy fish and other things, of which he had need. And she at the request of the said Reginald, going out, on her return the same day, found herself shut out: but immediately she, by a certain ladder, entered that house by the window of a certain gallery of the said house. And they declare that the said wife with the servants and chattels of the said Nicholas, there dwelt, without any removal by the said (Abbot and convent) until the said Nicholas being recovered from the said sickness, to the said house returned and entered that house. And in the presence of his neighbours, there called together, the said charter and letter . . . entirely contradicted, and Gilbert, his servant, who put the same Abbot in possession . . . "

The mutilated state of the Record does not allow us to know the fate of Gilbert.

A second entry, Rot. 5, records the recovery of the messuage on the part of the King, and that it was worth forty shillings per annum. The first memb., Rot. 2. of the Municipal Records, is a bond dated 1295, from Ralph Rechel, who obtained, according to the recital, a grant of the house from the King, to pay Matilda, late wife of Nicholas le Vinetur, one mark per annum, the dower to which she was legally entitled. The deed is witnessed by the Mayor and Burgesses, William Orfeur, Richard le Sandwell, and Geoffrey the Clerk, who were jurymen on the trial.

At Fol. lxviii. of first Ledger, is the following remarkable entry.

"On Tuesday, in the 40th year of the reign of King Edward III., it was ordained that every child of a burgess, who at the time appears to be the oldest, after the decease of his father, on claiming the freedom [of the Borough] shall have the same on paying $10\frac{1}{3}^d$., without any further payment; namely, to the Mayor 1^d., to the clerk $\frac{1}{2}^d$., to the under bailiff $\frac{1}{4}^d$., to the gilds-men [gildains] 8^d., and to the Master of St. John's $\frac{1}{2}^d$., he making oath, etc."

The following is a translation of a deed in Norman French, contained in the Records of Wycombe, being an award made by Joan, Countess of Hereford, 1407.

"This indenture of three parts witnesseth that whereas divers debates and discordes have arisen between the Mayor and the Commonalty of Wycomb, and Raulf Lude, Esquier, for that the said Mayor and Commonalty have claim of twenty and one shillings of rent for certain tenements the which the said Rauf holds of the said Mayor and Commonalty in the town aforesaid, and suit at their Court of Wycombe two . . . at the Feasts of Saint Michel and Hokday,* and two shillings and threepence for one meadow, the which the said Rauf holds of them in the Town aforesaid. And also the said Mayor and Commonalty have claim of the said Rauf and demand one ancient rental touching the Mayor and Commonalty of the said Town, the which the said Rauf hath in his possession. And also the said Mayor and Com-monalty have plaint, that the said Rauf hath built one house upon the waste land of the said Town, of which debates and claims, as well the said Mayor and Commonalty as the said Rauf, have submitted them to the ordinance and determination of the most noble and gracious Dame, Joan de Bohunne, Countess of Hereford, and to hold and perform the award, ordinance, and determination, of the said Countess, the said parties are bound to the said Countess and other certain persons each party of them.

"Whereupon the said most noble Dame, by the advice of her Council, hath examined all the matter and all the evidences of the one party and the other, unto her shown, and inspects the said evidences, and hears the reasons on both sides. And the said Countess hath awarded and ordained, that the said Rauf and his heirs shall pay the said rent of one and twenty shillings for all the tenements which the said Rauf holds of them in the Town aforesaid, as . . . the said Rauf and the said Mayor and Commonalty in like manner to have the said two shillings and three pence . . . Thomas Lude, father to the said Rauf, whose heir he is . . . his heirs hath . . . parcel of the said tenure in the said town, holds the right . . . in the said . . . by which release the said tenements are . . . tenements to the said Mayor and Commonalty as touching the said two tenements at the rent of . . . the said Mayor and Commonalty and the said Rauf duly discharged from their Court. And the said Mayor and Commonalty have . . . have been seised of the said suit. That the said Countess shall . . . certain persons."

The Countess of Hereford was a great benefactress to the monasteries of Essex, as appears from the State Rolls. She was grandmother to Henry V., and a resident in her own right at Bassetsbury Manor.

Before remarking on the documentary history of the Middle Ages, in

---

* Hockday, the second Tuesday after Easter, in commemoration of the slaughter of the Danes on that day, and their expulsion from England, A.D. 1100.

E

connection with the subject in hand, a few topographical observations may not be out of place. The borough is situated principally on the highway (via regia) from London to Oxford; and is divided into four wards, Easton Ward, Paul's Row Ward, out of which High Street Ward was probably taken, and Frogmore Ward; now the most populous of the four Wards. Separate rates were made for each ward, when the Poor Law Act, of the 43rd of Elizabeth, came into operation. The ancient British road through Chiltern passed by Desborough Castle, the back of Newland, through the now depopulated suburb of Horseyn or Horsenden, and the Windsor way through Wycombe Abbey Park, close to Great Penns Mead, bounding the borough on the south.

The easternmost piece of land in the borough adjoining the Rye and Halliwell, or Holywell, Mead on the west (both already referred to), is a meadow belonging to the Chapel of St. Mary, which was (inter alia) assigned by Queen Elizabeth to the Corporation, who leased it in the latter part of the 13th century to Roger Outred, then Mayor, as tenant at will. In 1346, Roger's son, William, resigned it to the Mayor and burgesses. In 1369, we find the Wardens of St. Mary letting it to John Bynewell, and describing it as adjoining William Outred's meadow, i.e., that belonging to the mill, and the Pontfolde, which was in later years called Penn or Great Penns Mead. In 1540, the wardens granted it to John Brasebrydge, Esq., the Mayor, particularising its situation minutely, for a term of thirty years. The meadow was leased by the Corporation to Lord Shelburne, who, in a subsequent arrangement with the Corporation, gave a portion of it up to the Rye, the rest being added to and remaining part of Halliwell Mead, now belonging to Lord Carington. The ditch separating it from the Rye may yet be traced, and the borough boundary stones on the east mark its limits in that direction, dividing it from Halliwell Mead.

The Rye is a commonable pasture of about thirty acres, being an appurtenance to the lands belonging to the Hospital of St. John, and conferring no small benefit on the inhabitants of the town. Its antiquity is great. The origin of the rights in connection with it has been erroneously ascribed to Queen Elizabeth, and the popular tradition is, that "that glorious Dame," on the occasion of a temporary sojourn at Wycombe, being inconvenienced by the non-supply of milk at the royal breakfast table, caused this meadow to be given to the town, in order that such an occurrence might be obviated for the future; but as we find the Rye as early as the 13th century was a common meadow belonging to the Corporation, we are compelled to discredit the tradition. It was really the common pasture of the tenants of the ancient demesne of Wycombe, prior to the incorporation of the borough : and on the incorporation, the burgesses entered into the rights of the tenants. A family, taking name from the Rye, was established here during the 13th and 14th centuries. We find the meadow of Geoffery atte Rye adjoining Our Lady Mead and Halliwell Mead in 1346. This Geoffery probably was the occupier of the Rye Mill. In the Rye, the inhabitants of the borough by ancient prescription have the right of common for two cows and a heifer in the day time only. An Old Topographer* says :—

"All the inhabitants of the borough have liberty at all times to walk, and use sports and pastimes, such as running, leaping, wrestling, riding, back swords, and other plays, at their pleasure, without being trespassers. The liberty of using these exercises is very much valued by the common people."

From a memorandum in 1518 (vide "Ecclesiastical Antiquities"), Rowland Messenger, Vicar of Wycomb, would seem to have discovered some grounds for setting up a claim to the Rye, alleging it to be the property of the Church, but he made no attempt to establish the claim. From time immemorial the borough election days and law days (so called) of the mayor and burgesses were there held. At the law days and views of frank-pledge, all the leases were renewed, and fresh grants made in the presence of the inhabitants; resolutions and orders were openly made and proclaimed, and other public business transacted. This custom may reasonably be supposed to have been a relic of the moots or gemotes of the Anglo-Saxons. Pound Mead is included in, and situate at the east end of the Rye, nearly adjoining the Dyke on the North, and Great Penns Mead on the West, the mounds of which are still traceable. This mead was, in 1633, in the possession of the Standish family, who sold it to Thomas Archdale of Loakes House; he again sold it to the Reverend John Biscoe, of St. Thomas Parish in Southwark, in whose family it remained till his grandson, Samuel Jacques of Uxbridge, sold it to the Mayor, bailiffs, and

* Author of a curious MS., descriptive of the Borough of Wycombe in the beginning of the last century ; penes the author.

burgesses, in 1719, for £150, which sum was raised by the sale of oak on Town Farm, and oak and ash on Kingshill Lands. The Corporation leased it to Bigoe Hensell, goldsmith, who converted it into a hop ground, but the speculation did not pay, and he surrendered his lease. Rot. Wyc. Burg.

The Hayward's House, near the Rye, is an old tenement, concerning which there are several singular entries in the Registers; one is in a Rent Roll, temp. Phil. and Mary, from which it appears that rent was taken for it :—

"Item ; of Thomas a Lee, Cowherd, for his howse sumtyme an hermitage, V:."

No records of the hermitage or hermits remain ; but, as at a very early period hermitages were frequently found at the entrance to our ancient towns, without doubt hermits did take up their abode at this spot. We find the house at a subsequent period described as the " Hermitage," or " Snail," and also as an Almshouse, belonging to the Hospital of St. John.

The two mills near the Rye are both of extreme antiquity, the one at the north-west end of the Rye is called Bridge Mill, and the other at the north-east, Pann Mill ; these mills, though included within the boundary of the borough, were always considered as belonging to the Parish of Wycombe, and were assessed to the parochial rates. They are excepted in Alan Basset's grant of the borough. The owners of these mills have each the right of common in the Rye for a mare or gelding. In Ledger No. I., fo. 144, we find the following order :—

"Memorandum the ninth daye of October, in the first yere of the reigne of our sovereigne Ladye, Quene Elizabeth, beinge the lawe daw in the gelde halle, John Sterlynge then being maier, it was ordeyned and agreide by the whole howse, that the Myllmen that be or shall be of Panne Myll, and of Cristofer Paitefer's Myll, shall have no horse, geldynge, nor mare, goinge in the Rie, onlesse he or they Do loode and serve the towne withe the same horse, geldynge, or mare, upon the payn of fforfiture of his or their common in the seide Rie ; and that at no tyme or tymes, he or they shall have any other kynde of horse or mare goinge there, but such only as serve the towne as afore ys seide."

In the year 1380, one of these mills belonged to Thomas atte Lude, who terminated a dispute concerning his right of common in respect of the mill, by granting the Mayor and burgesses a rent of one shilling, issuing out of a shop in the market place in tenure of John Geky, as a consideration for a confirmation of his right, at the same time acknowledging that he had previously no right of common there, unless by special favour of the burgesses.

Separated from the Rye, which extended to Horsenden Lane, and which was the entrance to it, is Easton Street, formerly called "Easton Towne," in early deeds "Estynton," giving name to the ward. This ward contains that part of the town eastward of Crendon and Horsenden Lanes. Here was formerly held a fair on the Day of St. Thomas the Martyr: "For all manner of pepuls for cum to the forsayde fayer free, w'oute any maner of staullayge payde that day to the bayllys," which was the "holde custome of thys borough of Wycomb and by the Kyng's graunts," to the Mayor and burgesses, "tyme aute of mynde," as appears by an order of the Court "held on the Thursday before the feast of St. James the postyll," 1527, wherein the Mayor, bailiffs, and burgesses lament that "now ther cummythe but few, or ells none of thys towne and borough thethyr for to kepe and maynteyne the forsayd ffayer ther in that place, whareas of holde costume was wont for to be kept, but kepythe ther schopys and ther stallys at home ther as they doo dewll her w'in the sayd towne," and make a stringent order "that from thys tyme fforwarde, that no maner of man nor woman w'in the sayd towne kepe ther schoppys and ther stallys at home ther as they doo dewlle. Nor make nowe Schowe forthe into the strete on that day, but resorte into the ffayer ther as yt is wonte to be kypte, apon payne of ev'' Borges so afending Xs, and of ev'' fforynar, III'. and IIII''., the one halff to the Baylyffs and the othyr half to the Chamberr of Wycomb." Notwithstanding this severe enactment, the fair in Estyntowne has long been a thing of the past.

Crendon Lane is so called from its leading up the ancient British road to the depopulated hamlet near the Upper Temple Farm, called Croyndon or Crendon. The charter of Henry III. mentions Crendon's-hatch with Hazelmere. The houses in Horsenden Lane were purchased by John, Earl of Shelburne, and were afterwards demolished. His Lordship obtained a lease of the lane as waste ground from the Mayor and burgesses, and included the same in the grounds of Wycombe Abbey, in the middle of the last century, the fee of which was purchased by the late Lord Carington.

The High Street, also giving name to a ward, is a continuation of Easton Town, westward, terminating at the Guildhall. Most of the shops (shopæs) of the burgesses in the 13th century appear to have been in "Altâ Stratâ;" so little has the name or the locality changed. This, the topographer of the beginning of the 18th century described as the "Beauty of the Borough, for here the houses exceed in magnificence most of the buildings of the borough, for goodness of brick, mortar, and other materials, of which the modern houses are built," it may be (he proceeds) "Great Britain can't show better." It is rather curious that in the reign of Henry VII. the Vicars of Hughenden and Wooburn had town houses in the High Street; the house of the former was situate on the site of Wine Vaults now belonging to Mr. Leadbetter, and the latter on the site of the house at the corner of Crendon Street, lately erected by Mr. Robert Vernon. This house originally belonged to the Corporation, to whom, in 1319, it was granted by William Oughtred. It was let in 1388 to "Will. Depham, Sir Robt., Vicar of Wouborne, and Sir Geof. Laver, priest, with certain privileges."

The High Street had a curious collection of old inns, some of which have disappeared; there was the George, adjoining the Red Lion Inn on the west, in which was the scene of a memorable election in 1723. An account of this Inn may be found in three scarce tracts extant, wherein it is described as "the neatest, the largest, and most convenient public house, or place to receive so great a company." The Red Lion Hotel, *i.e.*, the ancient portion of it, comprehends the whole of the building, including the gateway on the west side of the present hotel. In Churton's "Founders of Brasenose College," we find that John Cox of Kyrtleton, Oxon, wool merchant, gave a messuage called the Red Lyon in Cheping Wycombe, and 120 l. in money, to purchase land to provide two priests, being fellows; one of them an Oxfordshire, or south countryman, to make annually, each of them, a sermon at Kyrtleton, and to pray for the founder." The rent of the inn, 20 Edw. IV., was £8 6s. 8d. (Yate, pa. 119, 129.) In 1535 it was let for £3 only. (Extract from Valuation of First Fruits Office.) Churton considers inns generally at that time depreciated in value. There is an entry in a rent roll of the 16th century as follows: "Of the Principal of Brasenose for the Redde Lyon 2d." That part of the hotel which formed the ancient inn still belongs to Brasenose College. The Antelope, adjoining the Red Lion on the east, was a famous inn, erected c. 1480, on the site of two others, called the New Inn and the Saracen's Head. The

Royal Oak, which was burnt down nearly a century ago, was situate on the east side of what is now called Church Square, formerly the Hog Market. It was a famous house of call, at which the Mayor and Corporation were accustomed, up to the end of the last century, to hold their convivial meetings. The Maidenhead Inn stood at the corner of the lane called Hailey's, afterwards Maidenhead, and now Crown Lane; this inn was made somewhat locally notorious as the scene of the misconduct of Mr. William Child, an attorney, practising at Chesham, who, while conducting a case in the Borough Court of Record, in 1662, used insolent and indecorous language to the Mayor and Aldermen, for which he was struck off the roll of that court. The Three Cups, on the other side of Maidenhead Lane, stood on the site of the house occupied by Mr. Mason. The Falcon, the Cross Keys, and the Wheatsheaf, bespeak their own antiquity. The Katherine Wheel, opposite the Red Lion, was an ancient inn, chiefly built of timber, and elaborately decorated with carved work; it was burnt down in the year 1780, by an incendiary, who was a private in the Oxford Blues. The porch, covered with ivy, which now adorns the Hayward's House, formed the entrance to the inn. Here Charles II. once stopped on his way through Wycombe from Oxford, on the 30th September, 1663, accompanied by the Queen, the Duke and Duchess of York, Prince Rupert, the Duke of Monmouth, and many others of the nobility. From an old record we find—

"They did come into the town about 4 of the clock of the same day. They came from Oxford. The king in his progress going back again to London. The king did go out of the town between V. and VI. of the clock the next morning, and was at his palace at Whitehall before 9 of the clock in the morning. The queen did go out about VII. of the clock, and dined at Uxbridge, and then went to Whitehall."

There is a room at the back of the house occupied by William Rose, Esquire, then adjoining the premises of the Katherine Wheel, which is hung with tapestry, and which, according to tradition, was used by the King during his sojourn at Wycombe. In a note on the Coat of Arms of Cardinal Moreton, in a paper on the Cordwainers of Oxford, in the "Archæological Journal," VI. 279, occurs the following extract from a letter of Aubrey to Anthony Wood, dated London, Vigil of SS. Luke and Paul, 1681, as follows :—

"His coat somewhat resembles the Shoemaker's Armes, who give three goate's heades, as you may see in the sign Without Bocardo. This coate of Moreton is in a west chamber of the Katherine Wheele Inn, at Great Wiccomb in Bucks, w^th (as I remember) the Cardinal's Cappe."

The original letter is in the Ashmolean Museum at Oxford.

Paul's Row Ward includes the Guildhall, the Church and Parsonage, All Hallows Lane, Noyes Lane near the church gates at the south entrance, the north side of White Hart Street, formerly called Hoog Lane * and the streets called Paul's Row, Crown Lane, formerly called Hailey Lane, afterwards Maidenhead Lane, and St. Mary's Street.

The old Guildhall claims our attention as an important municipal building; it was erected in 1604, and stood on "twenty-two large posts, or pillars, of heavy oak." After serving the public purposes of the town many years, it was ultimately burnt down. Amongst the old records we find some scattered notices of a former Guildhall or Guildhalls are preserved; the earliest is in 1380, when a gallery (solarium) at the end of the Guildhall was granted to John Deye, at an annual rent of 3s. 4d., a stipulation being made " that the bailiffs should be at liberty to open and shut the door of the prison of the town, if required." Among the "rents belonging to the Chamber," temp. Philip and Mary, is an entry as follows : " Of Rowland Lyttleboy for his house under the geld hall X. III^d." There were also shops under the Guildhall of 1604.

Whilst on the subject of the Guildhall we may add another curious notice which is preserved.

"Nicolas Gerarde) The gelde halle dore to stande open, if any burgesse be comytted to
    Maior.   ) Warde."
"M^d. that the thursday next after the fest of Sent Thom'. the martir the XXth yere of Kyng Harr. the VIIth, in the full Gildaule before Nichūs Jerard Mayr of the burowgh and all the hole comynte of the same, that 'it is ordenyd and stabely acted the geld hall dor shall be stondying opyn ffrely wher as ony burgess be comitted to ward be the comaundemet of the Mayr for the tyme beying and inspeciall that other burgess may have licens to exorte and advise hym to the beste.'"

In addition to the old Guildhall, " were places or roomes called Clapper Court and Dungeon, of or belonging to the Counter or Geale thereunto adjoyneing." An oaken corbel from the old Guildhall is preserved in the

---

* Hoog is Dutch, or Old Saxon, for "High." Hoog Lane is the same as High Street. The High Street in most Dutch towns is still called "Hoog Laan."

Wycombe Guildhall in the olden time.

There can be little doubt that the site of the homestead of the ancient demesne lands of Wycombe was called Church Square, and was most probably occupied by Wigod de Wallingford, of whom mention has already been made. We find from the records of Wallingford, that "William the Conqueror, in 1067, instructed Robert D'Oiley to convert Wigod's Castle into a strong fortress, and Wigod, under pressure, removed to the Out-berry of Wycombe." We may here add, an old chronicler informs us, that "Wigod had the favour and confidence of Edward the Confessor, who paid a visit to his castle, and through his influence created Wallingford a Royal Burgh. After the battle of Hastings, Wigod invited the victorious monarch to pay him a visit at the castle; the invitation was accepted, and at this place the conqueror received the submission of Archbishop Stigand and the principal barons, before he marched with his army into London. Wigod died in the beginning of the reign of Henry I. When the burgesses became sui juris, it was in the middle of Church Square that they very naturally would erect their "Geld halle," and the space formed round this site may account for the curved line taken by Paul's Row, which, in the earliest times, must have been the lane surrounding the homestead, and leading to the open space, "La Grene." The cabins of the ceorls or serfs were undoubtedly grouped in various positions round the homestead. The meadow ground, which, in the last century, lay "behind the Katherine Wheel," would be part of the demesne meadows, and Bridge Mill, the natural place for people to cross and recross the river, so that the "Brigge," [bridge] was eventually erected at that spot. The position of the mill and the church clearly shows that the demesne homestead would be situated between them. And the castle mound, etc., would have been originally erected as a defence to the demesne below.

These conjectural observations the author must leave for the consideration of the antiquary, in the hope that should he be disposed further to pursue the subject, which is sufficiently interesting to engage his attention, he may be rewarded for his labours by the discovery of some further historical details confirmatory of the site of the ancient demesne of Wycombe.

The present Guildhall was erected at the cost of John Earl of Shelburne, in 1757, and was renovated by Sir G. H. Dashwood, Bart., M.P. for Wycombe, in 1859.

CONSTITUTION OF THE BOROUGH.

The early muniments of the borough describe it as an "ancient and populous borough" situated within the parish of Chipping Wycombe, but not coëxtensive therewith, having separate parochial officers and rates, yet with formerly but one church for the whole parish.

We may here mention that, prior to the year 1830, the borough was considered as a county within the county. A treasurer was appointed by the borough magistrates, who made orders from time to time on the overseers for the maintenance of borough prisoners, and for the incidental expenses of the gaol; but the non-intromittant clause in the charter of Philip and Mary containing no words expressly excluding the county magistrates from exercising concurrent jurisdiction within the borough, they, in the following year, claimed their original right of so doing, which right they have since occasionally exercised.*

Quarter Sessions were formerly held in the borough; they had, however, been in abeyance for some years, but were revived during the mayoralty of Mr. Ward, in 1801.

We have already remarked there is very little doubt that the borough was made a free burgh by Henry the First. It was governed by a court of burgesses up to the middle or latter part of the thirteenth century, when we find the first mention of Mayors, officially appointed as such. About that period the municipal body seems to have been composed of the Mayor, two bailiffs, two gildans, and the burgesses called the Commonalty. Aldermen do not appear until the fifteenth century; by the charter of Philip and Mary, they were called principal burgesses, and were twelve in number, including the Mayor. There was also a high steward appointed under this charter: the Corporation consisting of a Mayor, twelve Aldermen, a High Steward, and two Bailiffs.

The Arms of the Corporation are: Gu. on a mount Proper, a swan Arg. gorged ducally, and chained or.

The office of the bailiffs in early times seems to have comprised the following duties, namely, the collection of the rents belonging to the chamber; the keeping of the peace generally, including the custody of offenders,

---

* In support of the right of the county justices, see "The King against T. Sainsbury, 4th Term Reports, 451."

Waterlow Bros & Layton, London.

The Wycombe Corporation Arms.

From an Ancient Sculpture in possession of the Author.

the opposite side thereof, at the East end of the Tumbling Bay in the Rye, but which Stone has been removed and another ordered to be placed there; and from thence along the Bank of the said River, towards the New Mill, as far as a Stone, and from thence across the Rye (leaving a corner thereof to the left) as far as an Aspen Tree on the South side of the watercourse, taking in the said Tree, and continuing in an Eastern direction a few yards, as far as a Stone on the Eastern side of the Wall dividing the Rye from the Antelope Meadow; and from the said Stone turning in a Southerly direction across the said Antelope Meadow, as far as another Stone, Twenty-four yards from the Hedge, which Stone had been improperly removed, and placed in the Hedge, but which was replaced; then turning back again from the said Stone towards the Rye, to a Stone there on the West side of the hedge, dividing the said Meadow from the Rye, and so straight up the Rye towards the West, to another Stone there; then turning towards the Dyke, and keeping in a straight line to a Stone in the Rye Bank of the Dyke, continuing the said straight line into the centre of the Dyke, then turning down towards the West, and keeping the said straight line down the centre of the Dyke, as far as, and opposite to, a Stone, near a Lombardy Poplar Tree in Rye Mead, on which there is a X; on the Northern side of the Dyke across the Rye Mead, towards the Town of Wycombe, to a Stone between a large Elm in the Shrubbery there, called the Dark Walk, on the Southern side of the Mill Stream, opposite to Mr. Wilkinson's Garden, and so from the said Stone to another Stone, in the North Bank of the Dyke, in the said Dark Walk opposite the Fruit Garden belonging to Lord Carington, and from thence across the Dyke, to a large Spruce Fir Tree in Lord Carington's Park, and from thence to a large Elm Tree on the North front of the Abbey, nearly opposite the Entrance Hall, where the company were regaled with Bread, Cheese, and Beer, the gift of the said Lord Carington, and from thence in a straight line to a mark on the inner side of the Wall, on the Western side of the Road leading from Marlow to Wycombe, thence in a straight line across the Footpath leading from the said Marlow Road into New Land, to the South side of the Ash Tree standing in West Field, about Forty yards from the said Mark on the Wall, taking in the said Tree, and from thence along the ancient boundary at the bottom of West Field, to a Stone about Fifteen yards South of the South-West corner of the Garden Wall, by the North side of the Footway, and so along the said Ancient Boundary to the Stone at the South-East corner of the Orchard, late of Mr. Harman, now of Mr. Charles Busby, abutting upon the said West Field; and thence along the South side of the said Orchard, and along the South front of Four cottages, belonging to the said Charles Busby, in a line therewith across New land, to an ancient mark at the South end of a cottage, belonging to Edward King, and so through the said House, taking the same into the Borough unto and along a watercourse running on the South side of a Meadow, called Morecraft's Meadow, now Buildings and Garden ground, to a Stone there, about Twenty yards from a garden belonging to Thomas Mealing, and from thence across another Meadow, in a Westerly direction, to a Stone, on the North side of Watery Lane, about three yards from the South corner of the said Garden, and continuing along the North side of the said Watery Lane, as far as the South-West corner of Mr. Finch's Meadow, and into and along the Western boundary thereof to the   corner of the same, taking in the said Western boundary thereof as far as a mark on a Willow tree, and from thence on the other side thereof, about Fifty yards to the South-West corner of a Meadow belonging to Mr.   Enoch, taking in the South Boundary thereof; from thence along the Boundary of the said Meadow, and so down the South side of the Back Water of Bowdery's Mill, leaving the said Mill on the North, and from thence continuing in the same direction, until the same back water enters the Mill Tail, and along the South bank of the said Mill Tail as far as a Stone there, thence crossing the said River in a straight line, into the Ancient Watercourse, running into the said Mill Tail on the North side of the said River, and into and along the said Watercourse, as the same passes through the Fell-monger's Yard, and through the house of the late Mr. Samuel Treacher on the North side of the Street of Wycombe, leading towards Oxford, and so continuing in the said Watercourse across the said Street, through the passage of the Public house on the North side of the said Street, called the Angel; and in the course thereof, as it bends there to the Eastern side of the Dove House Mead, and also along the Eastern side of the Meadow, late belonging to Mr. Gibbs, and now of Mr. Edmond Heninghem, as far as the South-West corner of the Saw Yard Wall, where a Poplar is marked on the Eastern side of the said watercourse, and from thence along the North side of the said Wall, as it bends there, and continuing the said Wall, and into and along a watercourse, through Violet Court, and so along the said watercourse, until it enters another watercourse on the Western side of the Road leading to Hitchendon; and from thence across the said Hitchendon Road, to a X in the wall of the Garden, belonging to the House formerly occupied by Mrs. Jamieson, and now by Mrs. Wilkins, late the property of Mr. John Manning, and now of Mrs. King, and across the said Garden Four feet nine inches from the said house, to a mark on the Wall on the Western side of the Orchard, lately belonging to Mr. Carter, now rented by Mr. John Turner, Surgeon, where is a Stone on the Eastern side of the said Wall, and from thence across the said orchard in a straight line towards Temple Field, to a post about fifteen yards distant from the Eastern Hedge of the said Orchard, and from thence in a Southerly direction, in a straight line as far as a Stone there, near to an Alder Bush, where a Stone was ordered to be placed, and thence over the Eastern hedge of the said Orchard, to the Stone at the corner of Temple Field, where the boundaries of the said Borough commence."

"Perambulation of the Ancient Outward Boundaries of the Parish of Chepping Wycombe, made on Wednesday and Thursday, the 25th and 26th October, 1820.

"Wednesday, 25th October, 1820. Entered from the West Wycombe Road, the close opposite Cubbidge's Mill [a X], went up the north side of the hedge, this close called Lower Brook Field. Across the old chalk pit into the second close [Upper Brook Field] by the north side of the hedge. a X on entering the third close [Further Black Croft] on the top of the hill, by the north side of the hedge; X enter the south corner of Tinker's Wood, and down the south side of the wood, out at Chittle Hill, keep along the top bearing south-west, Lord's Close being on the other side of the hedge, second close (still Chittle Hill) keep straight on to 8 Acres Close, belonging to my Lord [Carington], on the other side of the hedge, Further Beddow's belonging to the Temple Manor on the other side of the hedge. .

"Entered near the bottom of Chittle Hill, 12 Acre Close (arable), at the south corner, and keep a little way down in that direction by the hedge a X at Chittle Spring, east corner of 12 acres; entered a meadow at the east corner over Chittle Spring (meadow belongs to Mr. Widmore) along the south hedge side, over the brook into the next little meadow, same direction by south hedge, a X on the Ash Tree; on entering this close across the Hitchendon Road, over the opposite bank and hedge, and X. Hold straight east across the clover field called Kitchen Field. Through the hedge near the south corner of the Fallow Field a X; across this close to a stone in the hedge about 50 yards on the left of the east corner of the close. Through the hedge from the stone to the east corner of the next close (Turnips), into

Green Street, Green Street a ✗. Bear due east up the street ✗ by the pond, and under the oak tree on the right, belonging to the Terrier's estate. The right hand ditch is the boundary a ✗ at Close Gate, belonging to Benjamin Shrimpton, on the right hand side of the street. A ✗ in White's garden [a seeming encroachment] on the right hand side of the street near the cottages. Through the hedge out of Green Street into Benjamin Shrimpton's orchard, occupied by West; a ✗ on a sapling in a dry pond—✗ a pigstie. Tree in the same orchard adjoining the cottage along the south hedge side, ✗ a tree near a cottage at the south corner of the orchard, out into the road near the turnpike—the cottage belongs to Charles Axton of Amersham, and is occupied by Hugh Jackson [house about 30 yards east of the turnpike] ✗ on the opposite (south) side the road in front of Jackson's cottage, which cottage is intersected; Jackson is a wheelwright. Another ✗ on the south side of the road just within the encroachment, and a little nearer the toll gate.

"A long dispute about which tree at the back of Jackson's cottage was to be marked.

"Through the pond at the south side of the Amersham Road, east, across the close. Through the hand gate; Through Barton's Farm yard, and marking the barn door. Along the south hedge of Wycombe Heath, ✗ an oak tree, and a neighbouring gate. Enter the wood on the heath, marking the trees on the south-west hedge, a ✗ at the north of Rushmere Pond, and through the pond another ✗. The north corner of Penn Wood, due south from Rushmere Pond to Potter's Cross, along a dry ditch dividing Penn Wood on the left, from Wright's Coppice on the right. Go through a cottage and garden side of a pond, still hold on the course of the dry ditch, due South Potter's Cross, make a ✗ south of the pond; south to Tyler's Green, north corner of Mr. Hearn's shrubbery, a ✗ east side of Mr. Hearn's house, holding south to a little lane, round a pond, west to John Tilbury's, southeast into Moses Wingrove's orchard, across it in same direction, across John Wingrove's orchard, the road running straight parallel on the left of us. The Bell at Tyler's Green, a ✗ under the tree in front of it. The 5th row of trees from Penn House Wall, is in Wycombe straight south under them they ✗ an elm tree, south of Widmer Pond, in the 4th row from Penn House, go through Widmer Pond, due south, and lunch at the Red Lion, Penn.

"From Widmer Pond down the horse road south, ✗ the ash tree at the first gate, and also the soil on the south (right) of the tree.

"Mr. Prickett and Mr. Bearcroft took possession of an encroachment on Tyler's Green occupied by Weller.

"The boundary is decided to be about 10 yards south-west of the ash tree, i.e., on the right hand side of the road. The road being considered to be in Penn Parish, and the ✗ accordingly made east of Robert Wright's Homestead, on the road side the hedge. Entered Robert Wright's Close, keeping close to the east side the hedge, which hedge is an old encroachment. To Beaconhill or Pistells Pond. Through the pond south the hedge on the west. Through the Willows, the house occupied by Edmond Hancock, on the east, going through his garden, a ✗ south of Hancock's garden pales. Go southward through the wash and pits, keeping close by the edge, west; go through Henry Stratford's orchard, also through the Widow Hawes's garden, still keeping the south, and marking an apple tree in the garden; intersecting near the middle of Widow Hawes's house, and marking between the door and window on the south; cross a lane, and enter the hedge of Henry Stratford's garden (an encroachment), continue a southern course through Miss Lovett's encroachment, and through the middle of John Hazell's garden, Beaconhill (where the pole stood), A ✗.

"Through Grove's Encroachment, the road on the east, still south, about 10 yards within

G

the east hedge.   A X on the common still Beaconhill due south, downwards to a Pollard Oak, going through the front, a trifling encroachment in this line.   From Pollard's Oak, straight down Snigg's Lane southwardly, Town Farm [a complaint of no cheese cakes from either house right or left] ; keep on down Snigg's Lane.   Entered James Spicer's garden, keeping the east hedge on the left hand, took about 5 or 6 yards of it, leaving Edmund's House on the west or right hand.   Snigg's Lane Road belongs to both parishes, each repairing one half ; made a X on the east side of Snigg's Lane, just before the entrance into Loudwater Lane, leading into Deerham's Farm.

"From Snigg's Lane nearly south, down Wooburn Lane, to the mud hole about 200 yards and made a X.

"Entered the hedge at the mud hole, and held south by the hedge side, going into Dupre's Close on the east side of Sam¹. Griffin's, Deerham Farm, continue the same course through the second close.   Third close, the hedge rather north-west near the end of this close, entered a coppice, keeping close to the hedge, which runs westerly ; cross westerly to a Balk.   The balk west, and go south to the end of the balk, and then cross a stone wall into John Smith's orchard (Knaves Beech), then straight to Smith's house.   Keep close to Smith's House wall, the wall standing west, and coming out at the bottom of Smith's garden, south into the London Road.

"Cross the road to the north end of the pond, cross the hedge and go westwardly (the hedge south) to Knaves Beech, mark the tree (an ash).   From the beech, proceed south to the Wire Mill Head, in the corner of the Close, marking a tree on the north side the pond.   Proceed westwardly the side of the rivulet, to the corner of the Close [Little King's Mead], northward by the rivulet side to the garden fence of Hedge Mill.

"Through the river into the mill yard, in at the back door of Spicer's house, mark the middle beam of the back kitchen, and out at the front door.   From Spicer's, or Hedge Mill, south up the back lane to an ash tree, opposite Mr. Davis's Mill, the fir tree marked, no ash tree now standing.   From the ash tree south-west up the hill, the hedge on our right, enter Pye Grove, going southward, up to an old ditch or balk, which lies west ; keep up an old dry ditch almost due south, through the wood, the furze being a little to the south-east.

"Through a pond to a large oak tree, with ancient marks upon it, close to the south hedge of the wood.   Over the hedge of Mincham Wood into the lane leading to Flackwell Heath ; cross the road, and bear due west from the oak tree, across a turnip field to a gap in the hedge, formerly a gate.   Got over the gap into Flackwell Heath, and made a X ; due north across the Heath to another X [many encroachments on the right hand, inspected by the freeholders] ; X in James Partridge's garden (an encroachment) through to the orchard belonging to the Green Man, and through the house (*i.e.*,) through the parlour window, marking the beam, and thence (marking a cherry tree in the orchard), out at the north end of the orchard a X [here they bumped old Dell].

"Go north from last mentioned orchard, across the Heath, and enter Mr. Haye's orchard, crossing the orchard northwardly to some white cottages, which are marked ; then north across another orchard, marking an apple tree, over the hedge into a sort of cross road, by a house called the Lawsuit House, and a X made on the little Green.   The Lawsuit House standing north west.   Go in a line due north, by the side of the Lawsuit House (which we leave on the left hand) across a little close by the side of a lane, to the road again, through the hedge X and keep the road due north X at the pits by the road side, enter garden occupied by John Weedon, leave Weedon's house on the right hand side, and through the next garden, leaving garden fences close on the left hand, out at the cross path and ✕; through Thomas Baker's garden and house, northwardly out at the pits, and ✕ by the roadside, through the middle of Smith's and Moody's gardens on the left hand side of the road. Through Moody's house and orchard to the mud hole, and a ✕, keep Flackwell Heath and Stony Rock Lane from Flackwell Heath End to Wynch Bottom, a ✕ made opposite Spicer's garden. From Spicer's at Wynch Bottom in a north-west direction towards Handy Cross, keeping the highway [or lane without gates] all the way to Handy Cross, a ✕ at the outlet of the lane into the Marlow Road on the south side the road, cross the road northerly (leaving the cottages on the left) to Holmer's Lane a ✕.

"From Handy Cross to Olders, or Holmer's Farm north, by the hedge side, the hedge east. Second Close, hold as before by the hedge side, the hedge east. Holmer's Farm being the 3rd Close, hold as before northerly, then north-east, then again northerly. To Holmer's orchard, a ✕ on the north-east, and of the orchard, cross orchard hedge, and continue north over next Close (Holmer's Farm), cross the lane leading from Cressicks to Booker at the gate ✕ continue north or north-west down the hedge side of next Close. Hedge east, enter the next close at the corner of this, and bear down the hedge side north-east, the hedge south-east. At north-east corner, enter turnip close down the hedge side. Hedge north to the end of the close, continue south-east down half next close, enter a gap to next close, bear north-east, then more eastwardly through the close passing Pond Riding.

"Then into next close by the hedge-side, the hedge being south. Hold on the same course (north-east), through the next close by the hedge, the hedge south-east [part of this is a horse road], enter the gap at the end of this close into Oakridge Wood. Go north-east by the wood side, which is southward, a ✕ at the gap by Mr. Allnutt's 12 acres and Lower Meashes; at this gap enter 12 acres and go to the hedge south-east [but qy? if the outskirts of Oakridge Wood hereabouts are not in West Wycombe parish]; enter the gap near the wood about 50 yards before the end of 12 acres, and ✕, enter the west corner of Pitt Field, and go up the woodside, the wood hedge nearly south, holding on eastwardly. Enter Lord Carrington's piece (a long piece) at the north-east of Oakridge Wood, keep under the hedge of this piece north-east. The hedge south-east excluding the piece. East corner of Lord Carrington's piece, Pitfield a ✕, go east down Booker Lane, pass Green Street Lane, marking a ✕ at the north-east end of the lane in passing. Go on down Booker Lane into West Wycombe parish, John Turner's garden on the right or east of the land, through the yard of Cubbidge's Mill, through the shop, over the coal house, and south of the bridge a ✕."

In 1398, we find the following order :—

"That no man of whatever condition shall be delaying (commorans) in the town of Wycombe after ten o'clock at night. Any wanderer ought to go out of the town unless he have reasonable cause for wandering therein. And if any one be so found wandering about after the said hour, he shall be immediately seized and imprisoned by the servants of the town, and detained in prison until he be set at liberty by the Mayor (or some one holding his place) and the commonalty."

This order was no doubt made under the provisions of the Statute of Wynton, 13th Edward I., Stat. 2. Cap. 4., which declares,

"That from henceforth, to wit, from the day of the Ascension unto the day of St. Michael, in every city, six men shall keep at every gate; and in every borough twelve men shall watch the town continually all night from the sun setting unto the sun rising, and if any stranger do pass by them, he shall be arrested until morning; and if no suspicion be found he shall go quit; and if they find cause of suspicion, they shall forthwith deliver him to the Sheriff, and the Sheriff may receive him without damage, and shall keep him safely, until he be acquitted in due manner." [See also 5th Edward III., Cap. 14, which confirms the above enactment.]

The whole of the records of the Borough Court during the Lancastrian period have perished, and a long blank of seventy years brings us to the time of William Redehode, before mentioned.

The following is an award made apparently about 1470, which is somewhat interesting in an architectural point of view.

"This ys the Awarde, lawde, dome, and Juggement of Thomas Pym, Mayre of y towne of Wycombe, Xpofre Wasse, Willm Redehode, Richard Cary, Wal' Collard, Arbitrors, indifferently chosyn bytwene Thomas Baydon the elder, and Willm Aley, of and upon all man' contversyes, stryves, etc., . . . atis had and moved bytwene them, and in especyall for a Dormand [joist or beam] of a howse bytwene them.

"Wherein we the said Arbitrors give dome and Juggement, that the same Thomas Baydon shall suffre the same Willm Aley to Dormond upon hym savyng the same Thomas Baydon harmless, both Wedyr Tyght and Wynde Tyght w^t sufficient defence of smoke; Restyng no purloyne uppon the same Thomas Baydon's Howse; but bere the said purloynes uppon his owne grounde, at his owne ppre costes and charge."

"ffurthermore we geve lawe de warde and Juggement, that the same Thomas Baydon shall not make nou Wyndow, ne hole, nor convey no lyght, under hys owne walplate, wherby he may have any man' sight into the grounde of the same Willm Aley; and which of them breke this oure awarde shall lese 20 lb. wex, to the behofe of the Chirche of all halowys of Wycombe, to be leveyed by the Churchemen of the seid Chirche, for the tyme beyng."

Another award of similar nature, dated 18th January, 1503, by Nicolas Gerard, and Thomas Nasche, between Gefery Pusey, and John Peytefer, provided that Gefery shall—

"Relese all man' of Watyrfallis, evis droppis, palis, postis, the wiche the same John newe hath bilde."

The first order for Weavers, 1316, declared that all weavers who wish to work within the liberty of this borough, shall not pay in future to the Gildans for doing their office 12d. per annum for every loom working, but from henceforth, shall be free in all things concerning the Guild of traders, except stallages. This order seems to have been made to induce the weavers to settle in the borough. The next order, temp. Henry VIII., is less liberal in its provisions. It commences with the not very appropriate invocation :—

. " J̅hus m̅ͬcy.
" An acte for wevers and fullers."

" FForasmoche as it hath plesed the Kyng's grace to direct his gracious letter of Comyssyon or letter myssyf unto the mayre of this Borough for the tyme beying, or ellys in tyme to com, shal be and to the Burgessys of the same, to order and execute all and singler the p'miss⁵ of the abovesayd Comyssion, or letter myssyf according to thee auncyent pvelage and gode customys of the same borough lyke as in the sayd comyssyon or letter myssyf playnly dothe apere, remayn-yng in the tresory of the same, berying Dat." . . .

" Wherefor we Roberd Aishebroke now mayr, w' th aldermen burgess aboveseyd, by one assent and consent, the 6ᵗʰ day of Marche in the secund yere of the regn of King Henr: the 8ᵗʰ in the Gildaule have pvided and ordened for a ferme and a continuall ordinauns and comynwell of the said borough, that no ps̅o̅n or ps̅o̅ns occupy̅y̅g the crafts or occupac̅o̅ns of wevyng,* ffullyng, schall from this forthe ocupy intromet nor medyll more than in . . . of one of the same occupac̅ons. Also that no pson ne psons ocupy nor intromete w' in the said Burgh ; Except those psons that have be prentyce, or ellis brought up in their youth w' craftysmen of the same occupacon. Provided allway that this ordynance schall not be dowtfull in hynderauns or hurtyng of pson or pesons to inhabite them w' in this borough, beyng or ocupyeing ony of the aboveseid ocupacons, notw'stondyng the ordinaunce and pvision abovenamed. Moreov' it is pvided and ordeyned by the said May', Aldermen, and burgesses, that what man' of pson or psons will take upon them to use or ocupy in ony of the aboveseyd craftys, or ocupacons, con-trary to the pvision and ordynaunce above specyfyed, schall renne in penalte, and fforfetur of x li sterlyng, then and as ofte as it schall happyn ony pson of ocupacon or craftis aboveseid to offend doyng contrary to the said pvision and ordynaunce ; and the said x li to be leveyed of and upon the godys and the catalls of the said offendo's, by commande̅met of the May' for the tyme beyng, and aldermen of the same borough, whe'of the one pte so levyed schall remayn and stond to the use of the pische churche of the same town, the second pte to the use of the Chamb', and the third pte unto the baylys ffor the tyme then beyng by even porcons.

" Also it is pvided and for a ferme ordynaunce stablysched, by the said May', Aldermen, and burgess s, at the aforename‾day and place, that none of the aforenamed ocupyers of ony of the crafts of wevyng, ffullyng, or dyyng, or clothyng, put not forthe none of ther werk to dy, weve, nor full, othirwyse then to craftsmen of the same borough ocupyyng that ocupacons. And if that the ptyes so puttyng forthe ther work, well and truly may be pved w' a resonabill price for the same, w'in the seid Borough upon the payn of fforfetur of 3li 6ˢ 8ᵈ, then, and as ofte as ony of the aboveseid ptyes do offend and contrary the same pvision and ordinace And the said 3li 6s 8d to be levyed in manner and forme afore rehersed ; and to the same use as afore is lymyted. Provided allwey by the sayd Mayr Aldermen and burgess s if ony clothear be deceved, hyndred, or ells hurte, in the defaulte of Dyar, ffuller, or ells wefer, that then the pte so hurte, schall be recompensed, and alowed of his hurts, at ony tyme beyng aldremen and

---

* It is very clear that from a very early period an extensive cloth manufactory was carried on in Wycombe, as from the ancient record already referred to, we find there was a fulling mill in Wycombe in the reign of Henry IV. ; and we gather from history that others were afterwards erected in the same locality.

burgess, to levey of the godys, and catalls, of the same wardens, to the use and behof of any such clothear so hyndered to the valowe of his Damage."

"An order conc'ninge wevers of other mens worke within this Borough.

"John Ster-
linge, Mayor."

" M^d the 8th day of Julii in the seconde yere of the reign of ower sovereigne Ladye Quene Elisabethes grace, it is fully established and agreide by the assent and consent of John Sterlinge then Maior, with the Aldermen, Bayliffs, and Burgess s, of this Borough, that all man' of men beinge wevers within this Borough, that now dothe, or shall after the feast of ——— next comynge after the date hereof, use to weve other mennes worke, shall not from thenceforthe weave or cause to be woven any kersey, or kerseys, of his or their owne worke, upon the payne and penaltie of the forfiture for ev' such kersey, or kerseis, so woven, of his or their owne, as is aforeseide 40s of good and lawfull money of England, to be leviede of and upon the goods and cattalles of everye suche offendor, by the commandement of the Maior for the tyme beinge."

March the 14th in the same year the Mayor confirmed the foregoing order of Ashbrook's.

April 20th, 4 Jac. I., 1606. An order was made on all foreigners who come to dwell within the town, to pay such fines as shall be assessed and levied by the Mayor :—

"And it is further ordered that every foreyner and straunger and inhabitaunte in this towne, shall paye for theire Loomes, y^t have Loomes, and they that have noe Loomes, to paye for their Shoppwindowes VI^d a yeare for every Loome."

The first order concerning Brewers is dated 1527, and is as follows :—

" The brewer not to tiple.

" Also be yt Inactyd and orderyd before the said Mayer and all borgessys, and the cominalte of the sayd towne and borowe, from thys day forward that no man' of man, nor woman, that shall brew to sale and typpyll hit w^{t}in hym or hyr, but send it into the towne to the typpellars, for to be solde acordyng to the Mayers prysse, upon payne so affending the ffyrste tyme 10^s. fowarnyd the seconde tyme, 13^s. 4^d., and the thyrd tyme 20^s., for to be levyd apon suche gudds, and catallys, as thay have here, or ells can be founde w^{t}in thys towne, or borowh, aforsayd. And yf ther be any Burges agyn thys ower ordinaunce and acte, that we have afore made, that than the Mayer for the tyme beyng shall comyte hym or hyr to warde, and dyscharge hym of hys Burgeswycke, or ells hyr of hyr fredome. And so to presyn them as forinars and not as burgess, and to forfeyt to the chambur of this towne 40^s. for hys mysedoyng agyn the gud order of this towne, and our acte made aforsayd, and for to syt in prison 3 dayes, and 3 niwteys, after the costome of thys towne as a fforynar, and so for to put yor Sewerte to the Mayer and hys brethern for to paye all soche merceements, or fynys as ys afore rehersyd, made and grauntyd be us. Also no maner of typpellar from thys daye forwarde, shall brew to salle and typpell y^t w^t in hym or hyr a pon payne, the fyrst tyme 10^s, the second tyme, 13^s 4^d, the thyrd tyme 20^s, for to be levyd apon ther gudds and catalls as they have here or ells can be founde w^t in this borough aforsayd. And the sayd typpellars wyll not abaye oure sayd acte, deyde, and ordenaunce, thus made her, but wyll very byl the Mayer for the tyme beyng callyng them afore hym for to know why they do not abaye the order that ys aforemade, by the sent of the comen howse of thys borowgh. And they wyll not so abay yt, then the Mayer shall comyt them to warde, and so to prison hym or hyr 3 dayes and 3 nytes as ys afore rehersyd. And also yf ther be any man or woman that dothe make labur and sewte, owte of thys towne contrary agyn the order, and Inactyd and made by us afore rehersyd, that than the Mayer shall calle them afore hym and hys brethern, and to banesche them thys towne and for to dewell no more yn yt. And also yff the Mayer be at any chargys in executyng of thys acte whe all wyll by a holle assent grauntyth for to paye hym all hys costs and charges at the townes costes and charges payd to hym by the Chamberlynes for the tyme beyng howte of the Chamber money, or ells any othyr offyeer for the tyme as yt shall be thowthe best, by the dyscrescyon of the said Mayer and hys bretherne."

This extreme jealousy on the part of the Guild of any " sewte " made against their order out of the town, is further illustrated by the following regulation :—

COMPLAINTE MADE WᵗOUT lYCENCE OF MAIOR.

" Mᵈ that it is inacted and ordeyned in the geld hall before the mayr John Aley and his bretheryn, and all the comynalte of the same Borowgh, that if ony Burges in tyme coming from this day forthe, make or cause to be made ony labor, by compleynt to ony pson or psons, wᵗout licens of the Mayr, that ony burgess so offendyng to forfeyte for his defaute 40ˢ and 3 dayes psonment. And ony forenar so offendyng to forfeyte 10ˢ and 6 dayes psonment, the payn to be levyed by the bayles for the time beying, the one d̄e to the Chambr, and the other to the baleys." **"John Alleye, Maior."**

" The same order is ratified and affirmed.

" Mᵈ that on the election day ther holden, the 13 day of March in the ffyfte yr̄e of the reign of our soveign Lord Kyng Edward the syxt, before Mr. Richard Cary then Mayer and his brethern, it is enacted by the whole howse wᵗ the consent of the seid Mayer and his brethern, that the act above wretyn is ratiffied and affyrmed to stond in full strenght and effect forevᵗ." **" Richarde Cary, Maior," 1551.**

" Memorandum yᵗ yᵉ 19ᵗʰ of May 1647, the act above written is further confirmed by us whose names are subscribed,

" James Bigg Mayor	Mathew Petefer	Nicholas Bradshaw
Edward Bedder	George Bradshaw	Henry Elliott, baylefe
John Gybbons	John Collins	
	Geᵃ Moore "	

The next order affecting Brewers is dated April 10th, 1559, and is as follows :—

" Memorandum it is mooreovᵗ orderede and agreide, the daye and yre before specifiede by the seide maior bailiffs and burgess's that all manᵗ of comon brewers of ale and bere that shall be admytted from henceforth wᵗin this borough, shall from tyme to tyme be bounde in a recognisaunce every of them in 5 li unto the maior, for the tyme, beinge that he or they shall not tiple or sell ale or bere within his or their howses upon the forfiture of the seide 5 li. And also **" Thomas Kele, Maior."**

that all man' of typlers shal be bounde in lyke man' not to brewe in their howses, to sale upon the lyke payne. And for the comyttinge of any such offence by any suche brewer, or typler, contrary to this order, it shall be lawfull at the commandement of the Maior for that tyme being to levie of and upon the goods and cattalles of ev^y suche offender to the value of the seide some, and all other orders to stand, made, and concerning the brewers and tiplers that are in this book."

An order on Butchers is as follows :—

" Robert Gravet, Mayor."

" M^d that at the lawe daye in the Rye being the 26th day of Aprell in the 4th and 5th yeres of the reignes of Kinge Philippe and Queene Marye before Robert Gravet Mayor and his brethern, and the burgesses there came in the bochers dwellinge within the Borough and did fully covennt, and graunt, that from this present tyme they will paye, or cawse to be payde, yerely unto the bayliffs, the some of 13' 4^d, and the seide bochers havinge therfore $\overline{ob}$ of ev^y cowe or stere hide, that straungers shall bringe in to be solde, and for everye oxe hide brought by the seide straungers, 1^d, and for every dosen of calve skynnes 1^d, and for ev^y standinge of the seide straungers bochers 1^d."

Another order is as follows :—

" Cheping Wicombe,"

" Ad vis. franc pleg. ib$\overline{m}$ tent in le Rye 27th dii Aprilis, Anno 21st Eliz. Regine coram Willo Mundye genos maiore Will° Twayts Ruland Eles Thurstayne Wynche Ruland Brasbridge John Litleboy and Thomas Eles, balliis.

" Wm Mundy, Esq., Mayor," 1579.

" It. this daie yt ys ordered by the mayer bailyffs and burgeses, that the butchers dwellinge w'in this borrowe, shall pay yerely to the bailyffs there, for thier billynge 6' 8^d and the owte bochers 6' 8^d more to be charged equally accordinge to their billynge this order to . . . duringe and untill other order shal be taken."

" John Gibbons, Gent., Mayer." 1599.

" At the leete holden in the Guyldhall of this boroughe the fower and twentith day of Aprill in the one and ffortithe ycre of Queen Elizabeth.

" No Butcher shall kyll any neate or beast, or sell, or offer to sell the same, wthin this borough, unles the same neate or beast, have stoode, lyen or ben, undriven and unchased by the space of ffower and twenty howers next before the same neate or beast bee so kylled, uppon payne of fforfeyture of twentye shillinges to the maier bayliffes and burgesses of this borough for every offence, contrary to this ordinaunce. Nor shall have, or keepe, above one stall in the markett of this Boroughe uppon the like payne. And yt is likewise ordered that no Butcher dwellinge out of this boroughe shall sell or offer to sell any beefe in the markett of the boroughe unless he bringe the hide and talowe of the same beast to the same markett, and will sell the same to any pson y' shall offer to give him a reasonable pryce for the same. Nor shall sell or offer to sell any manner of ffleshe in the markett on any markett daye betwene Michaellmas, and Shrovetyde, after fower of the clocke in the afternoone. Nor on any markett daye betwene Shrovetyde and Michaellmas, after sixe of the clocke in the afternoone, uppon payne of fforfeyture of five shillinges to the Maior bayliffs and burgesses of this boroughe, for every offence against this ordinannce, wch penalties shal be levied uppon the goodes and chattels of such butcher so breakinge any of the same ordinaunces.

" It is allso on the same day by the same authorytye ordered and established that no higler, nor any other pson, or psons, using to buy any victualls to the end to sell the same againe, shall buy any fflesh, powltrye, butter, cheese, egges, or such like victualls in the markett of this boroughe, before the markett bell have runge, uppon paine of fforfeyture of the same ffleshe, powltrye, butter, cheese, egges, or other victualls, so bought contrary to this ordinaunce, to the Maior, bayliffes, and burgesses of this boroughe."

The next order brings us to the time of the erection of the shambles in the Hogmarket.

"At the Courte leete holden the nynthe daye ot Aprill ano dni. 1627, John Littlepage esquire then maior. It is ordered that no fforraine butcher shall showe any meate on any stalle on any market daye hereafter, that shal be erectede in any other place or places in the sayde burrowe, until the comon shambles alreadye builte for that purpose shall be furnishede w[t] butchers, excepte it be the stall of William Haddinet employde to that use, for wh. he payethe 12[d] by the yeare.

John Littellpage Mayor
William Guy Senior
William Ayer
Robert Bisco
Richard Gibbins
John Davenport
John Bigg
George M. Dier   } Bailifes
Nathanaell Weedon }

"These shambles were built on an octagonal plan in 1622 by the advise and appointm[t] of W[m] Aire, Alderman."

We may take it for granted that William Aire was the architect of the building. The building was pulled down in 1761, to make way for the present structure, which was built from the design of Adelphi Adams.

At the end of the Register is the following stray memorandum :—

" It[m] it is ordered the 17th day of Jun 1590, that every butcher standinge in the market to sell beffe, shall weye onlye by the comōn scalles and wayghts apoynted by 2 sworne men therto ewsse, shall yeld and paye unto the sworne men for ther paynes and travills therin for every day 2[d]; and if it hapen any butcher a stranger, to kill or sell above one oxe, bullock, or cowe, then the same butcher to pay for every day 3[d]."

An act made Aprill 24-1564 imposes a tax of 20[s] yearly on ony Shoemaker residing in the Town. In consideration whereof, " yt is orderid and agreide, that there shall noo foren Shomaker come into the mkett to make any shewe their, with their shois to the hurt and hinderaunce of the seide towne shomakers except onely y[t] it shal be lawfull to all the saide fforren shomakers to come in and to make their shewe uppon the twoo ffaier dayes w[t]out interruption of any pson or psons w[t]in this borough."

" W[m] Thwayts, Mayer."

A precisely similar enactment was made regarding Hat makers, and hat sellers, Dec. 18, 1620, Thomas Gibbons, Mayor, imposing on them a tax of six shillings only.

We next quote an order on Foreign Tailors in the year 1609.

"John Little-page, Mayor."

"Mᵈ that at the leete holden the 16ᵗʰ daye of October in the year of the Reigne of o' Sove-raigne lord James by the grace of God of England, France, and Ireland, and Seaventh, and of Scotland, the three and ffortith. The taylors inhabiting wᵗʰⁱⁿ this boroughe came and com-playned that they were much oppressed wᵗʰ the nomber of fforeyne Taylors continuallye com-ming into the libertys, and much impoverished, and hindered in the exercise of theire trade thereby. Whereuppon yt was ordered by the then maior, aldermen, and baliffes present and consenting at the requeste and humble suite of the said taylors, that from thenceforthe noe fforreyne Taylor excepte he were eyther borne, or hadd seaven yeares served as an apprentice to a taylor wᵗʰin the boroughe, should come to dwell or to keepe any shoppe wᵗʰin this boroughe, uppon payne to have his shoppe windowes shutt uppe, by the Serjeante for tyme beinge. And if, after his shoppe windowes so shutt uppe, and uppon commandemᵗ of the then Mayor to forbeare the exercise of the trade or misterei, he shall presume to contemptuouslye either to open his windowes or to use his trade or misterei, wᵗʰin his owne dwelling howse, or shoppe, then uppone payne to be imprisoned by the then Maier untill he have bothe satisfied the Maior for his contempte, by submission, and shall be obedient to this order."

In consideration thereof the " Taylors agreed to pay for ever an annual taxe of 10s."

"The Tailors inhabiting within the Borough, complaining that they were much oppressed with the number of foreign Tailors coming within the liberty, and much impoverished and hindred thereby, an order was made on the 16th October, 7 James I., that in future such foreign Tailors should keep no shop in the town ; and in case of contravention of the order, their shop windows should be shut up by the Serjeant of the town ; if further resistance were made, they were to be committed to prison."

"Memorandum, that this 6th day of March, 1664, Nicholas Wilson gave security to dwell in the Burrough, and to follow his only vocation of distilling strong waters ; and did then assume and undertake not to follow any other calling by keeping of a retaile shop or the like ; and then at his admittance did pay a fine of 50s. to the towne.

"Jno. Boulter, Clerk."

Following the above order on Tailors in the pages of the Records, but preceding it in date by many years, is one intituled,

" Roger Bramstone, Maior, 1490."

" An order for wearinge of lyverye contrarye to the Statute.

" Mᵈ. that at the law day helld at Wykomb yn the yelld hall the Thorsday next afft' the fest of sent Luke the Avangell yn the yerre of our Lord God XIII C IIII and X, aforre Rog' Bramston then mayrr of the town, y' ys ordered, it be the avys of the sayd mayrre and hess bretherne, and granted be all the borgess and comonallte that be dwellyng w'yn thay sam town, That eff ther be any Borges dwellyng w'yn the sam town from thes day forthe, werre any leffray sayne or conysant contorare to the statuets of the lande, shall lees his fredom and xl. s of lawfoll monay of yngland, the on hallf to the Mayrre, the toder halff to the Baylyf for the tym beyng, to be levid upon the Goods and cattells be the sam baylyf of them soo fownden fawte, and allsoo eff ther be any dwellar w'yn the sam towne, nat beyng Borges, werre any leffray contrare to the statueds chall haff 7 days presonment w'owt any surte and to les 10', the on hallf to the Mayrre, the oder hallf, to the Baylyf for the tym beyng, to be leved be the sam Baylys apon the Goods and cattells of theis soo fownden fawte. Thes ackt to be form and Staboll and leve a Ball alls ofton tyms as any fawt ys fowndon yn manar and form as ys afor rehersed."

The statute referred to is the 1st Henry IV. cap. 7, 1399, confirmed by 7 Henry IV. cap. 14, and repealed by 3 Car. I. cap. 4. The most curious thing in the minute is its extraordinary orthography. From an inspection of the two entries which follow it, there is no doubt that it is in the handwriting of Roger Bramston, the Mayor already referred to. The two acts refer respectively to the oft-forbidden turning of pigs out on the " Kyngs hewway," and the selling of grain without payment of tribute; the latter providing that " ther shall noo psonds nooder of the Town nor of the Contey be let to buye all manor of grayn accordyng to the law w'owyt due trepett payeng To the baylys or to any of oder parsons."

" Thirsday after hokday, 1489."

Woodfetchers, in 1563, were ordered to be punished in the open stocks, according to the discretion of the Mayor.

In 1571 all " intenaunts being strangers, and acountyd, and knowen heggbrekers, to avoide the towne by pentecost next comyng, uppon payne of imprisonament and ev'y of the inhab'auncs suffering them to remayne and dwell in ther seid houses, to pay 20', and y' no intenaunts be receyved hereaft' into anie house, or houses, uppon payne of 20'."

The following enactments relate to the Mayor.

"WYCOMBE.

" M^d. that on the Thorsday next aft' the feste of Seynt Seythe * the 14th yere of Kyng Henry the VII, at the Law day held yn the yeld hall Before Rogg' Bramston, then beyng maire of the seyd Towne, hit is ordeyned and stablyshed and acte by the assent of the seyd maire and all the Burgess and comynnalte of the sayd Boroghe, that ther shall no maire be electe or chosyn from this day forthwarde, excepte he come owte of the howse callyd ye counsell howse of the sayd borghe, and if ther be ony burgeys of ye seyd borghe geve his voyce, or electyon, to any psone or psonys other wyse then is before rehersyd, to lese his fredom of ye

---

* It may be observed in passing, that the St. " Seythe " here mentioned, was the virgin Saint Oseth of Aylesbury in this county. For the account of her, see Dr. Lipscombe's "History of Bucks," vol ii., p. 3.

seyd borghe and a fyne of 10ˢ, half to yᵉ mayre for the tyme beyng, and that other halfe to the Chambʳ to be levyed by the Baylyffs for the tyme beying, of the goods and catells of such psone or psonys that so offendyth. And if ony foryner wᵗyn the seyd Burghe dwellyng, gȇve, or graunt, his voice or ellectyon to ony other psone or psonys otherwyse then before is named, shall have 7 days psonemet wᵗowet ony manʳ maynprise and lese a fyne of 5ˢ to be levyed by the baylyffs in manʳ and forme aforesayd."

The magisterial dignity of the Mayor having been grievously insulted, was justly revenged by the following enactment.

"PUNYSCHM͞ET FOR ILL DOERS
AGAYN THE MAYR." ("Mallefactʳ cont. maiorem")

"At the Courte holdyn in yelde hall the Thursday next before the ffest of Pentecosten, in the 10ᵗʰ yere of the reyngn of oure soveraign lorde Kyng Henr. the eyghtith, it is ordeyned by the mayre at that tyme beyng Thomas ffrere, Robᵗ Astbroke, and Willᵐ Chalfount, Aldermen of this borough, wyth the moste pte of the burgens, belongyng to ther comyn, and counselhouse, for as moche as now of late, di͞vs variaunces stryfys debats and grudgs hathe be moved and hadd betwene the abovesaid mayr and othir burgens, on the one pty, Richard Pede and Thomas Scherefeld burgens, on the other ptye, for divsᵉ wordys unfittyng spokyn agayn the said mayʳ by the abovenamed Richard Pede and Thomas Schereffeld uppon ther ill mynde and counsell pursued a citacon agayn the said mayr, and other of the said burgens of the same Towne out of the arches. And also the said Richard Pede and Thomas Scherefeld hathe comitted and spokyn di͞vs wordys unlefull agayn the said mayre, as seyng that they wolde have a`newe mayr, and no thyng thereof done in dede. Wherfor now it is aggreed by the assent and consent of the said Mayre and Aldermen and the more pte of the burgens of the comyn house, that the forsaid Richard Pede and Thomas Scherefeld, shall sursease and no ferthur pʳ serve in the said arches, or ells where agayn the said mayr and Burgens as is above wretyn upon the payn of 40s. of evʸ yche of them to be levied to the use of the hole Chambʳ. And furthermor upon the payn of lesying, and utterly dischargyng of ther fredom and Burgeswyk. And aftur that to be reported, and taken as fforeners, and to abide suche punyschemet as schal be then thought by the discrescon of the said Mayr, Aldermen, and other of the said Comyn house. And in lyke wyse all and evʸ Burgess' offendyng the Mayr for the tyme beyng, to have punysche͞met by the Mayr, Aldremen, and Burgess' of the comyn house accordyng to his, or there demerits, in tyme to com."

From an order, dated 1504, it is enacted "that evʸ mayr chosyn from that day fortheward, schall ocupye the rome but one yere togedyr for certin consideracons for the gode order, and rules of the seid borowgh." The next enactment, in 1505, provides "that he shal be charged by othe upon a book yerely."

We also find two orders, dated respectively 1505 and 1563, against the practice of canvassing for elections, which seems to have been introduced about this time; any burgess offending "wᵗ dewe p͞ve [with due proof] to lose 20', and that to be levied of his gods to the behove of the chamb', the one halfe, and the othir halfe to the repacon of the chirch," etc. The latter one increases the penalty to £10.

By an order, dated 21st September, 1608, "the Bailiffs should from thenceforth keep two Feasts yearly in the Guildhall for the Mayor and Burgesses, on the days on which the 'Leetes' are held ; under a penalty of 20', to be paid by each Bailiff on neglect thereof."

There is also an order made in 1613, by William Shrimpton, Esq., Mayor, that all apprentices shall be enrolled before the Mayor and Recorder, and to serve not less than seven years, after which they are to be free men and women of the borough ; the women, however, only so long as they shall live unmarried. In the same year occurs the election of John Scott to the office of a yealding or "gildan," who is to serve until some other be elected in his room.

At Folio liii., Ledger I., there is " An order for wearing the badges," of very considerable length. Among other things it is stated :—

" And whereas the poore people of the said Burrough are growne very numerous and are likely to increase dayly, to the great impoverishment of the tradesmen of the said Burrough, many of them through idleness, being able to work, yett will not, because they find an easier way of living by collection. And unlesse some speedy care be taken to prevent the excessive growth of such poore, all, or the greatest part of the tradesmen of the said Burrough in a short time are like to come to poverty, and to be unable to maintain themselves and familye by reason of such great taxes towards the relieffe of the poor."

The benefit of the " easie rates " when " the poor people wore badges," is then adverted to ; and it is therefore ordered by the Mayor, and the major part of the " Common Councell," that before the Overseers or Church-wardens give

" Any releiffe, collection, or money, to any poore man or woman of the said Burrough, they shall give a badge, being the sign of the swan, or the town armes, and shall cause him, her, or them, to wear the same upon his or her uppermost garment, at all times, soo as the same may been seen apparently and openly."

In case of refusal, no relief or " collection " is to be given ; as it is clear that the person refusing can live without it.

The Mayor, Bailiffs, and Steward, were, by the Charter of Philip and Mary, empowered to hold a Court of Record from three weeks to three weeks, to hear and determine all actions for the recovery of debts, etc., not exceeding the sum or value of £20; and here we may appropriately add the Oath to be taken by Attorneys practising in the Court.

"MAY 22, 1665.—THE FORME OF THE OATH THAT THE ATTORNEYES ARE TO BE SWORNE TO BEFORE THEY ARE ADMITTED TO PRACTICE IN THE COURT OF THIS BURROUGH.

"You shall sweare that from henceforth duringe the tyme y° shall continue to practice as an Attorney or Solicitor in this Court of the Burrough of Chepinge Wicombe, not to act any thing that may tend to the p'judice or damage of the same Burrough, or ingage yo'self in any cause or lawsuit that shall at any time be comenced ag' the Corporacon itselfe as it is a body politique or corporate by virtue of his mat'es late gracious Letters pattents, but shall endeavor to the best of yo' skill and power at all tymes (as occasion serves) to uphold and p'serve the privileges and imunities of the Burrough, and to be aydinge and assistinge to the Mayor for the tyme beinge and the Comon Councell ag' all psons that shall comence any suite in law or otherwise endeavor to oppose or disturbe them in p'curinge or maineteyninge of their just rights and priviledges, and that yo. shall pleade noe forreine pson to any accon that y" shall appeare in the said Burrough Court, soe helpe y" God."   Reg. Burg., N° i., F° 46.

This oath was probably consequent on the misconduct of Mr. William Child, of Chesham, who having been admitted to practice in the Court

"Several tymes very insolently and uncivilly behaved himselfe towards the Mayor and Aldermen of this Burrough, as namely, at a Court Dinner at the White Hart, where in his discourse he gave to Mr. Edward Bedder one of the Aldermen of this Burrough much undervaluing and slighting language, telling him in playne termes, 'It should not be as he would have it, neither should he comand or have his will,' with many other short curbing words misbecoming his place and p'fession."

And further :—

"Att the generall sessions of the publique peace holden for this County at the Guildhall of this Burrough the tenth day of Aprill last past, there beinge some businisse of consequence to be discust that related to a matter in difference between the burrough and the p'ish, the said Mr. Child being not reteyned in the cause, nor in the least concerned in it, yet nevertheless to show how willing and ready he was to doe the Burrough an injury, did then and afterwards, counsell the p'ishioners, and side and take pte with them agaynst the Burrough, and moreover deridingly in the open Hall did then say to the Mayor and Aldermen then p'snte ('you make your Charter a nose of Wax'), and further did then publish and speake (in a scoffing manner) several scurrelous words tending to the reproach and discredit of the Mayor and company on purpose to make men have them in derision."

And also on the 28th July, "at the signe of the Maydenhead, to show how far he had the Mayor and Court of Aldermen in contempt," said to Mr.

Lucas, a Justice of the Peace, and other Aldermen, several untranscribable expressions of contempt and ridicule, "for all of which several misdemeanours, slovenly languidge, malepart caridge, and fanatick-like deportment," the Mayor, Aldermen, and Common Council, formally expelled him from practising any more in the Court, but "out of favour to his clyants," allow him "tyme to bring those causes to a period that he is now concerned in, and are depending in the Court. But shall not for the tyme to come appeare to any new accōn for any psōn or p'sons whatsoever." Fº 27, 1662.

We cannot refrain from quoting in this place the disfranchisement of Mr. Henry Shepard, Feb. 6th, 1678, for "insolently misbehaving himselfe, by beinge drunke and offring affronts to sev'all gentlemen, namely Sir John Borlase, and others, the third day of this instant ffebruary at the signe of the Katherine Wheele, in this Burrough," being reported generally to be "a man of uncivill and rude behaviour at other times not becominge his place of a Burgess of this Burrough." "In token whereof," proceeds the Record "it is ordered that the great Bell shall be rung out accordinge to custome, in testimony of his misdemeanors, and for his disfranchisement."

According to ancient custom, which was continued up to the passing of the Municipal Corporation Act, the outgoing Mayor was "tolled out," by tolling of the great bell on the morning of the Mayor's election. After which the Corporation proceeded in state to St. Mary's Chapel, and in subsequent years to the Parish Church, when a sermon was preached suitable to the occasion, for which 6s. 8d. per annum was left by Mr. Wainwright to the Vicar of the Parish. On the Corporation returning from the chapel or church they proceeded to the Guildhall, the pathway being strewed with flowers, preceded by a drummer, who drummed the old Mayor out. The burgesses elected the Mayor in open common hall,* and at the close of the election, the Corporation went in procession round the Market Hall, when

* At fol. 141 of first Ledger we find the following curious entry :—" The Thursday after Midlent Sunday, 20 Henry VII., Nicholas Jerard is mentioned as Mayor. 'In the Gilde Haule holdene the day above wretyne, etc., that it is stabylly actide from this forthe that no burgesse, nor forener make no labour, nor desir no man to speke before the day of election of the Meyre, for no singular desir, but every manne to schewe ther voyces at ther owne mynde, without trobyll or unresonabille doynge ther in the tyme of ther election, under the payne of every burgess that so offendyth, with dewe prove, to lose XXˢ, and that to be levied of his godes to the behove of the Chambre the one halfe, and the other halfe to the reparacion of the Chirche. And every forener so offendyng to lose Xs., and to be levied in lyk wyse," etc.

the new Mayor was drummed into office, accompanied by a merry peal of bells from the Parish Church. After partaking of a luncheon, the Mayor and Council attended at the Bar Iron Warehouse, in White Hart Street, when each member of the Council was weighed, and his weight duly recorded. Such was the order of proceedings during the past generations, but how far back the practice thus described originated, it would be difficult to determine ; however we may assume that it was of remote antiquity.

We may here mention that from a very early period the Members of Parliament for the borough were, on their election, carried on men's shoulders round the Market Hall ; this practice was in later years superseded by the more graceful form of chairing the representatives round the borough in elegant chairs, tastefully decorated with their respective colours.

The burgesswick of Wycombe in the seventeenth century became quite a position of fashion among the county gentry, of whom we find very many enrolled therein, as having taken the oath of office, and in particular the following well-known personages :—

1658. Sir James Harrington, Knt.
1660. Sir Edmund Pye.
  ,,   Sir John Borlase, Marlow.
1668. Robert Danvers, Esq.
1672. John, Earl of Bridgewater, Lord Lieut. and High Steward of Wycombe.
  ,,   Sir Wm. Egerton, his son.
  ,,   John, Lord Lovelace.
  ,,   Wm. Lovelace, Esq.
  ,,   Richd. Lovelace, Esq.
  ,,   Sir John Borlase, Knt. & Bart.
  ,,   John Borlase, Esq.
  ,,   John Tipinge, Esq., Chequers, Stokenchurch.
  ,,   Thomas Clayton, Esq.

1684. Sir Dennis Hampson, Bart.
1688. Sir John Hoby, Bart., Bisham.
  ,,   Thomas Lewes, Esq., of West Wycombe, and Alderman of the City of London.
  ,,   Edm. Waller, Esq., Beaconsfield, son of the poet.
  ,,   Hon. Wm. Jephson, Boston House.
1691. Hon. Chas. Godfrey.
  ,,   Hon. Thos. Wharton.
  ,,   Sir Thos. Lee, Bart., Hartwell.
1698. Hon. Goodwin Wharton.
  ,,   Sir Thomas Skipwith, Bart.

To this we might add in the next century :—

The Hon. Wilbraham Tollemache, of Colvelly Hall, Cheshire.

58

which forms a portion of the properties of the Wycombe Municipal Charities. His seal exhibits a classic bust in a helmet, sinister, faced in profile.

The reign of Elizabeth is marked by nothing extraordinary in our annals. According to tradition, the Queen, in 1566, on the occasion of her Majesty's visiting the University of Oxford, on her return, did Edward Lord Windsor the honour of a visit at his seat at Bradenham, where she was sumptuously entertained; and Wood, in his "Athenæ Oxon.," vol. i., p. 416, informs us "that his Lordship's kinsman, Miles 'Windsor,' spoke an oration, which giving the Queen great content, she, in a high manner, commended it to the Spanish ambassador then present." Her Majesty and suite left Bradenham House on horseback, passing through some of the loveliest scenery in the county, by the way of the primeval forest of Walter's Ash, over Downley Common, and through Tinker's Wood, down the ancient way called Hobbes Lane, to Wycombe, where she was welcomed by the hearty greetings of her loyal subjects. The route from Bradenham to Wycombe is still traceable on the southern slope of the Downley Hill, and Tinker's Wood. The queen is said to have paid a visit to John Raunce, Esquire, at Bassetsbury Manor House, where she remained until the following day.

Queen Elizabeth's Charter in 1598, and James the First's in 1609, present us with nothing remarkable. The latter, indeed, abolished the office of High Steward and substituted that of Recorder. Yet we find, notwithstanding this, that the aldermen continued to elect noblemen and others to the honorary office of High Steward, viz., Scott the Regicide, in 1651, and the Earl of Bridgewater in 1672; the Lord Chancellor Jeffries in 1683, and Thomas, Marquis of Wharton, in 1715. And at the same time Recorders were also elected.

Among the miscellaneous orders of this period is one—

"That the towne seale shall always remayn in the tresurye, upon payne and penaltie of C lb. to be leviede upon the goods and catalls of the Maier for the tyme beinge for not fullinge of this order; if he, the seide Maier for the tyme beinge, do not when the occasion shall serve to occupye the seide seale for the townes busyness, then the seide seale immediately to be putte into the treasurye agayne w'out any further delay."

1624. Memorandum, "That the daie and yeare abovesaid it is condiscended, concluded, and fullie agreed by the Maier, Aldermen, and Bailiffs, of the said Burrough," etc., etc., "that burgesses shall have only one stall on market day except by payment of a foreigners stallage." "Geo Welles, Maier."

The burgesses, ever loyal to their sovereign, and staunch supporters of Protestantism, commemorated the Gunpowder Treason with great spirit, on the anniversary of the plot. Large bonfires were made in the four wards; one in front of the Guildhall; one as you enter Easton Street; one near the bridge in St. Mary's Street; and one opposite the Canal. The men of the different wards kept up a spirited skirmish with fireworks. The Mayor, aldermen, and bailiffs, assembled in the Guildhall to witness the rejoicings; after which they regaled themselves, as we are quaintly informed, "with cold spareribs and apple sauce." The loving-cup of spiced ale was passed round the festive board, loyal toasts were drunk with hearty enthusiasm, and the downfall of Popery predicted with groans.

Passing to the time of Charles the First, we find that during the civil war Prince Rupert at one time made a sally upon Wycombe; it was on the occasion of his acting under the advice of the adventurous Hurry (Urrie), when he determined to attack the Parliamentary forces, under Lord Wentworth of Bradenham House. At four o'clock on Saturday, June 17, 1643, his trumpets sounded to horse in the streets of the City of Oxford. The cavalry, joined by infantry from Islip, proceeded to Stokenchurch, leaving Thame, where Essex was quartered, to the left. It being now too late to reach Wycombe, they encamped in the woods. Early in the morning they attacked Postcomb, and sacked Chinnor, killing fifty men, and making sixty prisoners. Hampden advised Essex, but in vain, to call in the detachment from Wycombe; if he had, it would have been too late; for Rupert, avoiding the western approach to the town, "fell in," says Clarendon, "at the further end of the town towards London, whence no enemy was expected, and so no guards were kept there. A regiment of horse and of foot were lodged there, which were cut off or taken prisoners, and all the horses and a good booty brought away. From thence they marched backward to another quarter, within less than two miles of the general's own quarters." (Clarendon, Ed. Oxford, 1707, vol. ii., p. 261.)

The encounter before alluded to took place in the Rye, where the Parliamentary forces, under Lord Wentworth, opposed the skirmishing party. The latter had proceeded down the Back Lane, which gave access to the Rye, before its conversion into a watercourse; the conflict was of too unimportant a character to give it an historical significance, or to make it the subject of further observation.

We find the King himself next appearing in Wycombe as a prisoner. His sojourn at Holmby House was terminated by an order to bring him to the Parliamentary head-quarters at St. Albans, thence, after more vicissitudes, to Caversham, where he lodged at Lord Craven's. Here, Sir Philip Warwick says, " he could perceive the King was very apprehensive in what hands he was, but was not to let it be discovered." Thence through Henley, Marlow, and Wycombe, to Woburn.

The following entry of the journey of Charles is found in the Borough Records, Anno, 1647.

> " Kinge Charles marched through this Towne ffro Casūm toward Woborne in Bedfordshire (Mr. James Bigg then beinge Maior) and afterwards, was beheaded at Whitehall gate uppon the 30th day of January Anno 1648, *to the ppetuall infamy of the English nation."*

Oliver Cromwell granted a charter to this borough, which provided that eight burgesses should be elected as additional Common Councilmen yearly. The following is an entry of some of the annual elections :—

> " Monday, 5th July, 1658.
>
> " Att a Comon Counsell held for the Burrough of Cheping Wicombe the day and yeare abovesaid. The Mayor, Bailiffs, and Burgesses of the said Burrough (being then p'sent) by virtue of the new charter, did then elect and sweare theis pticular psons hereunder named, to be additional Comon Counsellmen wᵗʰin this Borough, for this ensuing yeare, viz'.—

Joseph Birrott	Joshua Grange
Hugh Shrimpton	William Bovington
Jerome Gray	Samuel Welles
William Bigg	William Freer."

The increase in the number of the council was no doubt wisely ordained to correct abuses which crept in, when the old select body, who were self-elected, had sole authority.

The fate of Oliver's charter is told thus :—

> " This charter was, on the Restoration, burnt by consent in front of the Guildhall, when Mr. Lucas was Mayor."

On the occasion of the royal proclamation of 1681, appealing to the whole nation, the Corporation forwarded to the King the following address, which is a curious and interesting specimen of the verbosity of the day :—

> " To the King's most excellent Maᵗⁱᵉ
>
> " The most humble adresse of yoʳ Matⁱᵉˢ most Loyall subjects the Mayor, Aldermen, Bayliffs, Burgesses, and other Inhabitants of yoʳ. Matⁱᵉˢ Antient Corpora͞con of Chepping Wycombe, in the County of Bucks.

" May it please yo' sacred Mat^{ie}.

" Most of o' late defeated Politicians,* disappoynted of theire dark designem^{ts}. by yo'. Mat^{ies} pfound wisdom and divine prision have endeavoured to disparage all loyall adresses either as uselesse and insignificant, or as discountenanced and unregarded, and that the glutt of them doth cloy and surfett rather then satisfie yo'. Mat^{ie}.

" Notwthstanding these slye pjected discouragements, wee have alwayes detested and rejected them togeather with theire now exploded scanty and forsaken abettors. And have ever incerted o' loyall selves amongst the resolute, grave and deliberate psōns. And wee doe most highly applaud the stout fidelios, the strenuous, brisk, and valiant youth, of this yo' now much undeluded nation. We therefore yo' Mat^{ies} most dutyfull and most devoted subjects, entyrely plesse : That wee will to the utmost stresse of o' sinews, to the latest gaspe of o' lives, and the last solitary mite in o' coffers, adhere to yo' mātie. And wee beseech yo' Mat^{ies} most gratious acceptance of o' most humble and unfeigned thankfullnesse for all yo' Mat^{ies} most princely purposes comprized in 'yo' mat^{ies} most gratious delarācon, yo' royall resolves for frequent parliaments. Yo' most pious intentions to perpetuate the ptestant religion amongst us, yo' equall governm^t in Church and State, by the Lawes establist. And the legall (though we hope in God, the many yeares remote and distant) discent of yo' royall diadem. Many have out stript us in the wing, but none shall exceed us in theire wishes; we envye much theire more earley applye, but none shall ever appeare more faithfull, though many in this have been more fortunate."

" God p'serve yo' Mat^{ies} from all rebellious Machinacōns.

" Amen."

" This address was deliv^d to his Matie by D^{tor.} Lluellyn att Windsore upon Bartholomew day, August 24th Anno 1681.

" Mr. Henry Bigg being then Mayor."

" Test. Jo. Bigg. T. Clerke."

"Dr. Gumble, who wrote the life of General Monk, and is said to have greatly assisted him in restoring the parliament, and breaking the power of the army, by which the return of King Charles the Second was effected, was vicar here, but not, I believe, by episcopal institution." (Gough's MSS.) There were great rejoicings in Wycombe on account of the Restoration.

Dr. Lluelyn practised medicine in Wycombe for many years. See an account of him in his epitaph amongst the monumental inscriptions hereafter given, and also his life in Anthony à Wood. He resided in the fine old Elizabethan house in Easton Street, now occupied by Mrs. Wheeler. He was the author of " Wickham Wakened, or the Quaker's Madrigal," in doggrel rhyme, and other Poems. See copy of the inscription on the tablet in the church to his memory, with the translation, hereafter given. Mrs. Crosse, his last surviving daughter, died in 1767 at the age of ninety-three.

---

* The " defeated politicians " alluded to in this marvellous composition were probably Shaftesbury, Algernon Sidney, and Somers.

His grandson, Richard, became a Fellow of Magdalen College, and Rector of Saunderton, and died in 1770, aged sixty-two. He is buried near his grandfather and father, in the vicar's aisle of Wycombe Church. We may add that Dr. Lluelyn's great grand-daughter, Mrs. Bowles, possessed the gloves which King Charles the First wore on the day of his execution.

In the seventeenth century, Wycombe was accounted one of the strong-holds of Quakerism. Here the great founders of the Society occasionally met their friends for conference and religious worship, at the house of Dr. John Raunce in White Hart Street, which stood on the site of the present National Schools; and some of these early Friends, with Thomas Ellwood, the companion of the immortal John Milton, were frequently entertained at the ancient White House in the High Street. The oak table around which they sat, and enjoyed the hospitalities of the worthy host, is still preserved in this old edifice.

In consequence of the well-known refusal to bear arms, or to take oaths, and also for alleged extravagance of manner, a special Act was passed for their repression; when more than four thousand were soon in prison, though as a fact, the Quakers were one of the smallest of the Nonconformist bodies, and of these, five hundred were imprisoned in London alone. Large as it was, the number rapidly increased; and the King's Declaration of Indul-gence, twelve years later, set free twelve thousand Quakers who had been incarcerated.

In early times Frogmore contained a House of Correction, near Temple End, which, most probably, was within the jurisdiction of the county; the governor receiving a salary of £5 per annum, which was paid by the church-wardens, it may be presumed out of moneys arising from some private bene-faction. To this House of Correction, Thomas Ellwood and Morgan Wat-kins, with four other Quakers, were committed by Ambrose Benett, Justice of the Peace, who surprised them at a meeting at Hedgerley, about a mile from his house. "Having got scent of the meeting," says Ellwood, "he catched up a stack-wood stick, big enough to have knocked any man down, and brought it with him, hidden under his cloak. After listening outside to Morgan, who was speaking, on a sudden he rushed in among us, with the stack-wood stick held up in his hand, ready to strike, crying out, ' make way there.'" He selected six for punishment, whom he would have committed to "Ailesbury gaol," had not Mrs. Parker desired him to consider in time, "*how he would answer the cry of our blood, if by his sending us to be shut up in that infected place, we should lose our lives there;*" for the pestilence was then at Aylesbury.

Ellwood was recommitted to the House of Correction, June 7th, 1666, for twelve weeks; during his imprisonment he betook himself, for an employment, to making of nets for kitchen service to boil herbs, etc., in.

Quakerism was in all probability strong in Wycombe about the time of the Commonwealth. The principal patron of Quakerism in these parts appears to have been Isaac Pennington, who lived at the Grange, Chalfont St. Peter, and as Ellwood's family were resident at Crowell, Oxon, he paid frequent visits to the Grange. He describes a meeting held at the Grove, Chalfont, where James Naylor, afterwards too well-known as "the blasphemer," held forth. Here (this was before his conversion to Quakerism) Ellwood was so much struck with the force of Naylor's reasoning, that he determined to hear more, and accordingly he came to a meeting at " High Wicomb" on the ensuing Thursday; and that his father and family might think him to have gone out coursing, he let his greyhound run by his horse's side.

He remarks,—

"When I came there, and had set up my horse at an inn, I was at a loss how to find the house where the meeting was to be, I knew it not, and was ashamed to ask after it. Wherefore having ordered the hostler to take care of my dog, I went into the street, and stood at the inn gate, musing with myself what course to take. But I had not stood long, ere I saw an horseman riding along the street, whom I remembered I had seen before at Isaac Pennington's, and he put up his horse at the same inn. Him therefore I resolved to follow, supposing he was going to the meeting, as indeed he was. Being come to the house (which proved to be *John Raunce's*), I saw the people sitting together, in an outer room, wherefore I stept in, and sate down on the first void seat, the end of a bench just within the door; having my sword by my side and black clothes on, which drew some eyes upon me. It was not long ere one stood up and spake, whom I was afterwards well acquainted with, (his name was *Samuel Thornton*) and what he spake was very suitable, and of good service to me; for it reached home, as if it had been directed to me. As soon as ever the meeting was ended, and the people began to rise, I, being next to the door, stept out quickly; and hasting to my inn, took horse immediately homewards."

This was in 1659. Ellwood says he was treated with more than ordinary kindness by Raunce, who was a physician, and by his wife Frances, whom he calls "both a grave and motherly woman, and having a hearty love to truth." He lay during a sickness afterwards at Raunce's house. Ellwood came constantly afterwards to meetings at Wycombe. " At the next meeting, which was held in a 'fair room' in the house of Jeremiah Steevens, instead of Raunce's, because the latter was too small, Edward Burrough, of London, ministered."

At length the municipal Authorities of Wycombe determined on the suppression of the Quakers, and in the early records of the Corporation we find the following entries :—

"MEMORAND : that the eight day of January 1664 beinge Sabbath day, Samuel Trone, Jeremiah Steevens, Nickolas Noy, John Littleboy, John Cock, George Ball and Joseph Steevens, all of this Burrough, Labourers, and beinge p'fessed and knowne Quakers, having this day assembled themselves together with divers women at the house of John Raunce in this Burrough, under p'tence of religious worshipp, contrary to a late Act of Parliam', and beinge brought before us, beinge two of His Mat'h Justices of the Peace for the Burrough aforesayd, have acknowledged and confessed the same, and thereuppon the sayd sev'all p'sons were this psent day by warrant under o' hands and seales committed to the house of correction, (which was a loathesome dungeon in Frogmore Ward in this Burrough) there to remayne for the terme of three months according to the seyd late Act of Parliam' it being the first tyme that they or either of them have been convicted of the same offence."

"Henry Elliott Mayer"
" Robert Whittone."

These suffering people do not appear to have been deterred from holding their meetings by an enforcement of the law, as on June 11th, 1665, four of them, viz., Trone, Cock, Littleboy, and Jeremiah Steevens, " it beinge Sabbath day, and in the tyme of Divine service," were found " with sevall other p'sons at an unlawfull assembly at the same house, and were again committed to the house of correction for six months." The severity thus exercised on the Quakers is alluded to in Dr. Lluelyn's doggrel poem, " Wickham Wakened."

REPRESENTATIVES IN PARLIAMENT FOR THE BOROUGH OF CHEPPING WYCOMBE.

EDWARD I.

28 Par. at Westminster, Stephen Ayott,* Thomas Taylur.
30 „ at London, Adam de Guldeford, Roger Allitarius.
33 „ at West., Roger Allitarius, John le Pistor.
34 „ „ Peter le Cotiler, John le Baker.
35 „ at Carlisle, Peter le Cotiler, Andrew Batyn.

* In his place, being infirm, John de la Lude.

EDWARD II.

1 Par. Northampton, Peter le Cotiler, Roger de Sandwell.
2 „ at West., Peter le Cotiler, Edm. de Haveringdown.
2 at West.
6 „ Thomas Gerveys, Matthew le Fuller.
6 „ Robert Paer, William le Cassiere.
8 „ Balliviis honoris Wallingford, nullum dedit responsum.
12 at York, Robert Smith, William le Fote.
16 at West., Richard le Haslere of Harlere, Bennet le Cassiere.
19 „ John le Taylor, John de Sandwell.
20 „ Roger Sandwell, Matthew le Fuller.

EDWARD III.

1 Par. at Linc., Richard atte Walle, John atte Donne.
(1 at York, *Cedula manca.*)
2 at Northampton, John atte Don, Henry de Mussenden.
4 at Winchester, John le Harriere, Richard Perre.
6 at West., Matthew Fuller, Richard Fottering.
7 „ Jordan de Wycombe, Richard Bennet.
8 „ Jordan de Wycombe, Richard Beneye, *qy.* Bennet.
9 „ John Ayot,[*] Richard Perkyn.
10 „ John le Harrare, Thomas Gervays.
10 Council at Northampton, John Agod, *qy.* Ayot, Richard Abyndon.
11 Par. at West., John le Clerk, John Pool.
12 at York, Stephen Ayot, John le Taverner.
12 at Northamp., Thomas Gerveys, Jordan de Preston.
12 at West., Thomas Gerveys, Jordan de Preston.
13 „ Thomas Gerveys, Jordan de Preston.
14 „ Jordan de Preston, Thomas Gerveys.
15 „ Robert Stenstoole, Robert Haughford. [†]
20 „ Robert Haughford, Ralf Barber.

---

[*] He was Lord of Shalleston in the hundred of Buckingham, which estate passed in marriage with his daughter and heiress to William Purefoy, whose family still possess it.

[†] Query Harleyford : there was, it is believed, a family of that name then residing there.

K

21 at West., John Martyn, Robert Cuttingham.

22 ,, Walter atte Leech, William Cassiere.

29 ,, Thomas Gerveys, Ralf Haughford.

31 ,, Thomas Gerveys, Robt. *qy.* de Haughford.

31 ,, John Mepertshale, Thomas Gerveys.

34 ,, Thomas Gerveys, Robert le Wheeler.

34 ,, Thomas Gerveys, Robert Spigwinell.

36 ,, Thomas Gerveys, William Frere.

39 ,, Thomas Cornwaile, Richard Barbour.

42 ,, William atte Dene, Thomas Cornewayle.

43 ,, Thomas Gerveys, William atte Dene.

45 Council at Winchester ——, William atte Dene.

46 Par. at West., William atte Dene, John Bledlowe.

47 ,, William atte Dene, Thomas Ballard.

53 ,, William atte Dene, Thomas Ballard.

RICHARD II.

1 Par. at West., William atte Dene, Rich. Sandwell.

2 at Gloucester, William atte Dene, Rich. Jurdaine.

3 at West., William atte Dene, Richard Sandwell.

5 ,, Thomas Ravell, Walter Frere.

6 ,, William Kele, William atte Dene.

7 at New Sarum, Stephen Watford, John Petymin.

8 at West., William atte Dene, Richard Kele.

9 ,, Stephen Watford, Richard Kele.

10 ,, Walter Frere, Richard Holyman.

11 ,, Walter Frere, Richard Holyman.

12 at Cambridge, Stephen Watford, William atte Dene.

15 at West., William Dene, William Depham.

16 at Winchester, William Depham, Walter Waltham.

18 at West., William atte Dene, Nicholas Depham.

20 ,, Richard Sandwell, Walter Waltham.

HENRY IV.

1 Par. at West., John Cottingham, William Clerke.

3 ,, Nicholas Sperling, John Sandwell.

Henry V.

1 Par. at West., Henry Spiling, Roger Moore.
2   ,,   William Hall, John Coventry.
3   ,,   William Clerk, Andrew Sperling.
5   ,,   Andrew Sperling, Robert Moore.
7 at Gloucester, Wm. Merchant, John Cottingham.
8 at West., Roger Moore, Thomas Merston.
9   ,,   John Harewood, Thomas Pusee.
9   ,,   Roger Moore, Richard Merston.

Henry VI.

1 Par. at West., Nicolas Stepton, John Coventry.
2   ,,   John Coventry, Roger Moore.
3   ,,   William Whapelade, John Cottingham.
4 at Leicester, Thomas Muston, William Stocton.
6 at West., John Coventry, John Justice.
8   ,,   John Wellesbourn,* John Bishop.
9   ,,   Roger Moore, William Fowler.
11   ,,   John Martyn, John Blackpoll.
13   ,,   John Durein, John Cottingham.
14   ,,   John Durein, John Cottingham.
15 at Cambridge, John Hill, Esq., Bartholomew Halling.
20 at West., John Radeshill, John Martyn.
25 at Cambridge, John Wellesbourn, John Martyn.
27 at West., John Wellesbourn, John Haynes.
28   ,,   William Stocton, Nicholas Fayrewell.
29   ,,   William Stocton, Thomas Moore.
31 at Reading, Walter Collard, David Thomasyn.

Edward IV.

7 at West., Thomas Mansell, Thomas Catbery.
12   ,,   Thomas Fowler,† Thomas Fayrewell.

* He was probably descended from Simon de Montfort, Earl of Leicester, and resided at Hitchenden [Hughenden].
† Sheriff, 19 Ed. IV., 2 Rich. III., and 3 Hen. VII.

17 at West., Thomas Gate, Thomas Wellysborne.

The writs, returns, and indentures, from 17 Ed. IV. to Henry VIII. are all lost.

HENRY VIII.

33 Par. at West., John Gatts,* William Dormer.

EDWARD VI.

1 Par. at West., Thomas Fisher, Armigyll Wade.
6   „   Henry Peckham, John Cheyney.

MARY.

1 Par. at West., Henry Peckham, Robert Drury.
1 „ at Oxford, Henry Peckham, Thomas Pymme.

PHILIP AND MARY.

1 and 2 Par. at West., John ——, Robert Drury.
2 and 3   „   Henry Peckham, Robert Drury.
4 and 5   „   Thomas Pymme, Robert Woodlease.

ELIZABETH.

1 Par. at West., Thomas Pymme, *qy.*
5   „   Thomas Fermore, Esq., Thos. Neale, *qy.*
13   „   John Russel, Robert Christmas.
14   „   Thomas Neale, Rowland Goales.
27   „   John Morley of London, George Cawfield of Gray's Inn.
28   „   Thomas Ridley, LL.D., George Fleetwood de la Vache.
31   „   Owen Oglethorp of Newington, Oxon., Francis Goodwin.
35   „   Thomas Tasburgh of Beaconsfield, Thos. Fortescue of the Inner Temple.
39   „   William Fortescue, John Tasburgh.
43   „   Richard Blunt, Henry Fleetwood.

---

* Sheriff, 38 Hen. VIII.

JAMES I.

1 Par. at West., John Townsend, Kt.,* Henry Fleetwood.
12 „   William Borlase.
18 „   Richard Lovelace, Arthur Goodwin.
21 „   Henry Cook, Arthur Goodwin.

CHARLES I.

1 Par. at West., Henry Cook, Thomas Lane.
1   „   Henry Cook, Edmund Waller.
3   „   William Borlase, Kt., Thos. Lane.
15 „   Edmund Verney, Kt. Marshal, Thos. Lane.
16 „   Edmund Verney, Kt. Marshal, Thos. Lane,
                Richard Browne, vice Verney, deceased.
1654. Thomas Scott† of Lambeth.
1656. Thomas Scot, Maj.-gen., Tobias Bridge.
1658–9. Thomas Scot, Maj.-gen., Tobias Bridge.

CHARLES II.

12 Par. at West., Edmund Petty, Richard Brown, Edmund Petty,
                Recorder, Thomas Scott, double return.
13 „   Edmund Pye, Kt. and Bart., John Borlase, Bart.,
                Robert Sawyer, vice Pye, deceased.
31 „   John Borlase, Bart., Thomas Lewis.‡
31 „   John Borlase, Bart., Thomas Lewis.
32 at Oxford, John Borlase, Bart., Thomas Lewis.

---

* Ancestor of the Marquis Townshend.

† Major-general Thomas Scott was a brewer's clerk, afterwards became an attorney at Aylesbury, and was elected as one of the representatives of Aylesbury in the Long Parliament, and subsequently, by countenance of the Grandees, was elected to represent this borough. He was so violent against King Charles the First, that he desired no other epitaph over his grave than "Here lies Thomas Scott, one of the King's Judges." He signed the warrant for the King's execution, and suffered death as a Regicide. See "Heath's Chronicle of the Civil Wars."

‡ Alderman of London, and Lord of the Manor of West Wycombe.

JAMES II.

1 Par. at West., Dennis Hampson, Bart., Edward Baldwin, Recorder,
and Lord of the Manor of Temple Wycombe.

WILLIAM AND MARY.

1 Par. at West., Thomas Lewis, William Jephson.
2   ,,   William Jephson, Thomas Lewis,
Charles Godfrey, vice Jephson, deceased.

WILLIAM III.

7 Par. at West., Thomas Lewis, Charles Godfrey,
Fleetwood Dormer, vice Lewis, deceased.
10   ,,   Charles Godfrey, John Archdale,
Thomas Archdale, vice John Archdale, who
refused to take the oaths, being a Quaker.
12   ,,   Charles Godfrey, Fleetwood Dormer,
13   ,,   Charles Godfrey, Fleetwood Dormer.

ANNE.

1 Par. at West., Charles Godfrey, Fleetwood Dormer.
4   ,,   Charles Godfrey, Fleetwood Dormer.
7   ,,   Charles Godfrey, Fleetwood Dormer.
9   ,,   Sir Thomas Lee, Bart., Charles Godfrey.
12   ,,   Sir Thomas Lee, Bart., Sir John Wittewrong, Bart.

GEORGE I.

1st Sir Thomas Lee, Bart., Sir John Wittewrong, Bart.
9th The Hon. Charles Egerton, The Rt. Hon. the Earl of Shelburne.
Feb. 1. 1725. Charles Collyer, vice Egerton, deceased.*
This Election was declared void.

---

* It has previously been mentioned, that the borough of Wycombe was not, in earlier times, altogether exempt from corrupt and illegal practices at Parliamentary Elections, which will be further indicated by the copies of publications issued from the press on the occasion of the contested election between the Hon. Charles Collyer and Harry Waller, Esq., for which see Appendix II.

See also a graphic account of the Marquis of Wharton's canvass of the borough, in the Liberal interest, which is corroborative of the above remark. Appendix III.

March 8.   The Hon. C. Collyer again elected.

March 17.   By order of the House, his name was erased, and that of Harry Waller inserted.*

GEORGE II.

1st   Harry Waller, William Lee.

1730   The Hon. Sir Charles Vernon, vice Lee, made one of the Judges of the King's Bench.

8th   Harry Waller, Edmund Waller.
   Sir Charles Vernon, vice Edmund Waller, who made his Election for Marlow.

15th   Edmund Waller, Harry Waller.
   Edmund Waller re-elected, having been appointed Cofferer of His Majesty's Household.

21st   Edmund Waller, Edmund Waller Jun.

28th   John Waller, The Rt. Hon. the Earl of Shelburne.

31st   Edmund Waller, vice John, deceased.

GEORGE III.

1st   Robert Waller, Lord Viscount Fitzmaurice.

1761   Isaac Barré, vice Lord Visc. Fitzmaurice, called to the House of Peers, now Marquis of Lansdowne.

9th   Robert Waller, The Rt. Hon. Isaac Barré.

15th   Robert Waller, The Hon. Thomas Fitzmaurice.

21st   Robert Waller, Lord Viscount Mahon.

25th   Robert Waller, Lord Viscount Mahon.

1786   The Rt. Hon. the Earl of Wycombe, vice Lord Visc. Mahon, called to the House of Peers, on the decease of his father, Earl Stanhope.

30th   The Rt. Hon. the Earl of Wycombe.   Admiral Sir John Jervis, K.B.†

---

* The Mayor made a false return.   See " Journals of the House."

† Sir J. Jervis after various promotions, was, in 1795, appointed to the command of the Mediterranean Fleet, with which he performed the great exploit of his life, by intercepting and defeating the Spanish Fleet off Cape St. Vincent, February 14th, 1797.   For this victory, Sir J.

1794 Sir Francis Baring, Bart., vice Jervis, made Steward of the Chiltern Hundreds.

36th Rt. Hon. the Earl of Wycombe, Sir John Dashwood King, Bart.

42nd Sir J. D. King, Bart., Sir Francis Baring, Bart.

47th Sir J. D. King, Bart., Thomas Baring, Esq.

48th Sir J. D. King, Bart., Thomas Baring, Esq.

52nd Sir J. D. King, Bart., Sir Thomas Baring, Bart.

58th Sir J. D. King, Bart., Sir Thomas Baring, Bart.

GEORGE IV.

1820 Sir J. D. King, Bart., Sir Thomas Baring, Bart.

1826 Sir J. D. King, Bart., Sir Thomas Baring, Bart.

WILLIAM IV.

1831 Hon. Robt. John Smith, Sir Thomas Baring, Bart.

1832 Hon. Chas. Grey, vice Sir T. Baring, Bart., resigned.

1835 Hon. Robt. John Smith, Hon. Charles Grey.

VICTORIA.

1837 George Robt. Smith, Esq., G. H. Dashwood, Esq.

1841 Geo. H. Dashwood, Esq., R. Bernal, Jun., Esq.

1847 Geo. H. Dashwood, Esq., M. T. Smith, Esq. On the death of Sir G. H. Dashwood, Bart.

1862 Martin T. Smith, Esq., J. R. Mills, Esq.

1865 The Hon. Chas. Robt. Carington, J. R. Mills, Esq. After the passing of the second Reform Bill, Captn. The Hon. W. Carington.

Jervis was raised to the Peerage by the title of Earl St. Vincent, and Baron Jervis of Meaford. Two Brass pieces of Ordnance taken from the enemy were presented, as a token of regard, by the noble and gallant Earl, to the late Isaac King, Esq., one of the Aldermen of the said Borough, and also a Magistrate for the County, and were subsequently presented by his Grandson, the late Rev. Isaac King, of Bradenham Rectory, to the Author.

"Copy STATE OF THE POLL, at the Election of two Burgesses to serve in the ensuing Parliament, for the Borough of Chepping Wycombe, in the County of Bucks. Taken before the Worshipful and Reverend John Manning, Mayor, on Saturday, June the Nineteenth 1790.

"CANDIDATES—Right Hon. Earl Wycombe, Sir John Jervis, Knight of the Bath, and John Dashwood, Esq.

		W	J	D
Sworn	Henry Howard, of Camberwell, Surrey, Farmer	—	—	
Ditto	Henry Alnut, Sen., Borough of Wycombe, Gent.	—		—
Ditto	Joseph Veary, Sen., of Ditto, Blacksmith	—	—	
Ditto	Samuel Baldwin, of Charing Cross, Westminster	—	—	
Ditto	Joseph Steel, of Well-End, Bucks, Gent.	—		—
	Rᵗ Hon. Isaac Barré, Stanhope-Sᵗ., Westminster	—	—	
Sworn	John Carter, Borough of Wycombe, Maltster	—	—	
Ditto	Josiah Powell, of Ditto, Gardener	—	—	
	Samuel Welles, of Ditto, Esquire			—
	Joseph Stevens, of Ditto, Miller	—		—
	Richard Witchurch, of Ditto, Esq.			—
	Joseph Shrimpton, of Ditto, Gent.			—
Sworn	Isaac King, Parish of Ditto, Esq.	—	—	
	Richard Welles, Borough of Ditto, Gent.			—
	Ferdinand Line, City of Bristol, Gent.	—	—	
	Christopher Widmer, Wycombe, Brandy Merchᵗ.	—	—	
	John Price, Talgarth, Brecon	—	—	
	Henry Grange, Borough of Wycombe, Esq.	—		—
	Daniel Squire, of Ditto, Gent.	—	—	
	Thomas Jones, Clerk, of Dinton, Bucks	—	—	
	William Lowe, of Piccadilly, London, Painter	—	—	
	Samuel Rotton, Borough of Wycombe, Esq.	—		—
	Thomas Birch, City of London, Linen Draper	—	—	
Sworn	Samuel Veary, Borough of Wycombe, Blacksmith	—		—
	Thomas Rose, of Ditto, Jun.	—	—	
	Thomas Weller, of Ditto, Carpenter		—	—
	Thomas Shrimpton, of Ditto, Esq.	—		—
Sworn	James Batting, of Ditto, Esq.	—	—	
	Samuel Manning, of Ditto, Esq.	—	—	
	James Price, Clerk, of Ditto	—	—	
	John Charsley, of Ditto, Attorney at Law	—	—	
Sworn	Thomas Rose, of Ditto, Apothecary	—	—	
	John Bates, of Wycombe Marsh, Esq.	—		—
	Richard Welles, City of London, Stationer			—
	Samuel Welles, Borough of Wycombe, Brewer	- -		--
	Joseph Shrimpton, Bedford Square, London, Esq.	—	· ·	
	William Peck, Lambs Conduit Sᵗ., London, Esq.			--
	Hon. Wilbraham Tollemache, City of Westminster	--	·	
	Hon. Thomas Fitzmaurice, Llweny, Sou. Wales	—	·	--

l.

		W	J	D
	Sir John Jervis, K.B.	—	—	
	Right Honourable Earl Wycombe		—	
	Thomas Clarke, Borough of Wycombe, Esq. . .			—
	John Bates, of Ditto, Esq.			—
	Thomas Clarke, University of Oxford, Gent. . .	—		—
	John Manning, Clerk, Borough of Wycombe . .	—	—	
	Joseph Bell, of Ditto, Esq.			—
Sworn	James Fastnage, of Ditto, Gent.	—		—
		34	26	22"

"Copy STATE OF THE POLL at the Election of a Burgess, to serve in Parliament, for the Borough of Chepping-Wycombe, in the County of Bucks. Taken before the Worshipful Thomas Clarke, Esq., Mayor, on Saturday the 1st of February, 1794.

CANDIDATES—Sir John Dashwood, Bar^t, of West Wycombe House, and Sir Francis Baring, Bar^t.

		D	B
Sworn	Henry Allnutt, Sen., Borough of Wycombe, Gent. . .	—	
Ditto	Right Hon. Col. Barré, Stanhope Street, Westminster .		—
Ditto	John Carter, Borough of Wycombe, Gent.	—	
Ditto	Samuel Welles, of ditto, Esq.	—	
Ditto	James Fastnage, of ditto, Gent.	—	
Ditto	Joseph Bell, of ditto, Esq.	—	
Ditto	Thomas Rose, of ditto, Apothecary		—
Ditto	John Bates, Esq., Reading	—	
Ditto	William Lowe, of Piccadilly, London, Painter . . .		—
Ditto	Daniel Squires, Borough of Wycombe, Gent. . . .		—
Ditto	Revd John Manning, of ditto, LL.B.		—
Ditto	Ferdinand Line, City of Bristol, Gent. . . .		—
Ditto	Thomas Birch, City of London, Linen Draper . . .		—
Ditto	Revd Richard Welles, Portsmouth	—	
Ditto	Samuel Romilly, Esq., Lincoln's Inn, London . . .		—
Ditto	John Bates, of Wycombe Marsh, Esqre	—	
Ditto	James Blackstone, Esq., V.P., Oxford		—
Ditto	John Tirel-Morin, Esq., Weeden Lodge, Bucks . .		—
Ditto	Joseph Shrimpton, Borough of Wycombe, Gent. . .	—	
Ditto	Andrew Biddle, of ditto, Brewer		—
Ditto	Thomas Shrimpton, of ditto, Esq.	—	
Ditto	Rev. Thomas Clarke, Buckland, Bucks	—	
Ditto	Rev. James Price, A.M., Vicar of Wycombe . . .		—
Ditto	Richard Welles, City of London, Stationer . . .	—	
Ditto	Robert Cosens, Tetsworth, Oxon, Grazier . . .		—
Ditto	James Batting, Esq., Borough of Wycombe . . .		—
Ditto	John Price, Talgarth, Brecon, Gent.		—
Ditto	Revd Thomas Jones, Clerk, of Dinton, Bucks . . .	—	

		D	B
Ditto	Thomas Aldridge, Esq., of Wycombe	—	—
Ditto	John Goodwin, of Wycombe Marsh, Paper Maker . .		—
Ditto	Samuel Veary, Borough of Wycombe, Blacksmith . .	—	
Ditto	Samuel Wells, Borough of Wycombe, Gent. . . .	—	
Ditto	Henry Grange, Borough of Wycombe, Esq. . . .	—	
Ditto	Joseph Stevens, of ditto, Miller	—	
Ditto	Richard Whichchurch, Esq., Mumfords, Bucks . . .	—	
Ditto	Rev. James Prosser, of Cheddington, Bucks . . .		—
Ditto	Ben. Vaughan, Esq., M.P., Finsbury Square, London . .		—
Ditto	John Rutt, Mould Maker, Wycombe		—
Ditto	William Vaughan, Esq., London		—
Ditto	Josiah Powel, of Wycombe, Gardener		—
Ditto	John Sherwood, Mark Lane, London, Contractor . .		—
Ditto	Sam. Sproston, Gent.		—
Ditto	George Harman, Borough of Wycombe, Cooper . . .		—
Ditto	Samuel Rotton, Borough of Wycombe, Esq. . . .	—	
Ditto	James Matthie, of ditto		—
Ditto	Samuel Manning, of ditto, Esq.		—
Ditto	Isaac King, parish of ditto, Esq.		—
Ditto	John Charsley, of ditto, Attorney at Law . . .	—	
Ditto	Right Hon. Earl Wycombe		—
Ditto	Henry Smith, Drapers' Hall, London, Gent. . . .		—
Ditto	Thomas Clarke, Esq., Mayor	—	
		22	29"

The following are the results of the Polls taken since 1794 :—

1832.	Hon. Robert Smith	170.
	Hon. Col. Grey	140.
	Benjamin Disraeli, Esq.	119.
1841.	Sir G. H. Dashwood, Bart	180.
	R. Bernal Osborne, Esq.	159.
	J. Freshfield, Esq.	130.
	W. Alexander, Esq.	80.
1852.	Sir G. H. Dashwood	259.
	Martin T. Smith, Esq.	204.
	Wm. Simpson, Esq.	111.

On the death of Sir G. H. Dashwood.

1862.	J. R. Mills, Esq.	220.
	D. Cameron, Esq.	158.

After the passing of the second Reform Bill, when the Borough returned one Member only :—

1868.	Capt. The Hon. W. Carington	701.
	J. R. Mills, Esq.	500.
1874.	Lieut. Col. The Hon. W. Carington	953.
	Mr. H. Broadhurst	415.
	F. Charsley, Esq.	19.

MAYORS OF CHIPPING WYCOMBE.

Edward IV.

14. Thomas Gale.	16, 17, 18. Richard Cary.
15. William Readhead.	19, 20, 21. Christopher Waes.

22, 23. Richard Cary.

Richard III.

1. The Same.	2. William Readhead.

Henry VII.

1.	William Readhead.	14, 15.	Roger Bramston.
2.	William Monday.	16.	John Alley.
3.	Thomas Pyman *q.* Pymm.	17.	Robert Astbrook.
4.	Roger Bramston.	18.	William Alley.
5.	Robert Astbrook.	19, 20, 21.	Nic. Gerrard.
6.	Thomas Pymm.	22.	Robert Astbrook.
7, 8.	Richard Cary.	23.	Nic. Gerrard.
9, 10.	Thomas Pymm.	24.	William Alley.
11, 12, 13.	Humphrey Wellisbon.		

Henry VIII.

1.	Thomas Freere.	5.	Robert Astbrook.
2.	Roger Bramston.	6.	William Chalfont.
3.	Robert Astbrook.	7.	Richard Burch.
4.	Richard Burch.	8.	William Chalfont.

9, 10.	Thomas Freere.	28.	William Juncklyn.
11.	Robert Astbrook.	29.	Christopher Pusey.
12.	William Chalfont.	30.	George Peytever.
13, 14.	Robert Astbrook.	31.	John Keele.
15, 16.	Richard Burch.	32.	John Brasbrich.
17.	Robert Astbrook.	33.	William Juncklyn.
18.	George Peytever.	34.	John Littleboy.
19.	William Juncklyn.	35.	Thomas Bottery.
20, 21, 22.	Robert Astbrook.	36.	George Peytever.
23.	William Juncklyn.	37.	William Alley.
24, 25, 26, 27.	Geo. Peytever.	38.	Thomas Chalfont.

Edward VI.

1.	John Welles.	4.	William Gravetts.
2.	Robert Pusey.	5.	Edward Cary.
3.	Simon Whitmell.	6.	George Paytefer.

7. John Raunce.

Mary.

1.	Thomas Chalfont.	4.	George Littleboy.
2.	John Raunce.	5.	Robert Gravett.
3.	Thomas Pymm.	6.	Thomas Keele.

Elizabeth.

1.	Thomas Keele.	14.	William Thwaites.
2.	John Sterling.	15.	Robert Collings.
3.	Rowland Witnall.	16.	Rowland Witnall.
4, 5.	—— ——.	17.	Thomas Keele.
6.	William Thwaites.	18.	Rowland Brasbrigg.
7.	George Littleboy.	19.	Robert Cullyn.
8.	Francis Sparkes.	20.	Tristram Winch.
9.	Tristram Winch.	21.	William Munday.
10.	Thomas Francis.	22.	Tristram Winch.
11.	Thomas Keele.	23.	Thomas Keele.
12.	Francis Sparkes.	24.	Robert Cullyn.
13.	Tristram Winch.	25.	William Munday.

26. Tristram Winch.
27. Francis Challener.
28. John Greenland.
29. Thomas Kempe.
30. John Gibbons.
31. Thomas Hayly.
32. Francis Challener.
33. John Fox.
34. John Welles.

35. John Greenland.
36. John Gibbons.
37. John Fox.
38. John Welles.
39. Thomas Welles.
40. John Greenland.
41. Thomas Gibbons.
42. Thomas Tayler.
43. Ambrose Conway.

44. William Shrimpton.

James I.

1. Gabriel Redman.
2. George Welles.
3. William Ayre.
4. Gabriel Redman.
5. Thomas Welles.
6. Michael Burgh.
7. John Littlepage.
8. Thomas Brandon.
9. Thomas Gibbons.
10. William Shrimpton.
11. Robert Eeles.

12. William Ayre.
13. Robert Biscoe.
14. John Littlepage.
15. —— ——.
16. George Welles.
17. Thomas Brandon.
18. Thomas Gibbons.
19. Richard Gibbons.
20. John Davenport.
21. Robert Biscoe.
22. George Welles.

Charles I.

1. William Guy.
2. John Littlepage.
3. John Bigg.
4. John Davenport.
5. Richard Gibbons.
6. Thomas Lock.
7. Richard Gibbons.
8. Thomas Ayre.
9. Matthew Pettypher.
10. Edward Winch.

11. John Gibbons.
12. Richard Nelson.
13. { Thomas Bedder. / Thomas Welles.
14. Thomas Hobbs.
15. George Bradshaw.
16. John Collins.
17. William Guy.
18. —— ——.
19. —— ——.

20. —— ——.
21. Edward Bedder.

22. James Bigg.
23. George More.

24. John Gibbons.

THE COMMONWEALTH.

1649. Nicholas Bradshaw.
1650. Stephen Bates.
1651. William Fisher.
1652. James Bigg.
1653. { John King.
       { John Gibbons.

1654. Nicholas Bradshaw.
1655. Henry Elliott.
1656. John Grove.
1657. Samuel Guy.
1658. Richard Nelson.
1659. George Timberlake.

CHARLES II.

13. Richard Lucas.
14. Thomas Gibbons.
15. Nicholas Bradshaw.
16. Thomas Gibbons.
17. Henry Elliott.
18. Edward Bedder.
19. James Bigg.
20. Richard Lucas.
21. Samuel Welles.
22. Thomas Gibbons.
23. Robert Whitton.
24. Martyn Luellyn.
25. { Nicholas Bradshaw.
     { Henry Bigg.
     { Richard Lucas.

26. Alexander Parnham.
27. Henry Bedder.
28. Edward Bedder.
29. Thomas Davies.
30. Charles Elliott.
31. John Wheeler.
32. Jonathan Randall.
33. Henry Bigg.
34. John Michell.
35. John Pettypher.
36, 37. John Lane.
38. Robert Whitton.

JAMES II.

1. Robert Whitton.
2. John Bigg.

3. Richard Rutt.
4. George Bradshaw.

5. Thomas Grove.

WILLIAM AND MARY.

1. Thomas Grove.
2. Thomas Fellows.
3. Thomas Stevens.
4. Thomas Barnes.
5. John Bigg.
6. Thomas Alford.

7. John Blacknall.

WILLIAM (ALONE).

8. Edward Marshall.
9. George Grove.
10. Thomas Fellows.
11. Thomas Barnes.
12. { George Clewer. / Ferdinando Shrimpton.
13. Thomas Stevens.
14. John Bigg.

15. Thomas Alford.

ANNE.

1. Thomas Alford.
2. Thomas Alford.
3. Thomas Stevens.
4. Benjamin Hinckman.
5. George Alford.
6. Ferdinando Shrimpton.
7. Thomas Wood.
8. The same.
9. Thomas Russin.
10. Hugh Shrimpton.
11. Ferdinando Shrimpton.
12. Thomas Stevens.

13. Benjamin Hickman.

GEORGE I.

1. Benjamin Hickman.
2. Henry Hunt.
3. Thomas Wood.
4. John Stevens.
5 and 6. Hugh Shrimpton.
7. John Smales.
8. Richard Shrimpton.*
9. Ferdinando Shrimpton.
10. John Smales.
11. Thomas Shrimpton.
12. Edward Bedder.
13. Ferdinando Shrimpton.

14. The same.

---

* In 1726, Richard Shrimpton, the Mayor, was served with an order of the House of Commons, for permitting Harry Waller, Esq., or his agent, to inspect the Records of that Borough (in consequence of a late election), and refused to obey the same; when he was ordered to be taken into custody by the Serjeant-at-Arms, and the books for entering the names of the freemen to be delivered to the Clerk of the House; and the House made the following

GEORGE II.

1. Ferdinando Shrimpton.
2. Joseph Tomlinson.
3. The same.
4. Edward Bedder.
5. Ferdinando Shrimpton.
6. The same.
7. John Welch.
8. Ralph Dean.
9. Edward Bedder.
10. The same.
11. John Bates.
12. John Clarke
13. Samuel Welles.
14. Joseph Shrimpton.
15. Richard Beacham.
16. John Welch.
17. Edward Bedder.
18. Ralph Dean.
19. John Bates.
20. Ralph Dean.
21. John Clarke.
22. Richard Bates.
23. Thomas Aldridge.
24. Richard Bates.
25. Richard Welles.
26. John Welch.
27. Joseph Shrimpton.
28. Richard Beacham.
29. Samuel Welles.
30. Thomas Rose.
31. John Bates, Jun.
32. Ralph Dean.
33. Thomas Aldridge.

GEORGE III.

1. Richard Welles.
2. Rev. James Price.
3. John Welch.
4. Joseph Shrimpton.
5. Samuel Welles.
6. Thomas Rose.
7. Thomas Rose, Jun.
8. John Bates.
9. Thomas Aldridge.
10. John Birch.
11. Samuel Shrimpton.
12. John Widmer.
13. Isaac King.
14. Samuel Shrimpton.
15. Rev. James Price.
16. Joseph Shrimpton.

resolutions thereupon :—" That in an entry of burgesses there had been made certain erasures; that persons had been admitted to vote who had no right so to do; that the Honourable Charles Collyer was not duly elected; that Harry Waller, Esq., was duly elected to serve in that Parliament; that the Mayor was guilty of divers arbitrary, illegal, and partial proceedings at the election; and that Edmund Marshall, who had presumed to read the proclamation against riots, whilst the burgesses were legally assembled for the electing a burgess to serve in Parliament, without having sufficient authority, was guilty of a high infringement of the freedom of elections. And it was ordered that the Mayor be committed to Newgate, by the Speaker's warrant; and that Edward Marshall be taken into custody of the Serjeant-at-Arms."

M

17. Thomas Rose.
18. Joseph Steel.
19. Samuel Welles
20. John Bates.
21. Samuel Welles.
22. Joseph Bell.
23. Thomas Clarke.
24. Isaac King.
25. John Shrimpton.
26. Samuel Manning.
27. Rev. James Price, Sen.
28. Thomas Rose.
29. Rev. James Price, Jun.
30. Rev. John Manning.
31. Daniel Squire.
32. Samuel Welles.
33. Joseph Bell.
34. Thomas Clarke.
35. Isaac King.
36. Samuel Rotton.
37. Andrew Biddle.
38. Benjamin Blackden.

39. Samuel Manning.
40. Rev. James Price.
41. Charles Ward.
42. Thomas Clarke.
43. Thomas Rose.
44. Isaac King.
45. Charles Ward.
46. Richard Barry Slater.
47. Andrew Edward Biddle.
48. William Baly.
49. Samuel Manning.
50. William Sproston.
51. John Carter, Jun.
52. William Parker.
53. Robert Wheeler.
54. William Rose.
55. Thomas Westwood.
56. Richard Barry Slater.
57. Rev. James Price.
58. Richard Barry Slater.
59. John Carter.
60. Robert Wheeler.

GEORGE IV.

1820. William Parker.
1821. William Rose.
1822. Richard Barry Slater.
1823. John Carter.

1824. John Matthie.
1825. Robert Wheeler.
1826. Isaac King.
1827. William Parker.

1828. William Rose.

WILLIAM IV.

1829. William Denny.
1830. Thomas Westwood.
1831. John Carter.
1832. Robert Wheeler.

1833. Thomas Westwood.
1834. {Robert Wheeler till Dec.
and   26th, when Town Coun-
1835. cillors were elected.

VICTORIA.

1836. James George Tatem (Jan. 1st. to Nov. 9th).	1856. William Henry Hayden.
1836. George Harman.	1857. Alfred Lane, Jun.
1837. Robert Wheeler.	1858. Buckmaster Joseph Tuck.
1838. John Carter.	1859. Robert Wheeler.
1839. Buckmaster J. Tuck.	1860. Robert Wheeler.
1840. George Lloyd Parker.	1861. Ralph Lansdale.
1841. John Turner.	1862. Thomas Wheeler.
1842. Alfred Lane.	1863. Joseph Hunt.
1843. William Jackson.	1864. Purton Weston.
1844. Joseph Hunt.	1865. Charles Strange.
1845. Charles Harman.	1866. Robert Wheeler.
1846. Robert Wheeler.	„ John Turner.
1847. William Blandy.	1867. Thomas Wheeler.
1848. William Rose.	1868. John Turner.
1849. John Nash.	1869. William Henry Hayden.
1850. Robert Wheeler, Jun.	1870. John Parker, Jun.
1851. John Turner.	1871. Joseph Hunt.
1852. Robert Wheeler.	1872. Francis Wheeler.
1853. Alfred Lane.	1873. Thomas Gilbert.
„ Joseph Hunt.	1874. Thomas Wheeler.
1854. Ralph Lansdale.	1875. William Vincent Baines.
1855. Thomas Wheeler.	1876. George Wheeler.
	1877. William Phillips.

In the year 1608, by an Order in Council, the Mayor was required to make a feast on his going out of office.

In 1654, the Mayor was allowed £40 per annum towards defraying the expenses incident to his office.

In 1661, the allowance was increased to £50, the outgoing Mayor, on the Thursday before Michaelmas day, to make a feast for the entertainment of the new Mayor, the aldermen, and burgesses.

In 1691, the Mayor's salary was reduced to £40.

In 1699, it was further reduced to £20, and in the same year increased to £30.

From 1782, the salary was again increased to £50.

In 1791, it was reduced to £20.

In 1816, it was increased to £30.

In 1819, it was reduced to £20.

In 1826 to 1835, the Mayor's expenses only were allowed.

In 1836, under the provisions of the Municipal Corporation Act, no allowance was made to the Mayor for any of his expenses.

HIGH STEWARDS.

20 Oct., 1651.	Thomas Scott, Esq., Maj.-Gen.
17 Aug., 1672.	John, Earl of Bridgewater, Lord-Lieut. of the County of Bucks.
23 Dec., 1686.	George Lord Jeffries, Baron of Wem, Lord High Chancellor of England.*
	John Lord Lovelace.
6 Feb., 1693.	Rt. Hon. Thomas Wharton, Compr. of their Majesties', Household, afterwards Marquis of Wharton.
18 April, 1715.	Rt. Noble Philip, Marquis of Wharton.

RECORDERS.

Thomas Waller, Esq.

Thomas Lane, Esq.

Edmund Petty, Esq.†

---

* This was the notorious Lord Chief Justice Jeffries whose country seat (which he rebuilt) was, Bulstrode Park, in this county. Mr. Justice Foster pronounced him to be "the very worst judge that ever disgraced Westminster Hall." Granger adds, "Juries were overborne, judgment was given with precipitation; even the common legal forms were neglected, and the laws themselves openly trampled upon by a murderer, in the robes of a Lord Chief Justice." On William, Prince of Orange, ascending the throne, Jeffries was discarded by the Court, and by his barbarities he had rendered himself obnoxious to all classes of the community. He disguised himself in the garb of a sailor, intending to quit the country. He was discovered drinking in the cellar of the Red Cow alehouse, in Anchor and Hope Alley, near King Edward's Stairs in Wapping; a mob collected round the house, seized Jeffries, and carried him to the Lord Mayor; who sent him with a strong guard to the Lords of the Council, and their Lordships committed him to the Tower. He entered the gates of that gloomy old fortress a robust man, but rapidly wasted to a skeleton, and died a miserable death on the 18th April, 1689. Truly "the wicked shall fall by his own wickedness."

† Edmund Petty was of a good family in Oxfordshire, quite distinct from the ennobled family of Petty, and having different arms.

John Clark, Esq., of Aston Rowant, 1674.

Edward Baldwin, Esq., removed by Order in Council, 10th February, 1687.

Sir James Etheredge, 1687, o. 1730.

Edmund Waller, Esq., 1689, resigned,

Fleetwood Dormer, Esq., 1695, resigned.

William Lee, Esq., 1718, resigned

Harry Waller, Esq., 1730.

Richard Whitchurch, Esq., 1768.

James Blackstone, D.C.L., Vinerian Professor in the University of Oxford. (A fine Portrait of Dr. Blackstone is in the Council Chamber of the Guildhall.)

Sir Giffin Wilson, Knt.

By the Act to amend the Representation of the People of England and Wales, 2 Will. 4, c. 45, the Borough of Wycombe, being included in Schedule B of the Statute, was deprived of one of its members.

By the Municipal Corporation Act, 5 and 6 Will. 4, c. 76, so much of all Laws, Statutes, and usages, and so much of all royal and other charters, grants, and Letters Patent then in force, relating to the several Boroughs named in Schedules A and B to this Act, or to the inhabitants thereof, or to the several bodies corporate named in the Schedules as were inconsistent with, or contrary to, the provisions of this Act, were thereby repealed.

The Borough of Wycombe, being included in Schedule B of the Statute, was deprived of the original right under its charters of holding Quarter Sessions, and of appointing a Recorder, and Coroner. And under the provisions of the Statute, the Corporation is to consist of four Aldermen and twelve Councillors, and out of the Aldermen or Councillors of such Borough, the Council shall elect a fit person to be the Mayor of such Borough, who shall continue in his office for one whole year, and by the Statute 6 and 7 Will. 4, c. 105, s. 4, and until his successor shall have accepted the office of Mayor, and shall have made and subscribed the requisite declaration.

By the 71st section of the 5 and 6 Will. 4, c. 76, it is enacted that all bodies corporate, seised of Charity Estates and Funds, should continue to hold the same until the first day of August, 1836, or until Parliament should otherwise order, and should immediately thereupon utterly cease and determine. And the Statute provides that if Parliament should not otherwise direct on or before the first of August, 1836, the Lord High Chancellor, or Lords Commissioners of the Great Seal, should make such orders as he or they should see fit for the administration, subject to such charitable uses or trusts, of such trust estates. No such Parliamentary direction respecting the charities having been made, a petition was, on the 22nd day of May, 1838, preferred by Messrs. George Harman, James George Tatem, two of the Aldermen of the Borough, and Alfred Lane, one of the Councillors of the Borough, to the Lord Chancellor, praying for the appointment of Trustees of the Charities, when fourteen persons were appointed Trustees.

Eighteen years afterwards, an appointment of twelve Trustees was made by the Master of the Rolls, to supply vacancies among the Trustees so appointed, and a scheme for the management and regulation of the Grammar School and Almshouse Charity was approved on the 26th July, 1856.

TERRIER OF ESTATES BELONGING TO THE CORPORATION.

COPY OF THE RENT ROLL

FOR THE

BOROUGH OF CHEPPING WYCOMBE.

Name of Tenant.	Property Liable.				Amount per Ann.		
Lord Carington.	Redfords Pieces	7	7	0			
	Sundries	5	5	0	13	19	11
	College Yard	1	7	11			
H. Edgerley.	Encroachm', House in occupation of Woodland				0	1	6
Jos' Hunt's Exors.	„ 4 Houses, Frogmoor Gardens				0	2	6
E. Hutchinson.	„ St. Mary Street				0	1	6
W. H. Mayne.	„ Oxford Street				2	15	0
William Mealing.	Rent of House, Newland				8	0	0
Joseph Varney.	Encroachment, White Hart Street				0	1	0
John Kibbels.	„ House, Easton Street				0	0	8
Ja'. Putman.	Rent of Warehouse, Town Hall				5	10	0
William Raffety.	Rent Charge, College Yard				0	10	5
Cha'. Strange.	do.				0	17	0
C. H. Tilly.	Encroachment, Palings, Easton Street				0	0	4
W. Tomlyn.	„ Window, St. Mary St.				0	1	6
Sam'. Turner.	Rent Newland				8	0	0
Tho'. Wheeler.	Encroachment, Easton Street				0	4	0
George Rance.	Rent Charge, Railway Terrace				14	0	0
W. Judson.	Shutter Box, Little Market House				0	2	6
County Court.	for holding Courts in Hall				4	6	0

THE WYCOMBE TOKENS.

"N°. 1. Thomas Atkines = his half peny, of Wickham, 1668 = T. E. A.

N°. 2. Thomas Bates = (Prince of Wales's Feathers) in Wickham 1661 = T. B.
Farthing.

N°. 3. Thomas Butterfield = (A Wheatsheaf) in Wickham = his half peny.

N°. 4. Tho. Dimarsh of High Wickham, 1668 = T. A. D.
Farthing.

N°. 5. William Fisher = (The Cloth Workers' Arms) in Wikcombe, 1652 = W. A. F.
Farthing.

N°. 6. Jeremiah Gray, IN. = (A Swan chained, Or) Hey Wickiam = I. M. G.
Farthing.

N°. 7. John Harding, IN. = Great Wickome = I. M. H.

N°. 8. Fransis Ingeby, IN. = 1666, Wickum Parrish = F. I.
Farthing.

N°. 9. John Juson at the = (Chequers) in High Wickham, 1669 = his halfe peny
         I. M. I.

N°. 10. Rich. Lucas of Wickham = R. D. L., 1670, rather dead than disloyal = (Lion
         Rampant).

N°. 11. Richard Lucas = (Lion Rampant) in Wickham, 1653 = R. D. L.

N°. 12. John Morris, 1666 = (a stick of Candles) in Wickham his half peny = I. M.

N°. 13. Richard Preist = R. E. P., 1662, in High Wickham = (a Crown).
Farthing.

N°. 14. John Rowell in High Wickham, 1667 = his halfe peny. I. M. R.

N°. 15. Robert Whitton = (a stag) of Great Wickham = R. K. W.

N°. 16. Edward Winch of Wiccombe = (Arms, on a fess, 3 crosses, pat. once on a
         comton, 5 fleurs de lys), his halfe penny = E. P. W.

N°. 17. Robert Frier = (a Rose) in Hie Wickham.

N°. 18. James Gomme, 1811 = (The Guildhall, and Corporation Arms) = token XII
         pence."

In the year 1817, the Charters and Letters Patent granted to the Corporation were translated and published by subscription, when a question was raised, in whom the right of election of burgesses was vested. The burgesses, as already mentioned, elected the Mayor in Common Hall, by a majority on a show of hands. The select body, viz., the Common Council, elected the burgesses under a presumed bye-law, not extant in writing. In Hilary Term, 1819, an application was made to the Court of Queen's Bench, in legal phraseology, for a rule to show cause why an information in the nature of a Quo Warranto should not be filed against Thomas Westwood, to show by what authority he claimed to be one of the burgesses of the borough. No cause being shown, the rule was made absolute in the following Easter Term; and an information was filed against the defendant, to which he pleaded, 1st, an ancient custom for the Mayor and Common Council of the borough to elect the burgesses ; the 2nd, 3rd, and 4th being in substance the same, founding the right of such election upon a presumed bye-law. Issue was taken to these several pleas, and on the trial of the same before Mr. Justice Richardson and a special jury at the Bucks Assizes in 1821, a verdict was found for the defendant generally upon all the issues. In Michaelmas Term, 1821, an application was made to the Queen's Bench to set aside the verdict, on the ground of all the issues being found for the defendant, which was manifestly wrong ; and the verdict should have been on one plea only. The Court granted this application as to the issues, upon the first and second pleas, with liberty to each party to amend their pleadings, without costs.

Following out the precise nature of these legal proceedings, in Michaelmas Term, 1824, the case came on for argument, when judgment was given for the Crown on the two first pleas, and for the defendant upon the third plea ; Mr. Justice Bailey dissenting, and the Lord Chief Justice expressing a doubt, and not pronouncing an opinion on the point.

The effect of this judgment was to set aside the custom alleged in the first and second pleas, and to establish the bye-law in the third plea as good and valid. Against this judgment a Writ of Error was carried to the House of Lords on the part of the Crown. The case was heard on the 20th and 28th May, 1829, when the judgment of the Court below was affirmed. The Corporate Body had therefore the right to repeal the bye-law. Thus ended the most protracted and costly litigation, which was, in fact, a combat between the Parliamentary representatives of the borough, and the burgesses, whether or not the borough should be continued a close, or restored to its original position of, a free borough, in conformity with the provisions of its ancient charters. The unsatisfactory state of the law of Corporations at this period, and which was rendered more glaringly apparent, by the case of The King *v.* Westwood, led to the introduction of the bill for the regulation of Municipal Bodies.

In the year 1833, the Mayor, Robert Wheeler, Esq., convened a special meeting of the burgesses, to consider the propriety of rescinding the bye-law, when it was resolved by a large majority to rescind the same. For this laudable and popular act on the part of the Mayor, as well as for the high estimation in which he was justly held by the inhabitants and burgesses, they presented him with a very handsome silver epergne, at a public dinner, held in the Guildhall, on the 16th May in the same year, with the following inscription engraved on it.

"Presented to Robert Wheeler, Esqre., by the Inhabitants and Burgesses of High Wycombe and its vicinity, in testimony of their respect and gratitude for his upright, patriotic, and successful exertions during his fourth Mayoralty, in procuring the repeal of the Bye-law which deprived the Burgesses of the rights granted them by the Charters; for his steady and consistent support to the great measure of Parliamentary Reform; and for his uniform zeal and liberality in promoting the improvements of the Town, and advancing the interests of the Inhabitants.

"Virtus repulsæ nescia sordidæ
Intaminatis fulgit honoribus."

Upon petition of the Town Council, under the authority of the Municipal Corporation Act, sec. 98, a Commission of the Peace, bearing date the 16th of August, in the 15th year of the reign of Queen Victoria, was granted to the Mayor of the borough, and the Mayor for the time being, William Rose, Randolph Crewe, and Thomas Treacher, Esquires. On the death of Mr. Treacher, Charles Fowler, and Charles Thomas Grove, Esquires, were appointed on the Commission, and some few years after, on the death of Mr. Fowler, Alfred Gilbey, Arthur Vernon, and Henry Stephens Wheeler, Esquires, were appointed as Magistrates for the borough.

By the Statute 41 Geo. 3, c. 15, entitled an Act "for taking an account of the population of Great Britain, and of the increase or diminution thereof," which was the first census taken in this country.

The following return was made by William Payne and William Parker, Overseers, and John Prestage and James Kingston, Churchwardens, in March, 1801 :—

| Number of Houses. | . | . | 458 within the Borough. |

Males   .   .   1088 ⎫
Females .   1261 ⎬ Total 2349 within the Borough.

Males   .   .   850 ⎫
Females .   1043 ⎬ Total 1893 within the Parish.

4242 Population 1801.

A return made by Joseph Burrough and John Hill, in 1811.
    Number of Houses.   .   .   474 within the Borough.

N

Males . . 1148 } Total 2490 within the Borough.
Females . . 1342 }

Males . . 1065 } Total 2266 within the Parish.
Females . . 1201 }

4756 Population 1811.

In 1811 there were 440 houses in the Parish.

A return made in June, 1821.

Number of Houses . . . 551 within the Borough.

Males . . 1333 } Total 2864 within the Borough.
Females . . 1531 }

Males . . 1311 } Total 2735 within the Parish.
Females . . 1424 }

5599 Population 1821.

In 1509, the population of the Parish was 1000.

The population of the Borough and Parish was

In 1831	.	.	.	.	6299
1841	.	.	.	.	6469
1851	.	.	.	.	7179
1861	.	.	.	.	8375
1871	.	.	.	.	10492

A brief account of the murder of Mr. Pontifix of Downley, March 22nd, 1736.

"This morning early, Marsh and Marshal condemned for the Murder and Robbery of Mr. Pontifix, the Farmer, near High Wycomb, were brought in a Cart from Aylesbury, to Rye Common, lying between the two Wycombs, and about eleven o'clock were executed on a Gibbet of an extraordinary height, being 28 feet high, that the Spectators, who were very numerous, might have the satisfaction of seeing justice done on two villains, who had deprived of life a Person highly esteem'd by all that knew him.

"They had been out 8 days upon the pad, when coming late into High Wycombe, to lie, they overheard some persons taking their leave in order to go home into the Country; upon which they conceal'd themselves till they were past, and then followed; which young Pontifix observing, and telling his Father that some persons were following them, he stood still at a stile above Bell Field, and leading to Downley, till they came up, and upon their asking the way to West Wycombe, he kindly informed them, and a moment after, Marsh turning back, shot the Farmer dead without further speaking.

"They both confessed the Robbery, but denied they had any intention to murder him;

WYCOMBE PARISH CHURCH.

EXTRACTS FROM THE CARTULARY OF GODSTOWE.

"ENDOWMENT OF THE VICARAGE OF WYCOMBE, ACCORDING TO THE REGISTER OF LINCOLN. [Translation.]

"The Vicar of Wycombe, shall have, in the name of his Vicarage, a moiety of all oblations of the altar, with the whole tithe of cheese, and all eggs, on Easter Eve, coming to the said church; and all tithes of geese, and tithes of gardens and orchards within the borough, Except the oblations and obventions of four days by the year, to wit, the day of the Purification of the blessed Mary, the day of the Preparation [*i.e.*, Good Friday], Easter Day, and the day of the Exaltation of the Holy Cross. And except all tithes of wool, flax, lambs, young pigs, and calves, when a whole calf shall happen, and except all tithes of fruits of gardens and orchards without the borough, and all tithe of Teasels which appertain to the business of Fullers, as well within the borough as without, Except also, all eggs save on Easter Eve forthcoming to the said church, and all offering of candles through the whole year, save the candle which comes on Sundays to the altar with the 'bread to be consecrated; All which things above excepted shall wholly appertain to the Abbess and Nuns of Godstowe. And the Vicar shall have a manse assigned to him on the West side of the house of the Abbess, and he shall pay Synodals, and the Nuns shall procure a lodging for the Archdeacon. And it is to be remembered that this endowment was abiding by scrutiny of the Register of Lincoln, under the Seal of Henry Bishop of Lincoln, under date at Lydyngton, the twenty-eighth day of May, in the year of Our Lord One thousand four hundred and three, and in the fifth year of the consecration of the said Henry."

"CONFIRMATION by Lord Hugh, Bishop of Lincoln of all our Churches.

"TO ALL the faithful in Christ to whom the present Writing shall come, Hugh, by the grace   [Translation.] of God, Bishop of Lincoln, Greeting in the Lord. Desiring to attend with devout favour to the just petitions of suppliants, especially are we bounden to afford the protection of our patronage to religious houses, lest those benefits, which by the bounty of the faithful have been conferred

---

any degree, contributed malt to the Church as a free offering, in addition to their tithes in kind. This malt was duly brewed by the Church Authorities, and on a stated festival, when the "Ale was fairly old," the Parishioners used to repair to the Church Yard, or some other convenient place, and celebrate the wake, or feast of the Dedication of the Church. "These festivals, however piously intended, grew by degrees into great excesses of eating and drinking and other irregularities; and which, by the way, were at the first in some sort indulged to the English by Gregory the Great, at the feast of the Dedication in lieu of their sacrifices while they were heathens, viz., that they might set up booths round the Church, and there feast and entertain themselves; a custom which was evidently borrowed from the Jewish ritual. See Nehemiah 8 c. 16 and 17 vs. Each person paid, according to his means, some small sum for the privilege of joining the festival." "The Buttyng [or tunning] of the Ale" was a duty of some importance, and it was natural enough to lay it, in the case of Wycombe, upon the Vicar, though the profits on the "ale" or carousal, went to the Rectory, *i.e.*, to the Abbess and Nuns of Godstowe. The amount paid by each guest, called his "scot," or "shot," became a regular phrase, and hence the name of "scot" or "shot ale." The holding of these festivals was prohibited by Canon 88. But they were in some measure revived for a time by the "Book of Sports." Gibson's "Codex," 191. Burn's "Ecclesiastical Law," Quarto edition, vol. ii., p. 277.

on holy and religious places, bee by the malignant depravity of anye either meddled with over-much, or by long lapse of time buried in oblivion; We, therefore, will it to come to the knowledge of you all, that we ratify, and by this present Charter do confirm unto the religious house of Saint Mary and Saint John the Baptist of Godestowe and to the women of Christ serving God there, towards their support for their uses in time to come for ever, the benefactions granted by the bounty of the faithful in Christ, which in their proper names we have caused to be set forth, that is to say: of the gift of Alexander, Bishop of Lincoln, of worthy memory, one hundred shillings yearly to be received in toll of the Market of Bannesberi; of the gift of King Henry, son of the Empress Maud, the churches of **Wicumbe** and of Blockesham, with all their appurtenances; of the gift of Ailwin son of Godegose, the Church of Saint Giles, with all its appurtenances, which is situate without Oxineford; of the Gift of Agnes, daughter of Payne fitz-John, the church of Dunigtune, with all its appurtenances; of the gift of Simon de Wahille, a moiety of the Church of Pateshille, with all its appurtenances. The aforesaid benefactions, therefore, as upon the same Nuns they have been reasonably conferred, to be fully converted to their own proper uses and to be served by their own proper Chaplains, We ratify, and by our Episcopal authority do confirm. We grant also to the aforesaid handmaids of Christ, that they shall be free and quit from all exaction and custom and grievance, Saving our Episcopal right and the dignity of the Church of Lincoln. Which thing, in order that it may be accounted firm and valid, We by this present writing and by Our Seal have caused to be confirmed. These Witnesses: Master Stephen, Chancellor; Master Roger de Rolvestone, Master Symon de Siwelle, Master Geoffrey de Lechelade, Canons of the Church of Lincoln; Thomas Walerand, Eustace Payan, Priests of Godestowe; Geoffrey, Deacon; John, Clerk; Thomas, Steward; Luke, Janitor; Henry de Eatune; Henry of York; William of Baggeherste."

"ORDINANCE of Lord Hugh, Bishop of Lincoln, concerning
our Churches of Saint Giles, of Bloxham and of **Wycombe**.

[Translation.] " TO ALL the faithful in Christ to whom the present writing shall come, Hugh, by the Grace of God Bishop of Lincoln, Greeting in the Lord. We will it to come to the knowledge of you all, that we with the authority of our Council have ordained perpetual Vicarages in the Churches of Wycumbe, of Bloxham, and of Saint Giles, Oxford, and at the presentation of our beloved daughters in Christ, the Abbess and Nuns of Godestowe, have admitted perpetual Vicars to the Vicarages so ordained, and have instituted them in the same. Moreover, the aforesaid Vicarages are ordained in this wise, to wit:—That the perpetual Vicar of the Church of Wycumbe shall have, in the name of his Vicarage, a manse assigned to him on the West side of the house of the Abbess in Wycumbe, and a moiety of all the oblations and obventions of the Altar, with the whole tithe of cheese and all Eggs on Easter Eve coming to the said Church, and all tithes of geese, and all tithes of gardens and Orchards within the Borough, Except the oblations and obventions of four days by the year, to wit, the day of the Purification, the day of the Preparation [i.e., Good Friday], Easter-day and the day of the Exaltation of the Holy Cross; and except all tithes of wool, flax, lambs, young pigs and calves, when a whole calf shall happen; and except all tithes of the fruits of gardens and orchards, without the Borough, and the whole tithe of teasels which appertain to the business of Fullers, as well within the Borough as without, Except also, all eggs (save on Easter Eve) coming to the said Church, and all offerings of candle through the whole year, save candle which comes on Sunday to the Altar with the bread to be consecrated. All which things above excepted shall wholly appertain to the Abbess and Nuns of Godestowe. And the Perpetual Vicar of the Church of Blokesham shall have, in the name of his Vicarage, the whole Altarage of that church and of the Chapel of Middelcumbe, Except tithes of wool, and lambs of the mother-church of Blokesham ; he shall have also the corn which is wont to be given when threshed to the said Church of Blokesham and Chapel of Middilcumbe, and which is called Chercheset ; and he shall have a manse which is situate between the manse which was of Payan de Bereford, and the manse which was of William Coleman. And the perpetual Vicar of the church of Saint Giles in Oxford shall have, in the name of his Vicarage, a moiety of all Altarage of that Church with the whole tithe of gardens, except wool, and flax, and lambs, and except candle on the day of the Purification of the Blessed Virgin, which the said Nuns shall wholly receive. He shall have, moreover, a manse where the Chaplain of the Church was wont to dwell, for which the Vicar shall pay to the said Church sixpence yearly. And in these three Vicarages so ordained, the aforesaid Nuns shall sustain all ordinary charges of the said three churches as are due * and accustomed, except Synodals, which the Vicars shall pay. Further all the Vicars, so often as they shall be admitted to the Vicarages aforesaid, shall take an oath of fealty to the before mentioned Nuns. The Chaplains also, if the said Vicars shall receive any to assist them in ministration together with themselves in the said churches, shall likewise swear in presence of the Vicars and of the Proctor of the Nuns sent thither by them for this purpose, that they will be faithful to them, so long as they shall be there, in the things which affect the said Nuns in those churches, Saving in all respects the Episcopal customs and the dignity of the Church of Lincoln. And in witness hereof we have caused our seal to be set to the present Writing. These Witnesses :—Robert, Archdeacon of Huntingdon ; Master William of Lincoln, Chancellor ; Master's William of Canterbury [or Cambridge]. Hugh of Greneford, and Nicholas of Evesham, William of Winchecumbe, and Oliver de Chedney, Clerks. Given by the hand of Thomas de Filketone, Chaplain and Chancellor of Lincoln, at Croppery, the day before the *Ides* † of December, in the twelfth year of our Pontificate."

35ᵗʰ Hen. III.
[Translation.]

"For the Nuns of Godstowe.

"The King to Archbishops, etc. Greeting.

"We have inspected the Charter of the Lord Richard the King our Uncle in these words, 'Richard, by the grace of God, King of England, Duke of Normandy, Aquitain, and Earl ot Anjou, to the Archbishops, Bishops, Abbots, Earls, Barons, Justices, Sheriffs, and all his Ministers, and faithful subjects of his whole land, Greeting ; know ye that we have granted, and in perpetual alms confirmed by our present Charter, to God and the Church of the Holy Mary, and Saint John the Baptist of Godstow, and the Monks there serving God, that Gift which the Lord Henry the King our Father made to them, and by his Charter confirmed, and all gifts which have been made to them, that is to say, of the gift of the Lord Henry our Father, the Vill of Wulgaricot and the place which is called Godstow, in which its Church has been founded with the assent and consent of Bernard of Sᵗ. Waleric and his heirs, who, that is to say, Bernard, granted the aforesaid Vill, and that place, to the Lord Henry our Father, and gave and delivered seizin by a Silk Cloth, with which a hood is made, with the whole domain and the right of the Advowson of the same Abbey, which he formerly had in the same, so that the aforesaid Abbey be for ever free, and in Capite of our Crown, as the Abbey of Saint Edmond and other Royal Abbeys, which are established through England, also of the gift of the Lord

---

* "De vita :" for *debita*, an error in the orig:
† Thirteenth.

Henry our Father the **Church of Wycomb**, with all its appurtenances, and other Churches, &c., therein named.

"Wherefore, we will and firmly command that the aforesaid Abbey of Godstow and the Nuns there serving God, have and hold all the before named and whatsoever had been acquired for godly distribution, in free and perpetual alms, well and in peace, freely and quietly, full, entirely, and honourably, in wood and plain; in Meadows, and pastures, in waters, and Mills, in ways, and paths, in pools, and streams, within Borough and without, and in all other places with soc, and sac, and Tholl, and Theam, and infanganethef [infangthefe *] entirely quit and free, and that their tenants be quit of Shires and Hundred Pleas, and actions, aides, and assizes, geld and Dam Geld, murder and robbery, scuttage and Hydage, gifts, and scots, and works of Castles, Houses, Walls, parks, Streams, ditches and bridges, and summage and Carriage, and of ward penny, and aver penny, and hundred penny and Thening penny, and that they be quit throughout all our land, and by water, of toll and passage, and frontage, and talliage and lastage, and of all other customs which appertain to us, and with all their liberties and free customs.

"And we prohibit that any one do them injury or molestation in anything, because the aforesaid Church of Godstow and the Nuns of the same place, and all their things and possessions, and their men, with all other things in England, are more especially under our own hand, protection, and custody. Witnesses, Hugh, Bishop of Durham, Richard of London, Godfrey of Winchester, Hubert of Salisbury, Elect, William, Earl of Arundel, William of Saint John, Stephen of Longchamp; Roger of Pratell; the Steward, Nicholas Bilet; Robert of Wytefeld. Given at Winchester, the seventh day of October, by the hand of William Longchamp, Elect of Ely, our Chancellor, in the first year of our reign. We moreover, the aforesaid, grant and confirmation holding firm and valid, do grant and confirm the same for us and our heirs as the aforesaid Charter reasonably testified. These being Witnesses, The Venerable Father Silvester, Bishop of Carlisle; John of Plessy, Earl of Warwick, Ralph the son of Nicholas, Robert Passelewe, Archdeacon of Lewes; Master W. of Kilkenny, Archdeacon of Coventry, Bertram of Crioyl, John of Lessynton; Roger, Robert Waller, and Roger of Lachington, William Geruum and others.

"Given under our hand at Woodstock, the eleventh day of July in the thirty-five &c".

TRANSLATION OF CONFIRMATION.

Ministers' Account, 32 H. 8.

County of Oxford.

"AN ACCOUNT of all and singular Bailiffs, Farmers, and all other the Ministers of our Lord, the now King Henry the 8th by the Grace of God, of England and France, Lord of Ireland, and on Earth of the English Church, the Supreme Head, concerning all Lordships, Manors, Towns, Townships, and also of all other possessions and Hereditaments whatsoever, to divers lately dissolved Monasteries and Priories in the aforesaid County, late by virtue and authority of Parliament suppressed and dissolved, belonging or appertaining in the hands of our Lord the King, now being, that is to say, from the feast of St. Michael the Archangel, in the year of our said Lord the King the 31st, to the same feast of Saint Michael the Archangel, from thence next ensuing, in the year of the same our Lord the King the 32nd., That is to say, for one entire year.

---

* A privilege allowed in the Saxon Governments to the Lords of certain Manors, to pass judgment on any theft committed within the fee.

Godstowe in the County of Oxford.

Office of Collector of Rents.

Chepynge Wycombe in the County of Bucks.

"THE ACCOMPT of Thomas Catliff, Collector of the Rents and Farms there, for the said period.

• • • •

"And of £16 13ˢ. 4ᵈ. of William Grene, the Farmer of the Rectory of the parochial Church of All Saints in Chepynge Wicombe aforesaid, with all and singular Houses, Barns and Edifices, to the aforesaid Rectory belonging or appertaining, and all and singular the tenths of Hay and Corn within the aforesaid Parish of Chepynge Wicombe, with the tenths of wood and wool, within the Parish aforesaid. And with all lands, tenements, meadows, leasowes, pastures, woods, commons, rents, and all emoluments, commodities and advantages to the aforesaid Rectory belonging or appertaining, in as ample manner and form, as Geoffrey Bishop, or Henry Turner, or either of them the said Rectors, had or occupied (the patronage and donation of the Vicarage of the same Church of All Saints of Chepynge Wicomb, and the Chantry called Bowers Chantry, within the aforesaid Church excepted), and altogether reserved, in the tenure of William Grene, so to him demised by Indenture dated the 12ᵗʰ day of March, in the 22ⁿᵈ year of King Henry the 8ᵗʰ, to have for the Term of 22 years, Rendering therefore yearly, as above, at the Feast of Sᵗ. Michael the Archangel, and Annunciation of the Blessed Virgin Mary, by equal payments, beyond £8 paid every year by the aforesaid Farmer, to two Chantry Priests called "the Charnell Priests," at the Feast of the Annunciation of the blessed Virgin Mary and St. Michael the Archangel, by even payments and 116ˢ. and 8ᵈ. by the aforesaid Farmer, in like manner paid to one Priest called Bower Priest, within the aforesaid Church, to perform at four times of the year, viz., at the Feast of the Nativity of St. John the Baptist, St. Michael the Archangel, the Birth of our Lord, and the Annunciation of the Blessed Virgin Mary, by equal portions; all charges as well ordinary as extraordinary, from the premises issuing, and the costs of the aforesaid Farmer, as is in the Indenture amongst other things contained:

The sum is

£16 , 13 , 4."

"Between the Abbot of Godestowe and Lord John Coleman.   [Translation.]

"On the 27ᵗʰ day of November, in the 5ᵗʰ year of the reign of King Edward the 3ʳᵈ, after the Conquest. It is agreed between the Abbot of Godestowe and the Convent of the same place on the one part, and Lord John Coleman, Rector of the Church of Glacton, and Lord Robert atte Walle de Newenden, perpetual Vicar of Makeseye, jointly and severally, on the other part, as follows :—That there should not be better condition of one, than the other, vizᵗ., That the said Abbot and Convent have given, granted, and to farm let, to the said John and Robert, and their executors, from the day of the Translation of St. Thomas the Martyr next after the day of the date of these presents, for the term of 10 years thence next following and fully to be completed, the Manor and Rectory of Wicumbe, together with all profits of corn, wool, and lambs, rents, lands and customs, and with all and singular commodities and tithes, during the said term to the said Rectory, in any manner belonging, appertaining, or falling, except all vestments and exchanges from the said Church arising, which to the Convent of Godestowe are reserved; to which certain agreement faithfully to keep, the said Abbot and Convent bind themselves, and their goods spiritual and temporal whatsoever in their manors, wheresoever they may be found in the said district."

|(*Portion omitted.*)|

O

COPY TERRIER.

"THE VICARAGE of Cheping Wiccombe in the County of Bucks hath a fair dwelling-house, standing on the West side of the parsonage house, and over against the North side of the Church. The house is built with timber, and where the walls have been decay'd they are repaired with Brick, elsewhere the Walls, plaistered walls. The house contains a large handsome Hall, with two large Windows against the South Sun. On the East side of the Hall there is a parlour indifferent large. On the West side of the Hall there is a parlour or dining Room neatly wainscoted, and a little Closet belonging to it. Behind the Parlour on the North side there is a Kitchen and two Butteries, and a place to brew in, and a Seller. Over the Hall and the Parlours there are fouer lodgeing Chambers, to two of which there are two Closets. And over the Kitchen, there is a lodgeing Chamber, and next to that Chamber, there is a hay loft, and next to the Hay Loft over the Seller there is a roome for wood, where also one may set an horse or cow. The House, Hayloft and Woodroom, are covered with Tileing. The two Parlours are floor'd with deal bordes, the Chambers are floor'd with boards of Oake. The Hall and the Kitchen and one of the Butteries, and the place for brewing, are floored with pavementing Tiles. There belongs to the Vicarage house a piece of ground lying round about it, containing in length 68 foot and ⅓ before the South side of the house, and on the west side of the house 184 foot, and on the North side of the House 188 foot, and on the East side of the House 150 foot. This piece of ground is fenced on the West side with a Brick Wall, on the South side with a tall stone Wall of Flints, to the Vicarage Gate, and from the Vicarage gate to the parsonage house, with a tall wooden fence of pales. And on the East side, it is fenced with a wooden fence or pales from the parsonage house throughout; on the north side it is fenced about half way with pales, and half way with a quick set hedge. The repairs of the walls, and Tiling of the house has been by the Churchwardens, at the charge of the Town, and parish, and usually put into the Church Rate. Besides this piece of ground and the church yard, and a little Cartway between the Churchyard and the Vicarage pales; there is noe Glebe Land as we know off belonging to the Vicarage. The Churchyard wall, which is built of Flint Stones, is repaired by the Parson, as farr as the parsonage ground goes, and from thence by the Churchwardens as farre as the stone wall goes. All Tythes of gardens, Orchyards, and grounds, within the Burrough, belong to the Vicarage. There is within the Town a Gift of Five pounds a year for ever, payable, out of two tenements next adjoyning to the Antilope on the West side, left to the Vicar by the Will of Mr. Richard Rut, for reading morning prayer on Munday's, Twesdayes, and Thursdayes, weekly, throughout the year. There is an ancient gift of a Noble a year left by one Mr. Wainwright, for preaching an election sermon on the Thursday before Michaelmas day, at the election of the Mayor, which the Mayor and Aldermen, considering it was but small, were pleased to order it, to be noe less than Ten shillings, which accordingly is payed me, by the Town Chamberlain.

"In the Parish, the Vicar has noe Tyth of grain, nor hay, nor wood, nor wooll. But by custome there is left him the Tyth of roots, and fruits, and of the fowles, or geese, and the Eggs of poultry. There is left also to him the Tyth of cattel, Calves, Lambs, Pigs, milk and cheese, also the Tyth of Bees, Wax and Honey, all which Tyths may be gathered in kinde, but beeing very troublesome, it is usually paid by composition with the Vicar, as they can agree. The custome for Easter Offerings is fower pence for Single persons, Six pence for a Man and his Wife. The dues of Mills are a Noble. For marriages, the custome is to demand Five shillings, At christenings, a Shilling is paid, which I suppose is for the Churching Offering, and the

Registering of the Child. For Buryals they pay a shilling. But we want our ancient Bill of Fees, which was lost I suppose in the time of Trouble. My predecessor and I have received a mortuary of Ten shillings for rich people, but some contend against it. The Vicarage payes to the Crown for Tenths, Two pounds, seven shillings, and eight pence halfepenny. To the Bishop for procurations at his Visitation, five shillings. To the Archdeacon for Synodals, three shillings. The Church has a pulpit, a reading Desk, a large Bible and common prayer Booke, a Booke of Homilyes, a Booke of Canons, the nine & thirty Articles, a Saints' Bell to ring to prayers, a chest for Almes; the steeple has a ring of six, of very good and tuneable Bells, a Clock and Chymes, a moon Diall inwards to the Church, on the outside a Clock Diall, and a Sun dial. The Chancell has rails before the Communion Table, at which Three score people may kneel at a time. The Communion Table, has a Table cloth lyeing upon it, & at the giving of the Sacrament, a white linnen Table cloth over it. There are three Pewter Flagons for Wine, a Silver Chalice, & Silver Cover. The inscription on the side of the Chalice is, 'This cup belongs to the Church of Cheping Wiccombe in the County of Bucks.' It was bought by Robert Noy, Richard Piggot, & Robert Bowdrys, Churchwardens in the year of our Lord 1671. The inscription on the cover is, 'This Cover belongeth to the Church of Cheping Wiccombe in the County of Bucks,' & was bought by Peter Sillers, Joseph Shingleton, John Bedder, & William Turner, Churchwardens, 1686. There is a pewter plate to lay the Communion Bread on. There are two pewter plates, each with a foot at the bottome to hold by, & an high edge round about the upper side, made for the purpose to receive the oblations before the Sacrament. There are two surplices. There is no Stock for any Repairs. The Clark, Sexton, and Grave-digger are appointed by the Vicar, & are maintained by what the people give them at Easter, & by ringing of the Bells, & attending on Christening, Buryals, & marriages. The Churchwardens pay the Grave digger Forty shillings a year, for sweeping & keeping clean the Church. The Silver Chalice above mentioned weighs Ten Ounces and an half. The Silver Cover above mentioned weighs Five Ounces and a fower penny weight."

"RICH. SHRIMPTON ⎱ Churchwardens.
THO. FELLOW ⎰

THOMAS CORDELL, Vicar of the Church of Cheping Wiccombe in the County of Bucks."

"The foregoing is a true Copy of an original Terrar remaining in the registry of the Lord Bishop of Lincoln at Lincoln.
RICHD. SMITH
Registrar of the Diocese of Lincoln."

"N.B.—The above named Thomas ⎱
Cordell was Instituted to
the Vicarage of Cheping ⎱
Wiccombe on the 3rd
August 1681. R. S." ⎰

Palace Lincoln
Septr 12. 1845."

COPY TERRIER belonging to the Vicar of Chepping Wicombe.

Date supposed to be about 1711.

"THE VICARAGE HOUSE contains 1 Hall, 1 Kitchen, 2 pantrys, 2 parlours. The best Wainscoted, & both floor'd with deal, 6 Chambers floor'd with Oak. The front of the House is 55 feet long by 28 feet. The Brew House, Stable and Hayloft, adjoining to the house, are

47 feet long & 16 feet wide. A wood house not far from the house is 17 by 13 feet. The house is built with Timber and dirt, but til'd.

"The Ground about the Buildings is on the west side 195 feet, fenced with a brick wall, and house on the East side is 160 feet, fenced about half way with a good brick Wall and a parsonage house, the rest is with pales. On the South end is 131 feet fenced 3 parts with brick and Stone Walls, the other part with pales. On the North side is 187 feet fenced with a quick hedge, and about the 6th part with pales. All this Ground comes to 3 roods, 15 poles, and 268 feet. There is a Brick and Stone wall on ye East side of the passage going up from the North end, to the house which parts it from ye Garden, 50 feet long & 5 feet high. On ye West side of ye passage, there is a quick to be kept cut. There is no more Glebe belonging to the Vicar except you look upon the Church Yard as such.

"All manner of Tithes within the Verge of the Corporation belong to ye Vicar, & all small Tithes in the parish, except that of wool. These Tithes are taken some of them in Kind, but generally compounded for & pay'd every half year in money. There is no modus for anything except barely for paper Mills, & Corn Mills, that have been such time out of mind. There is nothing paid out from the Vicar's Tithes. The fee for Marriage is 5^s/-, for Easter Offering 4^d, for Churching 1^s/-, for Mortuary 10^s/-, for burying in the Church, sometimes a Guinea, sometimes half a Guinea, but never less than ten Groats; for burying in the Church-yard, if no going into the Church, 1 shilling, but if there is, sometimes more. And there is a pension of 5^{lb} per annum for reading prayers, left by one Mr. Rut. The Clerk and Sexton have been chosen time out of mind by the Vicar; the Clerk's fee is a Groat a House at Easter, a Groat for Churching, a shilling for marriage, 5^s/- for the Great Bell, if the Corps is buried in Church, but 4^s/- if in the Churchyard, 2^s/6^d for the 7th Bell, 2^s/- for all the lessor, but the first, and that is 1^s/6^d. The Sexton has 2^{lb} per annum for sweeping the Church, 1^s/- for digging an Adult person's Grave, and 6^d for a Child's, if the Corps is buried in y^e Churchyard, but if in the Church 2^s/6^d for the former, & 1^s/6^d for the latter.

"There are 8 Good Bells belonging to the Church. The biggest weighing about 2700 weight. A good velvet cloth and cushion to the pulpit, a good brass candle stick, a silver cup and cover weighing 15 ounces $^3/_4$, 3 pewter Flaggons & 2 Salvers, a good linnen cloth & 2 Napkins, & a plain woollen cloth belonging to the Communion Table; 2 surplices & a hood, a Bible & 2 Common prayer Books, a good clock and chimes—".

"J. GUISE—FERD^o SHRIMPTON—JOHN HEALEY—Churchwardens".

"A true Copy having been examined with the Original Terrier remaining in the registry of the Lord Bishop of Lincoln.
ROBT. SWAN.
Reg.

Lincoln 10th Septr 1845".

In a Deed without date, but apparently of the middle of the 13th Century, the Burgesses of Wycombe granted Ade fitz Walder for their lives, to him, and for the Service he had done them, that they and their successors are his Attorneys to see and cause that the Grant which the Abbess and Convent of Godstowe granted him, be fully carried out, viz., that the said Abbess and Convent find for ever one fit Priest to celebrate the

Priestly Office in the Church of Wycombe, specially for the Soul of Walder his Father, and of Alice, his Mother, and for his Soul, and that of Agnes, his Wife, and of all faithful departed. And that all things contained in the Deed of the said Abbess and Convent be fully carried out.

In the reign of Edward I. (1274) John le Bowyer gave the Church of Wycombe 3 Torches of Wax, each 4 pounds weight, to be found, out of his Tenement, which he granted Walder de . . . between William Ger-veys' house, and Richard le Hurlers, and 3ˢ/- out of the said William Gerveys', and /12ᵈ out of late Gregory le Barber's. The said Walter to find out of the said houses and rents, 3 Torches, 2 on Lady day, and 1 on Christmas day, for ever.

We may here add what is probably the probate Copy of the Testament of William atte Coumbe, in Latin, written on parchment, and dated Tuesday, — A.D. 1354, whereby he leaves (inter alia) " to the Church of Bradenham one sheep; to the Church of Hugendene one sheep; and to the Church of Wycombe one sheep; to Sir Roger, Chaplain of the parish, 6ᵈ; to the Sacrist 3ᵈ; to the Clerk 2ᵈ. He leaves to the Wardens of the Church of Wycomb 2ˢ/ of yearly rent from the tenement of Richard le Carpenter, formerly, of John le Mareys [Marsh] to find one torch, and the raising [levationem] of the body of Christ, in the Chapel of the Blessed Mary of Wycombe. To the same Wardens also 6ᵈ yearly to be received from a certain Shop, which formerly belonged to Matthew le Fullere near the tenement of W. le Carpenter. Also to the same Wardens, one penny of rent from the tene-ment which belonged to Serche, towards the fabric of the Church. Also 20ˢ to be spent on the day of his burial, and the same on his Annivisary days. The residue of his goods he leaves to be distributed, at the discretion of his executors for his Soul, and the Soul of Thomas atte Coumbe, to his Uncle; one earthen pot [brec] excepted, which he leaves to the house of St. John the Baptist, of Wycombe. " And, for the execution of this testament, I do make, ordain, and appoint, Sir John Parson of Bradenham, and Edith my Wife to be executors."

With regard to the Architectural features of the present Church, there are some fine specimens of the early English Work. Many of the Windows with their tracery, as well as the beautiful arcading in the great South Porch, have been preserved. The structure originally consisted of the Nave, Aisles, and Chancel, with their high pitched, or gable roofs, and the Tower rising between the Chancel and the Nave. At the West end of the North Aisle, doorways have been discovered which evidently led to a building of two Stories, long since demolished, traditionally called "the Confessional," but correctly, the Revestry with Sextry above. We learn from Dr. Browne Willis's MSS. that the North Aisle was originally called the Vicar's Aisle, and had been widened for the erection of eight Altars which formerly existed. In 1518 there were, however, only six Altars in the Church, beside the High Altar, namely, St. Clement's, St. Nicholas', Name of Jesus, the Bower, and the Resurrection Altar, but to which must be added the Altar to St. Mary's Chapel, to be presently mentioned. The construction of the Nave is of the period of the 15th Century. The length of the whole building is 180 feet; the Nave is 48 feet high. The South Aisle was of a very little later date.

The South Aisle in the Chancel is the most modern part of the Church, and was called "the Bower Chancel," and originally was very beautifully decorated. There was a Chapel in the Church dedicated to St. Mary, which in all probability was situate in the Chancel, at the back of the High Altar.

In the 23rd, Edward III., by his Testament, Matthew, son of Matthew le Fuller, left a tenement in the High Street, to maintain a lamp to be always burning before the Altar of St. Mary in the Church of Wycombe. There were also eight Altars in the Aisles of the Chancel in 1526. In the early part of the 15th century considerable alterations took place, as all the piers and arches, the roofs in the Nave, the Aisles, and the clerestory windows disclose the work of the perpendicular period. The old Tower, which contained a peal of five bells of great weight, was removed. And the last great alteration, or rather addition, which we have to record, as completing the building as it now stands, was the erection of the present magnificent Tower, in the year 1522, under the superintendence of Rowland Messenger, who had been Vicar of Wycombe from 1508 to 1511, when he resigned the living. The Tower was completed with much rejoicing "ryngying of bellys, and pypying of Organs."

We may here mention that Rowland Messenger was also Prebend of St. Botolph's, Lincoln, and Rector of Winwick, Northamptonshire. It appears that he was a man of considerable Architectural skill, energetic, and somewhat notorious in his time; he was appointed by Cardinal Wolsey a Clerk, or Comptroller of the Works, on the erection of the Tower of Christ

Church College, Oxford, in 1525. Longland, Bishop of Lincoln, and Confessor to Hen: VIII., in the year 1532, under the provisions of the infamous Statute against Heretics 2 Hen: IV. c. 15 (which Fox, the Martyrologist asserts, never received the assent of the Commons), directed a Warrant to the Sheriff of Bucks, for the burning of the venerable Thomas Harding of Chesham, who had for some time been incarcerated in the prison attached to the Bishop's Palace at Wooburn, significantly called, "The little ease," on a charge of heresy, and particularly, for denying the real presence in the sacrament ; and the bishop appointed Rowland Messenger to take the oversight of his martyrdom.

Thomas Rave of Great Marlow, having abjured, says Fox, " when he came to Wycomb, there to do his penance, Rowland Messenger bound his fagot with a silken lace." This penance was the bearing of a fagot on a Market day, on the Shoulder, the penitent standing on the highest step of the Market Cross ; and from thence, bearing his fagot in a procession within the Church, and at High Mass kneeling on the highest step before the Altar.

By the Statute of Hen: II. already referred to, bishops were not only permitted to arrest and imprison, so long as their heresy should last, all preachers of heresy, all schoolmasters infected with heretical teaching, all owners or writers of heretical books, but a reprisal to abjure, or a relapse after abjuration, enabled them to hand over the heretic to the civil officers, and by these, (so ran this first legal enactment of bloodshed, which defiled our Statute book), he was to be burnt on a high place before the people.

In the *Plowman's Tale* (formerly ascribed to Chaucer) are the following lines relative to the prosecutions of supposed Heretics :—

> " These * hav more right in England here,
> " Than hath the King, and all his lawe ;
> " They hav purchased such powere,
> " To taken hem whom list or knawe ;
> " And say that heresie is there sawe, †
> " And so to prison wol heme sende.
> " It was not *so by elder lawe*,
> " God for His mercy it amende.
> " The Kinges lawe wol no man deme,
> " Angerliche without an answere,
> " But if any man these misqueme,

---

* Viz. [the bishops.]　　　† [say or talk.]

" He shall be baited as a bere ;
" And yet well worse they wol him tere,
" And in prison wollin him pende, •
" In gines, and in other gere,
" Whan that God woll, it may amende."

In the early part of the present century, a stone Sarcophagus of a very early period, about five feet long, was discovered in the North Wall of the Church. And lately, a fragment of zigzag moulding, which it is presumed belonged to the old Norman Church, and also a quantity of mediæval pavements were uncovered. And more recently in the South Aisle, near the little door, and about six inches beneath the surface, some more pavement of the same period has been discovered, on the removal of which, another stone Sarcophagus was found without a lid, lying west and east ; it is sculptured to receive the head and shoulders, and is about five feet eight inches in length, and in good preservation. The Aisles of the Church and Chancel were both divided by ancient carved screens, or parcloses, which were erected by Mr. William Redehode, to whom reference has already been made.

The screen of the South Chancel Aisle had a well preserved inscription in Oak as follows :—

" Praye for the Soules of Rycharde Redehode,
" Agnes his Wyfe, the whyche Richard bilded this parclose with tymbre in the yere off oure Lord God 1468, on—Soules—God."

These Screens were some few years since removed, which is much to be regretted by the admirers of Church Architecture. The inner Arch at the west end, now opening to the Tower, discloses the remains of the old west window, with its jambs prolonged, till they reached the ground ; this pointed Arch, which is an object at once striking and beautiful, partly carries the Tower.

The iron gates in front of the South entrance to the Churchyard were the gift of the Earl of Shelburne, and formerly stood at the St. Mary Street entrance to Loakes House.

In concluding our remarks on the Church, we may add, that this noble and stately edifice ranks first in importance among the Churches of the County,

• [hang.]

and was by Dr. Kay, the learned Bishop of Lincoln, denominated the Cathedral of Buckinghamshire.

In 1509 a dispute arose between Thomas Heywood, LL.B., Vicar of the Parish, and the Parishioners, as to the Vicar's neglect of parochial duties, which was referred to Dr. Smith, Bishop of the Diocese. And his Lordship decreed in his domestic chapel at London, May 18th, 1509, that on account of the number of souls being 1000, and the extent of the parish, the Vicar should be resident, and have an Assistant; and in case of absence, should provide two Curates, or Officiating Clergymen.

The following is a list of the earlier Vicars of Wycombe :—

Vicars.		*Patrons.*	
Philip			resigned.
Robert Maynard, 9 cal. April...	1273.	per conventum de Godstow	...resigned.
Odo de Watlington	1273.		resigned.
John de Clera, 15 cal. April...	1276.		
John le Palmere de Bloxham ...	1310.		
John de Broughton			died 1368.
Elias de Merston, May 2nd ...	1368.		
Will. Chestayne			died 1418.
Thos. Sprott, August 24th ...	1418.		
John Croxley			Exchanged for Islington with.
Richard Dalby, Sept. 9th ...	1433.		
Robert Waring			died 1470.
Hugh Clay, Oct. 30th	1470.	...per Regem.	by reason of his being in possession of the temporalities of the Nunnery, quitted for West Wycombe.
John Thayles, Dec. 4th	1471.......	per Regem.	resigned.
John Fisher, Jan. 19th	1472......	per conventum de Godstow	
Tho. Gilbert, LL.D., Dec. 28th, 1482.			
Thomas Botiler, ... occurs 1487.			
T. Heywood LL.B. March 26th, 1508.			resigned.
Rowland Messenger, March 12th, 1511.			resigned.
William Wright, March 6th ...	1539.		
Richard Philips, March 20th ...	1555.	... by Jane Raunce	resigned.
Thomas Bernard, August 1st, 1557.	... by John Raunce*		
John Dans, May 25th	1592.	... by Robert Raunce	
Philip Chamberlain	1594.	... by the same	

* NOTE.—Dr. Brown Willis supposes the Crown sold this Benefice to them, and that Raunce, the Patron, was only a lessee of the Crown.

P

Vicars.		*Patrons.*
Gerard Dobson,* Nov. 6th ...	1629.	... by ten Citizens of London.... ....
George Fownes, during the Commonwealth...		
Thomas Johnson, Nov. 15th ...	1660.	... by Matthew Archdale, Esq. ....
William Ley, May 20th	1664.	{ by Matthew } resigned for Woo- { Archdale, Esq. } burn.
Vincent Owen, June 7th	1669.	... by the same ....
Isaac Mills, A.M., Feb. 20th ...	1673.	... by the same ....resigned.
Thomas Cordel, Aug. 3rd	1681.	... .buried here April 22, 1711.
Samuel Guise, A.B., May 30th ...	1711.	... by Hen: Petty, Lord Shelburne. ......
And again	1724.	.................buried here Oct. 19, 1753.
Edmund Trot, LL.B.,† Dec. 6th	1753.	... by John, Earl of Shelburne............
James Price, B.A., Nov. 24th ...	1763.	... by William, Earl of Shelburne.........
And again, M.A., Jan. 6th	1784.	... the same ... buried here, Jan., 1788.
James Price, B.A. March 21st ...	1784.	... the same, Marquis of Lansdowne, K.G.

The 1st Ledger referred to, folio 3, contains—

" An Inventory of the Goods of the Parish Church of All Saints at Wycombe, made there A.D. 1475, in the time of Nicholas Grove, John Porter, William Harper, and Thomas Lytylpage the Younger, Wardens of the Church aforesaid : the following is a copy.

" A sewte of vestmentes of rede bawdekyne, beryng werke damaske branchis of Gold, with lyons and byrdis of the same. A sewte of stuffe berynge werke branchis of grene, with levis of golde. A sewte of rede velewet, powdyrde, with crowns of gold. A sewte of blewe bawdekyn, berynge werke grene branchis with byrdis of gold. A sewte of white bawdekyne, powdyrde with birdis of golde. A sewte of rede sylke, powderid, with white branchis. A sewte of blacke for Requiem Mas. A chesapylle of rede bawdekyne, powdered, with birdis of golde, with an awbe (alb) longyng therto. A sewte of grene velewet, except the cope, beryng a grene bawdekyne. A chesapyll and tenekylle of sylke, beryng branchis of blewe purpylle with apys of golde, with apparell therto. A sewte of blewe sylke, with rayes of golde, except the awbys and copis of playne white sylke. A white chesapyll, with apparell therto ; ii. chesapyllis of sylke with apparelle therto ; ii. olde chesapylles of sylke ; vii. pelowis of sylke and of bawdekyne ; iii. pallis of clothe of sylke, powderide with gold ; vi. auter clothis to lye uppone the hye auter. A palle for the hersse of blacke sylke ; a blacke saye clothe [perditur, lost.—Note] ; another of wollen [perditur, lost.—Note]. Item v. longe hoselynge towellis of diaper ; ii. waisshinge towellis for the hye auter ; a blacke frontell for the hye auter, with branchis of grene powderid, with squier-elles of gold. Item, a blewe frontell with branchis of grene, powderid, with hyndis of golde. Item, v. corperas cases of diverse clothis of sylke, vii. corporassis of casis lynnyne. Item, a purse of clothe of golde ; a purse of clothe of sylke, with the reliquis. Item, iii. baneris of sylke, with the stavis thereto, a crosse baner of sylke with a staffe of copur and gylte ; a crosse staffe peyntid ; iiii. banir clothis of lynnyne. Item, a canape of purpull sylke, with iiii. botons gylt ; a canape of white clothe ; vi. pynounse [pennons] of sylke ; iii. pendauntes of sylke ; iii. lecturne clothis. Item, iiii. steynide clothis for the hye auter, with iiii. curtayns, ii. steynid clothis, for the hye

---

* Dobson occurs in 1652, when the Living was worth £20 per Ann., and in 1752 the Parliament augmented it by a grant of £50 per annum, out of Queen Anne's Bounty.

† Dr. Trot ruined himself in rebuilding the Vicarage House, and died at St. Kitts, leaving a destitute widow.

auter, with iiii. curtayns, ii. steynid clothis, with a frontell counterfeet clothe of gold for the hye auter; ii. curtayns of purpylle sylke; ii. auter clothis for Lent, with the curtayns; iii. lecturne clothis for Lent. A staynid clothe of gold, powderid with gold and sylver for the Sepulcur, with a lynnyne clothe therto; a Sepulcur of tymber with a stole therto. A vayle of white, with a crosse of rede; ii. canstykkys of latone to stonde uppone the hye auter; ii. grete canstykkys of latone, to stonde in the queir. A sensare of latone, a shippe of latone; a pyx box of latone, with a box of ivorie. A crismatorie of sylk, that weyth xxvii. unces. A chalys with a patent of sylver and gylt, that weythe xvi. unces and i. quarter. A chalys with a patent of sylver and gylt, that weyth xviii. unces and i. quart. A chalys with a patent of sylver and gylt, that weythe xxvii. unces and dwt. A chalys with a patent of sylver and gylt, that weythe xxx. unces i. quarter. A chalys with a patent of sylver, that weythe xii. unces and dwt. A sensare with cheyns of sylver, that weythe xxxvii. unces. A sensare with cheynes of sylver, that weythe xxxiii. unces i. quarter. Item, ii. shippes of sylver, with ii. sponys of sylver, that weyth xx. unces, iii. quarters, and dwt. A crosse of sylver and gylt, that weythe lxxiiii. unces; a fote of a crosse, with a penacull of sylver and gylt, that weythe lxi. unces; ii. crewettes of sylver, that weyne ix. unces and quarter; ii. basyns of sylver, that weyne xxx. unces; ii. canstykkys of sylver, that weyne xlix. unces and half unce. Item, a pax of sylver and gylt with v. stonys, that weythe xv. unces; a lytyll box of sylver and gylt, that weyth 3 unces; a lytyll box of sylver with dyverse reliquis therin; a box of copur and gylt, and enamilde, with reliquis therin. A crosse of copur and gylt; another crosse of copur and gylt with iiii. stonys. A crosse of latene; another of tree [wood]: a surplice for the quere. Item, ii. Mass bokys to the hye auter; ii. grete Luggeris [Leigers, or Antiphonars] in the queire; iiii. Portowis [Portifories, or Portehors] a Responsor, with a lytyll Graylle; v. Grayles; vi. Prosessioneris; ii. Manuellis; i. Dirgeboke; ii. Pystyl bokys [Epistle books]; a Legent; i. Ordinalle; i. Martilage [Martyrology]; a Cathalicane [Catholicon]; a lantorne; an halywater stok of latone; ii. lecternys of tymber; ii. hoselyng bellys [houseling bells]; iii. bellis for the bedmanne [bedeman, or summoner]; ii. beris [biers] with ii. coffyns therto. Item, i. crowe of irene wei'ng ix. li. weight. Item, a sute of clothe of golde tyssu of the gyfte of Sir John Stoktone of Londone, with alle the aparelle. Item, ii. Copys of whighte damaske, the orferasse [orfrays] of bleu damaske, *ex dono Willelmi Redehode* [the gift of William Redehode]. Item, ii. blac copys of worstede, the orferasse of blew worstede, poudered, with letters of gold, *ex dono dicti Willelmi Redehode* [the gift of the said William Redehode]. Item, a palle of imperiall a—. Item a Processionary, coveryd with black damaske. Item, ii. awter clothis of blew worstede, powderyd, with flowyrs of golde and spangyls of sylver. Item ii. curteynes of blew sarsenet, frengyd with sylke. Item, a pyx of sylver gylt, with a lytyll pece of sylver, weyeing xvi. unces. Item, ii. candystykkes of latene, stondyng in Seynt Nicholas chauncelle. Item, a Kercheffe of plesans, with a bordur of sylke and golde, *ex dono Johannis Collarde*. Item, a gowne of purpylle sarsenet for Ihesus awter, *ex dono Johannis Collarde*. Item, a cloth of blac worstede for the herse, with a whyte crosse imbrowderyd in v. placis with the name of Jhesus. Item a canape of launde, with iiii. botons of nedylle worke, freyngyd rounde abowte with rede sylke and golde, *ex dono Margeriæ Bontynge* [the gift of Margery Bontynge]. Item, a lynnyne cloth, with a crosse of blac bokeram, for the roode. Item a towelle to hossyl [administer the Sacrament to] peple, conteyning by estymacion xix. yerdes with blewe porelles [q^y. tufts] at the end. Item a baner clothe of blew-sylke, chaungeable with a fegure of the Trinite, of the yefte of John Collarde. Chales with a patent of sylver and gylte, weyeng x. unces, of the yefte of William Redehode *ad dictam Capellan Beatæ Mariæ* [to the said Chapel of S^t. Mary]."

In folio 4.*b* by a like Inventory taken in the year 1503, **some of** the former items have disappeared and others are added. Among the latter :—

"A sewte of rede sylk with sterris, and the floure de luce. A sewte of blak with flouris of golde in the crosse. A cope of grene bawdekyn with lyones rampyone of gold. A Chesebylle of grene borde alisaundre [a cloth, probably resembling sandalwood] with a crosse of saye sylke. Myters of diverse sewtes, ii. stremers of sylke, one rede, another blewe, iii. qweryes noted, of the Visitacion of oure Lady, iii. qweyres of the Transfiguration of Jhesu, and the Masse also. Two bokes, on off Seynt Austen's workes, another of Seynt Gregories worke, iiii. wol. stremers to goe by the crosse uppone high days."

In folio 7.*b* follows an Inventory of the Church goods made on the 20th of January, 10th Henry VIII. (A.D. 1519), in the presence of Thomas Kare, Mayor. The last in general resembles the preceding ones : the "Hygh awltere" is mentioned ; the "Bowre awltere," the "Resurrection awltere." "Jesus awltere" ; "Saynt Clements awltere." Many "vestments" are mentioned ; among them "a vestment of grene dornekke," [Cloth of Tournay] "a stremer of bokerham, image of our Lady." A "baner of bokerham of Sayent Poule."

The 2nd Ledger, folio 1, contains the following record of—

THE CHURCH BELLS.

"An accompt of the w^{tt} of the old, and new Bells ; the charge of casting, and their inscriptions. Cast in the year 1711.

W^u of ye Old Bells. cwt.	Inscriptions.
6. 29 „ 0 „ 00	Jos. Pettiphur May'; Cha. Elliott Ald. ; Jno. Bigg, T. Clerk ; Tho' Grove, Cris. Landell, Sam. Freeman, Rob' Rastliff, c.w. 1683.
5. 20 „ 1 „ 04	Martin Lewellin May', Rob' Roy, Cris' Weeden, Richd Piggot, Rob' Bowdrey, Church W. 1672.
4. 15 „ 2 „ 11	"Love God" 1636.
3. 12 „ 0 „ 18	Multis Annis Resonet Campana Johannis 1583.
2. 9 „ 0 „ 18	Sit nomen domini Benedictum.
1. 8 „ 0 „ 10	Praise the Lord 1620."
in all 94 „ 1 „ 05	

bell w^u

Wᵗᵗ of the New Bells.

cwt.

8. 25 „ 1 „ 00   Samˡ Guise M.A. Vicar, Nath: Morgin, Wm. Packer.
Samˡ Wells, Fra. Williams, C. W. Richᵈ Phelps, Wade Mee, 1711.

7. 17 „ 3 „ 00   Hugh Shrimpton Mayʳ; Thoˢ Russin, Justice,
Thoˢ Wood T. C. Richᵈ Allen, Jnº Carter, Bail: R.P. fecit 1711.

6. 13 „ 1 „ 06   Messeurs Jno: Lane, Thoˢ Stevens, Geo. Grove, Fred: Shrimpton,
bell wᵗᵗ   Thoˢ Wells, Aldⁿ R. P. fecit 1711.

5. 11 „ 3 „ 08   Messeurs Benj: Hickman, Jos. Pettipher, Richᵈ Shrimpton.
Hen: Hunt, Aldⁿ. R.P. fecit 1711.

4. 9 „ 3 „ 00   God preserve the Church of England, and our gracious Queen,
Ann, R.P. fecit 1711.

3. 7 „ 3 „ 00   Richᵈ Phelps of White Chappell, London, cast these eight Bells in ye
year 1711.

2. 6 „ 2 „ 22   Edwᵈ Stevens, Clark: Luke Gurney, Sexton, R. P. fecit 1711.

1. 6 „ 3 „ 15   Wᵐ Shrimpton, T. Clark, Jnº Rose, Serjeant.

in all 99 „ 0 „ 23   Wᵐ Hailey, Beadle, R.P. fecit 1711."

"The taking down of yᵉ old Bells, altering yᵉ Frame, Wheels, stocks, Clappers, Brasses, Carriage from Spade Oke Wharfe to London, all other charge at London, casting the eight new Bells, and adding five hundred weight of new mettle; Carriage back to Spade Oke Wharfe. Hanging yᵉ new Bells, and all other charges (except carrying yᵉ old Bells to Spade Oke Wharfe and bringing yᵉ new Bells back from thence, was undertaken and performed by Mr. Richard Phelps of Whitechapell, Lond: Bell founder, for yᵉ sum of one hundred and fourty pounds."

The second bell was added to the above by the Earl of Wycombe, and the 3rd by Lord Henry Petty.

The following inscription is cast upon the tenor bell:

"May all whom I shall summon to the grave,
"The blessings of a well spent life receive.

The Revᵈ James Price Vicar,
Messʳˢ Richard Barton, Samˡ Bates, James Kingston,
Daniel Turner, Churchwardens, W. B."   (No date).

The old Chimes were constructed by Mr. George Harman, Sen. (an amateur of considerable mechanical skill), who also constructed the celebrated chimes in Cripplegate Church, London; the cost of the Wycombe Chimes was paid by the Marquis of Lansdowne. Mr. Harman was by nature of musical genius, for he also built an excellent chamber organ, which he presented to his son, the late Alderman Harman, conditionally, that he first played upon it the old hundredth psalm tune.

The Church has lately been restored; the interior of the nave and choir, completely, and the exterior, partially, under the direction of the eminent architect, Mr. Street.

A memorial window, of exquisite art, by Hardman, to the late Right Honourable Robert John, second Lord Carington, has been placed at the east end of the chancel, by the voluntary contributions of his Lordship's tenantry and friends.

A new Town Clock has recently been erected in the Tower of the Church, by public subscription, having four dial plates, one of which is illuminated; and with a new set of chimes, playing seven tunes; the list, to which is added the names of the gentlemen presenting the same, is as follows, viz. :—

			Tune			
Sunday	...	...	Easter Hymn	...	...	Mr. F. Wheeler.
Monday	...	...	Rousseau's Dream	...	...	Mr. J. O. Griffits.
Tuesday	...	...	O Rest in the Lord	...		Mr. J. Parker, Jun.
Wednesday	...	...	Sicilian Mariners' Hymn	...		Mr. F. Wheeler.
Thursday	...	...	Blue Bells of Scotland	...		Mr. B. Lucas.
Friday	...	...	The Last Rose of Summer			Mr. W. V. Baines.
Saturday	...	...	Home, Sweet Home	...		Mr. A. Vernon.

The chimes are played on the Church Bells every three hours.

In 1545 William Avis was Parish Clerk and Organ Player.

An Organ by Green was placed in the Church in 1783. Mr. Maberley, an ancestor of an old Wycombe family, of the name of Pontyfix, was for many years the Organist, and was succeeded by his nephew, Mr. Pontyfix. This Organ was a few years since removed, and a magnificent Organ, by Jones, was erected in the Vicar's Aisle, and contains the most valuable of the pipes of the old Organ.

THE ALTAR PIECE.

A brief sketch relative to this picture, and as to its presentation to the Church, may not be altogether uninteresting to the reader. The picture which represents St. Paul preaching to the British Druids,* was painted b

---

* As to the reasonable probability of St. Paul having preached in Britain, see Spee "Great Britain," and the authorities therein cited, p. 203; Bp. Newton "On the Prophecie vol. ii. p. 237; and "The Early British Church founded by St. Paul," by the Rev. Henry Sm Chaplain of Parkhurst Prison.

John Hamilton Mortimer, an English historical painter of great merit; and for it, as being the best historical picture, he obtained the first prize of one hundred guineas from the Society for the encouragement of Arts, Manufactures, and Commerce. Doctor Bates, of Little Missenden, who was the great friend and patron of Mortimer, on one occasion visiting him, went into his studio, and to his great surprise found Mortimer playing with a ball at the game of fives against this picture. The Doctor remonstrated with him for his temerity; Mortimer said he did not value the picture particularly, and that the Doctor was quite welcome to it; which offer he at once accepted. Doctor Bates presented the picture in 1778 to this Church.

In 1779 Mortimer was, without solicitation or expectation, created a Royal Academician by the especial grant of the King. His reputation was now established, and his celebrity increased by the production of his pictures of King John granting Magna Charta, The Battle of Agincourt, Vortigern and Rowena, and other admired works. "In the freedom of his pencil" (says Gould), "and the savage air of his banditti (his favourite subject) he approached nearly to the boldest efforts of Salvator Rosa." After an illness of a few days, Mortimer died on the 4th of February, 1779, aged 40, and was buried in Little Missenden Church; six months afterwards his remains were exhumed, and in honour of his great master-painting, they were interred in the chancel of this Church.

In anticipation of the restoration of the Church, the Churchwardens obtained a faculty authorising the removal of the Altar Piece. And it was resolved in Vestry that the same should be presented to the Corporation, which was accepted. And this splendid production of art now graces the Council Chamber of the Guildhall.

The Church Register dates from the year 1598.

The Churchyard was closed by order of the Secretary of State; and the Cemetery was opened in July, 1855, which being pleasantly situated on an eminence, commands a charming view of the town and its immediate neighbourhood, embracing the beautiful grounds of Wycombe Abbey; Hughenden Manor, the seat of the Earl of Beaconsfield, with the picturesque little Church, and Vicarage House attached; also West Wycombe Park, and the Church on the opposite hill; restored by Francis Lord le

Despenser, after the Italian style.   This Church has been ironically **described**
by Wilkes as " built on the *top* of a hill for the convenience and devotion of
the town at the *bottom*."   Or as another wit irreverently adds,—

> " A temple built aloft in air,
>   That serves for show, if not for prayer."

THE PRINCIPAL MONUMENTS, Etc., IN THE CHURCH.

In the North Aisle of the Chancel.—The principal object of interest
is an elegant mural monument by Scheemakers, to Henry Petty, Earl of
Shelburne.   It consists of an architrave, supported by double Corinthian
columns of gray marble, the whole placed upon a basement of fine white
marble ; between the pillars stands a sarcophagus of gray stone, upon which
reclines the dying Earl, supported on his right elbow, and by his side
Religion, with an open book.   Upon the front of the sarcophagus is a
medallion with the head of Sir William Petty (the Earl's father) in alto.
To the left of this group, an erect male figure, habited as a Roman warrior,
and seated by his side, an elegant female caressing an infant.   To the right
another group, showing a youth tended by two female figures, emblematical
of Wisdom and Virtue.   At the back of the centre group is a pyramidal
tablet of Sienna marble, surmounted with the family shield, and bearing two
cherubims, prepared to crown the expiring statesman.   Above the entabla-
ture are two female figures in a reclining attitude, and holding the attributes
of Justice and Truth.   All these statues, twelve in number, are in white
marble, and the size of life.   The inscription is as follows :—

> To the Memory of Henry Petty, Earl of Shelburne
> Son of Sir William Petty.   His Lordship married Arabella
> Boyle daughter of Charles Lord Clifford, son and
> heir apparent of Charles Earl of Cork and Burlington,
> by whom he had issue,
> Julia, who died unmarried, aged 23 years ;
> Charles, who died at the age of 12 years.   Ann, who married
> Francis Bernard, Esq., of Castle Bernard, in the kingdom of
> Ireland, and died at the age of 30 years, leaving no issue.
> James Lord Viscount Dunkerron,
> Who married Elizabeth Clavering, daughter and co-heiress of
> Sir John Clavering, in the bishoprick of Durham ;

James Lord Viscount Dunkerron, died in the 40th year of his age.
Elizabeth, his Wife, in the 32nd, and with their only son,
Who died an infant, lie buried underneath
This monument.
Henry Earl of Shelburne,
Having survived his wife and children, bequeathed his fortune
to John Fitzmaurice, second son of his Sister Ann,
Countess of Kerry, on condition of his taking the surname of
Petty, and died in the 78th year of his age.
He and Arabella his wife, lie buried under this monument.
This monument was erected by Slingsby Bethel, Esq., alderman
of London, and William Monck, Esq., of the Middle Temple, London,
his lordship's executors, 1784.

In contemplating this fine work of art, the eye is struck by the admirable foil afforded by the flowing draperies to the straight lines of architecture. It is principally of light veined marble, and is some 26 feet high. A finer composition is rarely met with, and the examination of it is equally gratifying and satisfactory. It is surrounded with an iron railing—we trust a needless protection.

In the south aisle, on a brass plate :—

Here under lyeth buried, the bodye of Margaret Trone, the daughter of — Trone, and Añ his wife, who deceased the first of November, 1588.

Also a beautiful monument, by Carlini, representing Lady Shelburne reclining on an urn, with her two children, the effect of which is truly imposing,—

Sophia
Daughter
of John and Sophia, Earl and Countess Granville,
Wife
of William Earl of Shelburne, Baron of Wycombe,
Mother
of John Henry Viscount Fitzmaurice
and William Granville Petty,
Died in the twenty sixth year of her age,
on the sixth of January, MDCCLXXI.
Her price was far above rubies,
Her children arise up and call her blessed ;
Her husband also, and he praiseth her.—Solomon.

Above the monument is her ladyship's achievement.

Q

The following curious and unique inscription is on a tablet in the north aisle of the Chancel. William Bradshawe, whom it commemorated, resided at the Bridge Mill. Four of his sons were graduates of Oxford (one of them of Brasenose, and another of Balliol); and on the death of the parents, each of them contributed these epitaphs in elegant Latin.

Epitaphium.
In obitum Gulielmi Bradshawe qui obiit Jul. 19. 1614
An: ætat: 103.   Et Margeriæ Uxoris ejus quæ obiit Jul. 15. 1620 An. ætat 96.
Et Gulielmi filii ipsorum Qui obiit September 9. 1596 An. Ætat: 29
Junxit amor vivos, defunctos jungit et urna,
Jungit cœlum animas corpora jungit humus :
Ista manent stabili semper connubia nexu :
Et mors ipsa nequit solvere vincla Dei
F. B. Sac. Theol: Doct.

Aliud
Quæ genuere vorant πρόνος et πρόνος, almaque: tellus
Sed (micrum est) iterum que vorat ipsa parit.
N. B. Sac. Theol: Bach.

Aliud
Mors tibi jam stimulum moriens Salvator ademit:
Mors vitam, at mortem vita secunda fugat.
R. B. Art. M'.

Aliud
In damno lucrum est, injuria finore ditat,
Corpora quæ recipit mortua, viva dabit.
J. B. Art. M'.

Translation.   In memory
of Wm. Bradshawe, who died July 19, 1614, aged 103; and of Margery, his wife, who died July 15, 1620, aged 96 ; and of William, their son, who died September 9, 1596, aged 29.

Love joined their lives, the tomb unites their dust,
The realms above unite their souls, we trust.
Such perfect bonds not death itself can sever,
Whom God thus fitly joins, he joins for ever.
F. B., D.D.

Like time, like fabled Saturn, mother earth
Devours her sons, but gives them second birth.
N. B., B.D.

Where is thy sting, O death? 'tis nought to me,
Thou endest life : another life ends thee.
R. B., M.A.

Where loss is gain, why dread we death's attack?
Earth takes us lifeless, deathless yields us back.
J. B., M.A.

F. Bradshawe, D.D., was a fellow of Magdalene College, Oxford.   See Anthony à Wood.

In the south aisle, on a white marble tablet, enriched with decorative emblems of his profession, viz., a casque or modern helmet, sword and spear, and within a wreath of laurel, the words, " Ladoeira," " Salamanca," is this inscription :—

Captain William White,
Of His Majesty's 13th regiment of Light Dragoons,
and D. A. Q. M. G. of Cavalry, under his Grace the Duke of Wellington,
was mortally wounded at the battle of Salamanca, the 22nd of July, 1812,
in the 30th year of his age.
Of whom his brave companions in arms have
borne this honourable testimony that " he fell nobly,
acting with distinguished bravery in a glorious cause, with a character
unblemished as a man and as a soldier, adorned with unsullied integrity, and
undaunted courage !" a testimony amply corroborated
by the official Gazettes of Sept 18th, 1810, and May 9th, 1812.
He survived until the night of the 23rd, and ere he breathed his last had the satisfaction
of knowing that he died, as he had lived, the companion of Victory.

Lieut. Gillespie White of the same regiment twin brother
of the above, and holding similar rank on the staff of the army
in Egypt, commanded by Sir Ralph Abercrombie K.B.
died at Damietta Oct. 15th 1801, at the age of 20 years.

Also, on a neat mural tablet, near the communion table, is the following inscription, held—

Sacred
To the Memory of
William Sproston, of
High Wycombe, Gentleman,
Who departed this life
The 26th day of January, 1841,
in his 78th year.

A faithful director of
The Royal Free Grammar School,
In this Borough
for 47 years.
" Go and do thou likewise."
This tablet is erected by his only
Surviving and beloved brother,
Samuel Sproston Esq., of Sproston Wood,
Wrenbury, in the County of Chester.

Also on a neat white marble sarcophagus, adorned with a sculptured figure of a serpent coiled, emblematical of wisdom and eternity :—

Sacred to the memory of the Rev. John Manning LL.B.
Formerly of St. Mary's Hall, Oxford, and
Alderman of this Borough.   He died
the 1st Oct., 1822, aged 67 years.

Within the Communion rails, on a brass plate :—

Here lyeth the body of Robert Kemp, who departed this life
the 28.. November, A.D. 1621.

Wife, children, wealth, this world, and life forsaken,
In silent dust I sleep; when once awaken,
My Saviour's might a glorious change will give—
So loosing all I gayne, and dying, live.
My fame I trust the world with, for 'tis true,
Posterity gives each man his due.

M. S.

Hic jacet Martinus Lluelyn,
Eruditus Medicinæ Doctor,
Ex Æde Christi olim Alumnus
Sæviente Civilis Belli Incendio
(Dum Oxonium Præsidio muniebatur)
Cohorti Academicorum fideli Præfectus erat
Adversus ingruentem Rebellium ferociam
Postea quam serenissimo Carolo Secundo inter juratos medicus
Et Collegii Medicorum Londinensis Socius
Aulæ Sanctæ Mariæ dudum Principalis
Dein hujusce comitatus Irenarcha
Nec non Municipii hujus semel Prætor

Regiæ Authoritatis et Religionis Ecclesiæ Anglicanæ legibus stabilitæ
Strenuus Assertor
Inconcussus Amator
Celeberrimus et Insignis Poeta
Qui res egregias et sublimes pari ingenio et facundia depinxit
Bino matrimonio fælix septem liberos superstites reliquit,
Lætitiam et Martinum ex priore, Georgium, Ricardum et Mauritium ex posteriore
Nuper amantissimo Conjuge
Nunc Mæstissima vidua Martha Georgii Long de Penn gen: filia.
Heu quam caduca corporis humani fabrica
Qui toties morbos fugavit, Ipse tandem
Morbo succumbit anhelus,
Doctorum et proborum maximum desiderium
Obiit 17 Martii 1681 annoque ætatis 66.

———————————————————

Translation.

Arms, a lion rampant crowned.

Impaling, a lion rampant inter 8 croslets with a bordure charged with ermine.

M. S.

Here lies Martin Lluelyn,
A learned Doctor of Medicine,
Formerly a student of Christ Church, Oxford.
During the Civil War,
at the siege of Oxford,
He was a lieutenant in the loyal company of Students,
Formed to oppose the ferocious rebels.
He was afterwards one of the sworn physicians of Charles II.
and Fellow of the College of Physicians in London.
He was Principal of St. Mary Hall, Oxford, afterwards J.P. for this County,
And once Mayor of this Borough.
A strenuous supporter and unshaken admirer
of the Crown and Church as by law established.
A most famous and illustrious Poet,
who treated of lofty subjects with an ability
and eloquence not unworthy of the same.
Twice married, he left seven surviving children,
Letitia and Martin by his first wife, George, Richard, and Maurice,
By his second, Martha daughter of George Long of Penn, Gent.,
late his loving wife, now his disconsolate widow.
Alas! how frail a creature is man!
He, who so often banished disease
At last becomes its victim,
Regretted by all learned and good men.
He died 17 March 1681.
Aged 66.

At the foot of the tablet is an epitaph to his daughter, **Martha Crosse**, who died Feb. 1, 1767, aged 93.

On a flat stone in the nave, beneath the chandelier, is the following inscription, much defaced :—

Barnes 1701.
Is Johny dead? though young and small in age,
Translated quickly, from this wordly stage,
Life's like a flower, which of itself will die,
And nipt with frost, soon hangs its head awry.
Death spares not any mortal, but is bold,
To take both Kings and Peasants, young and old;
Be watchful then, when God doth give you ear
Of death and judgment, none knows who is near.

On a very neat mural tablet in the north aisle : —

" The memory of the just is blessed."
Sacred
To the memory of Isaac King, Esq.,
One of His Majesty's Justices of the Peace for the County of
Bucks, and an Honorary Member of the Board of Agriculture.
He was a firm supporter of constitutional Liberty, sincerely
attached to the Established Religion of his Country;
a most affectionate husband and father, a faithful
friend, an honest and benevolent man.
Died Dec. 24th 1812.   Ætat. 72.

Also : —

Sacred to the memory of
The Rev: Isaac King, LL.B.
Twenty five years Vicar of West Wycombe,
In the County of Bucks,
Who
" After he had served his own generation by the will of God
fell on sleep."
Born March 21st 1776, died January 26th 1832.
This tablet was erected by his surviving widow and children
as a testimony of their affection.

"And God shall wipe away all tears from their eyes, and
there shall be no more death, neither sorrow, nor crying, neither
shall there be any more pain, for the former things are passed
away."—Revelation xxi. 4.

Also near the Communion rails—Azure, a maunch ermine, over all a
bend gules.   Bearing argent a chevron inter 3 crosslets gules in pretence.

Near
This place lies the body of Ferdinando Norton, Gent., formerly
one of His Majesty's band of Musicians,
and many years an inhabitant of this Borough.
He died January 5th, 1773, aged 76 years ;
Leaving many legacies to the poor, and to the Magdalen and
St. Luke's Hospitals, £300 each.
Also of Bridget his wife, daughter of Mr Thomas Woodroff,
Linen Draper, of London, she died June 25, 1771, aged 64 years.

To commemorate such valuable characters, so much esteemed
through life for their honesty, religion, and charity, this monument
is erected by their nephews and nieces, as a small mark of
gratitude and affection.

On a neat tablet close to the Communion rails :—

In Memory of
Ann the beloved wife of
Thomas Westwood, Esq., of this town
and eldest daughter
of Samuel and Isabella Welles,
Died Jan: 28, 1839, aged 83 years.
Also,
Of the said Thomas Westwood, Esq:,
who died July 21st 1839,
aged 64 years.
Many years an alderman of this Borough.

Also on a slab in the south aisle is the following inscription :—

" Here lies in hope of a blessed resurrection of the just to eternal life, the body of Richard
Shrimpton, Gentª, Alderman, and thrice Mayor of this Corporation, and Justice, when he died.
He departed this life June yᵉ 20th 1727 aged 77

" For being just unto his Friend,
his enemies hastened his end."

Also, a monument erected to perpetuate the—

Memory of
Mrs Sarah Shrimpton
The beloved wife of Thomas Shrimpton, Esq ;
a native of this borough.
She departed this life the 28th day of May, 1783,
to the inexpressible grief of her family and friends.
" Blessed are the dead which die in the Lord."

Hear what the voice from heaven proclaims,
For all the pious dead ;
Sweet is the savor of their names,
And soft their sleeping bed.

They die in Jesus, and are bless'd ;
How kind their slumbers are !
From suffering, and from sins releas'd,
And freed from ev'ry snare.

Far from this world of toil and strife,
They 're present with the Lord ;
The labours of their mortal life
End in a large reward.

Peace all our angry passions then !
Let each rebellious sigh,
Be silent at the sovereign will,
And every murmur die.

The sculpture over the above tablet is, by the elder Westmacott, 1784.

In the north aisle, on a neat mural tablet :—

John Shrimpton, Esq.,
Major of the Tower of London, and Alderman
of this Borough, died March 28th, 1787,
Aged 45 years.
He left the character of a brave officer in every part of
the world, and as an honest citizen, a
generous man, and a steady friend, was universally
regretted by this town, and corporation.

Sacred
To the memory of Joseph Shrimpton, Esq,
of this borough, who died 16th April, 1783, in the
72nd year of his age.
Also,
Of Esther Shrimpton, wife of the above Joseph Shrimpton,
Who died March 8th, 1782, aged 71 years.
"The righteous shall be in everlasting remembrance."

Near this place are deposited the remains of
George Clavering, Esq., of Greencroft, in
the parish of Lanchester, and County of Durham.
He was the second son of
Sir James Clavering, of Axwell Park,
in the said County, Bart.,
and died at High Wycombe, on his journey from Bath, the
22nd day of May, 1794, aged 73 years.

On a slab in the pavement of the north aisle :—

Mary, wife of Major-General John Gaspard Le Marchant, 1811.

Also, in the north aisle ; arms, azure, a chevron ermine inter 3 talbots passant or.—Impaling. In chief a lion passant, in base a chevron ermine inter 3 fer de molines sable. (Turner)—Crest : a wolf's head on a ducal coronet.

Here lyeth the body of Thomas Archdale, Esq.,
who departed this life Aug. 9th 1711, aged 36.

In Memory of
Richard Lluelyn, B.D., late fellow of Magdalen College, Oxon,
and Rector of Saunderton,
who died 25th Dec., 1770, aged 62.

K

In the south aisle, on a mural monument of marble :—

Near this place is buried Mrs Mary Wyngrove, wife of Mr George Wyngrove, of this town, and daughter of Christopher Newell, of Postcomb, in the parish of Lewknor, Oxon, Gentleman. She died 23rd Sep., 1758, aged 53 years.

Also,

In a vault in the chancel of this Church is deposited,
Fanny,
Relict of John Stone James, Esq., Barrister at Law, in which
profession his upright conduct and ability distinguished him.
After a pious, beneficent, and truly Christian life,
tranquilly resigned for immortality and endless bliss,
the 7th of July, 1831, in the 85th year of her age.
She rests here in holy hope, with three beloved daughters
and two sons :
Fanny, who died in the 21st, Harriet, in the 18th,
John, in the 16th, Robert, in the 14th, and Mary,
in the 12th, year of their age.

Lovely—as seraphs and as cherubs bright,
Pure as the dew—brilliant as morning light,
Thy native goodness and thy mental grace,
On fond remembrance leave a lasting trace.
Like rare exotics, whose attractive bloom
Unfolds to captivate—but withers soon.
So thou ! with nature's choicest gifts replete,
In higher climes thy full perfection meet.
Lamented is thy transient sojourn here,
Still o'er thy ashes falls affection's tear !
Ye watchful angels, guard their precious dust,
Till raised " by faith," from earth's surrend'ring trust.
And heaven ! do thou the miscreant's arm arrest,
That, impious, would that sacred spot molest.
Fierce let thine anger pour, in vengeance shed
Thy wrath upon invaders of the dead.
This consecrated pile, which sure should prove
The resting-place of piety and love,
Let none e'er enter that would dare
Disturb those ashes in this " House of Prayer."

On a mural monument, these arms in a lozenge :—

Oz. a lion ramp, or, debruised with an inescutcheon, Gules, three Catherine wheels, Or : on a Chief of the Last a bull's head cabossed, S. below :—

Devoted
By Mary Elizabeth Hazard,
of Terriers House, in this parish,
to the memory of the best of mothers,
Jane,
Relict of the Rev: George Lewis A.M.,
Rector of Echingham,
in the bishoprick of Chichester,
and Vicar of Westerham,
in the Diocese of Rochester.
She died May XXVI A.D. MDCCXCIV,
Aged LXIII years.

— — — — — — ——————

On a simple marble tablet, in the south aisle :—

To the Memory of Elizabeth King,
who died Dec. 7th, 1782, aged 24 years.

- — - -

Go, happy spirit, freed from sin and care,
Go claim the palm which patient sufferers wear;
Enjoy the meed victorious meekness gains,
Go take the crown triumphant faith obtains.

- ———

What artful vice and humble worth conceal
The day of dread disclosure shall reveal ;
Then shall thy life in sweet memorial rise
And God himself, the judge, award the prize.

H. MORE.

Here lyeth the body of John Sparkes, Esq.,
Near his father, Mr. E. Sparkes, and his brother, Mr. J. Sparkes,
Who both died before him, being about 70 years old.
He served High Sheriff for the County of Bucks.
He died the 17th April, 1707, in the 79th year of his age

Here lyeth the body of Edward Sparkes, Esq., who departed
this life January 20ᵗʰ, 1727, aged 38 years.

Also,
Here lye interred the bodies of
Elizabeth Sparkes, wife of John Sparkes, Esq., who departed
this life Oct. 27, 1711, aged 63, and of
Sarah Sparkes, daughter of the said John and Elizabeth Sparkes,
who departed this life Dec. 31ˢᵗ, 1711.

Arms—A chief in base, 6 pears or.

Here lyeth interred the body of Thomas Alford, of this town,
who departed this life 17ᵗʰ day of July, 1704,
in the 59ᵗʰ year of his age,
and during the second time of his mayoralty in this
Corporation.

On a mural monument : -

Devoted by Ann Bigg, to the lasting Memory
of her dear husband, John Bigg, Doctor of Physick.
He was a constant and true member of the Church of England,
a prudent and loyal subject, very temperate, perfectly chaste,
a maker of peace, both in his private capacity and in
his public offices, both in the Borough and County :
of a charitable and even temper, never
uttering a word like an oath or a curse : very ingenious :
eminent and successful in his profession, a most
affectionate husband, a tender father, whose
example through all the stages of life
is most worthy of imitation.

He died 15ᵗʰ June, 1701, aged 58 years,
Survived by one son, and two daughters, Ann and Catherine.

On a stone, under the communion table : -

Here lyeth the body of Samuel Welles, Attorney-at-Law,
Sole surviving son of Samuel Welles, Gent., and Martha his Wife,
who both lie interred near this place.

In the north aisle :—

Sacred
To the memory of Archibald John Murray,
third son of Digby Murray, Esq.,
who died 17th March, 1840,
aged 8 years and 11 months.

On a brass plate in the chancel :—

In memory of the
truly virtuous and faithful wives of John Lane of this Town,
Margery and Mary.
As earth to bodyes, soe heaven to sacred soule's the center,
Through this the one by death, yet that the other by heavenly
life doth enter,
As when all finite times by God's decree are spent,
Then shall such souls most gloriously resume what nature lent:
Undoubtedly such is, and such shall be the bliss of these two
saints;
Such pious actors of faith and religion's work no sin attaints,
As there by grace in Christ you live in glory's lasting fame,
So here by love your honoured virtues gaine a never-dying name.

In the south aisle of the church are these tablets :—

The mortal remains of
Henry Allen, a native of this Town,
were deposited with military honors at Secunderabad,
in the East Indies,
where he had served six years as an Ensign in
the 24th regiment of Infantry of the Madras Establishment.
In the bloom of his youth, after a short illness, he died
beloved and regretted, June 24th A.D. 1814,
aged 22 years.
In remembrance of whom
his surviving father dedicates this tablet.

In sure and certain hope
of the resurrection to eternal life.
Near this tablet repose the mortal remains of
Henry Allnutt, Esq.,
who died April 20th 1813,
aged 67.
Also, of Thomas Allnutt, his youngest son, who departed
this life Sept. 15, A.D. 1812, aged 20 years.

𝕾𝖆𝖈𝖗𝖊𝖉
To the Memory of
William Rose, Esq.,
Who departed this life July 1, 1846,
aged 70 years.
Having exercised, after his Father and Grandfather,
the profession of Medicine and Surgery,
forty years in this place ;
Valued throughout for his care and skill ;
Respected for his unblemished integrity, and
beloved for his kindness.
Resting solely on the merits of his Saviour, his walk and
conversation were humble ; and have left to his
affectionate and grateful family a precious
example of a christian spirit and
character, the most unostentatious and self denying.
" The memory of the just is blessed."

In the north aisle, on neat marble tablets, are these inscriptions :—

To the memory
of
John Hollis, Esq.,
Who during a long life, unremittingly
practised the benevolent virtues of his ancestors.
He expired at his residence in this town,
on the 26th day of Nov. 1824.
aged 81.
" He delivered the poor that cried, the fatherless, and him that had none to help him."

A Memorial for
Henry Grange, formerly of Aston Clinton, in this County,
who died in the 67th year of his age, on the 1st April, 1755,
and Rachel, his Wife,
who departed this life the 31st Aug., 1746,
aged 63 years.
Rachel, their daughter, died June 29th, 1774, aged 55 years.
Martha died January 5th, 1780, aged 55 years.
Also, Henry Grange, their only son, who died April 19th, 1796,
in the 76th year of his age, and
Ann, his widow, who, to the inexpressible grief of her
surviving daughter, closed this mortal life the 27th April, 1807,
aged 61 years

On a mural tablet, in the north aisle of the Church :—

Sacred to the Memory of
The Rev. Thomas Jones, A.M.,
Rector of Radnage and Vicar of Ilmire, in this County,
who departed this life, Feb. 26, 1833,
in the 83rd year of his age.
Also to the memory of Mary, Wife of the above
Rev. T. Jones, Feb: 1, 1844,
aged 71 years.
Also, to the memory of
Mary Susan, the beloved and
only child of the
Rev. Thomas and Mary Jones,
who departed this life,
after a short illness,
on Jan: 20, 1822,
aged 11 years.
"Gone but not lost."

To the Memory
of
Robert Nash, Esq.,
who departed this life on the 28th day of Sept., 1831,
aged 75 years.
Having for upwards of fifty years practised as a Solicitor.
"Such was his calling.
He was honest, kind, forgiving, meek,
Easy to be entreated; gracious, mild, and with all patience
And affection, taught, rebuked, persuaded, solaced, counselled,
Warned."
Also of
Mrs. Charlotte Nash, his Widow,
Who died 13th day of Sept., 1835, aged 76 years.
"The ornament of a meek and quiet spirit."

In other parts of the Church and chancel are these inscriptions :—
Arms—Gules, a fess or inter 3 hands couped at the wrist or. Crest—a naked hand holding a sword.

Near this place lies interred the body of
Joseph Peytever, alias Pettipher, Gent;
one of the Aldermen of this Borough,
who departed this life the
11th day of June, 1730, aged 50 years.

[It is remarkable that one or more of this name or family have served public offices, in every King's or Queen's reign since the reign of King Henry VI. (except the short reign of King Richard III.), as appears by the Ledgers of the Corporation.]

Left surviving one Son, Joseph, who departed this life,
Aug. 14th, 1748, aged 19 years.

On a stone :—

Devoted by Mr. Vincent Owen, some time Vicar
of this Church, to the memory of his dear Wife, Elizabeth,
the second daughter of Edmund Petty, Esq.,
who died May 24th, 1672,
in the 28th year of her age and lyeth here buried, of
whom the world was not worthy.
Deo gratias quod habui, imo habeo.

Near this—a stone to the memory of Edmund Petty, Recorder of the Borough, who died Dec. 16th, 1661.

Sacred
To the memory of Elizabeth, Wife of
Daniel Bennet, Esq., of Farringdon House, Berks,
and Daughter of the late Mr. William Ball, of this Borough,
who died Nov. 24th, 1815, aged 59 years.
She was an affectionate wife, a sincere friend, and a
true Christian.

Ermine, a chevron gules.
In memory of
Mr. Samuel Guise, Vicar of this Parish,
born March 26, 1681, died Oct. 16, 1753.

A Memorial
For
Jacob Wheeler,
late of yᵉ
Parishe of St. Andrewes, Holborne,
Shoomaker, deceased,
who was borne in this Towne,
and gave by will yearly to yᵉ Poore
of this Towne, for ye space of 47
years yet to come, theis charitable
benevolences following :—

> 5 gownes to 5 poore men.
> 100ˡⁱ to 100 poore people.
> 52ˡⁱ yearly for bread weekly to be
>   given in this place, to 13 other
>   poore folkes of this Towne, and
> 20ˡⁱ for a sermon annually to be
>   made in this Churche.

All which are to be performed by
yᵉ Company of Inholders of yᵉ citie of
London during yᵉ said terme of 47 years.
He died yᵉ 10 day Jvne, 1621, being
aged 54, and is buried in Sᵗ. Andrewes
Parishe above saide.
"Vivit post Funera Virtus."

————————————

In memory of
Susannah, Wife of the Rev. Thomas Jones,
of Dinton in this County, and only daughter of the
Rev. James Price, late Vicar of this Parish,
Ob. 27. Sep, 1802, Æt. 42.
Also, of Susan Philippa, only child of the
Rev. Thomas Jones and the above Susannah his wife,
Obit. 6 Oct., 1806, Æt. 18—.

————————————

On a flat stone, close to the parish chest, behind the Organ-loft, is this inscription :—

George Clewer
is dead.

————

March 19ᵗʰ, 1701.
Aged 55.

George Clewer died under the following remarkable circumstances : He was a native of Wycombe, and previous to his death, went to London, and seeing a piece of stone in a mason's yard, purchased it ; observing, it would do well for his gravestone ; and ordered these words to be engraven on it,—

"George Clewer
is dead."

The next day he started home and arrived as far as Uxbridge, when he was taken ill and died in a few hours. The identical stone with the inscription marks the spot where his remains were deposited.

The following arms were formerly in the Church :—

1. Within a bordure a fess inter 3 martlets.
2. Arms of Wycombe.
3. A lion rampant guardant crowned, in his sinister paw, a roundle. Argent 2 bends engrailed. Argent 2 bends gules impaling sable within a bordure a fess inter 3 martlets or.

During the Rebellion, all the ancient brasses were taken from the grave-stones. The register, the first part of which is very much mutilated, commences 10th September, 1598.

At the Dissolution, the Rectory was granted to Robert Bennet, Bishop of Hereford ; in his will, proved Dec. 8th, 1617, he leaves his lease of the tithes of Chepping Wycombe to his cousin Robert Bennet.

The Rectory afterwards became the property of Samuel Welles, Esq., who died August 15th, 1807, when the Trustees under a settlement sold the property in various lots.

THE CHAPEL OF ST. MARY, CALLED THE CORPORATION CHAPEL.

Of the Chapel of St. Mary, the Records furnish but few particulars. It is supposed to have been situate in a street called Bynethe brigge [Beneath, or Beyond Bridge]. This bridge is, without doubt, the bridge near the ancient mill originally belonging to Alan Basset, and called Bridge Mill, and the name of the Street was probably, after the erection of St. Mary's Chapel, altered from Byenethe brigge Street to St. Mary's Street; this Street led to St. Margaret's Hospital for Lepers, called the Loke.

In Dr. Browne Willis's MSS. is a Copy of an Indulgence from Richard de Graves, Bishop of Lincoln, dated at Tinghurst [Fingest], Bucks, 1273, for the reparation of St. Mary's Chapel in the Churchyard of Wycombe. And that considerable works were prosecuting with this building, in the fourteenth century. As there was (as we have already mentioned) a Chapel dedicated to St. Mary in the Parish Church of All Hallows, it would appear the Bishop refers to some other Church Yard than that of All Hallows; and this seems to be confirmed by the fact, that in the fourteenth century there was a Churchyard situate between St. Mary Street on the West, and Horsenden Lane on the east, and then described as "Horsyn Churcheyerd," which in all probability was belonging to some destroyed Church of a depopulated Village, or part of the town, known as Horsyn or Horsenden, and it is most probable that the Bishop referred to this Churchyard connecting St. Mary's Chapel with it. Not a vestige of the Chapel remains, and the exact site of it is not known; but it is presumed to have been where the two Alms Houses (lately sold) were standing on the West side of the Street. Several tesselated pavements of the fourteenth century have lately been uncovered in the locality of the "Horseyn Churcheyerd." The Chapel of St. Mary was rebuilt between the years 1338 and 1378, and was under the control of two Wardens, who were always burgesses of standing, and were indifferently styled "Wardens," "Churchmen" or Collectors of St. Mary's Chapel. But in the year 1338 we find four Wardens coming into office; and further they are styled "Wardens of the Work," (custodes operis Beatæ Mariæ). In their first year of Office, Andrew le Goys gave a messuage to be disposed of towards defraying the expenses of the repairs; and Gilbert le Marshall gave a rent charge on a meadow, and other small benefactions for the same object. The Municipal body added their contribution towards the works. And Alan at Wythege, one of the surviving Wardens, by his will in 1353, gave his house in Godstowe-fee in the borough, to be disposed of towards defraying the expenses of the repairs. In the same year Richard Coleman granted his messuage and land to the Wardens for the benefit of the Chapel. And in 1371 William Frere gave the messuage wherein he dwelt, situate in Newland, for the like purpose. In 1384, the

Mayor and Corporation provided a new Manse in Frogmore, for Sir John atte Stoke, Chaplain of St. Mary's, for which he was annually to render one red rose to the Guild, at Midsummer, and they confirmed to him the office and stipend of Priest of the Blessed Mary of Wycombe.

> " Full sweetly heard he confession,
> And pleasant was his absolution,
> He was an easy man to give pennance,
> There as he wist, to have a good pittance."
> *Chaucer.*

The Corporation attended the Chapel of St. Mary on their solemn law days, and other municipal meetings ; and on special occasions the Chaplain was wont to preach a Sermon.   The same Bell which summoned the Corporation to Chapel summoned them to their Councils and other Corporate assemblies.

At folio cxli. of the first Ledger we find the following entry, which is a translation from the Latin :—

" Also at a view of frankpledge holden in the Rye, before Richard Cary Mayor, with the consent of all the burgesses there, on the 8th day of May in the 17th year of the reign of King Edward, after the Conquest the Fourth, it was ordained and granted unto William Redehode, and his assigns, that these two Chaplains, called 'Our Lady Preist,' and the ' Boure Preist' who now are, or for the time being shall be, shall have and hold those two Chambers with the Gardens adjoining, and their appurtenances, late of Henry Colleshille, near to the tenement called, 'The Charnelle House,' on the north side of the Church Yard ; To have and to hold the said two chambers, with the Gardens adjoining and their appurtenances, to the aforesaid Chaplains so long as they hold and fulfil their Offices ; rendering yearly therefore to the said William Redehode and his assigns 13[s] 4[d] of lawful money of England, at the two usual terms of the year, namely the Feasts of St. Michael the Archangel, and of the Annunciation of the Blessed Virgin Mary, to be paid yearly by the hands of the Collector of the rents of the Chapel of the Blessed Virgin Mary, and of the renter of the Rectory there, &c."

The Priest of St. Mary's Chapel was evidently Clerk to the Corporation ; that is, he entered and transcribed their Records.   There are several evidences of this in the old Journals: among others, the same hand that entered an act concerning weavers, and fullers (temp. Hen. VIII.), has prefaced it by the invocation I. H. V.S., M[r] C.Y.

The Municipal Records show that the Lady Priest was simply hired to say Mass for the Guild, and that he held his Office during the pleasure of the Corporate Body.   His Manse in Frogmore was exchanged in 1475 for one in Godstowe fee, in All Hallows Lane, now called Church Side, and known by the name of the Town House. It was the duty of the Lady Priest to pray daily in the Chapel for the members of the Guild, while living, and for their souls, when dead. It is very questionable whether this duty was regularly performed, as Skelton has quaintly, but truly said, —

> " The Diriges are forgotten,
> Theyr founders lye there rotten,
> But where theyr soules dwell,
> Therewith I will not *mell*." [*meddle*]
> *Colyn Cloute,* 427.

William Redehode, in making his bargain with the Corporation for prayers in St. Mary's Chapel, stipulated, that for every omission of prayer for the Souls of himself and his family, the priest shall be fined 4ᵈ.

At folio cxl., Ledger 1, is the following entry :—

" At the Gildhall there holden in the 14ᵗʰ year of the reign of King Edward, after the Conquest the fourth, before Thomas Gates then Mayor, there being, with the consent and will of all the burgesses and tenants of the Chapel of the Blessed Mary the Virgin, it was there ordained " (the preceding translated from the Latin)—" that the Preyst hired, that syngeth, or seyth Mas at oure Lady Auter, and all other Preistis that shall be hired in 'tyme to come in the Chapell foreseid for ever to say Mas, and bytwene the offatorie, or [before], that he wasshe at the lavatorie, he shall turne hym at the auteris ende, and pray for the good state, welfare, and prosperitie of all the tennantes, menne and womenne, bretheryne and susteris, unto the said Chappell of Oure Lady, and for the good state, welfare, and prosperitie, of all the tenauntes, menne and womenne, bretheryne and susteris, unto the saide Chappell of Oure Lady, and for the good staat, welfare, and prosperitie, of Willyam Redehode and Jone his Wyfe, and of Margerie Fyssher, terme of theire lyves, and for all theire Kynred, being alyive. Wich done, *Misereatur etc. Paternoster cum Suffragiss,* and a Colet [Collect] *Deus caritatis &c.*—And after the deeces of the said William Redehode and Jone his Wyfe, and of Margerie Fyssher, to be prayed for with them that be departed out of this world, it is to be understonde that when the Preist hath prayed for the quicke, then he, standying stylle at the auteris ende, shall pray for the sowlis of all the tennantes, menne and womenne, and of all the sowlis of all the brethern and susteris and benefactors of the same Chapell ; and in especyell for the sowlis of Richard Rede-hode, and Agnes his Wyfe, and for the sowlis of all theire Kynrede ; for the sowlis of William Lancastelle, Emma his Wyfe, and for the sowlis of all theire Kynrede ; for the sowlis of John Covyntre and Jone his Wyfe, and of all theire Kynred ; for the sowlis of Henry Colleshill, and Agnes his Wyfe, and for all theire Kynred ; for the soule of Thomas Fyssher and for alle his Kynrede ; and for all Cristene sowlis he shalle sey *De profundis* with the Versiclis and Colet *Inclina* or *Fidelium,* as in a tabylle stondyth uppone the same auter opynly it apperyth. For the whiche dayly prayeris kept, the foresaid Henry Colleshill geve to the towne of Wycombe the reversion of his house, with the gardyne lying therto, bytwene the house of the Charnelle, that the preistis of the Charnelle dwelle in, on the est part, and the house of Thomas Gate, sometyme Jone Briggewateris, on the west part, the kynges hyeway on the south part; the whiche house the foresaid William Redehode hath repairde and made. Whiche costis and chargis draweth to the somme of xiiii. lb.—Also the foresaid William Redehode willeth and grannteth that after his deces be delivered to the keperis of Oure Lady auter, and collectoris of oure Lady Rent, a chalys, part gylt, with the scripturs on the fote—*Orate pro animabus Ricardi Redehode, Agnetis uxoris ejus, Willelmi Redehode, et Johannæ uxoris ejus,* weying x. unces and more of troye weyght; one preist to synge ther with on the workedayes. The foresaide Meyre, burgeys, and tenaunts, wollen and grauntyne that yf the preist that now is, that seyth Mas at oure Lady auter, and alle other preistis that shalle be hirede in tyme to come to syng at the foresaide auter, shal pray dayly for the foresaid lyvis and sowlis by name. And yf it so fortune and happe the foresaid lyvis and sowlis to be unprayed for by iii dayes in a month, the foresaid preist to lese [lose] iiii d. of his wagys to the reparacion of the same chaunselle, as ofte tymes as he and any other, in tyme to come, so dothe forgete the foresaid lyves and soulis, unprayed for. And yf it so be that the collectors of Oure Lady rent, the wiche shalle pay for all the wagys of the foresaid preist, rebate not so moche of his wagys as ofte tymes as defawte is founde, and acounte theruppone in there rekenyingis not do, than the Chirchemen, to the behovith [behoof] of the Chirche, to receyve the forsaide iiii d. of the preistis wages, to be payed by the hondis [hands] of the Collectors of Oure Lady rents, and they to acounte uppone the same.—Also the tabylle on the auter, with names to be repayrid at alle tymes when it nedith, on the cost of Oure Lady Rent."

Extract.

Dated circ : 1475. [Translation.]

"THIS is the Will of Edward Cary the elder. I will that immediately after my decease my feoffees make and deliver estate to Richard Cary my son, of and in one tenement, with its appurtenances, situate in the borough of Wycombe, in a certain Street called Frogmore, on fee of the Abbess of Godstowe, between the tenement of Robert Colyn on the north part, and the tenement late William Bernard on the south part as metes &c To have and to hold the aforesaid tenement with its appurtenances to the foresaid Richard Cary and Johan his wife and the heirs of the body of the same Richard lawfully begotten. And if it happen that the aforesaid Richard die without heirs of his body lawfully begotten, then the aforesaid tenement with its appurtenances to remain to Walter Cary, brother of the aforesaid Richard, and the heirs of his body lawfully begotten. And if it happen that the aforesaid Walter die without heirs of his body lawfully begotten, then the aforesaid tenement with its appurtenances, to remain to Margery Wykes, sister of the aforesaid Richard and Walter, and the heirs of her body lawfully begotten. And if it happen that the aforesaid Margery die without heirs of her body lawfully begotten, then the aforesaid tenement with its appurtenances, to remain to the Mayor and burgesses of the said town and their successors for ever, to the sustaining of the Chapel of the blessed Mary the Virgin there, and for the sustaining of a Chaplin there, to sing Mass for the sowls of the aforesaid Edward and Matilda his wife, Richard, Joan, Agnes, Walter, and Margery, and all their Ancestors, and all faithful departed, & all their friends &c."

To the latest days of the unreformed religion, the Chapel of St. Mary and its Priests and Wardens existed. At the Dissolution, it was, as we gather from the Inventory hereinafter referred to, rich in furniture, plate, jewels, and vestments. It possessed a magnificent image of the Virgin,

crowned with a crown of massive gold.   Most of these Ecclesiastical trea-
sures were votive offerings, given by Burgesses and their wives, and among
the donors, were William Redehode, Robert Astbroke and Mrs. Astbroke,
Miles Nichols, and " Mother" Filby.   The great Window of the Chapel
was glazed at the cost of the Executors of John Wilcocks, in pursuance of
the directions contained in his Will, dated 1506.

In the Ledger No. 1, fol. ix., is an Inventory dated the 20th of January
10 Henry VIII (A.D. 1519) "of the godes, jewellys, and ornaments, belong-
ynge to the Chapelle of oure Lady."   Among the items, the following may
be noticed,—" A Crowne for our Lady, silver and gylte, with stonys on the
border of the same.   Another crowne, lesse, with eyght stonys on the
bordere of the same.   An ouche of silver lyke a bokylle of silver, and gylte.
A pair coralle bedys with xl. stonys, of silvere and gylte, and rynge of
silver,"—a line run through it and added—" sold to Johan Putt."   " A pair
of blak bedys, with xxi. stonys of silver and too ringes of silver."—" The
rynges wher sold."—" A pair of bedys, rede amber, with one peny of silver
upone them."—" Ther lakketh the peny."

"Another pair bedys of yellow amber, with gaudes of jasper stonys.
A pair of bedys, amber, and glasse, with ii. ringes of sylver."—" The rynges
were solde."—" A pair of blacke gettys [jet] bedys and anothyr of ambur.
A Chaplet for our Lady, of tyssewe.   A garment to oure Lady of white,
with ermyns.   A Masseboke, prented.   A lytelle portewas, called our Lady
Portewas [portifory, an ensign or banner].   A curten clothe, for our Lady
lofte.   A gyrdylle, the pendentes with awkament [qy. tin] : iiii. thyrchoys
[turquoises] with a laude [a large bead].

Fol. xxi.   "Anno regni Regis Henrici Septime decimo octavo, xii. of November."—
"Inventory of the goods in the Chapel of the Blessed Mary the Virgin there, in the time of
William Aley and Hamlet Taylour, Wardens, delivered before Robert Aschebrok, Mayr."

The following are among the items mentioned :—

"II. chalys, one grete doybll gylde, a nothir parte thereof gylde, with a scripture [writing]
abowte the fote, praying for the sowlys of William Redhode and his friendis.   A Crowne of
silver upon oure Ladyes hede, and gylde.   A pece of coral, with ii. typpys of sylvere.   A bede-
stone of silver, anamelled."

The Redehode family are intimately connected with the history of
Wycombe in the latter end of the fifteenth century.   William was a rich
salter of London, having his Country seat in Paul's row, " Agenst the west

ende of the Churche of Wycombe," as we have already mentioned, called Coppydhall. He was also a great benefactor to the fraternity of St. Mary, and as we have seen, Masses were agreed to be sung in the Chapel of St. Mary for him and his friends. He repaired, at a cost of £14, a house left by Henry Coleshill to the borough authorities, and fitted it up as two Chambers (*duas cameras cum gardinis*) with gardens attached, for the residence of "Oure Lady Priest and le Boure Priest," in 1475. The deed of Covenants for Masses, dated 1475, contains a proviso for the delivery at his decease, to the "keeperis of oure Lady auter," "a chalys, part gylt, with this scripture on the fote, 𝕺rate p. anibus Ririi Rebehode, agn uris ejus Willi Rebehode & Johr uris ejus, weying x. unces and more of troye wyght." This Chalice is included in the Inventory of St. Mary's Chapel. Besides vestments, banners, altarclothes, curtains, and candlesticks, there were *II. latyn candilstyks apon the auter for priketts* besides two *grete ones* in the choir; a crowne of silver apon our ladyes hede and gylde; a brodegyrolle whyte corse the pendant, and the bokull dobyll gylde w' vi. stodes."

The Priest was to sing on the "worke dayes."

The following is a list of the earlier Priests of the Guild Chapel of St. Mary, Wycombe.

Stephen Egod, 1291.	Richard Butte, 1392.
Andrew Lyons, 1362.	Robert Brampton, 1506.
John at Stoke, 1375.	

A curious and interesting fact in connection with this Chapel is recorded by Foxe the Martyrologist, who says, "that Henry Phip was accused in the bishop of Lincoln's Court, for that being chosen Roodman, or keeper of the Rood Loft, of S'. Mary's Chapel, he should say, that he must go and tend a Candle before his block Almighty. For which he abjured his error in 1521 before bishop Longland."

At the suppression of the lesser Monasteries, under the provisions of the Stat. 27 Hen. 8th, Cap. 8th, St. Mary's Chapel with the "messuages, lands, tenements, meadows, feedings, pastures, rents, reversions, services, and hereditaments, whatsoever belonging thereto, in Wycomb, called or known by the name of the fraternity of the Blessed Mary, or by the name of our Lady Rents," was (inter alia) granted to the Crown.

And Queen Elizabeth, by her Letters Patent, in the 4th year of her reign, 21st July, 1562, granted the same to the Mayor, Bailiffs, and Burgesses, and their successors, towards the support and maintenance of a Grammar School, and four poor persons, which will more particularly be referred to when treating of the Hospital of St. John of Jerusalem.

The following is a record of the Chauntries at Chipping Wycombe, derived from the Certificates remaining in the Augmentation Office, as the same were taken 2 Edw: VI., 1549.

"A Chauntrie called the Bowere, in the Parish Church of Chipping Wycombe, is worth, by yere clere, over and beside certain reprizes, £4 ‖ 16 ‖ 0."

"Two Chauntries, called Charnells, within the said Town, are worth by the yere clere above certain reprizes, £12 ‖ 5 ‖ 10. Sir Thomas Huchinson and Sir Roger Hawkins are incumbents there. The said Incumbents of the age of 73 yeres, hath yerelie coming of the said Chauntries for their annuities or stipends by yere clere to either of them £6, and what other living the said Incumbents hath, is not presented."

"There was also a Chauntry dedicated to the Holy Trinity."

ACCOUNT OF LOUDWATER CHAPEL.
THE HAMLET OF LOUDWATER

is about three miles south east of Wycombe, on the London Road.

The Chapel was built by William Davis, Esq., in 1788; was consecrated by Dr. Pretyman, Bishop of Lincoln, June 25th, 1791, and endowed by Mr. Davis with lands, then of the value of £40 per annum.

In 1804 Mr. Davis added the south wing to the Chapel, and by his will he bequeathed £400 for its further endowment. He died at Loudwater, 17th Oct., 1818, aged 91. The building is quite plain, without ornament, about forty-five feet long, having on the roof, which is slated, a small turret, containing a single bell, and surmounted with a vane. The entrance is at the east end, and on each side are three semi-circular beaded windows, the walls being strengthened with as many buttresses. It stands in a small cemetery. Loudwater obtained £400 of Queen Anne's Bounty, and a Parliamentary Grant of £2,400, in addition to the private benefaction of £1,200. The Chapel was some years since further enlarged, and the

T

Parsonage House attached to it greatly improved by the late W. R. Davis, Esq.

The Reverend George Campbell Broadbelt, formerly Rector of Aston Sandford, was the first incumbent, and died in June, 1801. The Reverend William Pryce was presented to the living in Nov., 1801, and he held it up to his death in 1833. The Reverend James Prosser was presented to the living in the same year, and resigned it in 1841; he was succeeded by the Rev. Edward Arnold, who died about the year 1865, and he was succeeded by the Rev. W. P. Woollcombe, who continues the Incumbency.

CHARITABLE FOUNDATIONS.

Tanner in his "Notitia Monastica" says, "that previous to the 13 Hen. III. a Hospital for Lepers, dedicated to St. Margaret, and called the Loke," was founded in Wycombe. And on the 13th May, 1229, a Charter confirming the same was granted by Hen. III. "to the leprous brethren of the Hospital of St. Margaret of Wicombe, that they and their successors forever should have every year one fair at the aforesaid Hospital of St. Margaret, to continue for two days, that is to say, on the eve and on the day of St. Margaret, well and in peace, freely and quietly, with all liberties and free customs to such fair pertaining."

There was also a Hospital in Wycombe dedicated to St. Giles; King Hen. V. granted this Hospital to Thomas Giles; and in the next year granted it with St. Margaret's Hospital to Henry Swain, on the resignation of Thomas Giles; but subsequently the gift of the Mastership of St. Giles' Hospital was in the Collegiate Church of Windsor. Jacob Mallet, of Windsor, in 1516, resigned the Mastership to the College, reserving 40s. per annum during his life. He was executed for treasonable words spoken against King Hen. VIII., viz., "that the king had brought his hogs to a fine market." See Ashmole's "Berkshire."

In a Catalogue of the Religious Houses in England, contained in Speed's "Great Britain," p. 787, the Hospital of St. Margaret is described as being dedicated to a Priory, and valued at £22 6s. 7d.

OF THE HOSPITAL OF ST. JOHN BAPTIST AND THE ROYAL GRAMMAR SCHOOL.

There is every reason to believe that this Hospital was founded in the twelfth century; the existing architectural remains of the Hall indicating its Norman origin. The Hall is supposed to have been built about the year 1175. Dr. Lipscombe, in his History of Buckinghamshire, relying on the opinion of the late John Norris, Esq., of Hughenden House, erroneously denominates it a Norman Church. It was about 62 feet long, and appears to have consisted of a nave 16 feet wide between the pillars, and side-aisles 6 feet wide; and stood, or rather stands nearly north and south. There were three pillars on each side of the nave, alternately round and octagonal, supporting four plain semi-circular arches 13 feet in diameter, the two outer ones at each end resting upon brackets or capitals, built up in the north and south walls. Of the six pillars four remain; they are about 2 feet in diameter, $8\frac{1}{2}$ feet high, including the capitals, which are ornamented with sculptured foliage and shells; and on one of them is a dragon, which has unfortunately lost its head. One pillar has disappeared entirely; of another the capital only remains, supported by a brick wall. Of the arches, two on the east side of the nave remain entire, and three parts of a third; on the west are three, two of which had been bricked up to form an outside wall, and had windows cut through the tops of them; but enough of the original stone work remains to show that they were semi-circular like the others. The fourth arch has quite disappeared; and also the one which was opposite. The entrance to the Hall is at the south end fronting the street; and some years since, on the plaster at the entrance being removed, four small transitional Norman capitals were discovered, supporting a pointed receding arch; the shafts were gone, but have now been restored. Mr. Norris very handsomely defrayed the expense attending the restoration, and the original entrance again ornaments the street. A new scheme is in contemplation for the future government of the Grammar School and Almshouse Charity; a plan has been prepared by Mr. Arthur Vernon for the restoration of this Norman Hall, to be appropriated for the purposes of a school and class rooms for the Royal Grammar School, which has been highly commended and approved by the Charity Commissioners; the accompanying print represents the Hall restored. The school room, which is on the

"The Composityon of the hospytall of Saunte
John's of Wicōbe.

"Thys content of this Chart ys y⁺ Rob⁺ by the grace of God byschope of lyncholn tōke y⁺ popys letts⁺· yn thes wordys, Greygory Pope Svānt to the Svānts of God, sends to his welbelovyd brot⁺ Byschope of Lyncholm, halsying (greeting), & hys blessyng, wyllyng hym to know, y⁺ hys welbelovyd chyldren y⁺ Master & y⁺ brethern of the ospetaule of Saint John Baptist of Wycōbe mayde supplycatyon mekely . . . as mouche as they had . . . I made y⁺ yor y⁺ howse I wolde . . ."

The copy ends thus abruptly.

The lease purports to have the hospital seal appended, but it has been torn off. Many years after (to all appearance) the lease was written on the back.

The handwriting of the Bull looks like that of the thirteenth, or of the early part of the fourteenth century. Its date may be defined approximately by comparison of the list of Popes and Bishops of Lincoln, and is between 1235 and 1241. Bishop Robert Grostete held his see from 1235 to 1254. Pope Gregory IX. (who established the Inquisition), held the Popedom from 1227 to 1241. "We may," says Mathew Paris (cited in Dugdale's Monast. Ang. p. 322), "be justly proud of a connexion, even in so remote a way, with the excellent Grostete, one of the best bishops who ever sat on the Episcopal Bench."

The Records furnish us with a scanty list of the Masters of the Hospital, vizt. :—

Robert X 1265.

Adam de Warwick, late Rector of Bradenham, 1276.

Galfridus, 1304.

Richard de Caykay, 7 May, 1304.

John de Marham, 1343.

Hugo de Newton, March, 1343, late Prebendary of Banbury.

Michael de Northburgh, 1344, resigned 1354.

John de Hall, 1354.

John Atte Corner, 1355.

Hugo de Bridham, 1361.

John Talworth, 1382.

John Dede, 1440.

John Benet, 1456.

Hugo Clay, 1471, resigned.

William Blackpoll, 1471.

John Wykes, 1474.

Edward Hampden, 1478.

Galfrid Hemmingley, 1493.

Edward Wellesbourne, 1493.

William Trewe, 1522.

Christopher Chalfount, 1546, resigned 1553,

And who was the last Master of the Hospital.

It appears from deeds belonging to the Wycombe Municipal Charity Trustees, that in the second year of the reign of Edw. VI. the Hospital of Saint John Baptist was vested in Christopher Chalfount, Clerk, by virtue of his office as Master of the said Hospital for life, and which he granted to Sir Edmund Peckham and George Juncklyn on lease for 21 years, at the rent of £8 per annum. That by another indenture the said Christopher Chalfount disposed of his estate and interest in the said hospital to the said Sir Edmund Peckham, during the life of the said Christopher Chalfount, rent free. And that the said Edmund Peckham and George Philyps, Gentleman, executors under the will of the said George Juncklyn, deceased, did on the 1st April 3rd Edw. VI., 1548, in consideration of £30 paid to them by the Mayor, Bailiffs, and Burgesses of Chipping Wycombe, bargain and sell to the said Mayor, Bailiffs, and Burgesses, All the said Hospital, with the lands and premises; to the intent that the said Mayor and Burgesses should bestow all the yearly rents towards the foundation of a Grammar School, to be erected within two years from the date thereof. And in default thereof, then the said Sir Edmund Peckham and George Philyps should re-enter and possess the estate again. Sir Edmund Peckham died April 18th, 1560, or 4, and with Dame Anne his wife is buried under a splendid canopy tomb in Denham Church.

It also appears by the Borough Records, No. 1, fo. 22, that the Mayor and Burgesses established a Grammar School within the period prescribed, as by—

"An Agreement made the xxvᵗʰ daye of Mche in the fifte year of the reign of our Sovereign Lord Kynge Edwarde the VIᵗʰ; It was agreed First, the whoole howse of the Towne of Chiping Wicobe to keepe the Hospital of Saint John's wᵗ the appurtenances thereto belonginge, in the hole hands of the Towne, that ys to saye, Richarde Carye then Mayor wᵗ all his brethren and the Burgesses, to let and sett as they shall see cause in yt. And moreovᵗ weᵗ be all agreyde to pay the stepende of eyght powndes yerely to the saide Scole Mayster. And we all gyve to Mr.

Peckham hartye thankes for his good wyll, and for the apointinge of the Scole Maister at his pleas', and we the hoole howse be agreide that the saide M⁻ shall have the pleasure and pſite of a Cowe, or twayne in ower Comey accordinge to the custome of the Towne, and also to have V. Loode of Woode yerelye."

Whether the Grammar School, as thus established, was suffered to continue during the short, but unsettled years of Queen Mary's reign, is extremely doubtful; for Langley observes that "after the Dissolution, Queen Mary gave it (*i.e.*, the Hospital) to Sir Thomas Throgmorton." What rights the Crown had over the Hospital at this time, or as to the validity of the above grant, cannot at present be ascertained. But Sir T. Throgmorton could have held it only for a short period, as Queen Elizabeth had not been four years on the throne before the Mayor and Burgesses are found asserting their ancient right as Patrons of the Hospital, and evincing a laudable desire to see their school restored, and to have it established on a more sure and royal foundation. On the 18th of July, 1562, the Mayor, Bailiffs, and Burgesses granted the said Hospital, and lands belonging thereto, and also the rents which had belonged to the Fraternity of the Blessed Mary, and called the Lady Rents, to Queen Elizabeth, in order that the same might be created a Royal Grammar School. And the Queen, three days afterwards, *i.e.*, on the 21st July, by her Letters Patent, regranted to the Mayor and Burgesses, and their successors for ever, the said Hospital and lands, and the rents and revenues thereof, and also the said Lady Rents, to be applied towards the support and maintenance of the said school, and of four poor persons. The income of the Lady Rents amply provided for the alms people.

By Charter of King James I. already referred to, we find the Mayor, Bailiffs, and Burgesses were evidently groaning under the heavy burdens recently imposed on them by the Statute of the 43rd of Eliz. for the relief of the poor, and complained that the number of poor and needy people in the Borough was much increased, and did daily more and more increase, to the great charge of the Borough, and alleging that the Hospital lands and premises would well and competently suffice, as well as to maintain and support the said Grammar School, and four poor people, as also relieve more poor and needy persons in the same borough; license, power, and authority, therefore, were by the said Charter given to them and their successors, by their discretion, or of the major part of them from time to time, to take, expend, and dispose, of all and singular the Rents, etc. of the said Hospital, given and granted to the maintenance of the said Grammar School, and four poor people, according to the pious intention of the said late Queen in the same Borough to be sustained and relieved; as also to the relief and support of other poor and needy men in the same Borough, from time to time inhabiting and dwelling; and which was confirmed by the governing Charter of the 15th of Charles II. 1663.

	£	s.	d.
The Hospital was valued at the Dissolution at . .	7	15	3½
Remes, or Town Farm, was then let at . . .	4	0	0
The Master's stipend at the establishment of the school was, being the entire income of the Hospital	8	0	0

THE FOLLOWING IS A LIST OF THE EARLIER MASTERS OF THE ROYAL GRAMMAR SCHOOL.

The Reverend — Wrothe, 1548.
    „   William Wilkinson, A.M.
    „   Gerard Dobson, late Vicar of Wycombe, 1645, resigned 1646.
    „   Henry Wyat, A.M., afterwards Rector of Bradenham, 1646, resigned 1661.
    „   Philip Humphrey, 17th July, 1661.
    „   William Lardner,* A.M., formerly Rector of Bradenham, 1671.
    „   Joseph Howe, 1673, died 1701.
    „   Joseph Loveday, A.B., resigned 1707.
    „   Samuel Guise, 1707, died 1753.
    „   Thomas Heather, Jun., 1754, resigned 1762.

* Mr. Philip Humphrey, the late Master, having died very poor, his successor (Mr. Lardner) was bound, on his election by the Common Council, to pay to his Widow Katherine, ten pounds, in the course of the next two years, "provided she does not turne Quaker in the mean time, or otherwise become a Sectary, and not observe and obey the Liturgy of the Church of England."

The Reverend William Edwards, 1762, suspended 1771.

    „   Alban Thomas, 1771, died 1789.

    „   Daniel James, 1789, died 1793.

Mr. William Sproston, 1793, died 1841.

The Reverend Joshua Finlinson, 1841, resigned 1842.

Mr. Edwin Fox, 1843, resigned 1852.

The Reverend James Poulter, A.M. 1852.

Among distinguished men who were pupils at the Royal Grammar School, we may mention Edmund Waller, the poet; Sir Denis Le Marchant, Bart., M.P., late Clerk of the House of Commons, and author of the Biography of his father Major-Gen. John Gaspard Le Marchant; Lieut. General Sir John Gaspard Le Marchant, Bart., K.C.B., G.C.M.G., late Commander in Chief at Madras; Major Charles Douglas; Major James Dundas Douglas, Assistant Adjutant General in Afghanistan and Deputy Military Secretary to Government, killed in action near Pesh Bolak in the Afghan Campaign in 1840; General Sir Robert Percy Douglas, Bart., formerly Assistant Adjutant-General to the Forces, and Lieutenant-Governor of Jersey, and late Lieutenant-Governor and Commander-in-Chief at the Cape of Good Hope, 1864–8; H. W. Bristow, Esq. (son of Major-General Bristow), Professor of Geology, and one of the Examiners of the Council of Military Examination; J. O. Griffits, Esq., Q.C., Recorder of Reading; and we may add the names of Edward J. Payne, Esq., M.A., a fellow of University College, Oxford, and of Lincoln's Inn, Barrister-at-Law; and W. G. Hayden, Esq., M.D., who were educated by the present able Head Master of the School, The Reverend James Poulter.

The smaller Charities that come next in order were created under the Wills of *Ambrose Conway*, of Chipping Wycombe, Gentleman, also of

Dame Dorothy Pelham, Widow of Sir William Pelham, Knight, also of

The Right Hon. Robert Lord Dormer, also of

Thomas Church, Citizen and Draper, of London, also of

. . . *Weinwright*, sometime of London (will without date), and also of

William Littleboyes, Gent. (also will without date); whereby they respectively gave and bequeathed the several sums therein severally mentioned, for the purposes as set forth in the following entries, contained in the Ledger No. I. of the Corporation, folio 16, with the particulars of their investments and the application of the incomes arising therefrom.

"Burg: de Chipping Wicombe in Com. Bucks.

"Whereas Thomas Church, Citizen and Merchant of London, by his Will and Testament, bearing date the 16ᵗʰ Aug! 1616, did give and bequeath to the said Borough 100 Marks of lawful money of England; and also Ambrose Conway, by his last Will and Testament, did likewise give to the said Borough the sum of £10; and Sir Robert Dormer, Knight, did give to the said Borough the sum of 20 nobles, to be employed to the use of the poor of the said Borough; and also whereas the Lady Dorothy Pelham, by her last Will and Testament, did likewise give and bequeath to the same Borough the sum of £20 to be put forth at 18*d.* the pound, and the interest of the two parts thereof, viz. 20s., to be employed for the use of the poor, and the other 10s. thereof to be paid yearly to the Surveyor of the highways for the amending thereof, all which monies, with and amongst divers other moneys of the proper stock of the said Borough, were laid out upon the new erecting and building of the butchers' shambles in the said Borough, by the advice and appointment of William Aire, late Alderman of the same Borough; and whereas also there was had and used towards the building of the said Shambles, and the east corner of the old markethouse for a convenient sitting for the Judges of Assize, certain timber out of the hospital lands belonging to the said Borough: Now it is concluded and agreed by the Mayor and Aldermen of the said Borough this present day, that in consideration of the said Legacies and timber, there shall be yearly paid out of the said Shambles to the Overseers of the same Borough, to the use of the poor of the same Borough, the yearly rent or sum of £12 of lawful money of England, to be paid quarterly by equal portions; and that the residue arising out of the said Shambles shall be paid to the said Mayor, Bailiffs, and Burgesses of the said Borough, and their successors, in regard of their stock and charges disbursed upon the said Shambles and the ground whereupon they are erected; and that the Town Chamberlain for the time being shall yearly pay to the Surveyors of the highways the sum of 10ˢ in part of the gift of the said Lady Pelham."

The shambles have been pulled down, but the Corporation consented to pay £10 yearly in respect of these Charities.

In the above mentioned Ledger, folio 15, there is the following entry dated 23rd September, 1633 :—

"Mᵈ—That   Weinwright, sometime of London, deceased, in and by his last Will and Testament, bequeathed unto this Borough the sum of £20, to the intent that the Mayor of the said Borough for the time being should for ever pay to the use of the poor of the said Borough the sum of 23s. 4d., to be disposed of at the discretion of the said Mayor; and also 6s. 8d. more to be employed otherwise as the said Mayor should think most fit, yearly for ever, which said sum of £20 was by Richard Gibbons, Alderman, in the time of his late mayoralty, disbursed upon the new Mace of the said Borough: Now to the intent that there may be perpetual payment made of the said 30ˢ/- in manner aforesaid, it is hereby ordered, that the Mayor and Mayors of the said Borough for the time being shall yearly from henceforth, on the day of their going out of their Mayoralty, and election of the new Mayor, pay to the use of the poor of this Borough 23s. 4d., to be disbursed and disposed of where he shall think most fit, and that the other 6s. 8d. shall be paid to the Vicar of the Church of the Borough yearly on the day of the election of the said Mayor, unless the greatest part of the Company shall think fit otherwise to dispose of the same."

This yearly sum of £1 3s. 4d. is known by the name of Mace Money.

The above stipends were called half-yearly payments and Mace Money, amounting to £11 3s. 4d. per annum, and on the recommendation of the Charity Commissioners, are received by the Wycombe Municipal Charity Trustees, and applied for the purposes of the Charity.

Also in the above mentioned Ledger, folio 15, there is the following entry, dated 2nd September, 1633, signed by the Mayor, Bailiffs, and Aldermen :—

"Memorandum. That, whereas William Littleboyes, Gent., of a pious and charitable disposition, did by his last Will in Anno: Dni. —— give the sum of £100 to the Town of Chepping Wycombe, which he appointed to be employed at the discretion of Sir Randolph Mainwaring, Knight, deceased, and George Littleboyes, Esqrs, his brother, and their heirs for ever, towards the comfort of the poorest and most needy in that towne ; and appointed that the profit of the said £100 should be laid out weekly upon bread, to be distributed every Sabbath day to those persons whose necessities may be thought greatest, or their miseries the most extreme, by reason of their age or other incident infirmities, as by the said last Will appeareth ; And whereas the said sum of £100 was delivered into the hands of the Mayor and Corporation of this town, to the intent that they should purchase so much land as they could conveniently purchase for that sum, to the intent that the said gift might be perpetuated for ever by weekly payments, the said Mayor, Bailiffs, and Burgesses have, with the said £100, this day purchased from William Ayre, &c, a quantity of land lying at Coleshill, in the parish of Agmondesham, in the County of Herts, called by the name of Stock Grove, and containing about 13 acres, then in the occupation of Robert Bell, his Assignee or assigns, which is likely for ever to yield £5 ॥ 10 ॥ 0 per annum at least, Do hereby order and decree, that the whole profits of the said land shall for ever be employed by 2s. weekly, or more, as the profits will amount unto, to the relief of the poor of the said Town, according to the intent of the said last Will ; and to the intent the same may with more indifferency be disposed of, it is appointed that the ancientist churchwarden, and ancientist overseer of the poor of the said Town, for the time being, shall, with the consent of the Mayor for the time being, distribute the said rents weekly, as near the intent of the said Will as possibly they can ; and the Mayor shall at the end of the year, always at his going out of his Office, give account to the Common Council of the said Town, what the profit of the said Land hath been for his year, and how it is improved, and how bestowed, or employed, to the intent the said Charitable use may in nothing be defrauded."

In another Ledger, dated 1770, also containing the minutes of the proceedings of the Mayor and Common Council of the Borough of Chipping Wycombe, from that year unto the present time, there is an entry signed by the Mayor, Bailiffs, and certain members of the Common Council, from which it appears that the Corporation employed the said £100, together with £180 more, raised by them from the sale of a rent charge of £10 a year, in the purchase of lands and tenements at Coleshill, and vested the same in trustees upon trust that they should pay to the Overseers of the said Borough, for the use of the poor thereof, the rents and profits of the premises, so as the Overseers should cause £5 10s. of the rent to be weekly distributed, in bread, according to the true intent of William Littleboyes' Will, and if the Overseers should neglect or refuse so to do, then other persons fitting and willing to undertake the same were to be appointed to receive the rents and profits of the premises, and to apply the sum of £5 10s. according to the desire of William Littleboyes ; and that for several years then last past, the Overseers had applied the whole of the £5 10s. to the use of themselves, in common with other inhabitants of the said Borough, contrary to the true intent and meaning of the deed, and also the Will of William Littleboyes; and therefore the Mayor and Common Council ordered, on the 26th June, 1800, that in future the Overseers for the time being should weekly, on Sunday in every week for ever thereafter, distribute in bread to poor persons of the Borough, who should stand in most need thereof, an equal and proportional part of the said sum of £5 10s., agreeable to the Will of William Littleboyes; and the residue of the rents of the said Estate at Coleshill should be paid yearly to the Hospital Chamberlain of the said Borough for the time being, for the use and benefit of poor people belonging to the said Borough, agreeable to the same rules and orders as those by which the chamber rents were then paid and applied.

The Stock Grove Farm consists of 22 acres, and is let to Abel Slade, on lease for 21 years, from Michaelmas, 1861, at the yearly rent of £21 7s. 6d., which is received by the Wycombe Municipal Charity Trustees, who pay and apply the same as follows, viz. :—£5 10s. for bread for the poor, and the residue towards the support of the Grammar School and Almshouse Charity.

The bread is given away the last Sunday in every month.

BOWDEN'S CHARITY.

" Mary Bowden, of the Borough of Chipping Wycombe, by her Will, proved in the Prerogative Court of Canterbury, the 30th October, 1790, gave to the Rev. James Price and Isaac King, Esq., the sum of £1000, to be by them laid out and invested in the public funds, or in the purchase of lands, tenements, and hereditaments, in the County of Bucks, which should appear to them most advantageous for carrying the pious and benevolent disposition of the said Mary Bowden into execution, upon trust, in the first place, as concerning the sum of £30, part of the interest and produce to arise from the said sum of £1000 as aforesaid, to pay the same to the Rev. Alban Thomas, the then Master and teacher of the Free Grammar School, in the Borough of Chipping Wycombe aforesaid, in augmentation and addition to his then salary, and after his death, discharge, or resignation, to pay it unto such other person or persons as should be appointed in his stead Master of the said free grammar School, and to his successors for ever, and to apply the remainder of the said interest or profits so to arise from the said £1000 to the finding of clothes and fuel for such poor widow persons as should live in, and be entitled to, the benefit of the Almshouse at the bottom of the town of Wycombe, in equal shares; and the said testatrix by her Will appointed the said trustees her executors. A sum of £1,547 14s. 10d. Three per Cent. Reduced Annuities, was originally standing in the names of the Reverend James Price and Isaac King; on the death of Mr. King, Mr. Price, without the power of executing any deed of appointment of fresh trustees, in respect of this Charity, transferred the stock into the names of himself, Mr. William Rose, and Mr. John Carter; Mr. Price survived Mr. Rose and Mr. Carter; and on the death of Mr. Price, his surviving representative received and applied the income of the Charity. The attention of the Charity Commissioners was called to this Charity, suggesting the importance of a fresh appointment of trustees, when the Commissioners discovered that the £1,547 14s. 10d. Three per Cent. Annuities had been disposed of; and moreover that Mr. Price's representative had been guilty of a breach of trust, by appropriating the produce of the stock to his own use. The case was certified to the Attorney General, who on the 3rd of October, 1869, preferred his petition to the Lord Chancellor against Mr. Price's representative; the result of these proceedings was, that after payment of the costs of the suit, about six hundred pounds stock in the Three per Cent. Annuities, and five cottages situate at Buntingford, Herts, were recovered.

The Stock was transferred to the Official Trustee of Charitable Funds, and invested in Bank £3 per Cent. Annuities; and the five cottages were vested in the Wycombe Municipal Charity Trustees ; and they were let into the receipt of the rents and profits of the same. And out of the income of the Charity, so far as the same would extend, it was ordered by the Court that the yearly sum of £30 be paid to the Master for the time being of the Free Grammar School. And the remainder (if any) of such income, be paid to the poor Widows in the Almshouse named in the Will, and in such manner as directed by the Will of the said Mary Bowden, deceased.

TERRIER OF ESTATES,

THE PROPERTY OF THE WYCOMBE MUNICIPAL CHARITY TRUSTEES, AFTER SEVERAL EXCHANGES OF LAND HAVING, WITH THE SANCTION OF THE CHARITY COMMISSIONERS, BEEN EFFECTED OF A BENEFICIAL CHARACTER TO THE CHARITY.

	A.	R.	P.
Town Farm, formerly called Remes	190	1	4
Ginion's Field Farm (Marsh)	83	1	23
Hulnett's Meadow behind late Catherine Wheel; Pound Mead at the east end of the Rye; the Little Meadow, forming part of the Home Meadow (Lord Carington's), adjoining Loake's Lane; a piece of Arable Land in the Rye Field, adjoining Pound Mead; and the Hospital Meadow, or Rye Mead; and a Quit Rent of 14s. per annum	5	0	0
Priest Croft and Crabb Tree Mead (Marsh)	4	0	16
Ginion's House and Garden (Marsh)	0	3	26
Ditto Cottage and Garden	0	7	16
Ditto Cottage and Garden	0	7	16
Ditto Eleven Garden Allotments, each 13 r. 6 p. . . .	1	1	6
Land called Triggs, near Cryers Hill	8	0	32
Land, Cottage, and Buildings, at Kingshill	7	0	0
Spital Croft, Cottage, Barn, and Lands	24	3	10
"Stock Grove," Land, and Buildings, Coleshill . . .	22	3	30
Land near the Harrow, Hughenden	4	0	0
Sawpit House and Premises	0	0	15
House and Premises, Paul's Row, Wycombe (Wootton's) . .	0	0	4
Town House and Premises (Miss Drewett)	0	0	19
Rent Charge on Land at Wycombe Marsh, known as Brooklands, 11s.; for a description of these Lands, see the Court Rolls of the Manor of Temple Wycombe			
Rent of Borough Shambles and Mace Money £11 3s. 4d.			
Gross Annual Rental . . £632 11s. 4d.	355	3	17

In addition to this rent roll, there is £2,456 17s. 11d. Stock, invested in Consols, the result of sales of different Charity properties, which sum, with the accumulating dividends, is intended to be applied towards the restoration of the ancient Grammar School, and the erection of a Master's house, under the direction of the Charity Commissioners.

The Charity Commissioners in 1833 made a very exhaustive Report on these Charities, to which any reader is referred who may wish further to pursue the subject.

LANE'S CHARITY.

John Lane, late of Hammersmith, in the County of Middlesex, Esquire, by his Will dated 2nd January, 1674, devised two little Tenements in Cornell Lane (now called Crendon Street), in Chipping Wycombe, with their appurtenances, for almshouses for the habitation of two poor widows, or two other poor old people, as the major part of his friends and persons thereinafter named or appointed to be overseers thereof, should choose out of the poor inhabitants of Chipping Wycombe aforesaid; and he gave and appointed for the maintenance of the same charitable use, his messuage and lands thereunto belonging, and therewith then used, in Great Missenden, which he bought of William Pratt, and also the little close of land, which he bought of Robert Lane, in Great Missenden aforesaid; and his two tenements in Agmondesham (Amersham), which he bought of William Mead, and purchased in his own name, and in the name of Andrew Hale; and he appointed to each of his said poor almspeople 40s. in money, yearly, to be paid at or about the feasts of the Nativity of St. John the Baptist, Michaelmas, St. Thomas, and Lady-day, by equal portions; and every second year, or once in two years, the sum of 25s. to be bestowed in cloth for a gown for each of them, or 10s. one year and 15s. the other year of those two years, as in the discretion of the said trustees thereinafter named for the ordering and governing of the same, or the major part of them, should seem fit for the need or use of the said poor people; and for the better raising of the said maintenance and monies for the said poor, as also for raising the sum of 10s. yearly to be kept in the bank for the repairing of the said devised messuages, lands, and tenements, and other 10s. yearly for the charges of the yearly meetings of his trustees or three of them; the said Testator thereby nominated and appointed trustees and overseers therein named, and thereby directed, that if one or more of his said trustees should die, that then the major part of the surviving trustees should choose in the place of them so dying such person or persons as they should think fit for filling up the number of six; and the Testator devised to his said trustees, their executors, administrators, and assigns, his said messuages, lands and tenements, which he bought of William Pratt, and all his estate and interest therein, which was a lease therein to come for the term of about 380 years, and the said close bought of Robert Lane, and also his tenement in Agmondesham, to hold to them their heirs and assigns in trust, for the charitable use aforesaid, and willed that his heir or heirs should confirm his said gift and appointment. The Testator died in the year 1675, and his Will was proved in the Prerogative Court, on the 18th November in the same year. The property belonging to the Charity recently consisted of—

Two cottages in Wheldon Street, Amersham.

Also an allotment under the Amersham Inclosure, containing about two roods.

A house and carpenter's workshop, outbuildings, and garden, and 4 a. 2 r. 29 p. of pasture and arable land at Great Missenden, yielding an annual rent of £86 11s. 0d. (less income tax). All the properties have been sold, except the Almshouses, and the purchase money has been invested in the Consols, in the name of the Official Trustee of Charities; the dividends are applied for the benefit of the Charity.

The Almspeople receive 6s. per week each, and 2£ each at Christmas. The trusts of this Charity are declared by a Deed approved by the Court of Chancery.

MURLIN'S CHARITY.

John Murlin, late of High Wycombe, Gentleman, by a Codicil to his Will dated 15th January, 1799, gave unto his executors therein named the sum of £300 to be appropriated at interest on Government or mortgage security, or in the purchase of lands, as they should think best, in their names; and he directed that the interest and proceeds should be paid over and applied by his said trustees, for the support of the Methodist Chapel, and the poor of the Society and Congregation thereof, in High Wycombe, in such manner as his Wife, during her life, should direct, and after her decease, that the same should be paid and applied to and for the same purposes, equally, according to the discretion of his trustees.

placed in the hands of the Clergy of the Church of England. The number of Bibles granted to Wycombe is now 25.

THE ROYAL MILITARY COLLEGE

Was established in Wycombe in 1799, under the patronage of His Royal Highness the Duke of York. The Antelope Inn, which occupied the space between the Red Lion Hotel and the house belonging to Thomas Marshall, Esq., was converted into College premises. The Institution, founded on the plan of the Military Academy at Woolwich, embraced a complete system of military education for officers desirous of qualifying themselves to serve on the general staff. Lieut.-Colonel John Gaspard Le Marchant, of the 2nd Dragoon Guards, was appointed Lieutenant Governor and Superintendent General of the College, who, from his extensive knowledge of military tactics, was eminently qualified for the appointment; he composed a code of instructions for the sword exercise, which was approved by the Duke of York, and forms a permanent part of the regulations of the army. This led to his turning his attention to the swords worn by the cavalry; and the pattern he selected was adopted by the army. In 1796 he published, by His Majesty's command, a work on the Cavalry Exercise, which has since gone through five large impressions. Soon after he prepared a work on Military Education, which was submitted to, and highly approved by, the Duke of York; and this led to many interviews with His Royal Highness, resulting in the establishment of this College, and also one at Great Marlow for the junior department. In 1811 Colonel Le Marchant was promoted to the rank of Major General; by a regulation in the Army this promotion rendered the holding of the office of Lieutenant Governor incompatible; he therefore vacated the appointment, to enter upon the more arduous duties of commanding a brigade of cavalry, then about to embark for service in the Peninsula, where he distinguished himself as a gallant officer, and on several occasions received the public approbation of Lord Wellington.

Lord Wellington, in his despatch on the triumphant victory gained at the memorable battle of Salamanca, on the 22nd July, 1812, bore the honourable testimony, "that the success was dearly purchased by the loss of that most noble officer, General Le Marchant," who at the head of his heavy brigade of cavalry, under General Sir Stapleton Cotton, in a brilliant charge against a body of infantry (which they overthrew and cut to pieces; and in the moment of victory, while carrying the Standard of England through the ranks of France), fell mortally wounded, deeply regretted by his numerous friends and brother officers. Colonel James Butler succeeded General Le Marchant as Lieutenant-Governor of the College. General Francis Jarry (late *Aide-de-Camp* to Frederick the Great), Knight of the Military Order of St. Louis, was appointed Inspector General of Instruction; Major Douglas was appointed Commandant of the College, with the rank of Lieutenant-Colonel in the Army; Lieutenant-Colonel Fred. Mackenzie, Secretary thereof; and Charles Greenwood, Esquire, Treasurer. General Jarry resigned his appointment of Inspector General of Instruction in 1806, and died at his residence, Welleysbourne House, the 15th March, 1807, aged 75. His funeral was conducted with military honours, and his remains were interred in the Chancel of the Parish Church. Major Douglas succeeded General Jarry as Inspector General of Instruction. "The Army," says his biographer, "dates an era from Major Douglas's appointment to the Military College; for he supplied it with a 'new class of officers, who made it able to go anywhere, and do anything.'" "The training hand was unseen, but its work was apparent everywhere, and nowhere more than in the staff of Wellington. Our commanders have borne the same impress down to our own time, and it has been signalised by Hardinge, Gomm, Simpson, and Brown, in our latest struggles on the fields of India and the Crimea."

"Col. Douglas cultivated the minds of grown men who were versed in the uses of the world and the camp. He brought knowledge down to the humblest ability, and advanced it to a point that satisfied the highest, at the same time raising the moral tone of the students, by keeping before them the example of his own conduct." "And such was Howard Douglas, in the flower of his life—the guardian of virtue, the kind fosterer of merit."

Col. Douglas remained at his post through the year, and in February, 1808, without sacrificing his appointments at the College, he was appointed Assistant Quartermaster-General to the expedition to Spain, which set out in the following autumn. The death of his half-brother, Sir William, raised Col. Douglas to the baronetcy. After his engagement in the Walcheren Expedition, and the bombardment of Flushing, Sir Howard returned to his duties at the Military College. In 1811 he was appointed to reside in the provinces of Gallicia, for the purpose of communicating with the commanders of the Spanish armies, and of distributing such arms and stores as might be sent from this country; he accordingly repaired to the head-quarters of Lieutenant-General Lord Wellington, Commander-in-Chief of the British Forces in the Peninsula, and placed himself under his orders. He was also present at the Siege of Burgos, after the raising of which, he returned to England. He published a Work on Naval Gunnery. This treatise was followed by an Essay on Fortification. In 1824 he attained the rank of Major-General, and was appointed Lieutenant-Governor of New Brunswick, and Major-General in command of the troops in that province, together with those in Nova Scotia, Cape Breton, Prince Edward Island, Newfoundland, and Bermuda. He made great improvements in, and restored the prosperity of the colony. Fredericton owes to Sir Howard Douglas its college, for which he obtained a charter conferring the privileges of an university. The King gave his name to the College, appointing Sir Howard its first Chancellor. He was installed in the office on the 1st of January, 1829, which he held until 1835. He originated a school for naval gunnery; this school was established on board the *Excellent* at Portsmouth. He brought out improved editions of his Naval Gunnery, and published an Essay on Military Bridges. The King paid a tribute to his worth in a public Address at the Royal Military College at Sandhurst, in June 1834, and eulogised his services and literary productions, describing him "as an officer of first-rate ability and scientific attainments." In 1835 he was appointed Lord High Commissioner of the Ionian Islands. He initiated several improvements in the Islands, by the construction of roads; procured funds for a poor house and lunatic asylum, and for the improvement of prisons; as well as a large sum for purposes of public instruction. The town of Corfu had long suffered from a scarcity of water; he constructed a reservoir, employed soldiers to lay down pipes, and brought a plentiful supply of water to the town. The appointment to the Ionian Islands he held from 1835 to 1840. Soon after Sir Howard's return to England, he was elected Member for Liverpool in the Conservative interest, which seat he held from 1842 to 1847, when he retired. He supported the Cambridge Asylum (of which he became President), and other charities and institutions. "His services had won him the honours of the Bath, of which he was a Knight Commander in the Military Division, and a Grand Cross

during the bombardment of that city by the French Fleet in 1823. On the 22nd July, 1830, he attained the rank of Lieut.-Colonel. He became Colonel on the 9th November, 1846, Major-General 20th June, 1854, and retired from the army on 17th August, 1855.

General Bristow, who, since 1823, had been more or less identified with the cause of Spanish Independence, died at Madrid on the 23rd November, 1874, aged 89. His funeral was celebrated in the British Cemetery, and was attended by Mr. Layard, the English Minister ; Colonel George Fitch ; General Millaso del Bosch ; Duke of Castellejos, the only son of the late General Prim ; and other English and Spanish residents. The coffin was covered with the British flag, and at the moment of lowering it into the grave, full military honours, including a salute, were paid by a battalion of 500 soldiers, sent for that purpose, as a mark of respect to the deceased, by the Captain General of Madrid, General Primo de Rivera.

Whilst the College was flourishing at Wycombe, a military survey, and a model plan upon an elaborate scale, were prepared by the staff, under the supervision of Sir Howard Douglas, representing a complete fortification of the town and its immediate neighbourhood.

The establishment added very much to the attractions, as well as the trade, of the town. It continued here until the early part of the year 1813, when the Government transferred it to Farnham, in Surrey, and the Junior Department to Sandhurst, in Berks, in the preceding October.

EMINENT CHARACTERS OF WYCOMBE.

Wycombe has to boast, amongst others, of the following notable personages :

The first we remark upon is William of Wycombe, who must not be confounded with the celebrated William of Wykeham, Bishop of Winchester, and founder of New College, Oxford ; as the latter was a native of Wykeham, Hants ; the former, of Wycombe, Bucks.

Nothing is known of his parentage, except that he was born at Wycombe about the beginning of the reign of Henry I. In 1129 he became Chaplain to Robert Betun [or Bethune], thirty-third Bishop of Hereford, who was a native of Flanders, and formerly Prior of Llanthony. His learning was profound, as is evidenced in his life of Betun in Latin, in two books, printed in Wharton's "Anglia Sacra," in 1691. "He became odious to the monks of Llanthony on account of his severity of discipline, and his determination to procure the removal of their Monastery to its original place, whence it had been removed under the following circumstances: After the death of King Henry I. and Archbishop Anselm, there followed a time of great confusion and rapine, by means of which the Monastery of Llanthony was exposed to many robbers, and reduced to much distress; hereupon the Canons sent to the former Prior, Betun, then Bishop of Hereford, informing him thereof; who directed them all to come to him, which they did, and he entertained them in his own Palace, giving them the use of his Episcopal Chapel. Some of the most zealous, however, among them did not consent to this abandonment of the old Abbey, but remained there; and were particularly induced to do so, as that establishment afforded the only aid travellers could then procure in this district.

"When the Canons had lived two years with the Bishop, Milo, Earl of Hereford, gave them a place near Gloucester, where they founded a new Abbey, which was consecrated in 1136, and dedicated to St. Mary the Virgin. Earl Milo added to it many large possessions, and the Canons, growing rich and faring sumptuously every day, forgot their old Abbey, and declined to return to it; although their new Charter, which they had procured, distinctly provided that when peaceable times were restored, they should leave Gloucester (except thirteen of their number), and return to old Llanthony. This, Bishop Betun in vain endeavoured to induce them to do, for they only sent thither a few infirm old monks, who lived there in sad scarcity, almost on bread and water."

During the troubles of Stephen's reign, Hereford suffered greatly. The Cathedral was deserted and desecrated, and the Bishop himself was obliged to take flight in disguise; on his return, he cleansed and repaired the building. He was one of the best and worthiest Bishops of his age, a man of peace and religion, when by far the greater number of English Bishops were little better than turbulent Barons.

Wycombe, when appointed to the Priory by the Bishop, set himself earnestly to reform the Monastery, much to the distaste of the monks, who feared an interruption of their easy life.

Wycombe's earnestness found vent in an invective against the Earl of Hereford, whom he severely censured for his encouragement of the monkish delinquencies. Whatever the charges against the Earl were, Wycombe was

Clark removed to Upper Winchendon, the seat of Philip, Lord Wharton, who was the great ornament of the British Peerage, and the distinguished patron and sincere friend of the Nonconformists, where he found a "refuge from the storm, and a covert from the face of the spoiler." Mr. Clark afterwards retired to Wycombe, and took up his abode in Easton Street, and, after the manner of the Apostles, formed a Church in his house, which was the first Nonconformist Church established in Wycombe, and over which he presided up to the period of his death. He was much superior to his father in learning; and applied himself early to the study of the Holy Scriptures. He published Annotations on the Bible, which were the labour of his life; and also a Survey of the Bible, with other works. Dr. Calamy says of his Annotations, "that it is a work of great judgment, that it bears the lively signature of his exact learning, singular piety, and indefatigable industry; that it commonly fixes on the true sense of the place; diligently observes the connexion of things; freely represents the principal matters that occur; and contains the fullest account of parallel passages of any other then extant." It obtained the concurring testimony of Dr. Owen and Mr. Baxter; and a learned Primate recommended it to young divines, at their ordination. "Mr. Clark," says his biographer, "was a man of very considerable learning; a good critic, especially in the Scriptures; a great textuary; an excellent preacher; a great enemy to superstition and bigotry, yet zealous for unaffected piety and extensive charity. His soul cleaved to the purity of the Gospel and its institutions; and he disclaimed everything that looked like superstition. He, knowing God to be jealous for His worship, thought with Bishop Jeremy Taylor, ' that the teaching of Divine truths by symbolical things, and actions of human invention, was too low, too suspicious, and too dangerous, to be mingled with the Divine services, but the introducing of significant rites and ceremonies destroyed the Church, not only in her Christian liberty, but in the simplicity, purity, and spirituality of her religion, by insensibly changing it into a ceremonial and external service.' "—*Ductor Dubitantium*, l. iii. p. 668, sec. 7.

"He lived usefully and in much esteem, serving God with great patience, self-denial, prudence, and peaceableness; unweariedly seeking the furtherance of His kingdom, when it was made perilous to do so." He died suddenly, while conducting the public devotional exercises of the sanctuary, on February 24th, 1701, aged 75, and his remains were interred in the

Chancel of the Parish Church; but to use the words of one who composed this Epitaph to his memory :—

> "No costly tomb, nor monumental stone
>   Marks out the place where Clark, the Man of God,
>   Doth lie.   He needs them not; his name, his works
>   Still live on earth; and in that spirit world,
>   Where goodness ever dwells in memory,
>   He finds reward, the favour of his God;
>   Not that alone; for there with purest love
>   All join to welcome him whose days were spent
>   For Christ and Man, whose thoughts and words and deeds
>   Were consecrate to truth and goodness."

Mr. Clark was succeeded by the Rev. John Pownall, under whose ministry the Church and Congregation very considerably increased, so much so as to render it necessary, in the year 1714, to erect a Meeting House in Crendon Lane, which in subsequent years was twice enlarged, and school-rooms added to it, and it is now known as Crendon Street Chapel.

John Rowell, who resided in Wycombe about the year 1756, was by trade a plumber, and practised the art of Glass painting.   He was employed by the late Duke of Richmond at Goodwood, and executed many pieces for Dr. Maddox, Bishop of Worcester; particularly, "a history of Christ praying in the Garden," after a design of Dr. John Wall, of Worcester.   He painted a set of windows for Dr. Scawen Kenrick, in the Church of Hambledon, Bucks.   "The Nativity of Christ," and the "Roman Charity," were also executed by him in two large windows; the former was purchased of his widow by Mr. Chute, of The Vine, in Hampshire; the latter, by Viscount Fane.   The colours in some of his paintings stand very well; in others they have been observed greatly to fail.   He discovered the beautiful red which is so conspicuous in our old windows; but this secret is supposed to have died with him. *

Miss Hannah Ball was a resident in Wycombe from her childhood; in her Diary she informs us that she was born March 13th, 1733; blessed with parents who possessed Hagar's wish, "nor with riches crowned, nor poverty

---

* See Granger's "Biographical History," vol. iv. p. 335.

depressed." In one of Mr. Wesley's early visits to Wycombe she was prevailed on by a friend to hear him preach ; in her Diary she remarks, " I went at five o'clock in the morning, at which time the service commenced ; I was struck with the venerable appearance of Mr. Wesley, but more deeply affected with the words of his text, which were taken from Matt. xv. 28th, ' O woman, great is thy faith; be it unto thee even as thou wilt,'" and she thus became one of the first-fruits of his ministry in Wycombe. She adds, " I began my Diary in the year 1766 ; after three months' close exercise, I was brought by Divine assistance to resignation's shrine, with ' Father, Thy will be done.' From that time I found power to give the Lord all my heart." She very frequently corresponded with Mr. Wesley, and this she continued nearly to the close of his life. In another part of her Diary she observes, " I desire to spend the remaining part of my life in a closer walking with God, and in labours of love to my fellow-creatures,—feeding the hungry, clothing the naked, instructing the rising generation in the principles of religion, and in every possible way I am capable, ministering to them that shall be heirs of salvation." Miss Ball was the first person who established a Sunday School in Wycombe, in the year 1769 ; this circumstance is rendered the more remarkable from the fact of her taking nearly fourteen years' precedence of Mr. Raikes of Gloucester, the hitherto admitted founder of Sunday Schools, his school having been established in the year 1783. Miss Ball continued the school at Wycombe for many years ; and also met the children every Monday to instruct them, " earnestly desiring," as she adds in a letter to Mr. Wesley, " to promote the interest of the Church of Christ." Miss Ball attended the Parish Church with the children, and it was called Miss Ball's School.

She died August 16, 1792, in the fifty-ninth year of her age, and was succeeded by her sister, Miss Ann Ball, who continued her excellent work.

Thomas Orger was the son of Mr. George Orger, who was a Member of the Society of Friends, and resided at Hertford.

Mr. Orger removed to Wycombe in the year 1784, and placed his son at the Royal Grammar School, under the care of The Reverend Alban Thomas, by whose able tuition he made considerable proficiency.

In 1795 he entered a merchant's office at Sunderland, and accompanied the merchant on one of his voyages to St. Petersburg ; he subsequently returned to Wycombe, and established a printing office. In 1804 he married Miss Mary Anne Ivers, who was a celebrated actress of the day; and the following year he resided chiefly in London. In 1814 he entered himself as a student of civil law at Hertford College, Oxford. In 1824, on the recommendation of Dr. Crombie, Author of the Gymnasium, and Dr. Jones, the compiler of a Greek and English Lexicon, he obtained the degree of D.C.L. from the Marischal College, Aberdeen. In 1811 he published a translation of Ovid's Metamorphoses, with the original Latin text; and also a literal prose translation of the Odes of Anacreon. He educated a number of private pupils, and after Mrs. Orger's death, which transpired in 1849, he retired to Oxford, and resided with his son-in-law, Mr. Reinagle, the celebrated violoncellist, where he died of apoplexy, June 2nd, 1853.

John Hollis, Esq., the son of Isaac Hollis, was born in the old Elizabethan House, in Easton Street, already referred to. He was trained up in the principles of Protestant Nonconformity, and received a liberal education; he was on intimate terms with many literary men of his day, and particularly with the celebrated Dr. Samuel Parr. In the Doctor's Catalogue of his valuable and extensive library, he mentions Mr. Hollis as having given to him his work entitled "An Apology," in the year 1809; and in the summer of 1812 he sent him his other works. The Doctor remarks, that "Mr. Hollis leads a studious and blameless life at High Wycombe," where he sometimes visited him. "He is confessedly an unbeliever, but he never writes profanely; he is charitable and respectful in his judgment upon the character of Christians; he devotes his time and his fortune to doing good; and, be his errors what they may," Dr. Parr observes, "I am bound by the principles and spirit of Christianity to love and to honour such a moral agent as Mr. Hollis." In another note Dr. Parr adds, "that he knew Mr. Hollis personally, and considered him one of the most serious, upright, and benevolent of human beings; they often conversed upon the most important subjects; and whatsoever were the errors of Hollis, he supported them with much ability, and without any taint of acrimony or profaneness."

Mr. Hollis was also the intimate friend of that distinguished artist, John Opie, who was Professor of Painting in the Royal Academy; their friendship continued up to Opie's death, in the year 1807. Opie painted a fine portrait of his friend, which was engraved by Warren; and it is said that the execution of the engraving so delighted Hollis, that on seeing it, he exclaimed with considerable warmth of admiration, "Well, well, I declare we are all immortalized; yes, all of us are immortalized." His charity towards every class was commensurate with the dictates of his liberal soul, which ever devised liberal things, so that it may be justly said of him as of the patriarch Job, "When the ear heard him, then it blessed him; and when the eye saw him, it gave witness to him, because he delivered the poor that cried, and the fatherless, and him that had none to help him. The blessing of him that was ready to perish came down upon him, and he caused the widow's heart to sing for joy."

In Dr. Parr's Catalogue, Mr. Hollis's works are enumerated, amongst others :—

"Free Thoughts," consisting of remarks occasioned by Dr. Paley's Reply to Hume; "Hypercritical Strictures on certain passages in the Critical Review"; "A Letter to a Friend"; "The Reflections of a Solitary"; and a small volume of "Miscellaneous Poems," published anonymously "By a young Man." Mr. Hollis, in later life, remarked that "these poems were the production of a simple young man indeed." He published in an octavo volume his opinions on revealed religion, in a letter addressed to a friend. He was also the author of other works, copies of all of which he presented to Dr. Parr. He died on the 26th November, 1824, in the 81st year of his age. His coffin was placed in a stone case, and interred in the Nave of the Parish Church.

Mr. James Gomme was an auctioneer, and a Burgess of the Borough of Wycombe. He might be said to combine, as Dr. Johnson expressed it, "that which is rarely to be met with in persons of his class, the civility of the tradesman, and the manners of the gentleman."

He possessed considerable mental powers, and a retentive memory; he sought and enjoyed the society of literary men, and lived in habits of intimacy with Mark Noble, the antiquary, with whom he carried on a lengthened and most interesting correspondence. He was also on most friendly terms with Lord Dormer, Sir Isaac Heard, Sir George Naylor, and many other distinguished persons; and was particularly honoured with the friendship of the celebrated Edmund Burke. In 1795 Mr. Gomme wrote to the Biographer of Burke, and remarked that "corn became much increased in price, and the poor felt the pressure severely." Mr. Burke, who was ever feelingly alive to their wants, and never backward in exerting himself to afford relief, had a windmill in the park at Butler's Court, in which he directed good corn to be ground, had it made into bread at his own house, and retailed it to the poor at a very reduced price. "This," he said, "was a better plan than merely to make them a present of it. The bread was, of course, unadulterated, and excellent. He had it served at his own table. I partook of it there; and he requested me to take a loaf to Wycombe, in order to show to the more opulent people of that town and vicinity how much might be done, and with comparatively little trouble, for the benefit of the lower order of the community." Mr. Gomme adds, "Calling at Butler's Court one day, after passing through a drenching shower of rain, Mr. Burke pressed me to take a glass of strong sherry, which he said was of his own importation, and the very best he could procure." "I cannot," he added, "offer you brandy, for I will never pay a guinea per gallon for that, or for any other article, from that country (France)." "Shortly after this, it so happened," Mr. Gomme observes, "that I was invited to dine at Butler's Court. 'You will meet,' said Mr. Burke to me, 'the Bishop of St. Pol de Leon, of the Roman Catholic Church, and Dr. Walker King, a dignified clergyman *of our more fortunate and purer Church.*' This latter part of the sentence was pronounced emphatically, probably in allusion to the then unhappy state of the French Church and Clergy; and to Burke's having been suspected of being a Roman Catholic, when there was nothing whatever to countenance such a supposition, except his having some relatives of that persuasion, and his advocating their cause in Parliament and in the press. This stupid prejudice was not, however, confined to the lower class of people; for I once heard a person holding a considerable office under government term him, 'a kiln-dried Roman Catholic.' But to proceed, at table I accordingly met with the reverend persons Mr. Burke had mentioned, along with several others of his friends; but here let me say, I shall never forget the manner in which he descended the ground flight of stone steps to receive me, the cordial pressure of his hand, and the graceful and dignified demeanour of introducing me to his other guests.

"Burke had a way of doing these little things which struck me as being peculiarly his own, and calculated to make a strong impression on the mind of a stranger. He was particularly attentive in his own house, or at his own table, to any man who was of inferior rank; he would frequently address his conversation to such person, in order to overcome any diffidence he might feel, and, as the phrase is, *draw him out*, to exhibit any peculiar merit or talent he possessed. His own conversation, in his gayer moments, was various and excursive; he did not dwell long on common matters, but giving you some bright and brilliant thoughts, or happy phrases, which it seemed difficult to forget, would pass on to some kindred or relative topic, and throw out the coruscations of his wit or imagination upon that also, thus keeping up a kind of intellectual sharp-shooting on every subject that offered. It will be supposed there was some effort in this, and it is not improbable; but it was not obvious. His mind, however, seemed to be mostly on the stretch, and few things escaped it. I think it was impossible ever to mistake him for an every-day man; for in his efforts to sustain his reputation for superiority in private society, he sometimes failed in his hits, and stumbled into, or below, mediocrity; but he recovered in a moment his dignity and proper station."

" Mr. Burke founded the French Emigrant School at Penn, in 1796, for the destitute children of those who had perished by the guillotine, or the sword of the Revolution. The Abbé Moraine was the Superior, or Headmaster of the School, and was assisted by the Abbé Lefevre and the Abbé Chevallier."

Mr. Gomme states that " In April of that year the Emigrant School was opened, and Mr. Burke, for the remainder of his life, watched over the institution with the solicitude, not merely of a friend, but of a father. He visited it frequently, sometimes daily, being about three miles distant from his house, and often supplied the table of masters and scholars from his own. His smiles might be said to have gladdened the hearts of the exiles; I have witnessed many interesting scenes there of that nature; they were doomed, alas! too soon to lose their kind benefactor. At the annual distribution of prizes the senior scholar delivered a Latin oration in the presence of a large assembly of nobility and gentry, in the great hall, in which Mr. Burke was always alluded to as their patron and friend. He assigned to these youths a blue uniform, wearing in their hats a white cockade, inscribed, '*Vive le Roi*;' those who had lost their fathers had it placed on a bloody label; those who had lost uncles on a black one. The Marquis of Buckingham made the School a present of a brass field-piece, and a pair of colours which were displayed on public days, as a source of youthful pride, by these descendants of suffering loyalty. After the death of Mr. Burke, I was appointed Treasurer, and received from the Lords of the Treasury fifty pounds per month for the support of the establishment. Upon the restoration of the legitimate monarchy in France, in 1814, the money was remitted thence, until the dissolution of the Institution on the 1st of August, 1820; when, on the departure of the superior and the pupils, the colours were presented to me as a token of remembrance, and I retain them with satisfaction, from the interesting associations they recall."

From the above extracts, it is evident that Mr. Gomme shows great power of discernment in his descriptions of Mr. Burke's conversations. We must add that Mr. Burke introduced Mr. Gomme to Louis the Eighteenth, when the King resided at Hartwell, in this County; the King treated him with the greatest kindness, and after His Majesty's restoration and return to his dominions, transmitted to Mr. Gomme, as a testimony of his regard, the Cross of the Order of St. Louis. Mr. Gomme was a Fellow of the Society of Antiquaries, of London. We may add, that he was a portly man, of dignified appearance, and wore the costume of the last century. On the occasion of the funeral of His late Royal Highness the Duke of Kent, Mr. Gomme attended the mournful obsequies merely as a spectator; and as he approached the Royal Chapel of St. George, Windsor, in a pitiless shower of rain, he was, from his appearance, evidently taken by an official for a dignitary of the Church of England, and was accordingly ushered into the sacred edifice. He mentioned to the Author, that as he passed his Grace the Duke of Wellington and other great Officers of State, who were near the entrance to the Royal Chapel, he observed the venerable Lord Eldon standing on his hat, for the protection of his feet from the wet. He died 30th July, 1825, aged 59, and his remains were interred in a brick grave in the Nave of the Parish Church. He left a large collection of valuable curiosities, paintings, books, and MSS., which were sold by public auction in the Town Hall.

John Wilkinson, Esq., who resided in Wycombe for many years, was the son of a pious clergyman of the Established Church. He received a liberal education, and on the death of his father, his mother seceded from the Established Church, and joined the Society of Friends, in whose

z

principles she trained up her son, and of which Society he became a distinguished ornament, an Evangelical Minister, and was repeatedly the President of their Yearly Meetings. During the visit of the Emperor Alexander to this country in 1814, Mr. Wilkinson preached before His Imperial Majesty, his sister the Grand Duchess of Oldenburg, and suite, at the Friends' Meeting House in St. Martin's Lane, London. His subject was, the effects of vital religion, and the nature of true worship, beautifully applying the text, " He is their help and their shield," and afterwards concluded the service with earnest and appropriate prayer. Mr. Wilkinson formed one of the deputation of three to wait on the Emperor with a congratulatory address from the Society of Friends; when his Imperial Majesty took occasion to allude in the kindest terms to Mr. Wilkinson's sermon, and expressed how fully his spirit united with him in prayer at their Meeting. The Emperor remarked that he should never forget the opportunity, and as the deputation withdrew, he took each of them by the hand and said, " I part with you as a friend and a brother."

"Subsequently, during an interview with the late Thomas Clarkson, Esq., in Paris, the Emperor very kindly inquired after Mr. Wilkinson, and the two Friends who formed the deputation to wait on him in London, and said, ' the two hours' conversation that he had held with them were among the most agreeable hours he had spent in England; that the religious opportunity which he then had with them made a very serious impression on his mind, such an one, indeed, as he believed he should never forget, and he could not but have a high regard for the Society to which three such good men belonged.' In the year 1829 it pleased Almighty God to visit Mr. Wilkinson with an overwhelming affliction, in the removal by death of an only beloved and most interesting Daughter, at the age of thirteen years and eight months, which he bore with Christian fortitude, and the sweetest resignation to the Divine will."

In the autumn of 1832 Mr. Wilkinson delivered four discourses in London, which were taken down in short-hand, and published without his cognizance, as the Editor very justly remarks, "for their intrinsic excellence." There were also two sermons delivered by him at the Friends' Meeting House in Manchester, and one at Liverpool, and published under similar circumstances, which alike breathe a spirit of deep-toned piety and ardent zeal for the conversion of his fellow-sinners.

In addition to Mr. Wilkinson's intimate acquaintance with the classics, few men were more conversant with theology, ancient and modern history, and general literature; he also possessed no mean knowledge of the arts and sciences. He was distinguished by a noble and generous spirit, and an enlarged and benevolent heart; he was blest with a placidity of temper, most gentlemanly and urbane manners, and endowed with a mind of a superior order, abounding in intellectual resources, delighting in the beauties of nature, but, above all, adorned with humility and that Christian love which hallowed all the other gifts and graces Providence had so liberally bestowed on him.

In the month of February, 1836, Mr. Wilkinson seceded from the Society of Friends, and published a book entitled "Quakerism Examined," in reply to a letter of Samuel Tuke, in which he displayed the powers of his well-cultivated and vigorous mind. Subsequently he became a member of the Established Church. He was no bigot, but revered good men of every denomination. He was a liberal supporter of all the various societies having for their object the spread of the Gospel and the improvement of the moral and religious condition of his fellow-creatures. Love to all mankind was deeply engraven on his heart, and his charity towards every class was commensurate with the dictates of his liberal soul, which ever devised liberal things. That imperfections mingled in his character we cannot doubt, for he was human; but surely of him it may with truth be said,—

"E'en his failings lean'd to virtue's side."

All who had the happiness to share his intimacy will readily unite in this testimony; his friendships were those of the heart. He has left behind him an example that may instruct and encourage others. His praise is in all the Churches, and his memory will long be embalmed in the recollection of his many and sincerely attached friends. He died in the month of December, 1846, and his remains were interred in a brick grave in Hazelmere Church Yard. His Will (subject to Mrs. Wilkinson's life interest) contains the following munificent bequests :—

To the British and Foreign Bible Society	£3,000
„ London Missionary Society	2,000
„ Church Missionary Society	1,500
„ Baptist Missionary Society	1,500

To the Wesleyan Missionary Society	. . . . . .	£1,000
„ Religious Tract Society	. . . . . .	1,000
„ London Association in Aid of Missions of the United Brethren, called Moravians	}	1,500
„ Pastoral-Aid Society	. . . . . .	250
„ Irish Society of London, for Promoting the Education and Religious Instruction of the Native Irish, through the Medium of their own language	}	250

We should not omit to mention the principal manufactures of the Town and Parish, which are as follow :—

And first, of Paper, which was at an early period brought to such perfection, that to Mr. John Bates, of Wycombe Marsh, was awarded the Gold Medal of the Society of Arts, "for manufacturing paper equal to the French, for receiving impression from mezzotinto, and other engraved copper plates."

Wycombe is also celebrated for the manufacture of Chairs, which of late years has very considerably increased, so much so, that it is said, upon the average, in 1874, about seven chairs were made per minute in the town and neighbourhood for every hour of the day and night, being nearly one and a half millions in that year ; and they are exported to almost every Country in the world.

Another important manufacture is that of Pillow Lace. Although it is not in so flourishing a condition as in former years, yet it continues to be an extensive source of employment.

We may mention that in the year 1812 the Auxiliary Bible Society was established here, supported by many of the Nobility and Gentry of the County, and the whole of the Clergy, Nonconformist Ministers, and others of the town and neighbourhood.

In the list of subscriptions and donations, the name of Mr. Moses Solomon, an unconverted Jew, residing in Paul's Row, is included.

The amount of subscriptions and donations for the year 1812 amounted to £882 10s. 6d.

At a Public Meeting held in the Guildhall, on the 4th January, 1812, for the purpose of establishing a Royal Lancasterian School, Viscount Mahon occupied the chair, and in a very able speech stated the object of the meeting. After which, Mr. Fox, the Secretary to the Institution for Promoting the Royal British System of Education, addressed the meeting. The Hon. Robert Smith (the second Lord Carington), at the early age of seventeen, moved the various resolutions constituting the basis of the Society intended to be instituted. " In a neat but short speech " (says the Editor of the *Statesman* Newspaper) " he very modestly addressed the meeting, stating his approbation of the opinions already advanced by his noble relation and Mr. Fox, and expressed the pleasure he felt on the occasion, in being engaged in promoting so desirable an object." The meeting was supported by the Clergy, the Dissenting Ministers, the leading members of the Society of Friends, Robert Wheeler, Esq., and other influential persons of the Town and neighbourhood.

Sir Thomas Baring, Bart., M.P., was appointed President; the Right Hon. Lord Carrington, the Right Hon. Lord Gardner, Viscount Mahon, Sir John Dashwood King, Bart., M.P., and the Hon. Robert Smith, Vice-Presidents.

The footpaths of the Streets in the Borough were, in 1810, paved with Denner Hill Sand Stones, under the provisions of the Local Act of Parliament for paving and lighting the Borough.

On the 5th March, 1811, there was a grand torchlight funeral of the remains of Louisa, niece of General Sir Howard Douglas, Bart., which were interred in Wycombe Parish Church.

The Savings Bank was established in 1818.

On Nov. 9, 1832, Her Majesty the Queen, then H.R.H. Princess Victoria, accompanied by her mother the Duchess of Kent, passed through Wycombe on her way to Oxford, changing horses at the Red Lion Hotel.

The Town was first lighted with Gas in 1836.

The Wycombe Poor Law Union was established in 1835.

The Wycombe Amicable and Literary Institute, in 1844.

The Odd Fellows' Lodge, designated the " Loyal Bud of Hope," was opened at the Swan Inn, in 1845.

The Wycombe County Court, in 1847 ; John Herbert Koe, Esq., Q.C., Judge.

The Wycombe Branch Railway, connecting the town with the Great Western Line at the Taplow Station, was opened in 1847, which Line has since been extended to Oxford and Aylesbury.

On the 19th of February, 1863, Mrs. Alfred Lane, the widow of Mr. Councillor Lane, in carrying out her late husband's intention, presented, in the most handsome manner, to the Corporation a fine painting after Vandyck, of Philip, fourth Lord Wharton; of Lady Jane, his second wife (by whom he became possessed of the Goodwin Estates at Upper Winchenden and Wooburn); and of Henry, their fourth and infant son; the picture was included in the finest collection of portraits by Vandyck and Sir Peter Lely, in England, which adorned the gallery of his Lordship's palace at Wooburn, then in all its grandeur and magnificence. This grand picture is placed in the Council Chamber of our Guildhall. The old palace was taken down in 1750, and the present house was erected on part of its site. The other portraits were purchased by Sir Robert Walpole, and were afterwards transferred to the collection of pictures in the Winter Palace of the Emperor of Russia, at St. Petersburg.

In June, 1877, a splendid full-length portrait (by Graves) of His Royal Highness Albert Edward, Prince of Wales, K.G., G.C.I., etc., etc., robed as a Knight of the Garter, was presented to the inhabitants of the Borough and Parish of Chepping Wycombe, by the Right Honourable Charles Robert Lord Carington (who served as *Aide-de-Camp* to His Royal Highness during his Indian tour), in acknowledgment of the welcome given to his Lordship by his fellow-townsmen on his return, May 24th, 1876. This fine production of art graces the Guildhall.

The Author deems it a very suitable and gratifying conclusion to his history, to chronicle here the visit to this ancient town of Queen Victoria, on her way to Hughenden Manor, on Saturday, the 15th December, 1877, when Her Majesty was the guest of the Premier, the Right Honourable the Earl of Beaconsfield. Wycombe did its utmost on the occasion by way of appropriate demonstrations of loyalty. Flags, banners, and mottoes were everywhere displayed; triumphal arches were erected; and one of them was a construction of chairs, the staple manufacture of the town, of various artistic designs. Guards of honour from the Royal Bucks King's Own Militia, under Captain Powell, Leiutenant Rose carrying the Queen's colours; and the 1st and 2nd Companies of the Buckinghamshire Battalion of Rifle Volunteers, with their respective officers, Lieut. T. Lunnon, and Sub-Lieutenant Gilbey; being under the command of Lieut.-Colonel O. P. Wethered, were in attendance. The Right Honourable the Earl of

Beaconsfield; the Right Honourable the Lord Carington; Lieut.-Col. the Honourable W. Carington, M.P.; Sir Charles L. Young, Bart.; J. O. Griffits, Esq., Q.C.; the Mayor and Corporation in State; the Reverend Robert Chilton, Vicar; the Reverend James Poulter, Head Master of the Royal Grammar School, with the scholars of the foundation; Randolph Crewe, Esq., Chairman of the Parish Local Board, with several of its members as a deputation from that body, and many others, including an assemblage of the fair sex, were present at the Railway Station, to await Her Majesty's arrival. Punctually at a quarter past one o'clock the Royal train entered the station, the band of the Bucks Militia playing the National Anthem. Her Majesty, who was accompanied by Her Royal Highness Princess Beatrice, and looked remarkably well, was handed from the train by the Earl of Beaconsfield, who introduced the Mayor to the Queen; the Mayor presented to Her Majesty an Address from the Corporation, beautifully illuminated on vellum, which was as follows :—

"May it please your Majesty, we the Mayor, Aldermen, and Burgesses of the ancient Borough of Chepping Wycombe, as representing a population which has always shown itself loyal to the Throne, and deeply interested in every movement having for its object the promotion and advancement of the welfare of the nation at large, desire most cordially and loyally to convey to your Majesty our sincere and hearty congratulations upon your Majesty passing through our Town, on the occasion of a visit to our distinguished neighbour the Prime Minister of the Country; and at the same time to express our earnest desire that, under the smile of Divine Providence, your Majesty may long live to rule over a contented, happy, and loyal people, and that the peace and prosperity which has so signally marked your Majesty's gracious reign, may continue to distinguish the rule of this great nation and its dependencies, under your Majesty's guidance, for many years yet to come."

The noble Earl, speaking for the Queen, said that Her Majesty thanked the Burgesses for their address, and desired him to express her great satisfaction at finding herself, after a long lapse of years, once more in her loyal Borough of Wycombe. The Mayor then introduced his youthful daughter to the Queen, who, in a very graceful and simple manner, presented a beautiful bouquet to Her Majesty.

Lord Beaconsfield, on the conclusion of the ceremony, led Her Majesty to the open carriage, in which, amid the singing of "God Save the Queen," by the school children, and the ringing of the Church bells, she took her seat with Princess Beatrice, and the Dowager Marchioness of Ely, lady in waiting; General Ponsonby and Colonel Du Plat were in attendance on horseback, preceded by the carriage of the Premier. There was no escort, the whole cavalcade consisting of the gentlemen in attendance, the outriders, and the mounted police. Through the town the procession moved at a mere walking pace, amid the plaudits of thousands, and the waving of handkerchiefs from the windows of all the houses. After passing through the arch of chairs, and through the last of the triumphal arches erected by the entrance to Frogmore Gardens, which was surmounted with the now significant inscription, " Hail, Empress of India," the postilions broke into a trot, and the remainder of the journey of a mile and a half was quickly accomplished. The stay of Her Majesty lasted very little over two hours After luncheon, the Queen visited the Church and Church Yard, where the remains of the late Viscountess Beaconsfield are entombed ; there is a mural tablet on the exterior east wall of the Church to her memory. The Queen also planted a tree on the lawn of Hughenden Manor. By a quarter to four o'clock Her Majesty and the Princess had been conducted back nearly along the same route ; and on the royal party approaching the arch of chairs. Her Majesty stopped the carriage, and inspected and much admired this unique and artistic structure ; on reaching the railway station, the farewell cheers were as hearty as were the demonstrations of welcome. The return to Windsor was accomplished at half-past four o'clock.

APPENDIX.

I.

CHARTERS AND GRANTS

RELATING TO

The Borough of Chepping Wycombe,

IN THE

COUNTY OF BUCKINGHAM.

CHARTER ROLLS.

* 5 *John.* m. 24.	The Manor of Wycombe to Alan Basset.
12 *Hen. III.* m. 4.	Fair granted to the Hospital of Wycombe.
* 13 *Hen. III.* m. 7.	For the Lepers of St. Mary at Wycombe.
* *Ib.* m. 8.	Alan Basset.
* 21 *Hen. III.* m. 4 & 5.	The Burgesses of Wycombe.
35 *Hen. III.* m. 4.	The Church at Wycombe.
* 13 *Edw. I.* No. 59.	The Burgesses of Wycombe.
* 1 *Hen. IV.* p. 2. No. 6.	Borough of Wycombe.—Confirmation.
3 & 4 *Hen. V.* No. 2.	Free Warren in Wycombe, &c. granted to the Duke of Bedford.

INQ: AD $\overline{QD}$ DAMNUM.

8 *Edw. II.* No. 161.	Messuage in Wycombe, in the Honor of Wallingford.

PATENT ROLLS.

19 *Ed. III.* p. 3. m. 3.	For the Prior of St. John of Jerusalem. Certain Lands and Woods in Wycombe. About sixteen acres of Land, and one acre of Woodland.

* The Charters having this mark (*) prefixed, are those now printed.

4 *Ed. III.* p. 2. m. 5.	Manor of Wycombe, and a rent of £18 8s. 8d. granted to Thomas, Duke of Norfolk.
6 *Ed. III.* p. 2. m. 8.	Town and Manor of Wycombe. Grant to the Earl of Norfolk.
18 *Ed. III.* p. 1. m. 28.	Piece of Land in Wycombe granted to Egid. le Trampor.
16 *Ric. II.* p. 2. m. 19.	Chantry of the Holy Trinity at Wycombe.
28 *Hen. VI.* p. 1. m. 1 & 2.	Grant of Free Warren in Wycombe to Robt. Wittingham.

ESCHEATS.

9 *Ed. I.* No. 9.	Alisea le Despenser dies seized of the Manor of Wycombe, &c.

CLOSE ROLLS.

15 *Edw. I.* m. 6. dors.	Wycombe Farm.
19 *Edw. I.* m. 9.	Manor of Wycombe to Hugh le Despenser.
18 *Edw. II.* m. 38.	Lands in Wycombe to the Knights Templars.
19 *Edw. II.* m. 23.	Messuage in Wycombe.
20 *Edw. II.* m. 4.	Wycombe Manor.
6 *Edw. III.* m. 17.	Manor and Town of Wycombe. Surrender by the Earl of Norfolk to the King, of a Fee farm Rent.
Ib. m. 37.	Lands and Tenements in Wycombe.

18 *Edw. III.* p. 1. m. 25.	Two Water-Mills, &c. in the town of Wycombe.
43 *Edw. III.* m. 30.	Lands, &c. in Wycombe.
10 *Hen. IV.* m. 32.	Lands, &c. in the parish of Wycombe.
12 *Hen. VI.* m. 2.	Lands, &c. in the town of Wycombe.
18 *Hen. VI.* m. 35.	Lands, &c. in the town of Wycombe.
15 *Edw. IV.* m. 3.	Tenement and Land in the parish of Wycombe.
18 *Edw. IV.*	Dean and Canons of Windsor, the Manor of Bassetsbury, and Fee farm of the town of Great Wycombe, &c. (Ashmole's "Garter," p. 170.)

THE FIFTH OF JOHN.

10th JUNE, 1205.

Amongst the Records of the Court of Chancery preserved in the *Tower* of *London*, that is to say, on the Roll of Charters of the Fifth year of the Reign of King John, membrane 24, is thus contained :—

"THE CHARTER OF ALAN BASSET.

The Manor of Wycumbe granted to Alan Basset.

For £20 a year.

And the Service of one Knight.

"JOHN, by the grace of God, King of *England*, Lord of *Ireland*, Duke of *Normandy* and *Aquitain*, Earl of *Anjou*, To the Archbishops, Bishops, Abbots, Earls, Barons, Justices, Sheriffs, Reeves, Ministers, and all his Bailiffs, and faithful people, Greeting.—KNOW YE, that we have given, granted, and by our present Charter have confirmed, to our beloved and trusty *Alan Basset*, ALL the manor of *Wycumbe* with its appurtenances, except what *Robert de Vipont* there held, To HAVE and TO HOLD to the aforesaid *Alan* and his heirs, of us and our heirs, RENDERING therefore yearly, at our Exchequer, twenty pounds; that is to say, ten pounds at the Exchequer of *Saint Michael*, and ten pounds at the Exchequer of *Easter:* And moreover, doing therefore the service of one Knight for all service. Wherefore we will and firmly command, that the aforesaid *Alan*, and his heirs after him, shall have and hold the aforesaid Manor with the appurtenances, as is aforesaid, well and in peace, freely, and quietly, entirely, and fully, and honourably, with all liberties and free customs to the aforesaid Manor pertaining. WITNESS, *William* Earl *Marshall*, *William* Earl of *Arundel*, *William* Earl of *Ferrers*, *William de Breose*, *Peter de Stok*, &c.

"Given by the hand of *J. de Braunch*, Archdeacon of *Worcester*, at the tenth day of *June*, in the fifth year of our Reign."

(A true Translation.)

26th April, 1817.

W. ILLINGWORTH.
Deputy Keeper of the Records in the Tower.

THE THIRTEENTH OF HENRY III.

26th MARCH, 1229.

Amongst the Records of the Court of Chancery preserved in the *Tower* of *London*, that is to say, on the Roll of Charters of the Thirteenth year of the reign of King Henry the Third, membrane 9, is thus contained :—

"For ALAN BASSET, concerning the Manor of WYCUMBE.

"𝕳𝖊𝖓𝖗𝖞, by the grace of God, King of *England*, &c. To the Archbishops, &c. Greeting.—WE HAVE INSPECTED the Charter of the Lord JOHN, our Father, in these words : JOHN, by the grace of God, King of *England*, Lord of *Ireland*, Duke of *Normandy* and *Aquitain*, Earl of *Anjou*, To the Archbishops, Bishops, Abbots, Earls, Barons, Justices, Sheriffs, Reeves, Ministers, and all his Bailiffs, and faithful people, Greeting.—KNOW YE, that we have given, granted, and by our present Charter have confirmed, to our beloved and trusty *Alan Basset*, ALL the manor of *Wycumbe* with its appurtenances, except what *Robert de Vipont* there held, To HAVE and TO HOLD to the aforesaid *Alan* and his heirs, of us and our heirs, RENDERING therefore yearly, at our Exchequer, twenty pounds ; that is to say, ten pounds at the Exchequer of *Saint Michael*, and ten pounds at the Exchequer of *Easter:* And moreover, doing therefore the service of one Knight for all service. Wherefore we will and firmly command, that the aforesaid *Alan*, and his heirs after him, shall have and hold the aforesaid Manor, with the appurtenances, as is aforesaid, well and in peace, freely, and quietly, entirely, and fully, and honourably, with all liberties and free customs to the aforesaid Manor pertaining. WITNESS, *William* Earl *Marshall*, *William* Earl of *Arundel*, *William* Earl of *Ferrers*, *William de Breose*, *Peter de Stok*, *Robert le Roppel*, *John de Stok*. GIVEN by the hand of *J. de Braunch*, Archdeacon of *Worcester*, at   the tenth day of *June* in the fifth year of our reign. WE, therefore, this gift and grant ratifying and confirming the same for us and our heirs, do ratify and confirm to the aforesaid *Alan* and his heirs : THESE being WITNESSES, *Hubert de Burgh* Earl of *Kent*, Justiciar of *England*, *Philip de Albaniaco*, *Ralph Fitz Nicholas*, *Nicholas de Moles*, *John Fitz-Philip*, *Geoffry de Spencer*, and others.

"𝕲𝖎𝖛𝖊𝖓 by the hand of the venerable Father *Ralph*, Bishop of *Chichester*, our Chancellor at *Marlebridge*, the 26th day of *March*, in the 13th year of our Reign."

(A true Translation.)

26th *April*, 1817.

W. ILLINGWORTH.

Deputy Keeper of the Records in the Tower.

B B

Henry has inspected the Charter of John.

Recapitulated.

The Manor of Wycumbe granted to Alan Basset for £20 a year.

and the service of one knight.

Confirmed.

From the Fine Rolls in Turr. Lond., Bucks, 10 Hen. III., 125. (A translation by Dr. Lipscombe, corrected) :—

"**Between** the Burgesses of Wycumbe Querents, and Alan Basset, of certain damages and injuries which the said Alan had done to the said Burgesses, as they aver, contrary to the liberties which the same Burgesses say that they hold of the ancestors of the Lord the King. Alan granted to the same Burgesses the whole Borough and Town of Wycumbe with the rents, markets, and fairs ; and with all other things to a free Borough appertaining, and with the edifices of Knaves-thorn, and the rents, &c.; excepting the demesnes of the said Alan, and his lands in the foreigns ; and the mills there reserved in a fine passed between the aforesaid Alan Basset, and the Abbess of Godstowe, so as that the rents and customs which the men of the said Abbess were wont to render to the said Alan, may remain to the said Burgesses, and their heirs, in aid of the aforesaid Fee farm, to be paid according to the former fine passed between the same Alan and the aforesaid Abbess, saving always to the said Alan and his heirs all reasonable aids when the Lord the King and his heirs shall make talliage of the Domain lands throughout England. And be it known that the aforesaid Alan and his heirs acquit and release to the aforesaid Burgesses, &c., as against the said Lord the King and his heirs, the Fee farm of Twenty pounds, which the said Alan was thereupon indebted to the Lord the King ; and in like manner the service of one Knight's fee which the aforesaid Alan was accustomed to pay as his service, which the aforesaid Alan held of the Grant of King John. BE IT KNOWN LIKE-WISE that the fairs of Oxen annually on the lands of the said Alan, shall be and remain as they have been accustomed, saving to the said Burgesses and their heirs the customs thence issuant. And the said Alan and his heirs shall have all the Dung found in the Streets of Wycumbe, &c. And be it known that many Burgesses named in the fine aforesaid, and all other Burgesses named and acknowledged in the Town there, shall be in peace agreeable to the same."

THE THIRTEENTH OF HENRY III.

13th May, 1229.

Amongst the Records of the Court of Chancery preserved in the *Tower* of *London*, that is to say, on the Roll of Charters of the Thirteenth year of the Reign of King Henry the Third, membrane 7, is thus contained :—

"For the LEPERS* of Saint Mary of WYCUMBE.

"**Henry**, King, &c. Greeting.—KNOW YE, that we for the love of God, and for the health of our soul, and for others the souls of our ancestors and heirs, HAVE granted, and by this our Charter HAVE confirmed, to the leprous brethren of the Hospital of *Saint Margaret*,† of *Wicumbe*, that they and their successors for ever, shall have every year one fair at the aforesaid Hospital of *Saint Margaret*, to continue for two days; that is to say, on the eve and on the day of *Saint Margaret*, unless, &c. WHEREFORE we will, &c. that the aforesaid lepers and their successors for ever, shall have and hold the aforesaid fair at the aforesaid Hospital of *Saint Margaret*, well and in peace, freely and quietly, with all liberties and free customs to such fair pertaining as is aforesaid. WITNESS, &c.

Henry allows the Hospital

To have one Fair every year for two days.

"**Given** by the hand of the venerable Father *R.* Bishop of *Chichester*, our Chancellor at *Westminster*, the thirteenth day of *May*, in the thirteenth year of our Reign."

With all Liberties and free Customs.

(A true Translation.)

26th *April*, 1817.

W. ILLINGWORTH.

Deputy Keeper of the Records in the Tower.

---

* Prior to the reign of John we hear little in our Histories or Chronicles of the existence of leprosy in England. We find from "Rymer's Federa," vol. i. part i. p. 19, there were somewhere in the Diocese of Lincoln, houses to receive women who suffered from this terrible disease. Gul. Nubrigiensis, who died in 1208, makes mention of a noble hospital, for the reception of lepers, near Durham, as does Stowe, of hospitals for the same purpose, viz., the Loke, in Southwark, another at Mile End, and a third in St. Giles's.

"*Better than a lazere, or beggere.*"

—Chaucer, in the character of the Friar.

† So in the original.

THE TWENTY-FIRST OF HENRY III.

24th June, 1237.

Amongst the Records of the Court of Chancery preserved in the *Tower* of *London*, that is to say, on the Roll of Charters of the Twenty-first year of the Reign of King Henry the Third, No. 5, is thus contained :—

"For the Burgesses of Wycumbe.

"**The King,** To his Archbishops, &c. Greeting.—WE have inspected the final Agreement made in our Court before our Justices at *Westminster*, between the Burgesses of *Wycumbe* and *Alan Basset*, in these words : THIS is the final Agreement made in the Court of the Lord the King at *Westminster*, from the day of the purification of the blessed *Mary* in one month, in the tenth year of the Reign of King HENRY, Son of King JOHN, before *Martin de Pateshull, Thomas de Moleton, Thomas de Heyden, Robert de Lexinton, Geoffry le Sauvage, Warine Fitz-Johel*, Justices and other faithful subjects of the Lord the King then there present, between the Burgesses of *Wycumbe*, Plaintiffs, and *Alan Basset*, concerning the wrongs and injuries which the same *Alan* did to the same Burgesses, as they have said, against the liberties which the same Burgesses say they have of the gift of the ancestors of the Lord the King. And whereupon there was a plea between them in the same Court, that is to say, that the said *Alan* as much as in him and his heirs is, hath granted to the same Burgesses, ALL the Borough of *Wycumbe* with the Rents, Markets, and Fairs, and with all other things to a free Borough pertaining, without any reservation, and with all encrease and purchases which the said *Alan* hath made in the same Borough, and with the Buildings of *Enarenethorn* as the same *Alan* held such Buildings, and with the Rent of four shillings, which *Geoffrey Fitz Angod* used to pay, and with all other their appurtenances, and all things to that Borough pertaining, except the demesnes of the said *Alan* and his out lying Lands and his Mills, which entirely remain to the said *Alan* and his heirs, TO HAVE and TO HOLD to the said Burgesses and their heirs at Fee farm of the said *Alan* and his heirs for ever : RENDERING therefore yearly thirty pounds and one mark of Silver at two terms of the year, that

Agreement in the Court at Westminster in the 10th year of *Henry* the Third,

Between the Burgesses of Wycumbe and *Alan Basset.*

Alan granted to the Burgesses all the Borough, with the Rents, Markets, and Fairs ; And the purchases he has made, and the buildings of *Enarenethorn*, except his demesnes, outlying Lands, and Mills, for is to say, at the feast of *Saint Michael,* fifteen pounds and half a mark ; and at the feast of *Saint Mary,* in *March,* fifteen pounds and half a mark ; for all service and demand to the aforesaid *Alan* or to his heirs pertaining : And this Agreement was made between them, saving the fine made between the aforesaid *Alan* and the Abbess of *Godstowe,* so as, to wit, that the rents and customs which the men of the same Abbess are accustomed to render to the said *Alan,* shall remain to the same Burgesses and their heirs, in aid towards making up the aforesaid Fee farm, according to the fine before made between the same *Alan* and the aforesaid Abbess, saving to the said *Alan* and his heirs, his reasonable aids, when the Lord the King and his heirs shall talliage his demesnes throughout *England.* AND BE IT KNOWN, that the aforesaid *Alan* and his heirs, shall acquit the aforesaid Burgesses and their heirs, towards the Lord the King and his heirs, from the Fee farm of twenty pounds, which the same *Alan* thereof oweth to the Lord the King ; and likewise from the foreign service of one Knight's fee which the aforesaid *Alan* oweth out of this land of *Wycumbe,* which he hath of the gift of the Lord King JOHN : Also BE IT KNOWN, that the fair of cattle shall continue every year in the field of the same *Alan,* where and as it used before to be, saving to the said Burgesses and their heirs, the customs arising therefrom : And the said *Alan* and his heirs shall have the dung found in the Streets of *Wicumbe,* as the same *Alan* used before to have the same ; and if perchance the aforesaid Burgesses or their heirs shall not render to the said *Alan* and his heirs the aforesaid thirty pounds and one mark, at the terms appointed according as is aforesaid, or the talliages when they shall happen, it shall be lawful for the said *Alan* and his heirs to distrain the same Burgesses and their heirs, by their cattle found within the aforesaid Borough, and without, upon the fee of the said *Alan* and his heirs, until full payment of the aforesaid thirty pounds and one mark, and of the aforesaid talliage. And for this grant fine and concord, the aforesaid Burgesses have remised and quitted claim for themselves and their heirs to the same *Alan* and his heirs, all damages which they said they have [sustained] by the aforesaid wrongs and injuries. AND BE IT KNOWN, that *Adam Walder, Thomas Fitz-Pagan, John de Brightewell, John le Duc, William Cole, Robert de Shebinton, John Fitz-Robert, Walter Slegh, Walter le Drak, Ralph Faber, Baldwin le Seler, Nicholas Bruttemer, Hugh Faber, Geoffrey Fitz-Katherine, Richard de Dusteberg, Walter de Poterugg, William de Berkhamstead, Roger Fitz-Philip, Simon le Tanner, Adam Merl, Walter Fitz-Warin, Alexander le Duk, Geoffrey Bouche, Henry la Neir, Adam Bil, Peter Kippelust,* Burgesses of *Wycombe,* came into the same Court, and testified that all other Burgesses of the same town ratified that Agreement, and granted the same : WE therefore ratifying and confirming the aforesaid final Agreement for us and our heirs, do grant and confirm the same with our seal, as the chirograph between them thereof made, one part whereof remains in the hands of the same Burgesses, and the other in the hands of the heirs of the same *Alan,* and the foot of the same chirograph in our treasury, reasonably testifieth. THESE being WITNESSES, *William* elect [Bishop] of *Valenciennes, Simon de Montfort, William*

Marginal notes:

£30 and one mark a year.

The rents, &c. payable by the men of the Abbess of *Godstowe,* to remain to the Burgesses. Saving reasonable aids to *Alan* when the King talliages his demesnes. *Alan* to acquit the Burgesses of the £20 a year, and the service of one knight's fee to the King. The cattle fair to continue in *Alan's* field. The Burgesses to have the customs therefrom. *Alan* to have the dung in the streets. If the Burgesses should not pay their rent or talliages, *Alan* may seize their cattle.

The Burgesses quit their claim for damages.

Twenty-six burgesses testified in Court that all the other burgesses ratified this agreement.

The King confirmed the same. One part of the Chirograph remains with the burgesses, and the other part *de Ralegh, Brother Geoffrey* our Almoner, *Geoffrey Despencer, Henry de Capell,* and others.

with the heirs of Jlam, and the foot of it in the King's treasury.

" **Given** by the hand of the venerable Father *R.* Bishop of *Chichester,* our Chancellor at *Oxford,* the twenty-fourth day of *June,* in the twenty-first year of our Reign."

(A true Translation.)

25th *April,* 1817.   W. ILLINGWORTH.

Deputy Keeper of the Records in the Tower.

THE THIRTEENTH OF EDWARD I.

12th JUNE, 1285.

Amongst the Records of the Court of Chancery preserved in the *Tower* of *London*, that is to say, on the Roll of Charters of the Thirteenth year of the Reign of King Edward the First, after the Conquest, No. 59, membrane 18, is thus contained :—

"For the BURGESSES of WYCUMBE.

"**The King,** to his Archbishops, &c. Greeting.—WE have inspected the Charter of Confirmation, which the Lord *Henry*, of famous memory, late King of *England*, our Father, made to the Burgesses of *Wycumbe*, in these words : HENRY, by the grace of God, King of *England*, Lord of *Ireland*, Duke of *Normandy* and *Aquitain*, and Earl of *Anjou*, to his Archbishops, Bishops, Abbots, Priors, Earls, Barons, Justices, Sheriffs, Reeves, Ministers, and all his Bailiffs, and faithful subjects, Greeting.—We have inspected the final Agreement made in our Court before our Justices at *Westminster*, between the Burgesses of *Wycumbe* and *Alan Basset*, in these words : THIS is the final Agreement made in the Court of the Lord the King at *Westminster*, from the day of the purification of the blessed Mary in one Month, in the tenth year of the reign of King HENRY, Son of King JOHN, before *Martin de Pateshull, Thomas de Moleton, Thomas de Heyden, Robert de Lexinton, Geoffry le Sauvage, Warine Fitz Johel,* Justices, and other faithful subjects of the Lord the King then there present, between the Burgesses of *Wycumbe*, Plaintiffs, and *Alan Basset*, concerning the wrongs and injuries which the same *Alan* did to the same Burgesses, as they have said, against the liberties, which the same Burgesses said they have of the gift of the ancestors of the Lord the King. And whereupon there was a plea between them in the same Court, that is to say, that the said *Alan*, as much as in him and his heirs is, hath granted to the same Burgesses, ALL the Borough of *Wycumbe*, with the Rents, Markets, and Fairs, and with all other things to a free Borough pertaining, without any reservation, and with all encrease and purchases which the said *Alan* hath made in the same Borough, and with the buildings of *Enavenethorn*, as the same *Alan* held such buildings, and with the rent of four

The King has inspected the Charter of confirmation granted by *Henry* the third.

Recapitulated.

Agreement in the Court at Westminster in the 10th year of *Henry* the Third,

Between the Burgesses of Wycumbe and *Alan Basset.*

Alan granted to the Burgesses all the Borough, with the Rents, Markets, and Fairs ; And the purchases he has made,

and the buildings of *Eaureetkorn*.
Except his demesnes, outlying Lands, and Mills, for £30 and one mark a year.

The rents, &c. payable by the men of the Abbess of *Godstow*, to remain to the Burgesses.

Saving reasonable aids to *Alan* when the King talliages his demesnes.
Alan to acquit the Burgesses of the £20 a year, and the service of one knight's fee to the King.
The cattle fair to continue in *Alan's* field.
The Burgesses to have the customs therefrom.
Alan to have the dung in the streets.
If the Burgesses should not pay their rent or talliages, *Alan* may seize their cattle.
The Burgesses quit their claim for damages.
Twenty-six Burgesses testified in Court that all the other Burgesses ratified this agreement.

shillings which *Geoffry Fitz Angod* used to pay, and with all other their appurtenances, and all things to that Borough pertaining, except the demesnes of the said *Alan* and his outlying Lands and his Mills, which entirely remain to the said *Alan* and his heirs, To HAVE and TO HOLD to the said Burgesses and their heirs at Fee farm of the said *Alan* and his heirs for ever: RENDERING therefore yearly thirty pounds and one mark of Silver at two terms of the year, that is to say, at the feast of *Saint Michael*, fifteen pounds and half a mark; and at the feast of *Saint Mary*, in *March*, fifteen pounds and half a mark; for all service and demand to the aforesaid *Alan* or to his heirs pertaining: And this Agreement was made between them, saving the fine made between the aforesaid *Alan* and the Abbess of *Godstowe*, so as, to wit, that the rents and customs which the men of the same Abbess are accustomed to render to the said *Alan*, shall remain to the same Burgesses and their heirs, in aid towards making up the aforesaid Fee farm, according to the fine before made between the same *Alan* and the aforesaid Abbess; saving to the said *Alan* and his heirs, his reasonable aids, when the Lord the King and his heirs shall talliage his demesnes throughout *England*. AND BE IT KNOWN, that the aforesaid *Alan* and his heirs, shall acquit the aforesaid Burgesses and their heirs, towards the Lord the King and his heirs, from the farm of twenty pounds, which the same *Alan* thereof oweth to the Lord the King; and likewise from the foreign service of one Knight's fee which the aforesaid *Alan* oweth out of his land of *Wycumbe*, which he hath of the gift of the Lord King JOHN: ALSO BE IT KNOWN, that the fair of cattle shall continue every year in the field of the same *Alan*, where and as it used before to be, saving to the said Burgesses and their heirs, the customs arising therefrom: And the said *Alan* and his heirs shall have the dung found in the streets of *Wicumbe*, as the same *Alan* used before to have the same; and if perchance the aforesaid Burgesses or their heirs shall not render to the said *Alan* and his heirs the aforesaid thirty pounds and one mark, at the terms appointed according as is aforesaid, or the talliages when they shall happen, it shall be lawful for the said *Alan* and his heirs to distrain the same Burgesses and their heirs, by their cattle found within the aforesaid Borough, and without, upon the fee of the said *Alan* and his heirs, until full payment of the aforesaid thirty pounds and one mark, and of the aforesaid talliage. And for this grant, fine and concord, the aforesaid Burgesses have remised and quitted claim for themselves and their heirs to the same *Alan* and his heirs, all damages which they said they have [sustained] by the aforesaid wrongs and injuries. AND BE IT KNOWN, that *Adam Walder, Thomas Fitz-Pagan, John de Brightewell, John le Duc, William Cole, Robert de Shebinton, John Fitz-Robert, Walter Slegh, Walter le Drak, Ralph Faber, Baldwin le Seler, Nicholas Bruttemer, Hugh Faber, Geoffrey Fitz-Katherine, Richard de Dusteberg, Walter de Poterugg, William de Berkhamsted, Roger Fitz-Philip, Simon le Tanner, Adam Merl, Walter Fitz-Warin, Alexander le Duk, Geoffrey Bouche, Henry la Neir, Adam Bil, Peter Kippedust*, Burgesses of *Wycombe*, came into the same Court, and testified that all other Burgesses of the same town ratified that

Agreement, and granted the same : WE therefore ratifying and confirming the aforesaid final Agreement for us and our heirs, do grant and confirm the same with our seal, as the chirograph between them thereof made, one part whereof remains in the hands of the same Burgesses, and the other in the hands of the heirs of the same *Alan*, and the foot of the same chirograph in our treasury, reasonably testifieth. THESE being WITNESSES, *William* elect [Bishop] of *Valenciennes, Simon de Montfort, William de Ralegh, Brother Geoffrey* our Almoner, *Geoffrey Despenser, Henry de Capell*, and others. GIVEN by the hand of the venerable Father *R.* Bishop of *Chichester*, our Chancellor at *Oxford*, the twenty-fourth day of *June*, in the twenty-first year of our Reign.

Now WE, the grant and confirmation aforesaid ratifying and confirming the same for us and our heirs, to the aforesaid Burgesses and their heirs, do grant, and confirm, as the final Agreement aforesaid, and the Charter of Confirmation aforesaid, justly and reasonably testify, and as the aforesaid Burgesses and their Ancestors the liberties aforesaid have hitherto reasonably used. THESE being WITNESSES, the venerable Fathers *R.* Bishop of *Bath* and *Wells*, and *W.* Bishop of *Norwich, Edmund* our Brother, *William de Valance* our Uncle, *Edmund* Earl of *Cornwall, Gilbert de Clare* Earl of *Gloucester* and *Hertford, Roger le Bigod* Earl of *Norfolk* and Marshal of *England, John De Warren* Earl of *Surry, William de Beauchamp* Earl of *Warwick, Robert Tibetot, William Leyburn, Robert Fitz-John*, our Steward and others.

" **Given** by our hand at *Westminster*, the twelfth day of *June*."

(A true Translation.)

25th *April*, 1817.

W. ILLINGWORTH,

Deputy Keeper of the Records in the Tower.

Side notes: The King confirmed the same. One part of the Chirograph remains with the Burgesses, and the other part with the heirs of *Alan*, and the foot of it in the King's treasury. *Confirmed.*

C C

THE FIRST OF HENRY IV.

18th MAY, 1400.

Amongst the Records of the Court of Chancery preserved in the *Tower* of *London*, that is to say, on the Roll of Charters of the first year of the Reign of King Henry the Fourth, part the 2d, membrane 15, is thus contained :—

CONFIRMATION, WYCUMBE.

The King has inspected the Charter of Edw. I.

Recapitulated.

"The King to his Archbishops, Bishops, &c. WE have inspected the Charter of the Lord *Edward*, heretofore King of *England* our Progenitor, made in these words: EDWARD by the grace of God King of *England*, Lord of *Ireland*, and Duke of *Aquitain*, to his Archbishops, Bishops, Abbots, Priors, Earls, Barons, Justices, Sherriffs, Reeves, Ministers, and all his Bailiffs, and faithful subjects, Greeting.—WE have inspected the Charter of Confirmation which the Lord HENRY of famous memory, late King of *England*, our Father, made to the Burgesses of *Wycombe*, in these words; HENRY, by the grace of God, King of *England*, Lord of *Ireland*, Duke of *Normandy* and *Aquitain*, and Earl of *Anjou*, to his Archbishops, Bishops, Abbots, Priors, Earls, Barons, Justices, Sherriffs, Reeves, Ministers, and all his Bailiffs, and faithful subjects, Greeting.—WE have inspected the final Agreement made in our Court before our Justices at *Westminster*, between the Burgesses of *Wycombe* and *Alan Basset*, in these words : THIS is the final Agreement made in the Court of the Lord the King at *Westminster*, from the day of the purification of the blessed Mary in one Month, in the tenth year of the reign of King HENRY, Son of King JOHN, before *Martin de Pateshull*, *Thomas de Moleton*, *Thomas de Heyden*, *Robert de Lexinton*, *Geoffrey le Sauvage*, *Warine Fitz Johel*, Justices, and other faithful subjects of the Lord the King then there present, between the Burgesses of *Wycombe*, Plaintiffs, and *Alan Basset*, concerning the wrongs and injuries which the same *Alan* did to the same Burgesses, as they have said, against the liberties, which the same Burgesses said they have of the gift of the ancestors of the Lord the King. And whereupon there was a plea between them in the same Court, that is to say, that the said *Alan*, as much as in him and his heirs is, hath granted to the same Burgesses, ALL the Borough of

Agreement in the Court at Westminster in the 10th year of Henry the Third,

Between the Burgesses of Wycumbe and Alan Basset.

Alan granted to the Bur- ges all the

Wycumbe, with the Rents, Markets, and Fairs, and with all other things to a free Borough pertaining, without any reservation, and with all encrease and purchases which the said *Alan* hath made in the same Borough, and with the buildings of *Enavenethorn*, as the same *Alan* held such buildings, and with the rent of four shillings which *Geoffry Fitz Angod* used to pay, and with all other their appurtenances, and all things to that Borough pertaining, except the demesnes of the said *Alan* and his outlying Lands and his Mills, which entirely remain to the said *Alan* and his heirs, To HAVE and TO HOLD to the said Burgesses and their heirs at Fee farm of the said *Alan* and his heirs for ever: RENDERING therefore yearly thirty pounds and one mark of Silver at two terms of the year, that is to say, at the feast of *Saint Michael*, fifteen pounds and half a mark; and at the feast of *Saint Mary*, in *March*, fifteen pounds and half a mark; for all service and demand to the aforesaid *Alan* or to his heirs pertaining: And this Agreement was made between them, saving the fine made between the aforesaid *Alan* and the Abbess of *Godstowe*, so as, to wit, that the rents and customs which the men of the same Abbess are accustomed to render to the said *Alan*, shall remain to the same Burgesses and their heirs, in aid towards making up the aforesaid Fee farm, according to the fine before made between the same *Alan* and the aforesaid Abbess; saving to the said *Alan* and his heirs, his reasonable aids, when the Lord the King and his heirs shall talliage his demesnes throughout *England*. AND BE IT KNOWN, that the aforesaid *Alan* and his heirs, shall acquit the aforesaid Burgesses and their heirs, towards the Lord the King and his heirs, from the Fee farm of twenty pounds, which the same *Alan* thereof oweth to the Lord the King; and likewise from the foreign service of one Knight's fee which the aforesaid *Alan* oweth out of his land of *Wycumbe*, which he hath of the gift of the Lord King JOHN: Also BE IT KNOWN, that the fair of cattle shall continue every year in the field of the same *Alan*, where and as it used before to be, saving to the said Burgesses and their heirs, the customs arising therefrom: And the said *Alan* and his heirs shall have the dung found in the Streets of *Wicumbe*, as the same *Alan* used before to have the same; and if perchance the aforesaid Burgesses or their heirs shall not render to the said *Alan* and his heirs the aforesaid thirty pounds and one mark, at the terms appointed according as is aforesaid, or the talliages when they shall happen, it shall be lawful for the said *Alan* and his heirs to distrain the same Burgesses and their heirs, by their cattle found within the aforesaid Borough, and without, upon the fee of the said *Alan* and his heirs, until full payment of the aforesaid thirty pounds and one mark, and of the aforesaid talliage. And for this grant fine and concord, the aforesaid Burgesses have remised and quitted claim for themselves and their heirs to the same *Alan* and his heirs, all damages which they said they have [sustained] by the aforesaid wrongs and injuries. AND BE IT KNOWN, that *Adam Walder, Thomas Fitz-Pagan, John de Brightewell, John le Duc, William Cole, Robert de Shebinton, John Fitz-Robert, Walter Slegh, Walter le Drak, Ralph Faber, Baldwin le Seler, Nicholas Bruttemer, Hugh Faber, Geoffrey Fitz-Katherine,*

the other bur-
gesses ratified
this agreement.

Richard de Dusteberg, Walter de Poterugg, William de Berkhamsted, Roger Fitz-Philip, Simon le Tanner, Adam Merl, Walter Fitz-Warin, Alexander le Duk, Geoffry Bouche, Henry la Neir, Adam Bil, Peter Kippelust, Burgesses of *Wycombe,* came into the same Court, and testified that all other Burgesses of the same town ratified that Agreement, and granted the same: WE therefore ratifying and confirming the aforesaid final Agreement for us and our heirs, do grant and confirm the same with our seal, as the chirograph between them thereof made, one part whereof remains in the hands of the same Burgesses, and the other in the hands of the heirs of the same *Alan,* and the foot of the same chirograph in our treasury, reasonably testifieth. THESE being WITNESSES, *William* elect [Bishop] of *Valenciennes, Simon de Montfort, William de Ralegh, Brother Geoffrey* our Almoner, *Geoffrey Despenser, Henry de Capell,* and others. GIVEN by the hand of the venerable Father *R.* Bishop of *Chichester* our Chancellor, at *Oxford,* the twenty-fourth day of *June,* in the twenty-first year of our Reign. Now WE, the grant and confirmation aforesaid ratifying and confirming the same for us and our heirs, to the aforesaid Burgesses and their heirs, do grant, and confirm, as the final Agreement aforesaid, and the Charter of Confirmation aforesaid, justly and reasonably testify, and as the aforesaid Burgesses and their Ancestors the liberties aforesaid have hitherto reasonably used. THESE being WITNESSES, the venerable Fathers *R.* Bishop of *Bath* and *Wells,* and *W.* Bishop of *Norwich,* **Edmund** our Brother, *William de Valance* our Uncle, *Edmund* Earl of *Cornwall,* **Gilbert de Clare** Earl of *Gloucester* and *Hertford, Roger le Bigod* Earl of *Norfolk* and Marshal of *England, John De Warren* Earl of *Surry, William de Beauchamp* Earl of *Warwick, Robert Tibetot, William Leyburn, Robert Fitz-John* our Steward, and others. GIVEN by our hand at *Westminster,* the twelfth day of *June,* in the thirteenth year of our reign.

The King con-
firmed the
same.
One part of
the Chiro-
graph remains
with the bur-
gesses, and
the other part
with the heirs
of *Alan,* and
the foot of it
in the King's
treasury.

Confirmed by
Edw. I.

Confirmed by
Henry IV.

"Now WE, the grants and confirmations aforesaid, ratifying and confirming the same, for us and our heirs, as much as in us is, do accept, approve, and to the aforesaid Burgesses, their heirs and successors, do grant and confirm, as the final Agreement and Charters aforesaid justly and reasonably testify: MOREOVER being willing to do more ample grace to the same Burgesses, of our special grace, we have granted for us and our heirs, as much as in us is, to the same Burgesses, that ALTHOUGH they or their predecessors, any one or more of the liberties in the final Agreement and Charters aforesaid contained in any case arising hitherto have not used; NEVERTHELESS the same Burgesses, their heirs and successors, may for the future, fully enjoy and use those liberties, and every of them, without the hindrance or impediment of us or of our heirs, the Justices, Escheators, Sheriffs, or other Bailiffs, or Ministers, of us or of our heirs whomsoever: THESE being WITNESSES, the venerable Fathers *Thomas* Archbishop of Canterbury Primate of all *England, R.* Bishop of *London, W.* Bishop of *Winchester, H.* Bishop of *Lincoln, Edmund* Duke of *York* our most dear Uncle, *Thomas* Earl of *Warwick, Henry* Earl of *Northumberland, Ralph* Earl of *Westmoreland, John Searle* our Chancellor, *John Norbury* our Treasurer, *William Roos de*

Although any
of the liberties
have not been
used, the bur-
gesses may
enjoy them
in future.

Hamlak Knight, *John Grey de Coaenore* Knight, *Reginala de Grey de Ruthyn* Knight, *Thomas Rempston* Knight Steward of our Household, Master *Richard Clifford* Keeper of our Privy Seal, and others.

" **Giben** by the KING's hand at *Westminster*, the eighteenth day of *May*.

By the KING himself for forty shillings paid into the Hanaper."

(A true Translation.)

5th *May*, 1817.   W. ILLINGWORTH,

Record Office, Tower.

THE FIRST OF MARY.

15TH NOVEMBER, 1553.

The Queen has inspected the Charter of Edw. 1.

Recapitulated.

𝕸𝖆𝖗𝖞, by the grace of God Queen of England, France, and Ireland, Defender of the Faith, and Supreme Head of the Church in England and Ireland. To all whom these present writings shall come greeting. We have inspected Letters patent of confirmation of our Lord and Father Edward the I., heretofore King of England, made in these words: Henry, by the grace of God, King of England and France, and Lord of Ireland, to the Archbishops, Bishops, Abbots, Priors, Dukes, Earls, Barons, Justices, Sheriffs, Reeves, Ministers, and to all Bailiffs and faithful people greeting.—We have inspected a Charter granted in these words by our Lord and predecessor, Edward, King of England, Lord of Ireland, and Duke of Acquitain. To the Archbishops, Bishops, Abbots, Priors, &c., greeting. We have inspected a Charter of Confirmation which our Lord and predecessor Henry of gracious memory, and late King of England, granted to the Burgesses of Wycumbe in these words: Henry, by the grace of God King of England, Lord of Ireland, Normandy, and Acquitain and Earl of Anjou, To the Archbishops, Bishops, Abbots, Priors, &c., greeting. We have inspected a final Agreement made before our Justices at our Court of Westminster, between the Burgesses of Wycumbe and Alan Basset in these words. This is the final Agreement made in the Court of our Lord the King at Westminster in one month from the day of the Purification of the Blessed Mary in the tenth year of the reign of king Henry, son of King John, before Martin de Pateshall, Thomas de Woleton, Thomas de Heyden, Robert de Lexington, Balfro Lee Mannas, Warren Fitz Joel, Justices and other faithful subjects of the King then present. The Burgesses of Wycombe Complainants and Alan Basset concerning the wrongs and injuries which the said Alan Basset had done to the said Burgesses contrary to the liberties of the said Burgesses which they say they enjoy by grant of the ancestors of our Lord the King, AND whereupon it was pleaded between them in the same Court, to wit The said Alan Basset granted as much as in him and his heirs is to the said Burgesses ALL the Borough of Wycombe with the revenues markets and fairs, and all other things belonging to a free Borough or in any way appertaining, together with all increase and purchases which the said Alan

Agreement in the Court at Westminster in the 10th year of Henry the Third,

Between the burgesses of Wycumbe and Alan Basset.

Alan granted to the Burgesses all the Borough, with the Rents, Markets, and

hath made in the Borough, together with the Building of Enavenethorn as the said Alan held such Buildings and with the rent of Four shillings, which Balfro Fitz Angod was accustomed to pay and with all other their appurtenances and with all things pertaining to that Borough. The demesnes of the said Alan excepted, and his outlying lands and his mills which shall remain wholly to the said Alan and his heirs To HAVE AND TO HOLD to the said Burgesses and their heirs at fee farm of the aforesaid Alan and his heirs for ever, PAYING yearly thirty pounds and one mark of silver at two periods of the year, namely, at the feast of Saint Michael fifteen pounds and half a mark, and at the feast of the Blessed Mary in March fifteen pounds and half a mark for all service and demand of the aforesaid Alan or to his heirs pertaining, AND this Agreement is made between them, saving the fine made between the aforesaid Alan and the Abbess of Godstowe so as to wit Those rents and customs which her men are accustomed to render the said Alan shall remain to the Burgesses and their heirs in aid of the aforesaid fee first made according to the fine first made between the said Alan and the aforesaid Abbess, saving to the said Alan and his heirs his reasonable aids when the Lord the King and his heirs shall talliage his dominions throughout England, AND BE IT KNOWN that the aforesaid Alan and his heirs shall acquit the aforesaid Burgesses and their heirs towards the Lord the King and his heirs of the farm of twenty pounds which the said Alan then owed to the Lord the King, AND likewise of the fee of the foreign service of one knight which the aforesaid renders for the land of Wycombe which he held by the gift of our Lord King John, AND BE IT ALSO KNOWN that the cattle fairs shall continue to be held in each year on the Land of the said Alan, where it was always accustomed to be, reserving to the said Burgesses and their heirs the dues arising therefrom, and the said Alan and his heirs shall have the dung found in the streets of Wycombe as the said Alan before that was accustomed to have, AND if perchance the aforesaid Burgesses or their heirs shall fail in paying to the said Alan and his heirs the aforesaid thirty pounds and aforesaid mark at the appointed periods according as aforesaid or the talliages when they shall happen, it shall be lawful for the said Alan and his heirs to distrain on the said Burgesses or their heirs the cattle within or without the aforesaid Borough upon the fee of the said Alan and his heirs to the use and discharge of the aforesaid thirty pounds and one mark, and the aforesaid talliages, AND for this concession grant and agreement the aforesaid Burgesses remit and quit claim for themselves and their heirs of the said Alan and his heirs all damages which they say they have sustained through the aforesaid wrongs and injuries, AND BE IT KNOWN that Adam Walder, Thomas Fitz Pagan, John de Brightwell, John le Duc, William Cole, Robert de Shobinton, John Fitz Robert, Walter Sleigh, Walter le Drake, Ralph Faber, Baldwin le Weler, Nicholas Bruttemar, Hugh Faber, Balfro Fitz Catherine, Richard de Dusteburg, Walter de Pederug, William de Berkhampstead, Roger Fitz Philip, Simon le Tanner, Adam Serle, Walter Fitz Warrene,

---

Fairs; And the purchases he has made, and the buildings of *Enavenethorn*, except his demesnes, outlying Lands, and Mills, for £30 and one mark a year.

The rents, &c. payable by the men of the Abbess of *Godstowe*, to remain to the Burgesses.

Saving reasonable aids to *Alan* when the King talliages his demesnes. *Alan* to acquit the Burgesses of the £20 a year, and the service of one knight's fee to the King. The cattle fair to continue in *Alan's* field. The Burgesses to have the customs therefrom. *Alan* to have the dung in the streets. If the Burgesses should not pay their rent or talliages, *Alan* may seize their cattle. The Burgesses quit their claim for damages.

Twenty-six burgesses testified in Court that all the other burgesses ratified this agreement.

Alexander le Duc, Balfro Buche, Henry le Neir, Adam Byll, Peter Kippesone, Burgesses of Wycombe came into the same Court and that they and all the other Burgesses of the same Town have ratified and consented to the Agreement, We therefore ratifying and granting the aforesaid final Agreement for us and our heirs do approve and confirm with our seal as the chirograph made between them, one part remaining in the possession of the Burgesses, another in the possession of the heirs of the said Alan, and the foot of the said chirograph in our treasury reasonably testifieth. THESE being Witnesses, William elect (Bishop) of Valenciennes, Simon de Montfort, William de Raleigh, our Brother Balfro, our Almoner, Balfrò Despenser, Henry de Capel, and others. GIVEN under the hands of the Venerable Father, R. the Bishop of Chichester our Chancellor at Oxford on the twenty fourth day of June in the twenty first day of our reign. But we for the concession and confirmation of the aforesaid, ratifying and granting of the aforesaid for ourselves and our heirs to the before mentioned Burgesses and their heirs grant and confirm as a final Agreement aforesaid and charter of confirmation aforesaid justly and reasonably testifieth and as the aforesaid Burgesses and their ancestors, the liberties aforesaid have reasonably used. THESE being Witnesses, the Venerable Fathers, Richard, Bishop of Bath and Wells, and William, Bishop of Norwich, Edmund our Brother, William de Valence, our Uncle, Edmund, Earl of Cornwall, Gilbert de Clare, Earl of Glocester and Hertford, Roger le Bigod, Earl of Norfolk, Marshall of England, John de Warrene, Earl of Surrey, William de Beauchamp, Earl of Warwick, Robert Tibotot, William de Leyburn, Robert Fitz John, our Seneschalt [steward] and others. GIVEN under our hand at Westminster on the twelfth day of June in the twelfth year of our reign. BUT WE for the concession and confirmation of the aforesaid, ratifying and granting to them for us and our heirs as much as in us is Do accept and approve, and to the before mentioned Burgesses and their heirs we grant and confirm as the final Agreement and Charter aforesaid justly and reasonably testifieth besides being willing to confer a greater favour on the said Burgesses we grant it in our special grace for us and our heirs as much as in us and our heirs is to the said Burgesses the liberties enjoyed by them or their ancestors one and all as a final Agreement and Charter aforesaid, and if any cause of dispute should arise of what they have not hitherto been in full possession nevertheless the Burgesses their heirs and assigns with their liberties or any of them shall fully use and enjoy them without any hindrance or impediment of either our heirs, Justices, Escheators, Sheriffs, or others Bailiffs or Ministers of our Husband our heirs to every one of whom these witnesseth, Thomas, Archbishop of Canterbury and primate of all England, Richard of London, William of Winchester, Henry of Lincoln, Bishops, Edmund, Duke of York, our dear Uncle, Thomas of Warwick, Henry of Northumberland, Ralph of Westmoreland, Earls, John Serle Chancellor, John Norburry our Treasurer, William roos de Hamlec, John Grey de Codmore, Reginald Grey de Ruthen, Thomas Kempsone, Master of our Household, Knights,

Master Richard Clyforde, keeper ot our privy seal, and others. GIVEN under our hand at Westminster on the eighteenth day of May in the first year of our reign. BUT WE for the concession and confirmation of the aforesaid, ratifying and granting them for ourselves and our heirs as much as in us is we accept and approve but Now we grant and confirm to the Burgesses aforesaid of Wycombe as a final Agreement and Charter aforesaid justly and reasonably testifieth, IN TESTIMONY WHEREOF we have ordered these our letters patent to be drawn in WITNESS myself, GIVEN at Westminster on the fifteenth day of November in the first year of our Reign.

The Queen confirmed the same.

L. S.

THE FIFTH AND SIXTH OF PHILIP AND MARY.

27TH AUGUST, 1558.

First Part of Patents in the Fifth and Sixth Years of the Reign of King Philip and Queen Mary :—

Concerning the Mayor, Bailiffs, and Burgesses of Chepping Wycombe, of a grant to them and their Successors.

Wycombe has always been a market town and free borough of mayor, bailiffs, and burgesses.

THE KING AND QUEEN, To all to whom, &c. Greeting.—WHEREAS as We understand the town of *Chepinge Wycombe*, otherwise called *Wycombe*, in our County of *Buckingham*, as well by a Charter of the Lord *Henry* the Third, formerly King of *England*, ancestor of us the aforesaid Queen, and by Charters of other Progenitors of us the said Queen, formerly Kings of *England*, as by virtue and force of the custom there (from time whereof memory doth not exist) had and used, hath always been a market town and perpetual free Borough, and incorporated of the Mayor Bailiffs and Burgesses of the same town, for all the time aforesaid; and have had and obtained various liberties, franchises, acquittances, and immunities there continually, from the time abovesaid, and the same have used and enjoyed without interruption, and especially by the intent and meaning of the premises, have been always from the same time pleadable and impleaded by the name of Mayor Bailiffs and Burgesses, of the town of *Wycombe*, and have had and held many lands, tenements, and hereditaments, within the same Borough; and at present have and hold to them and their successors, as in right of the same Borough for ever. And all and all manner of lands, and tenements, and possessions whatsoever, being within the same Borough, for all the time aforesaid, from time to time deviseable, have been, and at present are, devised at the will of the possessors thereof, and the same Burgesses for the time aforesaid have had and used amongst

Might hold two Fairs yearly.

other things, that in right of the same Borough, two fairs may be there held in every year, that is to say, one to be holden on the Feast of the Translation of *Saint Thomas* the Martyr, and continue until noon of the morrow of the day of the same Feast; and the other to be holden on the Feast of the Exaltation of

Market and mercantile guild.

the *Holy Cross*, and to continue until noon of the morrow of the same Feast; and one market there to be holden in every week, that is to say, on Friday, and a

Mercantile Guild with a Hall and other customs and liberties to such Guild appertaining. So that no one who should not be of the same Mercantile Guild might be able to sell or buy within the same Borough, Flax, Wool, or Thread, or Skins, or Hydes, or any other thing to such Mercantile Guild appertaining, unless by those who should be of the same Guild. And also for the same time have had all Pleas and Plaints within the same Borough happening there, for whatsoever causes, except those which appertain to the Crown; with these liberties, that they should in no wise plead or be impleaded concerning their tenements being in the same Borough, by writ of *Mort d' Ancester*, but should be brought within the same Borough, by the law of the same Borough. And that it should be lawful for them for the debts of all persons arising within the same Borough, to distrain, and for their loans made within the same Borough. And that they should have of foreign men due Toll and due customs. And they have been free and quit for all the time aforesaid of Toll in all places throughout *England*. And that the assize of victuals made and constituted by good men of the said Borough, should be kept and preserved by their Bailiffs. And the same Mayor Bailiffs and Burgesses, by the name of Mayor Bailiffs and Burgesses of the Town of *Wycombe*, hold, and have long held, the same Town or Borough of us, and the Progenitors of us, the aforesaid Queen, formerly Kings of England, to fee farm; RENDERING therefore yearly, a certain yearly rent, which now by Charter of the Progenitors of us, the said Queen, is payable to the Dean and Canons of the Free Chapel of the Queen within our Castle of *Windsor* within the County of *Berks;* As in the said Charters, which certain of the Progenitors of us, the said Queen, have confirmed, is more fully contained. AND WHEREAS now our beloved and faithful subjects of our Town or Borough of *Wycombe* aforesaid, as well for the greater security and assurance of the premises, as for the rule and their better government and improvement of the same Town or Borough, have humbly besought us, that we would condescend not only to confirm, approve, and ratify, the Town or Borough aforesaid, and all and singular other the premises above expressed and specified, and also all the singular franchises, liberties, privileges, commodities, profits, and emoluments, whatsoever, to the same Town or Borough appertaining and belonging, or in the same Town and Borough from the time aforesaid used, approved, or allowed; but also, that by this our present Charter, we would condescend to incorporate anew the Town aforesaid and the inhabitants thereof, and to make and create them a Corporation of Mayor Bailiffs and Burgesses, in manner and form following: KNOW YE, that We consenting to the petition aforesaid, and considering that our aforesaid subjects, of whose fidelity and circumspection towards us, not only by the relation of our nobles, peers, and subjects; but also, of our certain and Royal knowledge, especially in the times of the rebellions of *John* late Duke of *Northumberland*, and Sir *Thomas Wyatt* Knight, lately attainted and convicted of High Treason and their Accomplices, against us lately attempted, have most faithfully adhered to us and have manfully resisted the same rebellions. And that our same subjects may be the better and more fully certified of our Royal and Queenly affection and favor, which we have towards them on that account; THEREFORE of our especial grace, and of our certain knowledge and meer motion, willing to make to our beloved subjects of the said Town or Borough of *Wycombe* a more ample Charter in that behalf, Do, as much as in us lies, accept, approve, and ratify, and by this our present Charter grant and confirm to the said now Mayor Bailiffs and Burgesses, their heirs and successors; ALL AND SINGULAR the liberties, franchises, privileges, acquittances, immunities, grants, free customs, rights and laws aforesaid, and other things aforesaid as well by the said Burgesses and their predecessors heretofore there used, as to the same Burgesses by the Charters of the Progenitors of us the said Queen in any wise granted: AND MOREOVER of our further and more abundant grace, WE have granted for us, the heirs and successors of us the said Queen, as much as in us lies, to the same now Mayor Bailiffs and Burgesses, and their successors, that although the same now Mayor Bailiffs and Burgesses, or their predecessors, may not hitherto continually have used any or either of the liberties, franchises, privileges, acquittances, immunities, grants, and customs, aforesaid, or any other things in any Charters or Letters of the said predecessors of us the aforesaid Queen contained and specified for any cause or impediment: NEVERTHELESS the same now Mayor Bailiffs and Burgesses and their heirs and successors, Burgesses of the said Borough of *Wycombe*, from henceforth fully, freely, and with impunity shall have and use all and singular the liberties, franchises, privileges, acquittances, immunities, grants, customs, rights, and pre-eminences, as well in the same Letters or Charters contained, as by the said now Mayor Bailiffs and Burgesses, or their predecessors, heretofore used, without the hindrance, impeachment, disturbance, molestation, vexation, disquieting, or impediment of us, or of the heirs or successors of us the aforesaid Queen, the Justices, Escheators, and Sheriffs, Coroners, Bailiffs, or other Officers or Ministers of us, or of the heirs or successors of us the said Queen whomsoever; any statutes, ordinances, provisions, establishments, acts or appointments enacted or made, or to be enacted or made, or judgments rendered, and Charters or Letters Patent of us, or of the ancestors or predecessors of us the said Queen, in times past, to the contrary made or granted, or other things, causes, or matters whatsoever to the contrary notwithstanding. AND FURTHER of our more ample grace, and of our certain knowledge and mere motion; WE WILL, ordain, constitute and grant, for us and the heirs and successors of us the said Queen, by these presents, That the said Town of *Wycombe* in our County of *Buckingham*, from henceforth may and shall be a free Borough Corporate, in deed, fact, and name, for ever of one Mayor, two Bailiffs, and Burgesses, by the name of Mayor Bailiffs and Burgesses of the Borough of *Wycombe*. And that the Mayor Bailiffs and Burgesses of the same Borough, shall be from henceforth one Commonalty, and one body corporate and politic in deed, fact, and name, for ever by the name of Mayor Bailiffs and Burgesses of the same Borough of *Wycombe*. And that, from henceforth for ever they may and shall be a body corporate, and one perpetual commonalty, in deed, fact, and name, and shall have perpetual succession. And the same Mayor Bailiffs and Burgesses, one Commonalty, and one body corporate and politic, of themselves really and fully We do create, erect, ordain, make, constitute, declare, and incorporate, for us and the heirs and successors of us, the said Queen for ever, by these presents. And the same Mayor Bailiffs and Burgesses by the name of Mayor Bailiffs and Burgesses of the Borough of *Wycombe*, from henceforth for ever, We will and command by these presents, to be called and named : and that by the same name, and under the same name, they shall and may be able to plead and be impleaded, sue and defend and be defended, answer and be answered, in all Courts and Places of us, and the heirs and successors of us the aforesaid Queen, and in other Courts and Places whatsoever, as well SPIRITUAL as TEMPORAL, as well in all and singular actions, suits, plaints, causes, and demands, real and personal, or mixt, as in all and singular other causes and business, and matters whatsoever. And that the same Mayor Bailiffs and Burgesses, and their successors, may and shall have a Common Seal for doing and treating of all and singular their affairs : And that it shall and may be lawful to them and their successors, at their pleasure, the same Seal to break, change, and make anew. AND ALSO WE WILL, and by these presents, for us and the heirs and successors of us the said Queen, constitute and ordain, that twelve Burgesses may and shall be and be named, principal Burgesses of the aforesaid Borough of *Wycombe* aforesaid ; all of which same Burgesses, WE WILL SHALL BE DWELLING AND INHABITING WITHIN THE BOROUGH OF WYCOMBE AFORESAID. AND ALSO We will, and by these presents, for us and the heirs and successors of us the aforesaid Queen, grant and ordain, that in the said Borough of *Wycombe*, there may and shall be one officer who shall be called and shall be, Steward of the same Borough, to do and execute all and everything which to his office doth appertain and ought to appertain, by himself or by his sufficient deputy or deputies ; That all and everything to his office appertaining may in due manner take effect : FURTHER KNOW YE, that WE of our especial grace, and of our certain knowledge and meer motion, Do assign, nominate, make, and ordain, by these presents for us, and the heirs and successors of us the aforesaid Queen, our beloved *Robert Gravet*, an honest man and inhabitant of the said Borough of *Wycombe*, faithfully by his oath to execute the office of Mayor of the Borough aforesaid, until Thursday next before the feast of *Saint Michael* the Archangel next ensuing, and from the same Thursday, until another Person elected shall be in due manner sworn faithfully to execute the same office. AND ALSO, We assign, nominate, ordain, and make, *Thomas Farmer*, Gentleman, to be the first and present Steward of the said Borough of *Wycombe*, to exercise, do, and execute justice, and other things which to the office of Steward doth appertain or ought to appertain, by himself or by his sufficient deputy or deputies. AND ALSO, WE HAVE assigned, nominated, made and ordained, our beloved *Thomas Raveninge* and *Rowland Rutte*, honest men, and inhabitants

May plead and be impleaded.

And have a common seal.

Principal burgesses to dwell within the borough.

Steward.

Robert Gravet first mayor.

Thomas Farmer first steward.

First bailiffs.

of the said Borough of *Wycombe*, to be the first and present Bailiffs of the Borough of *Wycombe* aforesaid, and faithfully by their oath to execute the office of Bailiffs of the same Borough of *Wycombe*, until the feast of the Annunciation of the Blessed *Virgin Mary* next ensuing; and from the same feast until other persons elected shall be in due manner sworn, faithfully to execute the same office. AND FURTHER, WE WILL, and of our certain knowledge and meer motion, for us and the heirs and successors of us the said Queen, by these presents, grant to the aforesaid Mayor Bailiffs and Burgesses of the Borough of *Wycombe* aforesaid, that they and their successors shall have and hold, and shall and may be able to have and hold a

Court before the mayor bailiffs and steward or their deputies

certain Court before the Mayor Bailiffs and Steward of the Borough aforesaid, or their or either of their sufficient deputy or deputies, being Burgesses of the Borough aforesaid, in a certain Common Hall, called THE GUILDHALL, or other place in the same Borough more convenient, to be holden from three weeks to three weeks, or oftener at their pleasure for ever. And that the same Mayor Bailiffs and Steward, or their or any of their sufficient deputy or deputies, shall have full power and au-

To determine all debts, &c.

thority to hear and determine, in the same Court by plaints, in the same Court to be levied, all and singular pleas, plaints, and actions, concerning all and all manner of debts, accounts, covenants, contracts, trespasses by force of arms or otherwise, in contempt of us or the heirs or successors of us, the said Queen, made covenants, detinues, contempts, deceits, wythernam, and other things and actions, real, personal, and mixt whatsoever, within the aforesaid Borough of *Wycombe*, and the limits, bounds, and liberties thereof, in any wise arising, or to arise, happening, or to happen; provided the same debts, accounts, covenants, contracts, and other actions,

not exceeding £20.

personal or mixt, shall not exceed the sum or value of twenty pounds. And the same Mayor Bailiffs and Steward, or their or any of their sufficient deputy or deputies for the time being, upon such questions, pleas, and plaints, and actions, shall have power, authority, and faculty, against the persons defending, against whom such plaints, pleas, or actions shall happen to be levied and moved in the afore-

By attachment and distress.

said Court, to draw them in plea by summons of attachment and distress, according to the law and custom of our kingdom of *England*, and for default of chattels and lands of the defendant within the Borough aforesaid, and the limits, bounds, and liberties thereof, where or by which they might be summoned, attached, or distrained by attachment of their bodies, and severally to hear all and singular the aforesaid matters, and to deduce and determine the like process, considerations, and executions of judgment, by which the like matters may be deduced and determined in our Court of our County of Buckingham, before our Sheriffs, Justices, or Ministers, of the same Court. And that the same Mayor Bailiffs and Steward aforesaid, or their or any of their sufficient deputy or deputies, Burgesses of the Borough of *Wycombe* aforesaid, for the time being, shall hear and determine all and singular the same matters, according to the laws, statutes, and constitutions of this kingdom of *England*, from time to time, within the said Borough of *Wycombe*. And that the said Mayor Bailiffs and Burgesses of the said Borough of *Wycombe*, and their successors, shall have and receive, and may have and receive, ALL fines, services, issues, and other profits whatsoever, of and in the Court aforesaid, arising, coming, accruing, or happening; to the behoof, and use, and profit, which to the said Mayor, and Bailiffs, and Burgesses, shall seem best to be expended. AND MOREOVER WE WILL, and for us and the heirs and successors of us the aforesaid Queen, by these presents, grant to the aforesaid Mayor Bailiffs and Burgesses of the said Borough of *Wycombe* and their successors, that they and their successors may and shall have full power, authority, and faculty, whensoever it shall please them to assign, nominate, constitute, and appoint, one fit person to the office of Under-Bailiff of the aforesaid Borough, to serve in the Court aforesaid, and for making, executing, and performing, proclamation, arrest, process, execution, and other things to the same office incumbent, belonging, or appertaining, within the aforesaid Borough and parish of *Wycombe*, and the limits, bounds, and precincts thereof. AND FURTHER of our more ample grace, for the better maintenance and support of the said Borough of *Wycombe*, WE WILL and for us, and the heirs and successors of us, the aforesaid Queen, by these presents grant, to the aforesaid Mayor Bailiffs and Burgesses of the aforesaid Borough of *Wycombe*; That the same Mayor Bailiffs and Burgesses, by the name of Mayor Bailiffs and Burgesses of the Borough of *Wycombe*, may and shall be persons able and capable in the law, without a writ of *Ad quod Damnum* to be obtained, prosecuted, and returned, in the Court of Chancery of us or the heirs or successors of us, the said Queen, to purchase, receive, and take to them and their successors or otherwise, lordships, manors, lands, tenements, rents, revenues, services, hereditaments, liberties, jurisdictions, and privileges whatsoever, situate, lying, and being within the Borough aforesaid, which are not holden immediately of us in capite nor by Knight's service, nor of any other person or persons by Knight's service; so that the same lordships, manors, lands, tenements, rents, hereditaments, liberties, franchises, rights, jurisdictions and privileges, shall not in the whole exceed the yearly value of twenty pounds. AND FURTHER WE WILL, and by these presents, for us and the heirs and successors of us, the aforesaid Queen, grant to the aforesaid Mayor Bailiffs and Burgesses of the said Borough of *Wycombe* and their successors, that the same Mayor Bailiffs and Burgesses and their successors, shall have and hold, and shall and may be able to have and hold for ever, one Market on every Friday in every Week, to be holden and kept in the said Borough of *Wycombe*; and two Marts or Fairs to be holden and kept there yearly, one of which marts and fairs shall begin at noon of the day of the Feast of the Translation of *Saint Thomas* the Martyr, and continue until noon of the morrow of the day of the same Feast; and the other of the same marts or fairs shall begin at noon of the day of the Feast of the Exaltation of the *Holy Cross*, and continue until noon of the morrow of the day of the same Feast, together with a Court of Piepowder, there to be holding during the

Marginal notes:

Fines to go to the corporation.

Under bailiff.

Corporation may purchase lands &c. within the borough,

If not held in capite, nor by knight's service, nor worth more than £20 a year.

Market.

Two fairs.

Court of Piepowder.

time of the same marts or fairs, together with stallage, piccage, toll, fines, and amerciaments, and all other profits, commodities, and emoluments whatsoever, to such market, marts, or fairs and Court of Piepowder, or by reason thereof coming, accruing, arising or happening, and with all commodities and free customs, to such market, marts, or fairs appertaining or belonging, to be taken and converted to the proper use and behoof of the said Mayor Bailiffs and Burgesses, and the commonalty of the aforesaid Borough of *Wycombe*, for the time being. WHEREFORE WE WILL, and firmly command, for us and the heirs and successors of us the aforesaid Queen, that the same Mayor Bailiffs and Burgesses, and their successors for ever, freely, peaceably, and quietly, shall use and have the aforesaid market and fairs, with all the commodities and free customs to such market and fairs appertaining or belonging. AND MOREOVER of our further Grace, WE WILL, and by these presents, for us and the heirs and successors of us the said Queen, grant to the aforesaid Mayor Bailiffs and Burgesses, and their successors, that they for ever shall have, use and enjoy, a

Gaol.

Mayor, bailiffs and steward may commit.

prison or gaol in any convenient place within the same Borough, to be limited and assigned according to their discretions for ever, and that they the aforesaid Mayor, Bailiffs and Steward, and every one of them, shall and may be able to commit to the prison or gaol aforesaid, safely and securely there to be kept, until they shall be delivered therefrom according to the form of law, all and singular persons who by the aforesaid Mayor Bailiffs and Burgesses or their Deputies, or the Stewards whomsoever within the same Borough at any time hereafter shall happen to be apprehended, or taken for any crime or offence deserving imprisonment. AND FURTHER KNOW YE, that We of our especial Grace, and of our certain knowledge and meer motion, for us and the heirs and successors of us the aforesaid Queen, Do grant to the aforesaid Mayor Bailiffs and Burgesses of the said Borough of *Wycombe* and their successors, view of frankpledge of all and singular the inhabitants and resiants, as

View of frankpledge,

well intirely as not intirely residing within the said Borough of *Wycombe*, and within the limits and bounds thereof, and all things which to view of frankpledge appertain or belong, or ought to appertain or belong, to be holden in the aforesaid Common Hall, or House called Guildhall, within the aforesaid Borough of *Wycombe*, twice in a year, that is to say, once within a month of *Saint Michael*, and again within a month of *Easter*, to be holden before the aforesaid Mayor Bailiffs and Steward of

Before the mayor or bailiffs and steward, or their deputies. Fines &c. to go to the corporation.

the Borough aforesaid, or their or any of their sufficient deputy or deputies, for the time being, in every year. And that the same Mayor Bailiffs and Burgesses, may and shall have ALL and all manner of fines, redemptions, issues and amerciaments, and all other profits of, or in the aforesaid view of frankpledge, in any wise coming, arising, or happening, to be taken and converted to the proper use and behoof of the said Mayor Bailiffs and Burgesses, and the commonalty of the aforesaid Borough of *Wycombe*, for the time being, so that no other person besides the Mayor Bailiffs and Burgesses of the town aforesaid, shall have or hold in any wise hereafter any view of frankpledge, or any other Court in the said Town or Borough, or any place thereof, unless only by the licence and consent of the said Mayor Bailiffs and Burgesses, or their heirs and successors thereto specially obtained or to be obtained. AND ALSO WE WILL, and by these presents for us and the heirs and successors of us the said Queen grant to the aforesaid Mayor Bailiffs and Burgesses of the Borough aforesaid, and declare by these presents, that the bounds and limits, metes, circuits and precincts, of the Borough aforesaid, shall extend and stretch as hereunder limited and specified ; that is to say, from a certain bridge called Wynkles Bridge in Frogmore, situate at the west end of the same Borough or Town, unto a certain meadow called Hallywell Mead, situate at the east end of a certain common pasture, called the Rye Mead, belonging to the said Mayor Bailiffs and Burgesses, and being parcel of the possessions, and from thence to a certain ditch, situate on the north part of a certain curtilage called Bourhayes, and from the same ditch unto a certain bridge in the street, called *Saint Mary* Street, near to a certain house or farm, called Lokes, which same bridge leads to the town of *Marlowe*, on the south part. AND that all and singular houses, edifices, lands, tenements, void grounds, and soil whatsoever within the bounds, metes and limits thereof, may and shall be, and shall be reputed to be, part and parcel of the said Borough of *Wycombe*, now by these presents into a body Politic as aforesaid erected and incorporated. AND FURTHER of our more ample grace, WE WILL, and for us and the heirs and successors of us the aforesaid Queen, by these presents grant to the aforesaid Mayor Bailiffs and Burgesses of the aforesaid Borough of *Wycombe* and their successors, that the same Mayor Bailiffs and Burgesses, and their successors, may and shall have within the Borough aforesaid, and within the metes, bounds, limits, and liberties of the same Borough, assize and assay of bread, wine, and ale, and of other victuals, and also of measures and weights whatsoever, and the amendment, punishment, and correction thereof, so often as and when it shall be expedient and necessary ; and also may and shall have ALL and all manner of fines, redemptions, and amerciaments, and all other profits therefrom coming or happening. AND that the same Mayor Bailiffs and Burgesses, and their successors, by their common council, or by the major part thereof, may and shall have authority, power, and faculty to frame, constitute, ordain, and make from time to time, laws, statutes, and ordinances whatsoever, for the government and rule of the artificers and other inhabitants, and for the victualling of the said Borough, and for the better rule and government of the same Borough and the inhabitants of the same : so that the said laws, statutes and ordinances shall not be repugnant nor contrary to the laws and statutes of our kingdom, nor to the prerogative of us and the heirs and successors of us the said Queen. AND ALSO of our ample grace, WE WILL and of our certain knowledge and meer motion, for us and the heirs and successors of us the aforesaid Queen, by these presents grant to the aforesaid Mayor Bailiffs and Burgesses of the aforesaid Borough of *Wycombe*, and their successors : that the same Burgesses of the said Borough for the time being, or the major part of them, from time to time every

Limits of the borough.

Corporation to have the assize of bread, wine, ale, measures and weights, &c.

And all fines therefrom.

Common Council may make laws.

Burgesses to nominate the mayor.

F. F.

year from henceforth for ever, on Thursday next before the Feast of *Saint Michael* the Archangel, shall assemble and shall and may be able to assemble, in the aforesaid Hall, called THE GUILDHALL, or in any other convenient place within the aforesaid Borough of *Wycombe*, and there shall and may be able to nominate and assign one honest and discreet man from the Burgesses and inhabitants of the said Borough, to be Mayor of the same Borough for one whole year then next ensuing; which same man, so elected to the office of Mayor, after his corporal oath in due manner made and taken, shall bear the office of Mayor of the same Borough of *Wycombe* for one year then next ensuing.   AND FURTHER WE WILL, and by these presents for us and the heirs and successors of us the aforesaid Queen grant to the aforesaid Mayor Bailiffs and Burgesses, that every person hereafter elected to the office of Mayor of the aforesaid Borough, shall take a corporal oath before his last predecessor in the same office, if the same predecessor shall be living and shall be then present; and if his same predecessor shall be dead, or shall be absent, before the steward or his sufficient deputy and other the Burgesses of the aforesaid Borough of *Wycombe*, there present for the faithful execution of the said office of Mayor.   And if and so often as it shall happen, any person being Mayor of the aforesaid Borough of *Wycombe*, to die or be removed from his office during the time which he shall be Mayor of the same Borough, that then and so often the Burgesses of the same Borough surviving, or for the time being, or the major part of them, shall assemble, and shall and may be able to assemble in the said house and place, at a certain day prefixed, within eight days next following the death or removal of the said Mayor of the said Borough, and there to nominate and elect one other honest man of the Burgesses and inhabitants of the said Borough to be Mayor of the said Borough, until Thursday then next ensuing before the Feast of *Saint Michael* the Archangel; which same man so elected and nominated, after his oath taken in manner and form aforesaid, shall bear and exercise the office of Mayor in the said Borough, until the said Thursday next before the Feast of *Saint Michael* then next ensuing.   AND FURTHER WE WILL, and of our certain knowledge and meer motion, for us and the heirs and successors of us the aforesaid Queen by these presents grant to the aforesaid Mayor Bailiffs and Burgesses, and their successors, that so often as and whensoever it shall happen any Burgess of the Borough aforesaid for the time being to die, or to dwell out of the said Borough, or be removed from his office of Burgess of the same Borough for any cause, that then and so often it shall and may be lawful for the Mayor Bailiffs and Burgesses of the aforesaid Borough, or the major part of them, from time to time, when and as it shall please them and seem expedient within fourteen days then next following the death or removal of the said Burgesses, or of any of them, to assemble in their said Guildhall at their pleasure, and there to nominate and elect one or more of the inhabitants of the said Borough of *Wycombe*, and then not being of the Burgesses of the same Borough, to be Burgess or Burgesses of the Borough aforesaid, during the life of them and each of them.   AND that

Mayor to take an oath.

If the mayor die or be removed, the burgesses to elect another within eight days.

If a burgess die, or dwell out of the borough, or be removed, the mayor bailiffs and burgesses to choose another within fourteen days.

every person so nominated and elected, from the time of such election, shall be a Burgess of the same Borough during his life, or otherwise if it shall so seem good and expedient to the said Mayor Bailiffs and other Burgesses of the said Borough of *Wycombe*, or the major part of them. And that every person so nominated and elected, and to be nominated and elected, to the office of Burgess of the Borough aforesaid, shall take a corporal oath before the Mayor and Bailiffs of the same Borough, well and faithfully to execute the office of Burgess of the Borough aforesaid. AND FURTHER WE WILL, and for us and the heirs and successors of us the aforesaid Queen, by these presents grant to the aforesaid Mayor Bailiffs and Burgesses of the same Borough and their successors, that so often as and whensoever it shall happen the steward of the same Borough for the time being, to die or be removed from his office of Steward of the same Borough, for any reasonable cause, that then and so often it shall and may be lawful to the Mayor Bailiffs and Burgesses of the said Borough, or the major part of the same Burgesses for the time being, from time to time, when and so soon as it shall please and it shall seem expedient to assemble in the said Common Hall, called the Guildhall, within the same Borough at their pleasure, within eight days next following the death or removal of the said steward, or at any other time at their pleasure, and there to nominate and elect one other fit person to be steward of the said Borough of *Wycombe* during his life, or otherwise, as to the Mayor Bailiffs and Burgesses of the said Borough of *Wycombe*, or the major part of them for the time being, shall seem good and expedient. And that every person so nominated and elected, and to be nominated and elected to the office of steward of the Borough aforesaid, by himself or by his sufficient deputy or deputies, shall well and faithfully exercise and do, and cause to be done and exercised, all things which to justice and other things which to the office of steward of the same Borough doth appertain. AND ALSO WE WILL, and for us and the heirs and successors of us the aforesaid Queen by these presents grant and ordain that there may and shall be in the said Borough, two Burgesses of the Parliament of us and the heirs and successors of us the aforesaid Queen; and that the aforesaid Mayor Bailiffs and Burgesses and their successors, upon a writ of us and the heirs and successors of us the said Queen, for the election of Burgesses of the Parliament to them directed, may and shall have power, authority, and faculty, to elect and nominate two discreet and honest men to be Burgesses of the Parliament of us and of the successors of us the aforesaid Queen, for the same Borough. And the same Burgesses so elected, at the charges and costs of the said Borough and of the commonalty thereof, shall send to the Parliament of us and of the heirs and successors of us the aforesaid Queen, wherever it shall be then holden in the same manner and form as in other Boroughs of our kingdom of *England*, or in our Borough of *Wycombe* aforesaid, hath been used and accustomed; which same Burgesses so elected and nominated, WE WILL to be present and to remain at the Parliament of us and of the heirs and successors of us the aforesaid Queen, at the

Burgesses to take an oath.

Steward to be elected by mayor bailiffs and burgesses.

Two burgesses of parliament to be elected by mayor bailiffs and burgesses.

And sent at the expense of the borough and commonalty.
In the same manner as hath been used.

charges and costs of the said Mayor Bailiffs and Burgesses of *Wycombe*, during the time which such Parliament shall happen to be holden, and in the like manner and form as other Burgesses of the Parliament for whatsoever other Boroughs or Borough within our kingdom of *England* can do, or have been accustomed to do. And which same Burgesses in such Parliament of us and of the heirs and successors of us the aforesaid Queen, shall have their voices as well affirmative as negative, and shall do and execute all and singular other things there as other Burgesses, or any other Burgess of our Parliament for whatsoever other Boroughs or Borough can have, do, or execute, or can or may be able to have, do, or execute. AND FURTHER WE

Mayor to be justice of the peace.

WILL, and by these presents ordain and grant that the said Mayor of the Borough aforesaid, for the time being, may and shall be Justice of us and of the heirs and successors of us the aforesaid Queen, to preserve the peace within the aforesaid Borough, and shall have full power and authority to preserve the peace of us and of the heirs and successors of us the aforesaid Queen, within the Borough aforesaid, and to do and execute all other things which to the office of Justice of the peace of us, and of the heirs and successors of us the aforesaid Queen, in any our counties of *England* doth appertain, to do and execute for the good keeping of the peace of us and of the heirs and successors of us the aforesaid Queen, and the quiet rule and safe government of the people of us and of the heirs and successors of us the aforesaid Queen, for all and singular articles and ordinances to keep and cause to be kept within the Borough aforesaid, according to the force, form, and effect of the statutes and ordinances thereupon enacted; and to cause to be punished all those whom they shall find acting and offending against the force and effect of the statutes and ordinances aforesaid, according to the law of our land; and to hear and determine all and singular those things according to the law and custom of our kingdom of *England*, as fully and intirely, and in as ample manner and form as the Justices of the peace in the county of *Buckingham*, or elsewhere within this our kingdom of *England* have heretofore had or exercised, or shall have and exercise hereafter, without the Borough and liberty aforesaid; so that the said justice of the peace within the aforesaid Borough of *Wycombe* aforesaid, for the time being, shall not proceed to the determination of any felony without the special command of us or of the heirs or successors of us the aforesaid Queen; saving to us

Fines to go to the Crown.

and the heirs and successors of us the aforesaid Queen, ALL and singular fines, amerciaments, redemptions, and other profits of the said office of justice of the peace coming or accruing. AND FURTHER, of our more ample grace, WE have

No sheriff to execute his office in the borough.

granted, and by these presents for us and the heirs and successors of us the aforesaid Queen, Do grant to the aforesaid Mayor Bailiffs and Burgesses of *Wycombe* and their successors, that they and their successors for ever shall have the return of all our writs and attachments and the execution thereof, so that no Sheriff or other Bailiff or Minister of the heirs and successors of us the aforesaid Queen, shall enter the same liberty for the execution of writs and summonses, or attachments, or to exercise any other office there, unless in default of the same Mayor Bailiffs and Burgesses and their successors, or other Ministers of us the aforesaid Queen there; AND MOREOVER of our especial grace, WE HAVE granted, and by these presents for us and the heirs and successors of us the aforesaid Queen do grant to the aforesaid Mayor Bailiffs and Burgesses, that the aforesaid Mayor to be elected for a time and for one year, as soon as he shall be so elected to be Mayor, may and shall be Escheator and Coroner of us and of the heirs and successors of us the aforesaid Queen, and Clerk of the Market of us and of the heirs and successors of us the aforesaid Queen, within the Borough aforesaid; and that he shall do and execute all and singular those things which to the office of Escheator, Coroner, and Clerk of the Market appertain and belong, to do and perform within the Borough aforesaid. And that he shall take an oath well and faithfully to perform and exercise the same offices of Escheator, Coroner, and Clerk of the Market, by the same Mayor, before the old Mayor Bailiffs and Burgesses of the Borough aforesaid, before he shall take upon himself the office of Escheator, Coroner, and Clerk of the Market. And that no other Escheator, Coroner, or Clerk, of us or of the heirs or successors of us the said Queen, shall in any wise enter into the said Borough or the precincts thereof, or there intermeddle, to do and perform any thing there which to the office of Escheator, Coroner, or Clerk of the Market doth appertain to do and perform. AND FURTHER of our more ample grace, and of our certain knowledge and meer motion, WE HAVE granted for us and the heirs and successors of us the aforesaid Queen, as much as in us lies, that the aforesaid Mayor Bailiffs Burgesses and honest men of the said Borough of *Wycombe* and their heirs and successors residing, dwelling, or inhabiting within the same Borough, shall be quit and discharged of Pavage, Passage, Lastage, Tallage, Carriage, Pesage, Piccage, and Terrage, throughout our whole kingdom of *England* and our dominions. WE HAVE ALSO granted to the same Mayor Bailiffs and Burgesses aforesaid, and their heirs and successors, that they shall have and receive all manner of fines for trespasses and other misdeeds whatsoever, and also fines for licence to agree, and all manner of other fines, redemptions, and amerciaments, from or by whatsoever cause accruing; and also issues forfeited of all such men, tenants, resiants, or dwellers in the said Borough of *Wycombe*, although the same men, tenants, resiants or dwellers, may be ministers of us or of the heirs or successors of us the aforesaid Queen. And that the same Mayor Bailiffs and Burgesses and their successors, shall have all and all manner of forfeitures, year day waste and estrepement, within the same Borough happening or arising, adjudged as well in the presence of us or the heirs or successors of us the aforesaid Queen, as elsewhere, in the absence of us or the heirs or successors of us the aforesaid Queen, before whatsoever Justices of us, or of the heirs or successors of us the aforesaid Queen. And that they shall be able to levy, perceive, and have, all that which to us our heirs and successors concerning such forfeitures, year day and waste, and estrepement might appertain, if this our present grant to the same

Unless in default of the mayor, &c.

Mayor to be escheator and coroner. And clerk of the market.

To take an oath.

Inhabitants quit of pavage, &c. &c. &c. throughout *England*.

Corporation to have fines for trespasses, &c.

Mayor Bailiffs and Burgesses had not been made, to the use of the same Mayor Bailiffs and Burgesses and their successors, by their Bailiffs or Ministers. And that they shall and may be able likewise from henceforth for ever to levy, perceive, and have, such fines, redemptions, and amerciaments, of all such tenants, resiants, or dwellers in the said Town or Borough of *Wycombe;* and also the issues by them or any of them forfeited, which shall happen to be made or adjudged, or forfeited before us and the heirs and successors of us the aforesaid Queen, or in the chancery of us or the heirs or successors of us the aforesaid Queen, or before whatsoever Justices and Ministers of us or the heirs or successors of us the aforesaid Queen, by Estreats of such Courts of us or the heirs or successors of us the aforesaid Queen, without the hindrance or impediment of us or the heirs and successors of us the aforesaid Queen, the Justices, Escheators, Sheriffs, Coroners, Bailiffs, or other Ministers of us or the heirs or successors of us the aforesaid Queen whomsoever.

Inhabitants not to be drawn into plea before the steward of the crown for the assize broken in the borough, nor for trespasses.

WE HAVE MOREOVER granted for us and the said heirs and successors of us the aforesaid Queen, to the aforesaid Mayor Bailiffs and Burgesses of the Borough aforesaid, that neither they nor their heirs and successors, nor any person dwelling in the same Borough, shall be drawn into plea before the Steward or Marshal of the Household of us or of the heirs and successors of us the aforesaid Queen, for the assize of bread, wine, and ale, in the same Borough broken, or for any trespasses by them or any of them without the Verge or within the Verge before or after the coming of the same Steward and Marshal, or either of them, to those parts, or at the time of the said Steward and Marshal being in those parts, to whatsoever person made or perpetrated, nor shall he or they be hindered or molested or in any wise aggrieved before the same Steward and Marshal, on those accounts or any of them.

Corporation to have fines by burgesses adjudged before the steward of the crown.

WE HAVE ALSO granted for us and the heirs and successors of us the aforesaid Queen, to the Mayor Bailiffs and Burgesses of the said Borough of *Wycombe,* and their successors, that they shall be able to levy, perceive, and have to the use and profit of the same Mayor Bailiffs and Burgesses, and of the whole Commonalty of the said Borough of *Wycombe,* ALL and all manner of issues, fines, redemptions and amerciaments, by any Burgess of the said Borough of *Wycombe* for the time being forfeited or adjudged before the Steward and Marshal of the Household of us and the heirs and successors of us the aforesaid Queen, for the time being.

Steward of the crown not to exercise his office in the borough.

WE HAVE ALSO granted, and by these presents firmly forbid, any Sheriff, Constable, or Bailiff, or the aforesaid Steward and Marshal of the Household of us or of the heirs or successors of us the aforesaid Queen, or any Minister or Officer of us or of the heirs or successors of us the aforesaid Queen, besides the Mayor and Bailiffs of the said Borough for the time being, in any wise to enter the same Borough, in any manner to exercise his office there, unless in default of the same Mayor or Bailiffs or any of them; but all that shall appertain and be done by the Mayor and Bailiffs and their successors

Corporation to have the chattels of felons &c.

from henceforth for ever. WE HAVE ALSO granted for us and the heirs and successors of us the aforesaid Queen, that the aforesaid Mayor Bailiffs and Burgesses and their successors from henceforth, shall have all manner of chattels of felons and fugitives, as well felons of themselves as others whomsoever, outlaws, attainted and convicted persons, and from whatsoever cause of all the men and tenants aforesaid, as well intire tenants as not intire tenants and resiants, and of all the dwellers and inhabitants within the said Borough of *Wycombe*, and goods and chattels waived, estrays whatsoever within the said Borough, deodands and treasure trove within the Borough aforesaid. And if any man of the tenants and residents of or in the same Borough, or any other person in the same Borough, for any his offence or misdeed whatsoever, ought to lose life or member, or shall fly and not stand to judgement, or shall commit any other trespass for which he ought to lose his chattels, in what place justice ought to be done, whether in the court of us or of the heirs or successors of us the said Queen, or in other courts, the chattels shall be of the same Mayor Bailiffs and Burgesses, and it shall be lawful for them to put themselves in seizin of the same chattels, and the same chattels to retain to their use without the hindrance or impediment of us or the heirs or successors of us the aforesaid Queen, the Justices, Escheators, Sheriffs, Coroners, or other Bailiffs or Ministers of us or of the heirs or successors of us the aforesaid Queen whomsoever. And that they the Mayor Bailiffs and Burgesses of the Borough aforesaid, shall have whatsoever goods and chattels, called Manuopera, taken or to be taken with any person being within the Borough aforesaid. WE WILL ALSO, and by these presents grant to the aforesaid Mayor Bailiffs and Burgesses of the said Borough of *Wycombe*, that they may and shall have these our letters patent under our great seal of *England* in due manner made and sealed, without fine or fee, great or small, to us in our Hanaper or elsewhere, to our use for the same in any wise to be rendered paid or done: Although express mention, &c. IN WITNESS whereof, &c. WITNESS, THE KING AND QUEEN at *Westminster*, the twenty-seventh day of *August*.

[margin note:] And waifs, estrays, deodands, treasure trove, and chattels forfeited by offenders.

[margin note:] And manuopera. This charter granted without fee.

THE FOURTH OF ELIZABETH.

18TH JULY, 1562.

Twenty-fourth Part of Close Rolls in the fourth year of the Reign of Queen Elizabeth.

The corporation patrons of St. John's hospital.

Have granted the same to the Queen.

As also our lady rents.

Of a writing between our Lady the Queen, and the Mayor Bailiffs and Burgesses of Cheppyng Wycombe.

TO ALL Christ's faithful People, to whom this present writing shall come. The Mayor Bailiffs and Burgesses of *Great Wycombe*, otherwise called *Cheppyng Wycombe*, in the County of *Buckingham*, true and undoubted Patrons of the Hospital of *Saint John* the Baptist in *Wycombe* aforesaid, Greeting in the Lord Everlasting. KNOW YE, that We the aforesaid Mayor Bailiffs and Burgesses, of our unanimous assent and consent HAVE given, granted, and by this our present writing confirmed, to our Lady *Elizabeth* by the grace of God, of *England*, *France*, and *Ireland* Queen, Defender of the Faith and so forth, ALL the scite, bounds, and circuit of the said Hospital of *Saint John* the Baptist, AND ALL the Hospital aforesaid. AND ALSO ALL and singular messuages, houses, edifices, lands, tenements, meadows, feedings, pastures, commons, rents, reversions, services, and hereditaments whatsoever, situate, lying and being in *Wycombe* aforesaid, and in the parishes of *Penne*, *Hichenden* and *Great Marlowe*, in the said County of *Buckingham*, and any of them and elsewhere wheresoever in the same County which to the said late Hospital did formerly belong or appertain, or which as part, parcel or member of the same late hospital were heretofore had, known, accepted, used, or reputed. AND ALSO ALL those our messuages, lands, tenements, meadows, feedings, pastures and hereditaments whatsoever, in *Wycombe* aforesaid, called or known by the name of the fraternity of the Blessed *Mary*, or by the name of our Lady Rents: AND ALSO ALL and all manner of woods, underwoods, and trees whatsoever, of, in, and upon the premises growing and being, and the land, soil, and ground of the same woods, underwoods, and trees ; and the reversion and reversions whatsoever of all and singular the premises above expressed and specified, and of every parcel thereof. AND ALSO the rents, reversions, and yearly profits whatsoever, reserved upon whatsoever demises and grants in any manner made of the premises or of any parcel thereof, To HAVE, HOLD, AND ENJOY the aforesaid scite, bounds, and circuit of the

THE FOURTH OF ELIZABETH.

21ST JULY, 1562.

Third Part of Patents in the fourth year of the Reign of Queen Elizabeth.

<table>
<tr>
<td>

The corporation minded to found a grammar school.

</td>
<td>

For the Mayor Bailiffs and Burgesses of the Borough of Wicombe of a grant to them and their successors.

</td>
<td>

THE QUEEN, To all to whom, &c. Greeting —WHEREAS, We now understand that our beloved subjects, the Mayor Bailiffs and Burgesses of the Borough of *Wicombe*, in our County of *Buckingham*, are minded and intend not only to make, found, erect and establish a certain Grammar School, of one Master or Pedagogue, for the good education and instruction of boys and youth, according to the ordinances and statutes by the same Mayor Bailiffs and Burgesses and their successors or any of

</td>
</tr>
</table>

them, therefore to be made, augmented or found, to be perpetually hereafter sustained and exhibited in the same Borough of *Wicombe*, in our said County of *Buckingham*:

And to support four poor persons.

but also, at their proper charges and expenses to support and maintain four poor persons within the same town for ever. AND WHEREAS ALSO, the same Mayor Bailiffs and Burgesses have humbly besought us, that We would condescend to grant our royal license to make, found, erect and establish the School aforesaid : We considering not only the premises, but also the pious, good, laudable, and devout intention of the aforesaid Mayor Bailiffs and Burgesses in the premises, and inwardly desiring as much as in us lies to augment all and singular those things which may in any wise concern the good education and instruction of boys and youth, and the relief of the poor, of our especial grace and of our certain knowledge and meer motion, HAVE granted and given license, and by these presents

The Queen grants the corporation Licence to form a school.

do grant and give license, for us our heirs and successors as much as in us lies, to the aforesaid Mayor Bailiffs and Burgesses of the said Borough of *Wicombe* and their successors; that they and their successors, or any of them, shall and may be able to erect, found, and establish, a certain Grammar School, of one Master or Pedagogue as is aforesaid, according to the ordinances and statutes by the same Mayor Bailiffs and Burgesses or their successors in that behalf, to be made, framed, ordered, and established in the said Borough of *Wicombe*, in our said County of *Buckingham*, to continue for ever hereafter. And that the same Mayor Bailiffs and Burgesses and their successors, may or shall be able to prefer, create, and ordain a proper person whomsoever to be Master or Pedagogue, and for Master and Pedagogue of the same School, according to the ordinances and statutes by the same Mayor Bailiffs and Burgesses or their successors, for the good and wholesome government and rule of the same School to be made, framed, and established. AND FURTHER of our grace we will, and by these presents for us our heirs and successors grant to the aforesaid Mayor Bailiffs and Burgesses, that they and their successors shall make, and shall and may be able to make, proper and wholesome statutes and ordinances in writing concerning and touching the ordering, and government, and direction of the Master of the School aforesaid, for the time being ; and the stipend and salary of the same Master and other things touching and concerning the same School, and the order, government, preservation, and disposition of the rents and revenues appointed, and to be appointed to the support of the same School, which same statutes and ordinances so to be made, WE WILL, and grant, and by these presents command inviolably to be preserved from time to time for ever, so that the same statutes and ordinances shall not be to the prejudice of us our heirs or successors, nor contrary to the laws, statutes or ordinances, of this our kingdom of *England*. AND WHEREAS the same Mayor Bailiffs and Burgesses of the said Borough of *Wicombe*, have humbly besought us that for their better sustenance, support, and maintenance of the School aforesaid, and of the Poor aforesaid, we would be pleased to extend to them our royal munificence, grace, and liberality : KNOW YE that we at the humble petition of the aforesaid Mayor Bailiffs and Burgesses of the said Borough of *Wicombe* and also in consideration of the late Hospital of *Saint John* the Baptist in *Wycombe* aforesaid, and of all and singular messuages, lands, tenements, rents, revenues, services, and other hereditaments whatsoever to the same late Hospital in any wise belonging or appertaining, and of all the messuages, tenements, and hereditaments whatsoever in *Wycombe* aforesaid, called or known by the name of the fraternity of the *Blessed Mary*, or by the name of *Our Lady Rents*, by the Mayor Bailiffs and Burgesses, patrons of the said Hospital, to us our heirs and successors lately given, granted, and surrendered, to do our pleasure therewith ; as by their deed remaining of record in our Chancery more fully doth and may appear : Of our more ample grace certain knowledge and meer motion, Have given and granted, and confirmed, and by these presents do give, grant, and confirm to the aforesaid Mayor Bailiffs and Burgesses of *Wycombe*, ALL the scite, bounds, and circuit, of the late Hospital of *Saint John* the Baptist in *Wycombe* aforesaid in our said County of *Buckingham ;* AND ALL the Hospital aforesaid, AND ALL and singular the messuages, houses, edifices, lands, tenements, meadows, feedings, pastures, commons, rents, reversions, services and hereditaments whatsoever, situate, lying and being in *Wycombe* aforesaid, and in the parishes of *Penne, Hychendon,* and *Great Marlowe,* in our said County of

And appoi
a master.

And make
statutes co
cerning th
master his
stipend an
other t

And the re
&c. for the
support of
same scho

The Quee
grants the
hospital of
St. John,

Buckingham, and every of them and elsewhere wheresoever, in the same County, which to the said late Hospital did formerly belong or appertain, or which as parts, parcel, or member of the same late Hospital have heretofore been had, known, accepted, used, or reputed. AND ALSO ALL those messuages, lands, tenements, meadows, feedings, pastures, rents, reversions, services and hereditaments whatsoever in *Wycombe* aforesaid, called or known by the name of the fraternity of the *Blessed Mary*, or by the name of *Our Lady Rents*. AND ALSO ALL and all manner our woods, underwoods, and trees whatsoever, of, in, and upon the premises growing and being, and the land, soil, and ground of the same woods, underwoods, and trees, and the reversion and reversions whatsoever of all and singular the premises above expressed and specified, and of every parcel thereof; and ALSO the rents, revenues, and yearly profits whatsoever, reserved upon whatsoever demises and grants in any manner made of the premises or of any parcel thereof. TO HAVE, HOLD, AND ENJOY the aforesaid scite, bounds, and circuit of the aforesaid late Hospital, and the aforesaid late Hospital and also the fraternity of the *Blessed Mary*, called our *Lady Rents* in *Wycombe* aforesaid; and all and singular the aforesaid messuages, houses, edifices, lands, tenements, meadows, feedings, pastures, rents, reversions, services, woods, underwoods, and all and singular other the premises above expressed and specified, with every of their appurtenances to the aforesaid Mayor Bailiffs and Burgesses and their successors, to the proper use and behoof of the same Mayor Bailiffs and Burgesses and their successors for ever; TO BE HOLDEN of us our heirs and successors, as of our Castle of *Windsor* in our County of *Berks*, by fealty only in free soccage and not in chief, for all rents, services, and demands whatsoever, for the same, to us our heirs or successors, in any wise to be rendered, paid, or done. AND FURTHER of our more ample grace, WE HAVE given and granted, and by these presents for us and our heirs, Do give and grant to the aforesaid Mayor Bailiffs and Burgesses of the Borough of *Wycombe*, ALL the issues, rents, revenues, and profits, of all and singular the premises above expressed and specified, with every of their appurtenances, from the Feast of the annunciation of the *Blessed Virgin Mary*, which was in the second year of the reign of the late King *Edward* the Sixth, our dearly beloved brother, until this time coming or accruing: TO HOLD to the same Mayor Bailiffs and Burgesses of our gift, without account or any other thing for the same to us our heirs or successors in any wise to be rendered, paid, or done: AND MOREOVER of our further especial grace, WE HAVE given and granted, and by these presents for us our heirs and successors, Do give and grant to the aforesaid Mayor Bailiffs and Burgesses of the Borough of *Wycombe* aforesaid and their successors, special license and free and lawful faculty, power and authority, to have, receive, and purchase, to them and their successors for ever, towards the support and maintenance of the School aforesaid, and of the poor persons aforesaid, as well of us our heirs and successors as of any other persons and person whomsoever, manors, messuages, lands, tenements,

---

Marginal notes:

And our lady rents,

To be held of *Windsor* castle, in free soccage.

The corporation to have all rents since lady day in the 2d. year of *Edw.* VI.

May purchase lands, &c.,

rectories, tythes, rents, and other hereditaments whatsoever, within our kingdom of *England* or elsewhere within our dominions, which are not holden of us our heirs or successors immediately in chief, or by knight's service, provided they shall not exceed the clear yearly value of thirty pounds, beyond the aforesaid messuages, lands, tenements, and other the premises above by these presents given and granted; the statute concerning lands and tenements not to be put in mortmain, or any other statute, act, ordinance, or provision, or any other thing, cause, or matter whatsoever to the contrary thereof, had, made, enacted, ordained, or provided, in any wise notwithstanding: PROVIDED ALWAYS, and further WE WILL, and by these presents ordain, that all the issues, rents and revenues of all the aforesaid lands, tenements, and possessions above by these presents granted, shall be converted or expended towards the support of the School aforesaid, and of the poor persons aforesaid, and to the reparation and support of the houses, lands, tenements, and possessions aforesaid, and not otherwise, nor to any other uses or intents. WE WILL ALSO, and by these presents grant to the aforesaid Mayor Bailiffs and Burgesses of the town of *Great Wycombe* aforesaid, that they may and shall have these our letters patent under our great seal of *England*, in due manner made and sealed, without fine or fee, great or small, to us in our Hanaper or elsewhere to our use for the same in any wise to be rendered, paid, or done: Although express mention, &c. IN WITNESS whereof, &c. WITNESS, THE QUEEN at *Westminster*, the twenty first day of *July*.

By the QUEEN herself, &c.

If not held of the crown in chief, nor by knight's service, nor worth more than £30 a year.

Rents &c. not to be applied to any other uses.

Granted without fee. 21st *July*.

CHARTER

GRANTED TO THE

MAYOR, BAILIFFS, AND BURGESSES

OF

THE BOROUGH OF CHIPPING WYCOMBE,

BY QUEEN ELIZABETH,

1ST MARCH, 1598,

IN THE FORTIETH YEAR OF HER REIGN.

Of a Grant to them and their Successors for the Mayor, Bailiffs, and Burgesses of the Borough of *Chepping Wycombe,* otherwise *Wicombe,* in in the County of *Buckingham.*

THE QUEEN, To all to whom, &c. Greeting.—WHEREAS our Borough of *Chepping Wycombe,* otherwise called *Wicombe,* in our County of *Buckingham,* is an antient and populous Borough, and the Mayor, Bailiffs, and Burgesses of the Borough of *Wycombe* aforesaid, have had, and used, and enjoyed divers Liberties, Franchises, Immunities, and Pre-eminences, as well by our Charter, and by the Charter of the Lord *Philip,* and our dearly beloved Sister *Mary,* late King and Queen of *England,* as by Charters of other our Progenitors and Predecessors, Kings of *England,* to them and their Predecessors heretofore made, granted, or confirmed, as also by reason of divers Prescriptions and Customs in the same Borough, from Time whereof the Memory of Man is not to the contrary used: AND WHEREAS We are informed that certain Defects, Ambiguities, and Uncertainties, are in the Charters and Letters Patent aforesaid, by Reason that some Things in the same contained were not granted plainly, expressly, nor by Words sufficiently proper for the good Rule, Government, and Advantage of the Borough aforesaid, according to the true Intent of the same Charters or Letters Patent: AND WHEREAS our beloved Subjects, the Mayor, Bailiffs, and Burgesses of the Borough of *Wicombe* aforesaid, have humbly besought us that we would be pleased to shew and extend to the same Mayor, Bailiffs, and Burgesses, our Royal Grace and Munificence in that Behalf, and that We, for the better Government, Rule, and Improvement of the same Borough, would condescend to ratify, confirm, approve, make, renew, constitute, or create anew, the said Mayor, Bailiffs, and Burgesses of the same Borough into one Body

Corporate and Politic, by our Letters Patent, as to us should seem most expedient ; WE THEREFORE, WILLING that from henceforth for ever in the same Borough there shall continually be had one certain and undoubted Method of and for the Keeping of the Peace, and the good Rule and Government of the People there; and that the Borough aforesaid from henceforth for ever shall be and remain a Borough of Peace and Quiet to the Dread and Terror of the Wicked, and in Reward of the Good; and that our Peace and other Deeds of Justice may be kept there without further Delay ; and hoping that if the Mayor, Bailiffs, and Burgesses of the same Borough, and their Successors, are able to enjoy by our Grant more ample Honor, Liberties, and Privileges, then they will consider themselves bound more especially and strongly to perform and exhibit to us, and to our Heirs and Successors, the Services which they are able of our special Grace and of our certain Knowledge and mere Motion, HAVE willed, ordained, constituted, and granted ; and by these Presents, for us, our Heirs and Successors, DO will, ordain, constitute, declare, and grant, That the said Borough of *Wicombe*, in our said County of *Buckingham*, from henceforth may and shall be a free Borough of itself, and that the Burgesses of the same Borough and their Successors from henceforth for ever may and shall be, by Force of these Presents, one Body Corporate and Politic, in Deed, Fact, and Name, of one Mayor, two Bailiffs, and the Burgesses, by the Name of Mayor, Bailiffs, and Burgesses of the Borough of *Chepping Wycombe*, otherwise *Wicombe*, in the County of *Buckingham*, one Body Corporate and Politic, in Deed, Fact, and Name, really and fully for us, our Heirs, and Successors, we do erect, make, ordain, constitute, confirm, and declare by these Presents ; and that by the same Name they shall have perpetual Succession ; and that they, by the Name of Mayor, Bailiffs, and Burgesses of the Borough of *Chepping Wycombe*, otherwise *Wicombe*, in the County of *Buckingham*, may and shall be for ever hereafter Persons able and capable in the Law to have, purchase, receive, and possess Lands, Tenements, Liberties, Privileges, Jurisdictions, Franchises, and Hereditaments, of whatsoever Kind, Nature, or Sort they may be, to them and their Successors, in Fee and Perpetuity, and also Goods and Chattels, and whatsoever other Things, of whatsoever Kind, Nature, or Sort they may be, and also to give, grant, demise, and assign Lands, Tenements, and Hereditaments, Goods and Chattels, and to do and execute all and singular other Deeds and Things by the Name aforesaid : and that by the same Name of Mayor, Bailiffs, and Burgesses of the Borough of *Chepping Wycombe*, otherwise *Wicombe*, in the County of *Buckingham*, shall and may be able to plead and be impleaded, answer and be answered, defend and be defended, in whatsoever Courts and Places, and before whatsoever Judges and Justices, and other Persons and Officers of us and of our Heirs and Successors, in all Suits, Plaints, Pleas, Causes, Matters, and Demands, real, personal, or mixt, as well spiritual as temporal, of whatsoever Kind, Nature, or Sort they may be, in the same Manner and Form as other our liege People of this our Kingdom of *England*, Persons able and capable in the Law, may and can

A Body Corporate, in Name of Mayor, Bailiffs, and Burgesses,

May possess Lands, &c.

May plead, &c.

be able to plead and be impleaded, answer and be answered, defend and be defended, and to have, purchase, receive, possess, give, grant, and demise: and that the aforesaid Mayor, Bailiffs, and Burgesses of the aforesaid Borough of *Chepping Wycombe*, otherwise *Wicombe*, in the County of *Buckingham*, and their Successors,

Common Seal. shall have for ever a common Seal, to serve for doing their Affairs and Business whatsoever, and of their Successors: and that it shall and may be lawful to the same Mayor, Bailiffs, and Burgesses, and their Successors, the same Seal at their Pleasure, from Time to Time, to break, change, and make anew, as to them shall seem meet: AND FURTHER WE WILL, and by these Presents, for us, our Heirs and Successors, grant and ordain, That from henceforth for ever there may and shall be, within the Borough aforesaid, one of the most honest and discreet Burgesses of the

Mayor. Borough aforesaid, in Form hereafter in these Presents mentioned, to be elected, who shall be and be named Mayor of the Borough aforesaid: and that in like Manner there may and shall be, within the same Borough, two honest and discreet Burgesses of the Borough aforesaid, in Form hereafter in these Presents mentioned,

Bailiffs. to be elected, who shall be and be named Bailiffs of the Borough aforesaid: AND ALSO WE WILL, and by these Presents, for us, our Heirs and Successors, grant and ordain, That from henceforth there may and shall be, within the Borough aforesaid,

Burgesses. from Time to Time, twelve honest and discreet Men, continually residing and dwelling within the same Borough, who shall be and be called Capital Burgesses of the said Borough: And that the Mayor, Bailiffs, and Burgesses of the same Borough, and their Successors, or the major Part of them, from Time to Time, for ever, shall and may be able to elect so many and such other Men inhabiting or not inhabiting within the Borough aforesaid, as to them shall seem to be most expedient, to be Burgesses of the said Borough: AND WE WILL, and by these Presents for us, our

Common Council. Heirs, and Successors, grant, That the aforesaid Bailiffs and Capital Burgesses shall be and be called the Common Council of the Borough aforesaid, and shall be from Time to Time assisting and aiding to the Mayor of the said Borough of *Chepping Wycombe*, otherwise *Wicombe*, aforesaid, for the Time being, in all Causes and Matters touching or concerning the Borough aforesaid: AND FURTHER WE WILL, and by these Presents, for us, our Heirs and Successors, grant to the aforesaid Mayor, Bailiffs, and Burgesses of the Borough aforesaid, and their Successors, That the Mayor, Bailiffs, and twelve Capital Burgesses of the Borough aforesaid, and their Successors for the Time being, or the major Part of them, of whom the Mayor for the Time being We will to be one, may and shall have full Power and

Ordering of Laws of the Borough. Authority to frame, constitute, ordain, and make, from Time to Time, such reasonable Laws, Statutes, and Ordinances whatsoever which to them shall seem to be good, wholesome, useful, honest, and necessary, according to their sound Discretions, for the good Rule and Government of the Burgesses, Artificers, and Inhabitants of the Borough aforesaid, for the Time being, and for declaring in what Manner and Order the aforesaid Mayor, Bailiffs, and Burgesses, and the Artificers, Inhabitants, and Residents of the Borough aforesaid, shall behave, and carry, and use themselves in their Offices, Mysteries, and Business within the same Borough, and the Limits thereof, for the time being, and otherwise for the further good and public Utility and Rule of the same Borough, and the Victualling of the same Borough, and also for the better Preservation, Government, Disposition, letting and demising of the Lands, Tenements, Possessions, Revenues, and Hereditaments to the aforesaid Mayor, Bailiffs, and Burgesses, and their Successors, by these Presents, or otherwise given, granted, assigned, or confirmed, or hereafter to be given, granted, or assigned, and other Things and Causes whatsoever touching or in any wise concerning the Borough aforesaid, or the State, Right, and Interest of the same Borough: and that they and their Successors, by the Mayor for the Time, and the Bailiffs, and Capital Burgesses aforesaid, being the Common Council of the same Borough, or by the major Part of them as aforesaid, so often as they shall frame, make, ordain, or establish such Laws, Statutes, and Ordinances in Form aforesaid, shall be able to impose and assess such and so many reasonable Pains, Penalties, and Punishments, by Imprisonment of the Body, or by Fines and Amerciaments, or by either of them, towards and upon all Delinquents against such Laws, Statutes, and Ordinances, or any or either of them, as and which to the same Mayor, Bailiffs, and Capital Burgesses, the Common Council of the Borough aforesaid, for the Time being, or the major Part of them as aforesaid, shall seem to be reasonable and requisite; and shall and may be able to levy and have the same Fines and Amerciaments, without the Impediments of us, our Heirs, and Successors: all and singular which Laws, Statutes, and Ordinances so as aforesaid to be made, WE WILL to be observed under the Pains in the same to be contained; so nevertheless that such Laws, Statutes, Ordinances, Imprisonments, Fines, and Amerciaments, shall not be repugnant nor contrary to the Laws, Statutes, Customs, or Rights of our Kingdom of England: And for the better Execution of our same Grant in that Behalf, WE HAVE assigned, nominated, constituted, and made, and by these Presents, for us, our Heirs and Successors, DO assign, nominate, constitute, and make our beloved *John Greneland*, now Mayor of the Borough aforesaid, to be the first and present Mayor of the Borough aforesaid, WILLING that the same *John Greneland* shall be and continue in the Office of Mayor of the same Borough, from the making of these Presents until the Thursday next before the Feast of St. Michael the Archangel next ensuing, and from the same Feast until another of the Burgesses of the Borough aforesaid shall be elected and sworn to the same Office, according to the Ordinances and Constitutions in these Presents hereunder expressed and declared, if the same *John Greneland* shall so long live: WE HAVE ALSO assigned, nominated, and constituted, and by these Presents, for us, our Heirs and Successors, DO assign, nominate, constitute, and make our beloved *Anthony Anthony* and *Thomas Bilson*, now Bailiffs of the Borough aforesaid, to be the two first and present Bailiffs of the Borough aforesaid, to continue in the same Office until the Thursday next before the Feast

Disposition of Lands, &c.

Penalties and Punishments.

First Mayor, Bailiffs, and Burgesses.

G G

of the Annunciation of the *Blessed Virgin Mary* next ensuing, and from the same Feast until two other Burgesses of the Borough aforesaid shall be preferred and sworn to the Office of Bailiffs of the said Borough, according to the Ordinances and Constitutions in these Presents hereafter expressed and declared, if the same *Anthony Anthony* and *Thomas Bilson* shall so long live: WE HAVE ALSO assigned, nominated, and constituted, and by these Presents, for us, our Heirs and Successors, do assign, nominate, constitute, and appoint our beloved *Tristram Wynche, Robert Cullen, William Mundy, John Gibbons, John Fox, John Wells, Thomas Wells, George Wells, Thomas Taylor, Ralph Eversley, William Littleboy,* and *John Littlepage,* Burgesses of the Borough aforesaid, to be the twelve first and present Capital Burgesses of the Borough aforesaid, to continue in the same Office during their Lives, unless, in the mean time, for bad Government or ill behaving themselves in that Behalf, they shall be removed from the same Office: AND FURTHER WE WILL, and by these Presents, for us, our Heirs and Successors, grant to the aforesaid Mayor, Bailiffs, and Burgesses of the Borough aforesaid and their Successors, That the Mayor, Bailiffs, and Burgesses of the Borough aforesaid for the time being, or the major Part of them, from time to time, for ever hereafter, may and shall have Power and Authority, yearly and every year, on the Thursday next before the Feast of St. Michael the Archangel, to assemble themselves, or the major Part of them, in the Guildhall of the Borough aforesaid, or in any other convenient Place within the Borough aforesaid, to be limited and assigned according to their Discretions, and there to continue until they, or the major Part of them there then assembled, shall elect or nominate one Burgess of the Borough aforesaid to be Mayor for the Year ensuing, to be elected and nominated in Form following; and that they shall and may be able there to elect and nominate, before they shall from thence depart, one Burgess of the Borough aforesaid, who shall be Mayor of the Borough aforesaid, for one whole Year then next ensuing; and that he, after he shall be so as aforesaid elected and nominated to be Mayor of the Borough aforesaid, before he shall be admitted to execute the same Office, shall take a corporal Oath upon the Holy Gospel of God yearly on the Day of Election, if he shall then be present; and if he shall be absent, then within one Month then next ensuing the said Day of Election, before the Mayor, his last Predecessor, and in his Absence before such of the aforesaid Capital Burgesses for the Time being, and other the Burgesses of the Borough aforesaid, who shall then be present in the Guildhall of the Borough aforesaid, or in any other convenient Place within the Borough aforesaid, to be limited and assigned according to their Discretions, rightly, well, and faithfully to execute the same Office in all Things touching the same Office; and that after such Oath so taken he shall undertake, and ought, and shall, and may be able to execute the Office of Mayor of the Borough aforesaid, until the Thursday next before the Feast of *St. Michael* the Archangel then next ensuing, and further until another of the aforesaid Burgesses of the Borough aforesaid shall be in due

Election of Mayor.

Manner and Form elected, preferred, and sworn to be Mayor of the Borough aforesaid : AND FURTHER WE WILL, and by these Presents, for us, our Heirs and Successors, grant to the aforesaid Mayor, Bailiffs, and Burgesses of the Borough aforesaid, and their Successors, That the Mayor, Bailiffs, and the aforesaid Capital Burgesses, or the major Part of them, from Time to Time, for ever hereafter, may and shall have Power and Authority, yearly and every Year, on the Thursday next before the Feast of the Annunciation of the *Blessed Virgin Mary*, to assemble themselves, or the major Part of them, in the Guildhall of the Borough aforesaid, or in any other convenient Place within the aforesaid Borough, to be limited and assigned according to their Discretions, and there to continue until they, or the major Part of them there then assembled, shall elect or nominate two Burgesses of the Borough aforesaid to be Bailiffs for the Year ensuing, to be elected and nominated in Form following ; and that they shall and may be able there to elect and nominate, before they shall from thence depart, two of the aforesaid Burgesses, who from thenceforth shall be Bailiffs of the Borough aforesaid, for one whole Year then next ensuing ; and that they, after they shall be so as aforesaid elected and nominated to be Bailiffs of the Borough aforesaid, before they shall be admitted to execute the said Office, shall take a corporal Oath upon the Holy Gospel of God yearly on the Day of Election, if they shall then be present, and if they shall be absent, then within one Month next ensuing the Day of Election aforesaid, before the Mayor of the Borough aforesaid, or in the Absence of the said Mayor, before the Bailiffs their last Predecessors, or either of them, in the Presence of such of the aforesaid Capital Burgesses of the Borough aforesaid, for the Time being, and other the Burgesses of the Borough aforesaid, who shall be then present in the Guildhall of the Borough aforesaid, or in any other convenient Place within the Borough aforesaid, to be limited and assigned according to their Discretions, rightly, well, and faithfully to execute the same Office in all Things touching the same Office ; and that after such Oath so taken they shall undertake, and ought, and shall, and may be able to execute the Office of Bailiffs of the Borough aforesaid, until the Thursday next before the Feast of the Annunciation of the *Blessed Virgin Mary* then next ensuing, and further until other of the aforesaid Burgesses of the Borough aforesaid shall be in due Manner and Form elected, preferred, and sworn to be Bailiffs of the Borough aforesaid : AND FURTHER WE WILL, and by these Presents, for us, our Heirs and Successors, grant to the aforesaid Mayor, Bailiffs, and Burgesses of the Borough aforesaid, and their Successors, That if it shall happen the Mayor of the Borough aforesaid, at any Time hereafter within one Year after he shall be preferred and sworn to the Office of Mayoralty of the Borough aforesaid, as aforesaid, to die or be removed from his Office, which same Mayor not well behaving himself in the same Office, WE WILL to be removeable at the Pleasure of the aforesaid Capital Burgesses, and of the other Burgesses of the Borough aforesaid, for the Time being, or the major Part of them, who shall be then present, so that the major Part of the Burgesses of the Borough aforesaid may or shall be then present, that then and so often it shall and may be lawful to

Election of Bailiffs.

Mayor removeable for Misbehaviour.

the aforesaid Capital Burgesses of the Borough aforesaid, for the Time being, to assemble themselves, or the major Part of them, within fourteen Days next ensuing the Death or Removal of the same Mayor in the Guildhall of the Borough aforesaid, or in any other convenient Place within the Borough aforesaid, and to elect, prefer, and nominate one other honest and fit Man of the aforesaid Burgesses, of the Borough aforesaid into the Mayoralty, and for Mayor of the Borough aforesaid, in the Place of him so dead, or removed from his Office ; and that he into the Office of Mayoralty so elected and preferred, having first taken a Corporal Oath in Form aforesaid, shall have and exercise the same Office during the Residue of the same Year, and until another Burgess of the Borough aforesaid shall be elected and sworn to the same Office ; and so as often as the Case shall so happen : AND if it shall happen the Bailiffs of the Borough aforesaid, or either of them, to die, or be removed from their Office of Bailiffs of the Borough aforesaid, which same Bailiffs, and each of them, not well behaving themselves or himself in their Office aforesaid, WE WILL to be removeable at the Pleasure of the Mayor and Capital Burgesses of the Borough aforesaid, for the Time being, or the major Part of them, that then and so often it shall and may be lawful to the Mayor and Capital Burgesses of the Borough aforesaid, for the Time being, or the major Part of them, within fourteen Days next after the aforesaid Bailiff, or Bailiffs shall so die, or be removed from his Office aforesaid, to assemble in the Guildhall of the Borough aforesaid, or in any other convenient Place within the Borough aforesaid, and to elect and prefer one or two of the Burgesses of the Borough aforesaid, into the Place or Places of the same Bailiff, or Bailiffs, so dead or removed from his Office ; and that he or they, so elected and sworn, shall have and exercise the same Office or Offices during the Residue of the same Year, and until another or others of the Burgesses of the Borough aforesaid shall be elected and sworn to the same Office of Bailiff or Bailiffs of the same Borough, having first taken a Corporal Oath in Form aforesaid ; and so as often as the Case shall so happen : AND if any or either of the Capital Burgesses of the Borough aforesaid, shall die, or be removed from his Office, who not well behaving themselves in their Office, WE WILL to be removeable at the Pleasure of the Mayor of the Borough aforesaid, and the major Part of the aforesaid Capital Burgesses of the same Borough, for the Time being, then that the Mayor and such of the rest of the aforesaid Capital Burgesses of the Borough aforesaid, who shall be assembled in the Guildhall of the Borough aforesaid, or in any other convenient Place within the Borough aforesaid, to be limited and assigned according to their Discretions, or the major Part of them so assembled, at the Pleasure of the Mayor and the Residue of the Capital Burgesses, shall and may be able to elect and prefer one, or as many as shall be deficient of the aforesaid Number of twelve of the best and most honest Burgesses of the Borough aforesaid, into the Place of the same Capital Burgess, or Capital Burgesses, so dead, or removed from his or their Office or Offices ; and that he or they, so elected and preferred, shall have and exercise the same Office to which he or they shall be so elected and preferred, so long as they shall well behave themselves in the same Office; and that the aforesaid Mayor so newly elected, before he shall execute the same Office of Mayoralty, shall take a Corporal Oath before such Burgesses of the Borough aforesaid, as shall then be present; and that the Bailiffs so newly elected, in like Manner, before they shall execute the same Office, shall take a Corporal Oath before the Mayor and Capital Burgesses of the Borough aforesaid, or the major Part of them; and so as often as the Case shall so happen: AND FURTHER WE WILL, and by these Presents, for us, our Heirs and Successors, grant to the aforesaid Mayor, Bailiffs, and Burgesses of the Borough aforesaid, and their Successors, That they and their Successors shall have in the Borough aforesaid for ever one honest and discreet Man, learned in the Laws of this Kingdom, to be elected and nominated in Form hereunder expressed, who shall be and be called Steward of the Borough aforesaid: AND WE HAVE assigned, constituted, and made, and by these Presents, for us, our Heirs and Successors, DO assign, nominate, ordain, constitute, and make our beloved *Sebastian Kele*, Gentleman, to be the first and present Steward of the Borough aforesaid, to continue in the same Office so long as he shall well behave himself in the same Office; and that the same *Sebastian Kele* shall and may be able to have, exercise, and enjoy the same Office of Steward of the Borough aforesaid, by himself, or by his sufficient Deputy or Deputies; and that the same *Sebastian Kele*, and his Deputy or Deputies, before they shall proceed to the Execution of his Office aforesaid, shall take a Corporal Oath upon the Holy Gospel of God before the Mayor of the Borough aforesaid, faithfully to execute the same Office in all Things touching the same Office; and that after the Death or Removal of the aforesaid *Sebastian*, the Mayor, Bailiffs, and Capital Burgesses of the Borough aforesaid, for the Time being, or the major Part of them, in a convenient Time shall and may be able to elect, nominate, and prefer one honest and discreet Man, learned in the Laws of *England*, from Time to Time, so often as to them it shall seem to be necessary, to be Steward of the Borough aforesaid; and that he who shall be so as aforesaid elected, preferred, and nominated into the Office of Steward of the Borough aforesaid, after the Death or Removal of the said *Sebastian*, shall and may be able to have, exercise, and enjoy the same Office of Steward of the Borough aforesaid, by himself, or by his sufficient Deputy, having first as aforesaid taken a Corporal Oath faithfully to execute the Office aforesaid, during the Pleasure of the Mayor, Bailiffs, and Capital Burgesses of the Borough aforesaid: AND FURTHER WE WILL, and by these Presents, for us, our Heirs and Successors, grant to the aforesaid Mayor, Bailiffs, and Burgesses of the Borough aforesaid, and their Successors, that from henceforth for ever there may and shall be in the Borough aforesaid one Officer, who shall be and be called Serjeant at Mace, to serve in the Court of the aforesaid Borough, and to execute and perform Proclamation, Arrest, and Execution of the Process, Mandates, and other Business to the Office of Serjeant at Mace, in the Borough aforesaid and the Parish of *Wicombe*, and the Limits, Bounds, and Precincts thereof appertaining, from Time to Time, at the Will and Pleasure of the Mayor, Bailiffs, and Capital Burgesses of the Borough aforesaid, which same Ser-

Steward.

Election of Steward.

Serjeant at Mace.

jeant at Mace shall be appointed, nominated, and elected by the aforesaid Mayor, Bailiffs, and Capital Burgesses of the Borough aforesaid, or by the major Part of them, so often as to the aforesaid Mayor, Bailiffs, and Capital Burgesses shall seem convenient and necessary; and shall be attending, from Time to Time, upon the Mayor of the Borough aforesaid for the Time being; and that the aforesaid Serjeant at Mace, so as aforesaid to be elected and nominated, may and shall be in due Manner sworn, well and faithfully to execute his Office aforesaid, before the Mayor, Bailiffs, and Capital Burgesses of the Borough aforesaid, or the major Part of them, for the Time being, of whom the Mayor for the Time being WE WILL to be one; and that after such Oath so taken, he ought, shall, and may be able to execute and perform the same Office during the Pleasure of the Mayor of the Borough aforesaid, and of the twelve capital Burgesses, or the major Part of them, of whom the Mayor WE WILL to be one: AND FURTHER WE WILL and ordain, and by these Presents, for us, our Heirs and Successors, grant to the aforesaid Mayor, Bailiffs, and Burgesses of the Borough aforesaid, and their Successors, That the aforesaid Serjeant at Mace, in the Borough aforesaid to be deputed, shall carry and bear a gilt or silver Mace, and engraven and ornamented with the Sign of the Arms of this Kingdom of *England*, every where within the said Borough of *Chepping Wycombe*, otherwise *Wicombe*, the Suburbs, Liberties, and Precincts thereof, before the Mayor of the Borough aforesaid, for the Time being: AND WE WILL, and by these Presents, for us, our Heirs and Successors, grant to the aforesaid Mayor, Bailiffs, and Burgesses of the Borough aforesaid, and their Successors, That they and their Successors from henceforth for ever shall have, and hold, and shall and may be able to have and hold in the Guildhall of the same Borough, or in

Court of Record to be held.

any other convenient Place within the Borough aforesaid, one Court of Record, on Monday in every third Week, or oftener, at their Pleasure, to be holden before the Mayor of the Borough aforesaid, and so many and such of the twelve Capital Burgesses for the Time being, as shall have been Mayors of the Borough aforesaid, if they are willing to be present, the Steward and Bailiffs of the same Borough, or one of the Bailiffs, or the sufficient Deputy, or sufficient Deputies of the Mayor or Steward of the Borough aforesaid, for the Time being; and that in the same Court they shall be able to hold by Plaints, in the same Court to be levied, ALL and all Manner of Pleas, Plaints, and Actions, concerning whatsoever Trespasses by Force and Arms, or otherwise, in Contempt of us, our Heirs and Successors, done or to be done, and of all and

Its Jurisdiction.

all Manner of Pleas upon the Case, Debt, Account, Covenant, Deceit, Detinue of Charters, Writings, and Muniments, and Chattels, taking and detaining of Cattle and Chattels, and other Contracts, for whatsoever Causes or Things, within the Borough aforesaid, and the Limits and Precincts thereof, arising or happening, provided the same Debts, Accounts, Covenants, Contracts, and other Actions, personal or mixed, shall not exceed the Sum or Value of forty Pounds; and that so often as any Person or Persons whomsoever shall be willing to implead any other Person or Persons whomsoever, possessing or holding Lands, Tenements, Rents, or Hereditaments within the

Borough aforesaid, the Limits and Precincts thereof, concerning the same Lands, Tenements, Rents, and Hereditaments, he or they so willing to implead shall prosecute our Writ of Right Patent, issuing out of our Court of Chancery of *England*, to be directed to the aforesaid Mayor of the Borough aforesaid, upon which same Writ in the Court aforesaid, before the Mayor of the Borough aforesaid, for the Time being, and so many and such of the twelve Capital Burgesses for the Time being, as shall have been Mayors of the Borough aforesaid, if they are willing to be present, the Steward and Bailiffs of the same Borough, or one of the Bailiffs, or the sufficient Deputy, or sufficient Deputies of the Mayor or Steward of the Borough aforesaid for the Time being, he or they, so as aforesaid willing to implead, shall make his Protest to sue his Plaint upon the aforesaid Writ, made in the Nature of a Writ of Assize, Novel Disseisin, Mort d'Ancestor, Attaint, or in the Nature of any other Action or Writ whatsoever at the Common Law, as the Matter and Case shall require ; and that such Pleas, Plaints, and Actions, as well real as personal and mixed, shall be there heard and determined before the Mayor of the Borough aforesaid, and so many and such of the Capital Burgesses of the Borough aforesaid for the Time being, who have been Mayors of the Borough aforesaid, if they are willing to be present, the Steward and Bailiffs of the Borough aforesaid, or one of the Bailiffs, or the sufficient Deputy, or sufficient Deputies of the Mayor or Steward of the Borough aforesaid, in the Guildhall of the Borough aforesaid, or in any other convenient Place within the Borough aforesaid, by such and the like Process and Means, according to the Law and Custom of our Kingdom of *England*, by which, and as shall be agreeable to our Law, and in as ample Manner and Form, and as in any other Court of Record, in any other Borough or Town Corporate within this our Kingdom of *England*, is used and accustomed, or may or ought to be done : AND WE WILL, and for us, our Heirs and Successors, by these Presents, grant and ordain, that the Serjeant at Mace of the Borough aforesaid, for the Time being, shall make and execute all Pannels, Juries, Inquisitions, Attachments, Precepts, Mandates, Warrants, Judgments, Process, and other Things whatsoever necessary to be done, touching the Causes aforesaid, or other Causes whatsoever touching or concerning the Borough aforesaid, within the Borough aforesaid and the Liberties thereof, as to them shall seem proper, according to the Exigence of the Law, and as in like Cases is used, or ought to be done in any other Court of Record, in any other Borough or Town Corporate within this our Kingdom of *England* ; and that the Mayor, Bailiffs, and Burgesses of the Borough aforesaid, and their Successors, shall and may have and receive all Fines, Services, Issues, and other Profits whatsoever, of and in the Court aforesaid, arising, coming, accruing, or happening to be expended to the like and such Use and Profit, as to the said Mayor, Bailiffs, and Burgesses shall seem best : AND FURTHER WE, of our special Grace and of our certain Knowledge and mere Motion, for us, our heirs and Successors, grant to the aforesaid Mayor, Bailiffs, and Burgesses of the said Borough of *Chepping Wycombe*, otherwise *Wicombe*, in the County of *Buckingham* aforesaid, and their Successors, View of

Frankpledge. Frankpledge of all and singular the Inhabitants and Residents, as well entirely as not entirely, residing within the said Borough of *Chepping Wycombe*, otherwise *Wicombe*, and within the Limits and Bounds thereof, and all Things which to View of Frankpledge appertain or belong, or ought to appertain or belong, to be holden in the Common Hall, called the Guildhall, or in any other convenient Place within the aforesaid Borough of *Chepping Wycombe*, otherwise *Wicombe*, twice in the Year, that is to say once within a Month, of *Saint Michael*, and again within a Month of *Easter*, to be holden before the aforesaid Mayor, Steward, and such of the Capital Burgesses as shall have been Mayors of the Borough aforesaid, who shall then be present, and the Bailiffs, or either of the Bailiffs of the Borough aforesaid, or the sufficient Deputy, or sufficient Deputies of the Mayor or Steward of the Borough aforesaid, for the Time being, in every Year; and that the same Mayor, Bailiffs, and Burgesses may and shall have all and all Manner of Fines, Redemptions, Issues, and Amerciaments, and all other Profits of and in the aforesaid View of Frankpledge, in any wise coming, arising, or happening, to the proper Use and Behoof of the said Mayor, Bailiffs, and Burgesses, and of the Commonalty of the said Borough of *Chepping Wycombe*, otherwise *Wicombe* aforesaid, for the Time being, to be taken and converted; so that no other Person besides the Mayor, Bailiffs, and Burgesses of the Borough aforesaid, shall in any wise hereafter have or hold any View of Frankpledge, or any other Court in the said Borough, or any Place thereof, unless only by the Licence and Consent of the said Mayor, Bailiffs, and Burgesses, or their Successors, thereto specially obtained, or to be obtained: AND FURTHER, of our more ample Grace, and of our certain Knowledge and mere Motion, WE HAVE granted for us, our Heirs and Successors, That the

Inhabitants free of Pannage. aforesaid Mayor, Bailiffs, Burgesses, and other Inhabitants of the said Borough of *Chepping Wycombe*, otherwise *Wicombe*, and their Successors, residing, dwelling, or inhabiting within the same Borough, shall be quit and discharged of Pannage, Passage, Lastage, Tallage, Carriage, Pesage, Piccage, and Terrage, throughout our whole Kingdom of *England*: WE HAVE ALSO granted to the same Mayor, Bailiffs, and Burgesses

Fines, &c. aforesaid, and their Successors, That they shall have and perceive all Manner of Fines for Trespasses and other Misdeeds whatsoever, and also Fines for Licence to agree, and all Manner of other Fines, Redemptions, and Amerciaments, from whatsoever Cause, and by whatsoever Cause arising, and also Issues and Forfeitures of all such Men, Tenants, Residents, or Dwellers in the same Borough of *Chepping Wycombe*, otherwise *Wicombe*, although the same Men, Tenants, Residents, or Dwellers, shall be Ministers of us, or of our Heirs or Successors; and that the same Mayor, Bailiffs, and Burgesses, and their Successors, shall have all and all Manner of Forfeitures, Year, Day, Waste, and Estrepement within the Borough aforesaid, arising or happening, adjudged as well in the Presence of us, our Heirs and Successors, as elsewhere in the Absence of us, our Heirs, or Successors, before whatsoever Justices of us, our Heirs, or Successors; and that they shall be able to levy, perceive, and have all that which to us or our Heirs concerning such Forfeitures, Year, Day, and Waste, and Estrepement, might appertain, if our present Grant to the same Mayor, Bailiffs, and Burgesses, had not been made, to the Behoof of the same Mayor, Bailiffs, and Burgesses, and their Successors, by their Bailiffs or Ministers; and that they, in like Manner, from henceforth for ever shall and may be able to levy, receive, and have such Fines, Redemptions, and Amerciaments of all such Men, Tenants, Residents, or Dwellers in the said Borough of *Chepping Wycombe*, otherwise *Wicombe*, and also the Issues by them or any of them forfeited, which before us, and our Heirs or Successors, or in the Chancery of us, our Heirs or Successors, or before whatsoever Justices and Ministers of us, our Heirs or Successors, shall happen to be done, adjudged, or forfeited by Estreat of such Court of us, our Heirs and Successors, without the Hindrance or Impediment of us, our Heirs or Successors, the Justices, Escheators, Sheriffs, Coroners, Bailiffs, or other Ministers of us, our Heirs or Successors whomsoever: AND FURTHER WE WILL, and by these Presents, for us, our Heirs and Successors, grant to the aforesaid Mayor, Bailiffs, and Burgesses of the Borough aforesaid, and their Successors, That the Borough aforesaid, and the Circuit, Bounds, and Precincts thereof, may and ought to extend and stretch themselves, as well in Length as in Breadth, to such and the like Metes and Bounds to which and as of old they have been accustomed, of Right and lawfully to extend and stretch; and that all and singular Houses, Edifices, Lands, Tenements, void Grounds and Soil whatsoever, within the Bounds, Metes, and Limits thereof, from henceforth may and shall be, and shall be reputed to be Parts and Parcel of the said Borough of *Wicombe*, now by these Presents erected and incorporated into a Body Politic as aforesaid: WE HAVE MOREOVER granted, and for us, our Heirs and Successors, DO grant to the aforesaid Mayor, Bailiffs, and Burgesses of the Borough aforesaid, and their Successors, That the Mayor of the Borough aforesaid, for the Time being, during the Time which he shall happen to be in his Office, shall be Justice of us, our Heirs and Successors, to preserve and cause to be kept the Peace in the same Borough, the Liberties and Precincts thereof, and also to keep and correct, and cause to be kept and corrected, the Statutes concerning Vagabonds, Artificers, and Labourers, Weights and Measures, within the Borough aforesaid, the Liberties and Precincts thereof; so that the Mayor of the same Borough, for the Time being, shall have from henceforth for ever Power and Authority to inquire, hear, and determine all Matters, Plaints, Causes, and Articles, which to the Office of a Justice of the Peace, Labourers and Artificers appertain; so nevertheless that the said Mayor, for the Time being, shall not in any wise hereafter proceed to the Determination of any Treason, Murder, or Felony, or of any other Matter touching the Loss of Life or Member, within the Borough aforesaid, the Liberties or Precincts thereof, without the special Mandate of us, our Heirs or Successors, and nevertheless he shall and may be able to do, inquire, hear, and determine all and singular other Offences, inferior Defaults, and Articles, which to the Office of a Justice of the Peace within the Borough aforesaid, the Liberties and Precincts thereof, appertain as fully and entirely, and in as ample Manner and Form as any other Justice of the Peace of us, our Heirs or Successors, in any County of our Kingdom of

Bounds of the Borough.

Mayor a Justice of the Peace within the Borough.

H H

England, as Justice of the Peace, can or may be able to inquire, hear, or determine : AND that the said Mayor, Bailiffs, and Burgesses of the Borough aforesaid, for the Time being, and their Successors, shall have from henceforth for ever, within the Borough aforesaid, the Liberties or Precincts thereof, a Prison and Gaol, proper to keep all those who shall hereafter happen to be taken, attached, or apprehended within the Borough aforesaid, or the Liberties thereof, for Felonies, Trespasses, or whatsoever other Crimes, Contempts, and Offences there perpetrated, as in that Behalf, in the same Borough, hath been heretofore used and accustomed ; so that they so being in the Gaol aforesaid, who cannot reasonably be delivered by the Mayor of the Borough aforesaid, for the Time being, according to the Liberties and Customs of the said Borough, shall be delivered by the Justices of us, our Heirs and Successors, assigned to deliver Gaols, or to take Assizes there, according to the Law and Custom of our Kingdom of *England*, and as hitherto hath been accustomed to be done : AND FURTHER WE HAVE granted, and for us, our Heirs, and Successors, by these Presents, DO grant to the aforesaid Mayor, Bailiffs, and Burgesses of the Borough aforesaid, and their Successors, That the Mayor of the Borough aforesaid, for the Time being, from henceforth for ever may and shall be Clerk of the Market within the Borough aforesaid, the Liberties and Precincts thereof, and shall do and execute, and shall and may be able to do and execute for ever, all and every thing which to the Office of Clerk of the Market there doth appertain to do, and to perform all and singular other Deeds and Things which to the same Office appertain to be done and performed, within the Borough aforesaid, the Liberties and Precincts thereof; and that the Mayor, Bailiffs, and Burgesses of the same Borough, for the Time being, for ever may and shall have the Assize and Assay of Bread, Wine, and Ale, and of other Victuals, Fuel, and Wood in the said Borough, the Liberties and Precincts thereof, and the Amendment of the same Assize broken, and also the Punishment, Correction, and Amerciaments, and Fines of all Persons there offending in the Abuse of Measures and Weights of Fuel or Wood, as well in the Presence as in the Absence of us, our Heirs and Successors ; so that the Clerk of the Market of the Household of us, our Heirs, or Successors, for the Assize of Bread, Wine, and Ale, broken and other Victuals, or such Weights or Measures, or for the doing of any other Thing touching or concerning the Office of Clerk of the Market, shall not in any wise enter or presume to enter within the Borough aforesaid, the Liberties or Precincts thereof : WE WILL ALSO, and for us, our Heirs and Successors, ordain and grant by these Presents to the aforesaid Mayor, Bailiffs, and Burgesses of the Borough aforesaid, and their Successors, That the Mayor of the same Borough, for the Time being, and his Successors for the Time being, during the Time which he shall be in the Office of Mayoralty, may and shall be Escheator and Coroner of us, our Heirs and Successors within the Borough aforesaid, the Liberties and Precincts thereof, and shall do and execute, and shall and may be able to do and execute, within the Borough aforesaid, the Liberties and Precincts thereof, all and every thing which to the Office of Escheator and Coroner there doth appertain to do ; and that he shall take an Oath

(margin: Gaol.)

(margin: Mayor Clerk of the Market.)

(margin: Escheator and Coroner.)

well and faithfully to do and exercise the same Offices of Clerk of the Market, Escheator, and Coroner, before the old Mayor and the Capital Burgesses, or the major Part of them, before he shall take upon himself the Offices of Clerk of the Market, Escheator and Coroner; so that any or either of the Escheators or Coroners of us, our Heirs and Successors in our County of *Buckingham*, shall in no wise intermeddle or presume to enter, nor shall any of them in any wise hereafter intermeddle or presume to enter, to do any thing which to the Office of Escheator or Coroner within the Borough aforesaid doth appertain, unless in Default of the Mayor of the Borough aforesaid for the Time being: WE HAVE MOREOVER granted for us, our Heirs and Successors, and by these Presents DO grant to the aforesaid Mayor, Bailiffs, and Burgesses of the Borough aforesaid, and their Successors, That neither they nor their Successors, nor any Person dwelling in the same Borough, shall be drawn into Plea before the Steward or Marshall of the Household of us, our Heirs and Successors, for the Assize of Bread, Wine, and Ale in the same Borough, broken, or for any Trespasses by them or any of them, without the Verge or within the Verge, before or after the coming of the same Steward and Marshall, or either of them, to those Parts, or at the Time of the being of the same Steward and Marshall in those Parts, to whatsoever Person done or perpetrated, nor shall they be hindered or molested in any wise, or aggrieved for those Occasions or any of them: WE HAVE ALSO granted, for us, our Heirs and Successors, to the aforesaid Mayor, Bailiffs, and Burgesses of the Borough aforesaid, and their Successors, That they shall be able to levy, receive, and have to the Use and Profit of the same Mayor, Bailiffs, and Burgesses, and of all the Commonalty of the said Borough of *Chepping Wycombe*, otherwise *Wicombe* aforesaid, all and all Manner of Issues, Fines, Redemptions, and Amerciaments, by any Burgesses of the said Borough of *Chepping Wycombe*, otherwise *Wicombe*, for the Time being, before the Steward and Marshall of the Household of us, our Heirs and Successors, for the Time being, forfeited or adjudged: WE HAVE MOREOVER granted, and by these Presents firmly forbid, that any Sheriff, Constable, or Bailiff, or the aforesaid Steward and Marshall of the Household of us, our Heirs or Successors, or any Minister or Officer of us, our Heirs or Successors, besides the Mayor and Bailiffs of the said Borough for the Time being, shall in any wise enter the same Borough in any wise to exercise their Office there, unless in Default of the same Mayor and Bailiffs, or any of them, but all that from henceforth shall appertain and belong to the Mayor and Bailiffs, and their Successors for ever: AND WE WILL, and by these Presents, for us, our Heirs and Successors, grant to the aforesaid Mayor, Bailiffs, and Burgesses of the Borough aforesaid, and their Successors, That they may and shall have the Return, as well of Assize as of all and all Manner of other Writs, Precepts, Bills, and Warrants of us, our Heirs, and Successors, within the said Borough, the Liberties and Precincts thereof, hereafter arising or happening, and the Execution thereof by the Bailiffs of the Borough aforesaid for the Time being: so that no Sheriff, Bailiff, Constable, or other foreign Minister of us, our Heirs or Successors, shall enter the Borough aforesaid, or

Prevention from Pleas, &c.

the Liberties or Precincts thereof, for the Return or Execution of the aforesaid Writs, Precepts, Bills, Warrants, Summons, or Attachments, or either of them, or to exercise in any other Thing his Office there, or with the same or any of them shall intermeddle, unless in Default of the same Mayor, Bailiffs, and Burgesses, or their Successors: AND FURTHER, of our more ample especial Grace, and of our certain Knowledge and mere Motion, WE HAVE granted, and by these Presents, for us, our Heirs and Successors, DO grant to the aforesaid Mayor, Bailiffs, and Burgesses of the Borough aforesaid, and their Successors, That they and their Successors shall have, hold, and keep, and from henceforth shall and may be **Market.** able to have, hold, and keep for ever within the same Borough one Market in every week throughout the Year, in and upon every Friday, as hitherto they have had and used; and also that they and their Successors shall have, hold, and keep, and from henceforth for ever shall and may be able to have, hold, and keep for **Fairs.** ever two Fairs or Marts by the Year within the same Borough, to be holden in every Year for ever; the first of which same two Fairs or Marts yearly, shall begin at Noon of the Day of the Feast of the Translation of *Saint Thomas* the Martyr, and shall continue until Noon of the Morrow of the Day of the same Feast; and the second Fair or Mart of the aforesaid two Fairs or Marts yearly, shall begin at Noon of the Day of the Feast of the Exaltation of the Holy Cross, and shall continue until Noon of the Morrow of the Day of the same Feast; together with a Court of Piepowder, there to be holden at the Times of the same Fairs or Marts; and together with all and all Manner of Tolls, Customs, Profits, Commodities, and Emoluments whatsoever, to such Fairs or Marts, and Court of Piepowder appertaining, belonging, accruing, arising, or happening; and that the Fairs or Marts aforesaid shall be holden in the Places of old used and accustomed; so nevertheless that the aforesaid Fairs or Marts shall not be to the Prejudice of other neighbouring Fairs or Marts near adjacent: AND ALSO WE WILL, and for us, our Heirs and Successors grant and ordain, That there may and shall be in the said Borough two Burgesses of the Parliament of us, our Heirs and Successors; and that the aforesaid Mayor, Bailiffs, and Burgesses, and their Successors, upon the Writ of us, our Heirs and Successors, for the Election of Burgesses of the Parliament to them directed, may and shall have Power, Faculty, and Authority to elect and nominate two **Return of two** discreet and honest Men Burgesses of the Borough aforesaid, to be Burgesses of the **Burgesses to** **Parliament.** Parliament of us and of our Successors for the same Borough; and the same Burgesses so elected at the Charges and Costs of the said Mayor, Bailiffs, and Burgesses, and their Successors, for the Time being, to send to the Parliament of us, our Heirs and Successors, wheresoever it shall be then holden, in the same Manner and Form as in other Boroughs of our Kingdom of *England*, or in our ancient Borough of *Wicombe* aforesaid hath been used and accustomed, which same Burgesses so elected and nominated, WE WILL to be present and to remain at the Parliament of us, our Heirs and Successors, at the Charges and Costs of the said Mayor, Bailiffs, and Burgesses, during the Time which such Parliament shall happen to be holden, in the like Manner and Form as other Burgesses of the Parliament, for whatsoever other Boroughs or Borough within our Kingdom of *England*, can do or have been accustomed to do; and which same Burgesses in such Parliament of us, our Heirs and Successors, shall have their Voices, as well affirmative as negative, and shall do and execute all and singular other Things there as other Burgesses, or any other Burgess of our Parliament, for whatsoever other Boroughs or Borough may have, do, and execute, or may or can be able to have, do, or execute, by whatsoever Reason or Means: WE HAVE ALSO granted, and by these Presents, for us, our Heirs and Successors, DO grant to the aforesaid Mayor, Bailiffs, and Burgesses of the Borough aforesaid, and their Successors, That the aforesaid Mayor, Bailiffs, and Burgesses, and their Successors, from henceforth shall have all manner of Felons and Fugitives, as well Felons of themselves as other Persons whomsoever, outlawed, attainted, and convicted, and for whatsoever Cause of all the Men and Tenants aforesaid, as well entire Tenants as not entire Tenants and Residents, and of all Persons dwelling or inhabiting within the said Borough of *Chepping Wycombe*, otherwise *Wicombe*, and Goods and Chattels waived and Estrays whatsoever, within the said Borough, Deodands and Treasure Trove within the Borough aforesaid; and if any of the Men, Tenants, and Residents of or in the same Borough, or any other Person in the same Borough, for any Offence or Misdeed whatsoever, ought to lose Life or Member, or shall fly and not stand to Judgment, or shall commit any other Trespass for which he ought to lose his Chattels, in whatsoever Place Justice ought to be done, whether in the Court of us, our Heirs or Successors, or in any other Court, the Chattels shall be of the same Mayor, Bailiffs, and Burgesses, and it shall be lawful for them to put themselves in seizin of the same Chattels, and to retain the same Chattels to their Use, without the Hindrance or Impediment of us, our Heirs, or Successors, the Justices, Escheators, Sheriffs, Coroners, and other Bailiffs, or Ministers of us, or of our Heirs or Successors whomsoever; and that the same Mayor, Bailiffs, and Burgesses of the Borough aforesaid, shall have whatsoever Goods and Chattels called Manuopera, taken or to be taken with whatsoever Person being within the Borough aforesaid: AND FURTHER KNOW YE that we, in Consideration that the Mayor, Bailiffs, and Burgesses of the Borough aforesaid, and their Successors, shall and may be able, the better to sustain and support the Charges in the Borough aforesaid, from Time to Time, and for the better Maintenance and Support of the Free Grammar School within the Borough aforesaid, of our especial Grace and of our certain Knowledge and mere Motion, HAVE granted, and by these Presents, for us, our Heirs and Successors, as much as in us lies, DO grant and give special Licence, and free and lawful Faculty, Power, and Authority to the aforesaid Mayor, Bailiffs, and Burgesses of the Borough aforesaid, and their Successors, to have, receive, and Purchase to them and their Successors for ever, as well of us, our Heirs, and Successors, as of whatsoever our Subjects and liege People, or of any other Persons or Person whomsoever, Manors, Messuages, Lands, Tenements, Rectories, Tythes, Rents, Services, and other Possessions, Revenues and Hereditaments whatsoever, which are not immediately holden of us, our Heirs or Successors in chief,

Purchase of Lands, &c.

nor of us, our Heirs, or Successors immediately, by Knight's Service, without the special
Licence of us, our Heirs, or Successors, provided the same Manors, Messuages, Lands,
Tenements, Rectories, Tythes, Rents, Reversions. and Services, or other Possessions,
Revenues, and Hereditaments, so to be had, received, and purchased, shall not exceed
in the whole the yearly Value of twenty Pounds. the Statute concerning Lands and
Tenements not to be put in Mortmain or any other Statute, Act, Ordinance, Provision,
or Restriction, or any other Thing, Cause, or Matter whatsoever, in any wise notwithstanding : WE HAVE ALSO granted, and given special Licence and lawful Faculty,
Power, and Authority; and by these Presents, for us, our Heirs and Successors, DO
give and grant to whatsoever Subject and Subjects of us, our Heirs, and Successors,
and to whatsoever Bodies Politic and Body Politic, and other Persons whomsoever
and every of them, That they and every of them shall and may be able to give, grant,
sell, leave, assign, or in any other Manner and Manners whatsoever, alien, devise, or
assure any Manors, Messuages, Lands, Tenements, Rectories, Tythes, Rents, Reversions, Services, and other Possessions, Revenues, and Hereditaments whatsoever, which
are not immediately holden of us, our Heirs or Successors in chief, nor of us, our Heirs
or Successors immediately, by Knight's Service, to the aforesaid Mayor, Bailiffs, and
Burgesses of the Borough aforesaid and their Successors, provided the same Manors,
Messuages, Lands, Tenements, Rectories, Tythes, and other Hereditaments whatsoever, so as aforesaid to be given, granted, sold, left, assigned, aliened, or devised, shall
not exceed in the whole the clear yearly Value of twenty Pounds by the Year; the
Statute concerning Lands and Tenements not to be put in Mortmain, or any other
Statute, Act, Ordinance, Provision, or Restriction, or any other Thing, Cause, or Matter
whatsoever, in any wise notwithstanding : AND MOREOVER, of our further especial Grace,
and of our certain Knowledge and mere Motion, WE HAVE given, granted, and confirmed; and by these Presents for us, our Heirs and Successors, DO give, grant, and confirm to the aforesaid Mayor, Bailiffs, and Burgesses of the Borough aforesaid, and their

**Former Privi-
leges con-
firmed.**

Successors, all and singular the Manors, Messuages, Lands, Tenements, Hereditaments,
Liberties, Free Customs, Privileges, Franchises, Immunities, Exemptions, Acquittances,
and Jurisdictions whatsoever, which the aforesaid Mayor, Bailiffs, and Burgesses of the
aforesaid Borough of *Chepping Wycombe*, otherwise *Wicombe* aforesaid, by whatsoever
Names or Name of Incorporation, or by whatsoever Incorporation, or by Pretext of whatsoever Incorporation heretofore rightly and lawfully, have had, held, used or enjoyed,
or ought to have, hold, use, or enjoy, by Reason or Pretext of any Charters or Letters
Patent, by us or by any of our Progenitors, in any wise heretofore made, confirmed, or
granted, or by whatsoever other lawful Means, Right, Custom, Usage, Prescription, or
Title heretofore lawfully used, had, and accustomed, to have and enjoy to the same
Mayor, Bailiffs, and Burgesses, and their Successors for ever; RENDERING therefore to
us, our Heirs, and Successors, the like such and similar Rents, Services, and Sums of
Money, and Demands, which for the same to us, our Heirs and Successors have been
heretofore due, paid, and of Right accustomed : WE WILL ALSO, and grant to the aforesaid

Mayor, Bailiffs, and Burgesses of the Borough aforesaid and their Successors, That they shall have, hold, use, and enjoy, and shall and may be able to have, hold, use, and enjoy for ever, all the Liberties, Free Customs, Privileges, Authorities, and Acquittances aforesaid, according to the Tenor and Effect of these our Letters Patent, without the Hindrance or Impediment of us, our Heirs, or Successors whomsoever; being unwilling that the same Mayor, Bailiffs, and Burgesses of the Borough aforesaid, or any or either of them, or any Burgesses of the Borough aforesaid, by Reason of the Premises, or of any of them, by us or by our Heirs, the Justices, Sheriffs, Escheators, or other Bailiffs or Ministers of us, our Heirs, or Successors whomsoever, shall be therefore hindered, molested, vexed, or aggrieved, or in any wise disturbed: WE WILL ALSO, and by these Presents, for us, our Heirs and Successors, grant to the aforesaid Mayor, Bailiffs, and Burgesses of the Borough of *Chepping Wycombe*, otherwise *Wicombe* aforesaid, That they may and shall have these our Letters Patent under our Great Seal of *England*, in due Manner made and sealed without Fine or Fee, great or small, to us in our Hanaper or elsewhere, to our Use for the same, in any Manner to be rendered, paid, or done, ALTHOUGH express Mention, &c. IN WITNESS whereof, &c. WITNESS, THE QUEEN, at Westminster, the first Day of March.

By Writ of Privy Seal, &c.

CHARTER

GRANTED TO THE

MAYOR, BAILIFFS, AND BURGESSES

OF

THE BOROUGH OF CHEPPING WYCOMBE,

BY KING JAMES THE FIRST,

17TH JUNE, 1609,

IN THE SIXTH YEAR OF HIS REIGN.

Of a grant to the Mayor, Bailiffs, and Burgesses of the Borough of *Chepping Wycombe,* and their Successors.

THE KING, to all to whom, &c. Greeting.—WHEREAS our Borough of *Chepping Wycombe,* otherwise called *Wicombe,* in our County of *Buckingham,* is an ancient and populous Borough, and the Mayor, Bailiffs, and Burgesses of the Borough of *Wicombe* aforesaid, have had, and used, and enjoyed divers Liberties, Franchises, Immunities, and Pre-eminences, as well by Charters of the Lady *Elizabeth,* late Queen of *England,* and by a Charter of the Lord *Philip* and Lady *Mary,* late King and Queen of *England,* as by Charters of divers others of our Progenitors and Predecessors, late Kings of *England,* to them and their Predecessors heretofore made, granted, or confirmed, as also by Reason of divers Prescriptions and Customs in the same Borough, from Time whereof the Memory of Man is not to the contrary used: AND WHEREAS WE are informed that there are certain Defects, Ambiguities, and Inconveniences in the Charters and Letters Patent aforesaid, by Reason that some Things in the same contained, were not granted plainly, expressly, or in proper Words, for the good Rule, Government, and Advantage of the Borough aforesaid, according to the true Intent of the same Charters or Letters Patent: AND WHEREAS our beloved Subjects, the Mayor, Bailiffs, and Burgesses of the Borough of *Wicombe* aforesaid, have humbly besought us that we would be pleased to shew and extend to the same Mayor, Bailiffs, and Burgesses, our Royal Grace and Munificence in the Behalf, and that We, for the better Government, Rule, and Improvement of the same Borough, would condescend to ratify, confirm, approve, make, renew, constitute, or create anew the said Mayor, Bailiffs, and Burgesses of the same Borough into one Body Corporate and Politic, by our Letters Patent, with the Addition of certain

Liberties, Privileges, Immunities, and Franchises, as to us shall seem most expedient: WE THEREFORE WILLING, that from henceforth for ever there shall be continually had in the same Borough one certain and undoubted Method of and for the keeping of the Peace, and the good Rule and Government of the People there; and that the Borough aforesaid from henceforth for ever shall be and remain a Borough of Peace and Quiet, to the Dread and Terror of the Wicked, and in Reward of the Good, and that our Peace and other Deeds of Justice may be preserved there without further Delay; and hoping that if the Mayor, Bailiffs, and Burgesses of the same Borough, and their Successors, are enabled of our Grant to enjoy more ample Honour, Liberties, and Privileges, then they will esteem themselves bound more especially and strongly to perform and exhibit to us, and our Heirs and Successors, the Services which they are able, of our especial Grace, and of our certain Knowledge and mere Motion, HAVE willed, ordained, constituted and granted, and by these Presents, for us, our Heirs and Successors, DO will, ordain, constitute, declare, and grant, That the said Borough of *Wicombe*, in our said County of *Buckingham*, from henceforth may and shall be a Free Borough of itself; and that the Mayor, Bailiffs, and Burgesses of the same Borough, by whatsoever Name they have been heretofore incorporated, and their Successors, from henceforth for ever may and shall be, by Force of these Presents, one Body Corporate and Politic, in Deed, Fact, and Name, by the Name of Mayor, Bailiffs, and Burgesses of the Borough of *Chepping Wycombe*, otherwise *Wicombe*, in the County of *Buckingham*; and them by the Name of Mayor, Bailiffs, and Burgesses of the Borough of *Chepping Wycombe*, otherwise *Wicombe*, in the County of *Buckingham*, one Body Corporate and Politic, in Deed, Fact, and Name, really and fully for us, our Heirs and Successors, We do erect, make, ordain, constitute, confirm, and declare by these Presents, and that by the same Name, they shall have perpetual Succession; and that they, by the Name of Mayor, Bailiffs, and Burgesses of the Borough of *Chepping Wycombe*, otherwise *Wicombe*, in the County of *Buckingham*, may and shall be for ever hereafter Persons able and capable in the Law to have, purchase, receive, and possess Lands, Tenements, Liberties, Privileges, Jurisdictions, Franchises, and Hereditaments, of whatsoever Kind, Nature, or Sort they may be, to them and their Successors, in Fee and Perpetuity, and also Goods and Chattels, and whatsoever other Things of whatsoever Kind, Nature, or Sort they may be, and also to give, grant, demise, and assign, Lands, Tenements, and Hereditaments, Goods and Chattels, and to do and execute all and singular other Deeds and Things, by the Name aforesaid; and that by the same Name of Mayor, Bailiffs, and Burgesses of the Borough of *Chepping Wycombe*, otherwise *Wicombe*, in the County of *Buckingham*, shall and may be able to plead and be impleaded, answer and be answered, defend, and be defended, in whatsoever Courts and Places, and before whatsoever Judges and Justices, and other Persons and Officers of us, and of our Heirs and Successors, in all Suits, Plaints, Pleas, Causes, Matters, and Demands, real, personal, or mixt, whatsoever, as well spiritual as temporal, of whatsoever Kind, Nature, or Sort

Declared a Body Corporate.

May possess Lands, &c.

May plead, &c.

I I

they may be, in the same Manner and Form as other our liege People of this our Kingdom of *England*, Persons able and capable in the Law, to plead and be impleaded, answer and be answered, defend and be defended, and to have, purchase, receive, possess, give, grant, and demise, may and can be able; and that the aforesaid Mayor, Bailiffs, and Burgesses of the aforesaid Borough of *Chepping Wycombe*, otherwise *Wicombe*, in the County of *Bucks*, and their Successors, shall have for ever a Common Seal, to serve for doing their Causes and Business, and of their Successors whomsoever; and that it shall and may be lawful to the same Mayor, Bailiffs, and Burgesses, and their Successors, the same Seal at their Pleasure from Time to Time to break, change, and make anew, as to them shall seem meet: AND FURTHER WE WILL, and by these Presents, for us, our Heirs and Successors, grant and ordain, that from henceforth for ever there may and shall be within the Borough aforesaid, one of the most honest and discreet Burgesses of the Borough aforesaid, to be elected in Form hereunder in these Presents mentioned, who shall be and be named Mayor of the Borough aforesaid; and that in like Manner there may and shall be within the same Borough two honest and discreet Burgesses of the Borough aforesaid, to be elected in Form hereunder in these Presents mentioned, who shall be and be named Bailiffs of the Borough aforesaid: AND ALSO WE WILL, and by these Presents, for us, our Heirs, and Successors, grant and ordain, that from henceforth for ever there may and shall be within the Borough aforesaid, from Time to Time, twelve honest and discreet Men, continually inhabiting and dwelling within the Borough aforesaid, who shall be and be called Aldermen of the said Borough; and that the Mayor, Bailiffs, and Burgesses of the same Borough, and their Successors, or the major Part of them, from Time to Time, for ever, shall and may be able to elect so many and such other Men, inhabiting or not inhabiting within the Borough aforesaid, as and which to them shall seem most expedient to be Burgesses of the said Borough: AND WE WILL, and by these Presents, for us, our Heirs and Successors, grant to the aforesaid Mayor, Bailiffs, and Burgesses of the Borough aforesaid, and their Successors, that the aforesaid Aldermen and Bailiffs of the Borough aforesaid, and their Successors, shall be and be called the Common Council of the Borough aforesaid, and shall be, from Time to Time, assisting and aiding to the Mayor of the said Borough of *Chepping Wycombe*, otherwise *Wicombe* aforesaid, for the Time being, in all Causes and Matters touching or concerning the Borough aforesaid: AND FURTHER WE WILL, and by these Presents, for us, our Heirs, and Successors, grant to the aforesaid Mayor, Bailiffs, and Burgesses of the Borough aforesaid, and their Successors, that the Mayor, Aldermen, and Bailiffs of the Borough aforesaid, and their Successors, for the Time being, or the major part of them, (of whom the Mayor for the Time being WE WILL to be one) may and shall have full Power and Authority to frame, constitute, ordain and make, from Time to Time, such reasonable Laws,

Marginal notes:

Common Seal.

Mayor.

Bailiffs.

Aldermen.

Burgesses.

Common Council.

May ordain Laws, &c.

Statutes, and Ordinances whatsoever, as to them, according to their sound Discretions, shall seem to be good, wholesome, useful, honest, and necessary for the good Rule and Government of the Burgesses, Artificers, and Inhabitants of the Borough aforesaid, for the Time being, and for declaring in what Manner and Order the aforesaid Mayor, Aldermen, Bailiffs, and Burgesses, and the Artificers, Inhabitants, and Residents of the Borough aforesaid, shall behave, conduct, and carry themselves in their Offices, Mysteries, and Business within the same Borough, and the Liberties thereof, for the Time being, and otherwise for the further Good and public Advantage and Rule of the same Borough, and the Victualling of the same Borough, and also for the better Preservation, Government, Disposition, letting and demising of the Lands, Tenements, Possessions, Revenues, and Hereditaments, to the aforesaid Mayor, Bailiffs, and Burgesses, and their Successors, by these Presents, or otherwise, given, granted, assigned, or confirmed, or hereafter to be given, granted, or assigned, and other Things and Causes whatsoever, touching or in any wise concerning the Borough aforesaid, or the State, Right, and Interest of the same Borough; and that they and their Successors, by the Mayor for the Time being, and the Aldermen and Bailiffs of the Borough aforesaid, being the Common Council of the Borough aforesaid, or by the major Part of them as aforesaid, whensoever they shall frame, make, ordain, or establish such Laws, Statutes, and Ordinances, in Form aforesaid, shall be able to impose and assess such reasonable Pains, Penalties, and Punishments, by Imprisonment of the Body, or by Fines and Amerciaments, or by any of them, against and upon all Delinquents against such Laws, Statutes, and Ordinances, or any or either of them, as and which to the same Mayor, Aldermen and Bailiffs of the Borough aforesaid, for the Time being, or the major Part of them as aforesaid, shall seem to be reasonable and requisite, and shall and may be able to levy and have the same Fines and Amerciaments, without the Impediment of us, our Heirs and Successors; all and singular which Laws, Statutes, and Ordinances, so (as aforesaid) to be made, WE WILL to be observed, under the Pains in the same to be contained; so nevertheless that such Laws, Statutes, Ordinances, Imprisonments, Fines, and Amerciaments, are not repugnant nor contrary to the Laws, Statutes, Customs, or Rights of our Kingdom of *England*: AND for the better Execution of our same Grants in this Behalf, WE HAVE assigned, nominated, constituted, and made our beloved *Thomas Welles*, now Mayor of the Borough aforesaid, to be the first and present Mayor of the Borough aforesaid, WILLING that the same *Thomas Welles* shall be and continue in the Office of Mayor of the same Borough, from the making of these Presents, until the Thursday next before the Feast of *Saint Michael* the Archangel next ensuing, and from the same Feast until one of the Aldermen of the Borough aforesaid shall be elected and sworn to the same Office, according to the Ordinance and Constitution in these Presents expressed and declared, (if the same *Thomas Welles* shall so long live): WE HAVE ALSO assigned, nominated, and constituted, and by

May let Lands, &c.

Penalties and Punishments.

First Mayor.

these Presents, for us, our Heirs and Successors, DO assign, nominate, constitute, and make our beloved *John Damporte* and *Robert Biscoe*, now Bailiffs of the same Borough, to be the two first and modern Bailiffs of the Borough aforesaid, to continue in the same Offices of Bailiffs of the same Borough, until the Thursday next before the Feast of the Annunciation of the *Blessed Virgin Mary* next ensuing, and from the same Feast until two other of the Burgesses of the Borough aforesaid shall be preferred and sworn to the Office of Bailiffs of the same Borough, according to the Ordinances and Constitutions in these Presents hereunder expressed and declared, if the same *John Damporte* and *Robert Biscoe* shall so long live; WE HAVE ALSO assigned, nominated, and constituted, and by these Presents, for us, our Heirs and Successors, DO assign, nominate, constitute, and make our beloved *John Welles*, *Thomas Taylor*, *Ambrose Conway*, *William Shrimpton*, *Michael Burr*, *Gabriel Redman*, *George Welles*, *William Ayer*, *William Littleboy*, *John Littlepage*, *Richard Hynde*, and *Thomas Brandon*, Burgesses of the Borough aforesaid, to be the twelve first and present Aldermen of the Borough aforesaid, to continue in the same Offices during their Lives, unless, in the mean time, for bad Government or ill behaving themselves in that Behalf, or for not inhabiting and residing within the Borough aforesaid, they shall be removed from the same Offices: AND FURTHER WE WILL, and by these Presents, for us, our Heirs and Successors, grant to the aforesaid Mayor, Bailiffs, and Burgesses of the Borough aforesaid and their Successors, That the Mayor, Aldermen, Bailiffs, and Burgesses of the Borough aforesaid for the Time being, or the major Part of them, from time to time, for ever hereafter, may and shall have Power and Authority, yearly and every Year, on the Thursday next before the Feast of *St. Michael* the Archangel, to assemble themselves, or the major Part of them, in the Guildhall of the Borough aforesaid, or in any other convenient Place within the Borough aforesaid, to be limited and assigned according to their Discretions, and there to continue until they, or the major Part of them there then assembled, shall there elect or nominate one of the Aldermen of the Borough aforesaid to be Mayor of the Borough aforesaid, for one whole Year then next ensuing; and that then and there they shall and may be able to elect and nominate, before they shall from thence depart, one of the Aldermen of the Borough aforesaid, for the Time being, who shall be Mayor of the Borough aforesaid for one whole Year then next ensuing; and that he, after he shall be so as aforesaid elected and nominated to be Mayor of the Borough aforesaid, before he shall be admitted to execute the same Office, shall take a corporal Oath upon the Holy Gospel of God yearly on the Day of Election, if he shall be then present; and if he shall be absent, then within one Month then next ensuing after the said Day of Election, before the Mayor, his last Predecessor, or in his Absence before such Aldermen of the Borough aforesaid for the Time being, and the rest of the Burgesses of the Borough aforesaid, who shall be then present in the Guildhall of the Borough aforesaid, or in any other convenient Place within the Borough aforesaid, to be limited and assigned

Marginal notes:

First Bailiffs.

First Aldermen.

Nomination of Mayor.

according to their Discretions, rightly well and faithfully to execute the same Office in all Things touching the same Office; and that after such Oath so taken he shall and may be able to execute the Office of Mayor of the Borough aforesaid, until the Thursday next before the Feast of *St. Michael* the Archangel then next ensuing, and further until one other of the aforesaid Aldermen of the Borough aforesaid in due Manner and Form shall be elected, preferred, and sworn to be Mayor of the Borough aforesaid, according to the Ordinances and Constitutions above, in these Presents mentioned: AND FURTHER WE WILL, and by these Presents, for us, our Heirs and Successors, grant to the aforesaid Mayor, Bailiffs, and Burgesses of the Borough aforesaid, and their Successors, That the Mayor, Aldermen, and Bailiffs of the Borough aforesaid, for the Time being, or the major Part of them, from Time to Time, for ever hereafter, may and shall have Power and Authority, yearly and every Year, on the Thursday next before the Feast of the Annunciation of the *Blessed Virgin Mary*, to assemble themselves, or the major Part of them, in the Guildhall of the Borough aforesaid, or in any other convenient Place within the Borough aforesaid, to be limited and assigned according to their Discretions, and there to continue until they, or the major Part of them then assembled, shall elect or nominate two Burgesses of the Borough aforesaid to be Bailiffs of the Borough aforesaid, for the Year then next ensuing, to be elected and nominated in Form following; and that they shall and may be able there to elect and nominate, before they shall from thence depart, two of the aforesaid Burgesses, who from thenceforth shall be Bailiffs of the Borough aforesaid, for one whole Year then next ensuing; and that they, after they shall be so as aforesaid elected and nominated to be Bailiffs of the Borough aforesaid, before they shall be admitted to execute the same Office, and each of them, shall take a corporal Oath upon the Holy Gospel of God yearly on the same Day of Election, if they shall be present, and if they shall be absent, then within one Month then next ensuing the Day of Election aforesaid, before the Mayor of the Borough aforesaid, or in the Absence of the said Mayor before the Bailiffs their last Predecessors, or either of them, in the Presence of such of the aforesaid Aldermen of the Borough aforesaid, for the Time being, and the rest of the Burgesses of the Borough aforesaid, who shall be then present in the Guildhall of the Borough aforesaid, or in any other convenient Place within the Borough aforesaid, to be limited and assigned according to their Discretions, rightly well and faithfully to execute the same Office of Bailiffs of the same Borough, in all Things touching the same Office; and that after such Oath so taken they shall and may be able to execute the Office of Bailiffs of the Borough aforesaid, until the Thursday next before the Feast of the Annunciation of the *Blessed Virgin Mary* then next ensuing, and further until others of the aforesaid Burgesses of the Borough aforesaid shall be in due Manner and Form elected, preferred, and sworn to be Bailiffs of the Borough aforesaid, according to the Ordinances and Constitutions in these Presents above mentioned: AND FURTHER WE WILL, and by these

Nomination of Bailiffs.

Presents, for us, our Heirs and Successors, grant to the aforesaid Mayor, Bailiffs, and Burgesses of the Borough aforesaid, and their Successors, That if it shall happen the Mayor of the Borough aforesaid, at any Time hereafter, within one Year after he shall be preferred and sworn to the Office of Mayoralty of the Borough aforesaid, as aforesaid, to die or be removed from his Office, which same Mayor not well behaving himself in the same Office, WE WILL to be removeable at the Pleasure of the aforesaid Aldermen and the rest of the Burgesses of the Borough aforesaid, for the Time being, or the major Part of them, who shall be then present, so that the major Part of the Burgesses of the Borough aforesaid are or shall be then present, that then and so often it shall and may be lawful to the aforesaid Aldermen of the Borough aforesaid, for the Time being, to assemble themselves, or the major Part of them, within fourteen Days then next ensuing the Death or Removal of the same Mayor, in the Guildhall of the Borough aforesaid, or in any other convenient Place within the Borough aforesaid, and to elect, nominate, and prefer, one honest and fit Man of the aforesaid Aldermen of the Borough aforesaid to be Mayor, and for Mayor of the Borough aforesaid, in the Place of the same Mayor so dead, or removed from his Office; and that he, so elected and preferred into the Office of Mayoralty, having first taken a Corporal Oath in Form aforesaid, shall have and exercise the same Office during the Residue of the same Year, and until one other of the Aldermen of the Borough aforesaid shall be in due Manner elected and sworn to the same Office; and so as often as the Case shall so happen: AND if it shall happen the Bailiffs of the Borough aforesaid, or either of them, to die, or be removed from their Office of Bailiffs of the Borough aforesaid, which same Bailiffs, and each of them, not well behaving himself in his Office aforesaid, WE WILL to be removeable at the Pleasure of the Mayor and Aldermen of the Borough aforesaid, for the Time being, or the major Part of them, that then and so often it shall and may be lawful to the Mayor and Aldermen of the Borough aforesaid, for the Time being, or the major Part of them, within fourteen Days next after the aforesaid Bailiff or Bailiffs shall so die, or be removed from his Office aforesaid, to assemble themselves in the Guildhall of the Borough aforesaid, or in any other convenient Place within the Borough aforesaid, and to elect and prefer one or two of the Burgesses of the Borough aforesaid, into the Place or Places of the same Bailiff, or Bailiffs, so dead or removed from his Office; and that he or they, so elected and preferred, having first taken a Corporal Oath for the same Office of Bailiff of the Borough aforesaid, in Form aforesaid, shall have, and exercise the same Office or Offices during the Residue of the same Year, and until another or others of the Burgesses of the Borough aforesaid shall be elected and sworn to the same Office of Bailiff and Bailiffs of the same Borough, having first taken a Corporal Oath in Form aforesaid; and so as often as the Case shall so happen: AND if any or either of the Aldermen of the Borough aforesaid shall die, or be removed from his Office, which same Aldermen, or any or either of them not well behaving himself in his Office, WE WILL to be removeable at the Pleasure of the Mayor of the Borough aforesaid, and the major

Marginal notes:
If Mayor die, or be removed,

another to be elected.

If Bailiffs die, or be removed,

others to be elected.

If Aldermen die, or be removed,

Part of the aforesaid Aldermen of the same Borough, for the Time being, that then the Mayor and such of the rest of the aforesaid Aldermen of the Borough aforesaid, who shall be assembled in the Guildhall of the Borough aforesaid, or any other convenient Place within the Borough aforesaid, to be limited and assigned according to their Discretions, or the major Part of them so assembled, at the Pleasure of the Mayor and Residue of the Aldermen of the same Borough, shall and may be able to elect and prefer one or more of the best and most honest Burgesses of the Borough aforesaid, in the Place or Places of the same Alderman or Aldermen of the Borough aforesaid, so dead, or removed from his Office, to supply the aforesaid Number of twelve Aldermen of the same Borough; and that he or they, so elected and preferred, having first taken a Corporal Oath, rightly, well, and faithfully to execute the same Office before the Mayor of the Borough aforesaid, for the Time being, or before the Bailiffs of the same Borough, or either of them, shall have and exercise the same Office or Offices to which he or they shall be so elected, preferred, and sworn, so long as he shall well behave himself in the same Office; AND FURTHER WE WILL, and by these Presents, for us, our Heirs, and Successors, grant to the aforesaid Mayor, Bailiffs, and Burgesses of the Borough aforesaid, and their Successors, That they and their Successors from henceforth for ever may and shall have within the Borough aforesaid one honest and discreet Man, learned in the Laws of *England*, who shall be and be named Recorder of the Borough aforesaid: AND WE WILL, and for us, our Heirs and Successors, by these Presents, grant, That the Recorder of the Borough aforesaid, for the Time being, shall do and execute all and every thing which any Steward of the same Borough, by Virtue of his Office of Steward of the same Borough, could or ought heretofore to do and execute, and not otherwise, being unwilling that after the Date of these our Letters Patent, any one shall be elected, preferred, and nominated into the Office of Steward of the Borough aforesaid; but that the Recorder shall be elected and preferred in the Stead and Place of the same Steward, from Time to Time, for ever, to execute all and every thing which to the Office of Steward did heretofore appertain, and not otherwise; and for the better Execution of our Will and Grant in that Behalf, WE HAVE assigned, nominated, constituted, and made, and by these Presents, for us, our Heirs and Successors, DO assign, nominate, constitute, create, and make our beloved *Thomas Waller*, Esquire, to be the first and present Recorder of the Borough aforesaid, to continue so long as he shall well behave himself in the same Office, and during the Pleasure of the Mayor, Aldermen, and Bailiffs of the same Borough; and that every Person to be elected and nominated into the same Office of Recorder of the Borough aforesaid, before he shall be admitted to execute the same Office, shall take a Corporal Oath before the Mayor of the Borough aforesaid, for the Time being, and so many of the Common Council of the Borough aforesaid, who shall be willing then to be present, rightly, well, and faithfully to do and execute all and every thing which to the Office of Recorder, so as aforesaid elected in the Place of the Steward, appertain in and by all things: AND FURTHER WE WILL, and by these Presents, for us, our Heirs and Successors, grant to the aforesaid Mayor, Bailiffs, and Burgesses of

others to be elected.

Recorder.

Office of Steward abolished.

Thomas Waller, Esq. appointed Recorder.

the Borough aforesaid, and their Successors, that from Time to Time, and at all Times, after the Death or Removal of the aforesaid *Thomas Waller*, it shall and may be lawful to the Mayor, Aldermen, and Bailiffs of the Borough aforesaid, for the Time being, or the major Part of them, (of whom the Mayor for the Time being WE WILL to be one) to

Recorder how to be appointed.

elect and prefer one other honest and discreet Man, learned in the Laws of *England*, to be Recorder of the Borough aforesaid, to continue in the same Office during the Pleasure of the Mayor, Aldermen, and Bailiffs of the same Borough for the Time being, having first taken a Corporal Oath in Form aforesaid; and so as often as the Case shall so happen: AND FURTHER WE WILL, and by these Presents, for us, our Heirs, and Successors, grant to the aforesaid Mayor, Bailiffs, and Burgesses of the Borough aforesaid, and their Successors, That the Mayor and Recorder of the Borough aforesaid, for

Predecessor of every Mayor to be Justice of the Peace.

the Time being, and the last Predecessor of every Mayor of the same Borough for the Time being, for ever hereafter, may and shall be Justices of us and of our Heirs and Successors, and each of them may and shall be a Justice of us, our Heirs, and Successors, to preserve the Peace of us and of our Heirs and Successors, in the same Borough, the Liberties and Precincts thereof, and also to preserve, correct, and keep, and cause to be corrected or kept, the Statutes concerning Artificers and Labourers, Weights and Measures within the Borough aforesaid, the Suburbs, Precincts, and Liberties thereof; and that the said Mayor and Recorder of the Borough aforesaid, for the Time being, and his last Predecessor, or any two of them, (of whom the Mayor of the Borough afore-

His Duties and Powers.

said, for the Time being, WE WILL to be one) shall have full Power and Authority to inquire concerning whatsoever inferior Offences, Defects, and Articles, within the Borough aforesaid, the Liberties and Precincts thereof, done, moved, or perpetrated, or hereafter to be done, moved, or perpetrated, which the Justices and Keepers of the Peace in any County of our Kingdom of *England*, by the Laws and Statutes of our same Kingdom of *England*, as Justices of the Peace, only ought or may be able to inquire; so nevertheless that they, or any, or either of them shall not in any wise proceed to the Inquisition, Trial, or Determination of any Treason, Murder or Felony, or any other Thing or Matter touching the Loss of Life, or Member, within the Borough aforesaid, the Suburbs, Liberties, and Precincts thereof: AND FURTHER WE WILL, and by these Presents, for us, our Heirs and Successors, grant to the aforesaid Mayor, Bailiffs, and Burgesses of the Borough aforesaid, and their Successors, That the Mayor, Recorder, and last Predecessor of every Mayor of the same Borough, for the Time being, so as aforesaid, being in the Office of Justice of the Peace, or any two of them, (of whom the Mayor of the Borough aforesaid, for the Time being, WE WILL to be one) by their Warrant in Writing, subscribed and signed, and to be signed with their own proper Hands, shall and may be able to send all such and so many Persons who hereafter shall be taken, arrested, attached, or found in the aforesaid Borough of *Chepping Wycombe*, otherwise called *Wicombe*, the Liberties and Precincts thereof, for Treason, Murder, Felony, Homicide, or Robbery, done or to be done, or for Suspicion of Felony, to the common Gaol of our County of *Buckingham*, there to remain to be tried, and to answer for their Offences before the Justices of us, our Heirs and Successors, of Oyer and Terminer, or our Justices assigned, or to be assigned, to deliver the Gaol in the said County of *Buckingham*, WILLING, and by these Presents commanding, as well the Sheriff of the County of *Buckingham* aforesaid, as the Keeper of the common Gaol of the same County of *Buckingham* aforesaid, for the Time being, That they and every of them upon such Warrant by the aforesaid Justices of the Peace, within the Borough of *Chepping Wycombe*, otherwise called *Wicombe*, for the Time being, or any two of them, (of whom the Mayor of the Borough aforesaid for the Time being, WE WILL to be one) to be made, and to them or either of them to be directed, shall receive and safely keep all and such Persons so as aforesaid by the aforesaid Justices of the Peace within the Borough aforesaid, hereafter to be taken, arrested, attached, or found in the aforesaid Borough of *Wicombe*, the Liberties or Precincts thereof, for the aforesaid Murder, Homicide, Robbery, or other Felony, done or to be done, or for Suspicion of Felony, and so as aforesaid to be sent to the aforesaid common Gaol of the aforesaid County of *Buckingham*, there to remain to be tried, and to answer before the Justices of us, and of our Heirs and Successors, of Oyer and Terminer, or the Justices assigned, and to be assigned, to deliver the Gaol of the County aforesaid, for the Time being; and these our Letters Patents, or the Inrollment thereof, shall be to the aforesaid Sheriff and Keeper of the common Gaol of the County of *Buckingham* aforesaid, for the Time being, for the same sufficient Warrant and Exoneration in that Behalf: AND FURTHER WE WILL, and by these Presents, for us, our Heirs and Successors, grant to the aforesaid Mayor, Bailiffs, and Burgesses of the Borough aforesaid, and their Successors, That they and their Successors shall have, hold, and keep, and shall and may be able to have, hold, and keep, within the Borough aforesaid, every Year for ever, four Fairs or Marts; the first of the said Fairs or Marts to begin on the Feast of *Saint John* the Baptist, and to continue through the whole of that Feast; and the second Fair to begin on the fourteenth Day of September, and to be holden and continue through the whole of that Day; and the third Fair of the same four Fairs or Marts, on the Day of the Feast of *Saint Simon* and *Saint Jude*, the Apostles, and to be kept and continue through the whole of that Day of the Feast of *Saint Simon* and *Saint Jude*; and the fourth Fair of the same four Fairs or Marts to begin on the Saturday next before the Feast of *Lent*, and to be kept and continue through the whole of that Saturday; together with a Court of Piepowder there to be holden in the Time of the same Fairs or Marts, and with all Liberties and free Customs, Tolls, Stallage, Piccage, Fines, Amerciaments, and all other Profits, Commodities, Advantages, and Emoluments whatsoever, to such Fairs or Marts, and Court of Piepowder appertaining, arising, accruing, or happening, or in any wise appertaining or belonging; so nevertheless that the aforesaid Fairs or Marts shall not be to the Prejudice or Damage of other Fairs or Marts adjacent: AND FURTHER WE WILL, and by these Presents, for us, our Heirs and Successors, grant to the aforesaid Mayor, Bailiffs, and Burgesses of the Borough aforesaid, and their Successors, That they and their Successors shall have, hold, and keep, and shall and may be able to have, hold,

Fairs.

Court of Piepowder.

Market.

and keep, within the Borough aforesaid, one Market in every Week in every Year for ever, on Friday, to be kept and holden within the Borough aforesaid; and that in the Time of the same Market all and singular Persons coming and resorting to the same Market shall and may be able to buy, sell, and expose to Sale from henceforth for ever all and singular Wares, Merchandize, Grain, and Things whatsoever, as all and all Manner of Oxen, Sheep, Hogs, Horses, Mares, Geldings, and Colts, and all and all Manner other Animals and Cattle alive and dead whatsoever, at their Pleasure, according to the Laws, Customs, and Statutes of our Kingdom of *England*, paying the Tolls and Customs therefore due to the same Mayor, Bailiffs, and Burgesses of the Borough aforesaid, for the Time being, To the proper Use and Behoof of the same Mayor, Bailiffs, and Burgesses, and their Successors, towards the Support and Maintenance of the Charges and

Court of Piepowder.

Expences of the same Borough; together with a Court of Piepowder, there to be holden at the Time of the same Market, and with all and all Manner of Liberties and free Customs, Tolls, Stallage, Piccage, Fines, Amerciaments, and all other Profits and Commodities, Advantages and Emoluments whatsoever to such Market and Court of Piepowder appertaining, arising, accruing, or happening; so nevertheless that the same Market shall not be to the Damage or Prejudice of other neighbouring Markets there

No Foreigner, except a Victualler or Tanner, to hold a Stall without a Licence.

near adjacent; and that no Foreigner who shall dwell out of the Borough aforesaid, unless he shall be a Victualler or a Tanner, from henceforth shall make, take, or use any Stalls within the Borough aforesaid, at the Time of the Market there, without the Licence of the Mayor and Aldermen of the same Borough, or the major Part of them, of whom the Mayor for the Time being WE WILL to be one: AND FURTHER WE WILL, and by

Borough confirmed in Rights, Liberties, Lands, &c.

these Presents, for us, our Heirs and Successors, give, grant, and confirm to the aforesaid Mayor, Bailiffs, and Burgesses of the Borough aforesaid, and their Successors, all and all Manner of Liberties, Franchises, Immunities, Exemptions, Privileges, Acquittances, Jurisdictions, Lands, Tenements, Wastes, void Grounds, Commons, and Hereditaments whatsoever, which the Mayor, Bailiffs, and Burgesses of the Borough aforesaid now have, hold, use, and enjoy; or which their Predecessors, or any of them, by whatsoever Names or Name, or by whatsoever Incorporation, or by Pretext of whatsoever Incorporation heretofore have had, held, used, or enjoyed, or ought to have, hold, use, or enjoy, of any hereditary Estate, by Reason or Pretext of any Charters or Letters Patent, by any of our Progenitors and Ancestors, late Kings or Queens of *England*, in any wise heretofore made, granted, or confirmed, or by whatsoever other lawful Manner, Right, Title, Custom, Usage, or Prescription heretofore lawfully used, had, or accustomed; although the same, or any or either of them, heretofore have not been used, or have been abused or discontinued, and although the same or any or either of them are or have been forfeited or lost, to HAVE, HOLD, AND ENJOY, to the aforesaid Mayor, Bailiffs, and Burgesses of the Borough aforesaid, and their Successors for ever; except nevertheless always and out of these our Letters Patent, and this our Grant wholly reserved, all and all Manner of Rents, Services, Sums of Money, and Demands whatsoever, which to us or to any of our Progenitors or Predecessors, or to any other Person or Persons for or in respect of the

Premises, or any or either of them have been heretofore accustomed to be rendered or paid, or ought to be rendered or paid: WHEREFORE WE WILL, and by these Presents, for us, our Heirs and Successors, firmly enjoining, ordering, and commanding. that the aforesaid Mayor, Bailiffs, and Burgesses of the Borough aforesaid, and their Successors, shall have, hold, use, and enjoy, and shall and may be able fully and entirely to have, hold, use, and enjoy, for ever, all the Liberties, free Customs, Privileges, Authorities, Jurisdictions, and Acquittances aforesaid, according to the Tenor and Effect of these our Letters Patent, without the Hindrance or Impediment of us, our Heirs and Successors whomsoever; being unwilling that the same Mayor, Bailiffs, and Burgesses of the Borough aforesaid, and their Successors, or any or either of them, by Reason of the Premises, or of any of them, by us, or our Heirs or Successors, the Justices, Sheriffs, Escheators, or other Bailiffs or Ministers of us, our Heirs and Successors, whomsoever, shall be therefore hindered, molested, vexed, or aggrieved, or in any wise disturbed; WILLING, and by these Presents commanding and ordering, as well the Treasurer, Chancellor, and Barons of our Exchequer at Westminster and other the Justices and Officers of us, and of our Heirs and Successors, as our Attorney and Solicitor General, for the Time being, and every of them, and all other our Officers and Ministers whomsoever, that neither they nor any or either of them shall prosecute, or continue, or make, or cause to be prosecuted or continued any Writ or Summons of Quo Warranto, or any other our Writ, Writs, or Process whatsoever, against the aforesaid Mayor, Bailiffs, and Burgesses of the Borough aforesaid, or any or either of them, for any Causes, Things, Matters, Offences, Claim, or Usurpation, or any of them, by them or any of them, due, claimed, used, attempted, or usurped, before the Day of the making of these Presents; WILLING ALSO, that the Mayor, Bailiffs, and Burgesses of the Borough aforesaid, or any of them, shall in no wise be molested, or hindered by any or either of the Justices, Officers, or Ministers aforesaid, in or for the due Use, Claim, or Abuse of any other Liberties, Franchises, or Jurisdictions, within the Borough aforesaid, the Limits or Precincts thereof, before the Day of the making of these our Letters Patent, or be compelled to answer to them, or either of them: AND WHEREAS our dearly beloved Sister the *Lady Elizabeth*, late Queen of *England*, by her Letters Patent, sealed under her great seal of *England*, bearing Date the twenty-first Day of July, in the fourth Year of her Reign, DID give and grant to the Mayor, Bailiffs, and Burgesses of the Borough of *Wicombe* aforesaid, all the Scite, Bounds, and Circuit of the late Hospital of *Saint John* the Baptist, in *Wicombe*, and all the Hospital aforesaid; and all Messuages, Lands, Tenements, and Hereditaments in *Wicombe* aforesaid, and in the Parish of *Penne*, *Hichenden*, and *Great Marlowe*, in the County of *Buckingham*, and elsewhere wheresoever in the same County, which to the said late Hospital did then lately belong; and all her Messuages, Lands, Tenements, and Hereditaments in *Wicombe* aforesaid, called by the Name of the Fraternity of the *Blessed Mary*, or by the name of our *Lady Rents*, which same Messuages, Lands, Tenements, and Hereditaments, so by the aforesaid late *Queen Elizabeth* to the same Mayor, Bailiffs, and Burgesses given and

Grammar School.

granted, were solely for the perpetual Maintenance of one Grammar School in *Wicombe* aforesaid; and also for the perpetual Maintenance and Relief of four poor People, to be relieved in the same Borough; as by the same Letters Patent amongst other Things more fully doth appear: AND WHEREAS WE are credibly informed by the Information of the now Mayor, Bailiffs, and Burgesses of the said Borough, that the Number of poor and needy People in the same Borough is much increased, and daily doth more and more increase, to the great Charge of the same Borough: AND ALSO WE are likewise informed, that the said late Hospital of *Saint John* the Baptist, and the aforesaid Messuages, Lands, Tenements, and Hereditaments, by the said late *Queen Elizabeth*, as aforesaid given and granted, to the perpetual Maintenance and Support of the Grammar School, and four poor people in *Wicombe* aforesaid, will well and competently suffice, as well to maintain and support the aforesaid Grammar School and four poor People, according to the Ordinance and Intention of the said late Queen in the said Borough; as also to relieve more poor and needy Persons in the same Borough; WE desiring to relieve the great Charges and Expences of the same Borough, and also willing that the poor and needy People of the same Borough should be succoured by all good and convenient Ways and Means; and nevertheless willing that the aforesaid Grammar School and the aforesaid four poor People, by the aforesaid Letters Patent of the aforesaid late *Queen Elizabeth* to be relieved in the same Borough, shall be chiefly and before all others perpetually sustained and maintained, according to the Ordinances and Intentions of the same late *Queen Elizabeth*, in the same Letters Patent mentioned, of our especial Grace and of our certain Knowledge and mere Motion, HAVE given and granted, and by these Presents, for us, our Heirs and Successors, DO give and grant Licence, Power, and Authority, to the aforesaid Mayor, Aldermen, and Bailiffs of the Borough aforesaid, and their Successors, That they and their Successors, by their Discretion, or of the major Part of them, from Time to Time, shall take, expend, and dispose of all and singular the Issues, Rents, Revenues, and yearly Profits whatsoever of all and singular the aforesaid Messuages, Lands, Tenements, and Hereditaments; so by the aforesaid late Queen as aforesaid given and granted to the Maintenance of the aforesaid Grammar School and four poor People, as well to the perpetual Support and Relief of the aforesaid Grammar School and four poor People, according to the pious Intention of the said late Queen, in the same Borough to be sustained and relieved, as also to the Relief and Support of other poor and needy Men in the same Borough, from Time to Time, inhabiting and dwelling; and also to the Support of the Charges and Expences of the same Mayor, Bailiffs, and Burgesses, in and about the Defence of their Title in and to the aforesaid Hospital, Messuages, Lands, Tenements, Rents, and other the Premises to the same Mayor, Bailiffs, and Burgesses, by the aforesaid late *Queen Elizabeth*, so as aforesaid given and granted, and to no other Uses, Intents, or Purposes: WE WILL ALSO, &c. without Fine in the Hanaper, &c. ALTHOUGH express Mention, &c. IN WITNESS, whereof, &c. WITNESS, THE KING, at Westminster, the seventeenth Day of June.

By Writ of Privy Seal.

CHARTER

GRANTED TO THE

MAYOR, BAILIFFS, AND BURGESSES

OF

THE BOROUGH OF CHEPPING WYCOMBE,

BY KING CHARLES THE SECOND,

16TH NOVEMBER, 1663.

IN THE FIFTEENTH YEAR OF HIS REIGN.

THE KING, to all to whom, &c., Greeting.—WHEREAS our Borough of *Chepping Wycombe*, otherwise called *Wicombe*, in our County of *Buckingham*, is an ancient and populous Borough, and the Mayor, Bailiffs, and Burgesses of the Borough of *Wicombe* aforesaid, have had, used, and enjoyed divers Liberties, Franchises, Immunities, and Pre-eminences, as well by Charters of divers of our Progenitors and Predecessors, late Kings or Queens of *England*, to them and their Predecessors heretofore made, granted, or confirmed, as also by Reason of divers Prescriptions and Customs used in the same Borough, from Time whereof the Memory of Man is not to the contrary: AND WHEREAS our beloved Subjects, the Mayor, Bailiffs, and Burgesses of the Borough of *Wicombe* aforesaid, have humbly besought us that we would be pleased to show and extend our Royal Grace and Munificence to the same Mayor, Bailiffs, and Burgesses, in that Behalf, and that We, for the better Government, Rule, and Improvement of the same Borough, would condescend to ratify, confirm, approve, make, restore and constitute the said Mayor, Bailiffs, and Burgesses of the same Borough into one Body Corporate and Politic, by Letters Patent: WE THEREFORE WILLING, that from henceforth for ever in the same Borough there shall be had continually one certain and undoubted Method of and for the keeping of the Peace, and the good . Rule and Government of the People there; and that the Borough aforesaid from henceforth for ever shall be and remain a Borough of Peace and Quiet, to the Dread and Terror of the Wicked, and in Reward of the Good, and that our Peace and other Deeds of Justice there may be preserved without further Delay; and hoping that if the Mayor, Bailiffs, and Burgesses of the same

Of a Grant of a Charter to the Mayor, Bailiffs, and Burgesses of the Borough of *Chepping Wycombe*, to them and their Successors.

Borough, and their Successors, are made able by our Grant to enjoy more ample Honours, Liberties, and Privileges, then they will consider themselves bound more especially and strongly to perform and shew such service as they are able to us, and to our Heirs and Successors, of our especial Grace, and of our certain Knowledge and mere Motion, WE HAVE willed, ordained, constituted and granted, and by these Presents, for us, our Heirs and Successors, DO will, ordain, constitute, declare, and grant, That the said Borough of *Wicombe*, in our said County of *Buckingham*, from henceforth may and shall be a Free Borough of itself; and that the Mayor, Bailiffs, and Burgesses of the same Borough, by whatsoever Name they have been heretofore incorporated, and their Successors, from henceforth for ever may and shall be, by Force

A Body Corporate. of these Presents, one Body Corporate and Politic, in Deed, Fact, and Name, by the Name of Mayor, Bailiffs, and Burgesses of the Borough of *Chepping Wycombe*, otherwise *Wicombe*, in the County of *Buckingham*; and them by the Name of Mayor, Bailiffs, and Burgesses of the Borough of *Chepping Wycombe*, otherwise *Wicombe*, in the County of *Buckingham*, one Body Corporate and Politic, in Deed, Name, and Fact, really and fully for us, our Heirs and Successors, We do make, ordain, constitute, confirm, and declare by these Presents, and that by the same Name, they shall have perpetual Succession; and that they, by the Name of Mayor, Bailiffs, and Burgesses of the Borough of *Chepping Wycombe*, otherwise *Wicombe*, in the County of *Buckingham*, may and shall be for ever hereafter Persons able and capable in the Law to have,

May possess Lands, &c. purchase, receive, and possess Lands, Tenements, Liberties, Privileges, Jurisdictions, Franchises, and Hereditaments, of whatsoever Kind, Nature, or Sort they may be, to them and their Successors, in Fee and Perpetuity, and also Goods and Chattels, and whatsoever other Things of whatsoever Kind, Nature, or Sort they may be, and also to give, grant, demise, and assign, Lands, Tenements, and Hereditaments, Goods and Chattels, and to do and execute all and singular other Deeds and Things, by the Name aforesaid; and that by the same Name of Mayor, Bailiffs, and Burgesses of the Borough of *Chepping Wycombe*, otherwise *Wicombe*, in the County of *Buckingham*, they

May plead, &c. shall and may be able to plead and be impleaded, answer and be answered, defend, and be defended, in whatsoever Courts and Places, and before whatsoever Judges and Justices, and other Persons and Officers of us, and of our Heirs and Successors, in all Suits, Plaints, Pleas, Causes, Matters, and Demands, real, personal, or mixt, whatsoever, as well spiritual as temporal, of whatsoever Kind, Nature, or Sort they may be, in the same Manner and Form as other our liege Subjects of this our Kingdom of *England*, Persons able and capable in the law, can and may be able to plead and be impleaded, answer and be answered, defend and be defended, and to have, purchase, and receive, possess, give, grant, and demise; and that the aforesaid Mayor, Bailiffs, and Burgesses of the aforesaid Borough of *Chepping Wycombe*, otherwise *Wicombe*, in the

Common Seal. County of *Buckingham*, and their Successors, shall have for ever a Common Seal, to serve for doing their Causes and Business, and of their Successors whatsoever; and that it shall and may be lawful to the same Mayor, Bailiffs and Burgesses, and their Successors, the same Seal at their Pleasure to break, change, and make anew, as to them shall seem to be best; AND FURTHER WE WILL, and by these Presents, for us, our Heirs and Successors, grant and ordain, that from henceforth for ever there may and shall be within the Borough aforesaid, one of the most honest and discreet Burgesses of the Borough aforesaid, to be elected in Form hereunder in these Presents mentioned, who shall be and be named Mayor of the Borough aforesaid; and that in like Manner there may and shall be within the same Borough two honest and discreet Burgesses of the Borough aforesaid, to be elected in Form hereunder in these Presents mentioned, who shall be and be named Bailiffs of the Borough aforesaid: AND ALSO WE WILL, and by these Presents, for us, our Heirs, and Successors, grant, ordain, and confirm, that from henceforth for ever there may and shall be within the Borough aforesaid, from Time to Time, twelve honest and discreet Men, continually inhabiting and residing within the same Borough who shall be and be called Aldermen of the said Borough; and that the Mayor, Bailiffs, and Burgesses of the same Borough, and their Successors, or the major Part of them, from Time to Time, for ever, shall and may be able to elect so many and such other Men, inhabiting or not inhabiting within the Borough aforesaid, as and which to them shall seem most expedient to the Burgesses of the said Borough: AND WE WILL, and by these Presents, for us, our Heirs and Successors, grant and confirm to the aforesaid Mayor, Bailiffs, and Burgesses of the Borough aforesaid, and their Successors, that the aforesaid Aldermen and Bailiffs of the Borough aforesaid, and their Successors, shall be and be called the Common Council of the Borough aforesaid, and shall be, from Time to Time, assisting and aiding to the Mayor of the said Borough of *Chepping Wycombe*, otherwise *Wicombe* aforesaid, for the Time being, in all Causes and Matters touching or concerning the Borough aforesaid: AND FURTHER WE WILL, and by these Presents, for us, our Heirs and Successors, grant and confirm to the aforesaid Mayor, Bailiffs, and Burgesses of the Borough aforesaid, and their Successors, that the Mayor, Aldermen, and Bailiffs of the Borough aforesaid, and their Successors, for the Time being, or the major part of them (of whom the Mayor for the Time being WE WILL to be one) may and shall have full Power and Authority to frame, constitute, ordain and make, from Time to Time, such reasonable Laws, Statutes, and Ordinances whatsoever, as to them shall seem to be good, wholesome, useful, honest, and necessary, according to their sound Discretions, for the good Rule and Government of the Burgesses, Artificers, and Inhabitants of the Borough aforesaid, for the Time being, and for declaring in what Manner and Order the aforesaid Mayor, Aldermen, Bailiffs, and Burgesses, and the Artificers, Inhabitants, and Residents of the Borough aforesaid, shall behave, conduct, and carry themselves in their Offices, Mysteries, and Business, within the same Borough, and the Limits thereof, for the Time being, and otherwise for the further Good and public Advantage and Rule of the same Borough, and the Victualling of the same Borough, and also for the better Preservation, Government, Disposition, letting, demising of Lands, Tenements, Possessions, Revenues, and Hereditaments, to the aforesaid Mayor, Bailiffs, and Burgesses, and their Successors, by these Presents, or

Mayor.

Bailiffs.

Burgesses.

Common Council.

May ordain Laws,

otherwise, given, granted, assigned, or confirmed, or hereafter to be given, granted, or assigned, and other Matters and Causes whatsoever, touching or in any wise concerning the aforesaid Borough, or the State, Right, and Interest of the same Borough; and that they and their Successors, by the Mayor for the Time being, and the Aldermen and Bailiffs of the Borough aforesaid, being the Common Council of the same Borough or by the major Part of them as aforesaid, so often as they shall frame, make, ordain, or establish such Laws, Statutes, and Ordinances, in Form aforesaid, shall be able to impose and assess such reasonable Pains, Penalties, and Punishments, by Imprisonment of the Body, or by Fines or Amerciaments, or by either of them, towards and upon all Delinquents, against such Laws, Statutes, and Ordinances, or any or either of them, as and which to the same Mayor, Aldermen and Bailiffs of the Borough aforesaid, for the Time being, or the major Part of them, shall seem to be reasonable and requisite; and the same Fines and Amerciaments they shall and may be able to levy and have without the Hindrance of us, our Heirs and Successors; all and singular which Laws, Statutes, and Ordinances, so (as aforesaid) to be made, WE WILL to be observed, under the Pains in the same to be contained; so nevertheless that such Laws, Statutes, Ordinances, Imprisonments, Fines, and Amerciaments, shall not be repugnant nor contrary to the Laws, Statutes, Customs, or Rights of our Kingdom of *England*: AND for the better Execution of our same Grants in this Behalf, WE HAVE assigned, nominated, constituted, and made, and by these Presents, for us, our Heirs and Successors, DO assign, nominate, constitute, and make our beloved *Robert Whitton*, now Mayor of the Borough aforesaid, to be the first and present Mayor of the Borough aforesaid, WILLING that the same *Robert Whitton* shall be and continue in the Office of Mayor of the same Borough, from the making of these Presents, until the Thursday next before the Feast of *Saint Michael* the Archangel next ensuing, and from the same Feast until one of the Aldermen of the Borough aforesaid shall be preferred and sworn to the same Office, according to the Ordinances and Constitutions in these Presents expressed and declared, (if the same *Robert Whitton* shall so long live): WE HAVE ALSO assigned, nominated, and constituted, and by these Presents, for us, our Heirs and Successors, DO assign, nominate, constitute, and make our beloved *Thomas Preslee* and *Edward Bedder* the younger, now Bailiffs of the same Borough, to be the two first and present Bailiffs of the Borough aforesaid, to continue in the same Offices of Bailiffs of the same Borough, until the Thursday next before the Feast of the Annunciation of the *Blessed Virgin Mary* next ensuing, and from the same Feast until two other Burgesses of the Borough aforesaid shall be preferred and sworn to the Offices of Bailiffs of the said Borough, according to the Ordinances and Constitutions in these Presents hereunder expressed and declared, if the same *Thomas Preslee* and *Edward Bedder* the younger shall so long live: WE HAVE ALSO assigned, nominated, and constituted, and by these Presents, for us, our Heirs and Successors, DO assign, nominate, constitute, and make our beloved *Nicholas Bradshaw, Thomas Gibbons, Edward Bedder* the elder, *James Bigg, Henry Elliott, Richard Lucas, Edward Winch, Edward Humfrey, Robert Fryer, Jonathan Randall, Samuel Wells*, and *John*

lties and shments.

First Mayor.

First Bailiffs.

First Aldermen.

hall of the Borough aforesaid, or in any other convenient Place within the Borough aforesaid, to be limited and assigned according to their Discretions, and there to continue until they, or the major Part of them there then assembled, shall elect and nominate two Burgesses of the Borough aforesaid to be Bailiffs of the Borough aforesaid,

for one Year then next ensuing, to be elected and nominated in Form following; and that they shall and may be able there to elect and nominate, before they shall from thence depart, two of the aforesaid Burgesses, who from thenceforth shall be Bailiffs of the Borough aforesaid, for one whole Year then next ensuing; and that they, after they shall be so as aforesaid elected and nominated to be Bailiffs of the Borough aforesaid, before they shall be admitted to execute the same Office, shall take, and each of them shall take a corporal Oath upon the Holy Gospel of God yearly on the Day of Election, if they shall then be present, and if they shall be absent, then within one Month then next ensuing the Day of Election aforesaid, before the Mayor of the Borough aforesaid, or in the Absence of the said Mayor, before the Bailiffs their last Predecessors, or either of them, in the Presence of such of the aforesaid Aldermen of the Borough aforesaid, for the Time being, and the rest of the Burgesses of the Borough aforesaid, who shall then be present in the Guildhall of the Borough aforesaid, or in any other convenient Place within the Borough aforesaid, to be limited and assigned according to their Discretions, rightly, well, and faithfully to execute the same Office of Bailiffs of the same Borough, in all Things touching the same Office; and that after such Oath so taken they shall and may be able to execute the Office of Bailiffs of the Borough aforesaid, until the Thursday next before the Feast of the Annunciation of the *Blessed Virgin Mary* then next ensuing, and further until others of the aforesaid Burgesses of the Borough aforesaid in due Manner and Form shall be elected, preferred, and sworn to be Bailiffs of the Borough aforesaid, according to the Ordinances and Constitutions in these Presents above mentioned : AND FURTHER WE WILL, and by these Presents, for us, our Heirs and Successors, grant and confirm to the aforesaid Mayor, Bailiffs, and Burgesses of the Borough aforesaid and their Successors, That if it shall happen the Mayor of the Borough aforesaid, at any Time hereafter within one Year after he shall be preferred and sworn to the

Office of Mayoralty of the Borough aforesaid, as aforesaid, to die, or be removed from his Office, which same Mayor not well behaving himself in the same Office, WE WILL to be removable at the Pleasure of the aforesaid Aldermen and of the other Burgesses of the Borough aforesaid, for the Time being or the major Part of them who then shall be present, so that the major Part of the Burgesses of the Borough aforesaid may or shall be then present, That then and so often, it shall and may be lawful to the aforesaid Aldermen of the Borough aforesaid, for the Time being, to assemble themselves, or the major Part of them, within fourteen Days then next ensuing the Death or Removal of the same Mayor, in the Guildhall of the Borough aforesaid,

or in any other convenient Place within the Borough aforesaid, and to elect, nominate, and prefer one honest and fit Man of the aforesaid Aldermen of the Borough aforesaid, to be Mayor and for Mayor of the Borough aforesaid, in the Place of the same Mayor so dead or removed from his Office, and that he so elected and preferred to the Office of Mayoralty, having first taken a corporal Oath in form aforesaid, shall have and exercise the same Office during the Residue of the same Year, and until one other of the Aldermen of the Borough aforesaid shall be in due Manner elected and sworn to that Office, And so as often as the Case shall so happen : And if it shall happen the Bailiffs of the Borough aforesaid, or either of them, to die or be removed from their Offices of Bailiffs of the Borough aforesaid, which same Bailiffs and either of them not well behaving themselves in their Office aforesaid, WE WILL to be removable at the Pleasure of the Mayor and Aldermen of the Borough aforesaid, for the Time being, or the major Part of them, That then and so often it shall and may be lawful to the Mayor and Aldermen of the Borough aforesaid, for the Time being, or the major Part of them, within fourteen Days next after the aforesaid Bailiff or Bailiffs shall so die or be removed from his Office aforesaid, to assemble themselves in the Guildhall of the Borough aforesaid, or in any other convenient Place within the Borough aforesaid, and to elect and prefer one or two of the Burgesses of the Borough aforesaid into the Place or Places of the same Bailiff or Bailiffs, so dead or removed from his Office, and that he or they so elected and preferred, having first taken a corporal Oath to execute the same Office of Bailiff of the Borough aforesaid, in form aforesaid, shall have and exercise the same Office or Offices during the Residue of the same Year, and until another or others of the Burgesses of the Borough aforesaid shall be elected and sworn to the same Office of Bailiff and Bailiffs of the same Borough, having first taken a corporal Oath in form aforesaid, and so as often as the Case shall so happen : And if any or either of the Aldermen of the Borough aforesaid shall die or be removed from his Office, which same Aldermen and every or any of them not well behaving themselves in the same Office, WE WILL to be removable at the Pleasure of the Mayor of the Borough aforesaid, and the major Part of the aforesaid Aldermen of the same Borough for the Time being, That then the Mayor and such of the Residue of the Aldermen of the Borough aforesaid, who shall be assembled in the Guildhall of the Borough aforesaid, or in any other convenient Place within the Borough aforesaid, to be limited and assigned according to their Discretions, or the major Part of them, so assembled at the Pleasure of the Mayor and the Residue of the Aldermen of the same Borough, shall and may be able to elect and prefer one or more of the best and most honest Burgesses of the Borough aforesaid, in the Place or Places of the same Alderman or Aldermen of the Borough aforesaid, so dead or removed from his or their Office or Offices, to supply the aforesaid Number of twelve Aldermen of the same Borough ; And that he or they so elected and preferred, having first taken a corporal Oath, rightly, well, and faithfully to execute the same Office before the Mayor of the Borough aforesaid, for the Time being, or before the Bailiffs of the same Borough, or either of them, shall have and exercise the same Office or Offices to which he or they shall be so elected,

If Bailiffs die, or be removed,

others to be elected.

If Aldermen die, or be removed,

others to be elected.

preferred and sworn, so long as he shall well behave himself in the same Office: AND FURTHER WE WILL, and by these Presents for us, our Heirs, and Successors grant and confirm to the aforesaid Mayor, Bailiffs, and Burgesses of the Borough aforesaid and their Successors, That they and their Successors from henceforth for ever may and shall have within the Borough aforesaid, one honest and discreet Man learned in the Laws of England, who shall be and be named Recorder of the Borough aforesaid: AND WE WILL, and for us, our Heirs and Successors, grant and confirm, That the Recorder of the Borough aforesaid, for the Time being, shall do and execute all and every Thing which any Steward of the same Borough by Virtue of his Office of Steward of the same Borough, could or ought heretofore to do and execute, and not otherwise; Being unwilling that, after the Date of these our Letters Patent, any Person shall be elected, nominated, or preferred to the Office of Steward of the Borough aforesaid; But that a Recorder shall for ever be elected and preferred, in the Stead and Place of the same Steward, from Time to Time, to execute all and every Thing which to the Office of Steward heretofore did appertain, and not otherwise; And, for the better execution of our Will and Grant in this Behalf, we have assigned, nominated, constituted and made, and by these Presents, for us, our Heirs, and Successors, do assign, nominate,

Recorder.

John Clerke, Esq. nominated Recorder.

constitute, create, and make our beloved *John Clerke*, Esquire, to be the first and present Recorder of the Borough aforesaid, to continue, provided he shall well behave himself in the same Office, during the Pleasure of the Mayor, Aldermen, and Bailiffs of the same Borough; And that every Person so to be elected and nominated to the same Office of Recorder of the Borough aforesaid, before he shall be admitted to execute the same Office, shall take a Corporal Oath before the Mayor of the Borough aforesaid, for the Time being, and so many of the Common Council of the Borough aforesaid who shall then be present, rightly, well, and faithfully, in and by all Things to do and execute all and every Thing which to the Office of Recorder, so as aforesaid elected in Place of the Steward, appertain: AND FURTHER WE WILL, and by these Presents, for us, our Heirs, and Successors, grant and confirm to the aforesaid Mayor, Bailiffs, and Burgesses of the Borough aforesaid, and their Successors, That from Time to Time, and at all Times, after the Death or Removal of the aforesaid *John Clerke*, it shall and may be lawful to the Mayor, Aldermen, and Bailiffs of the Borough aforesaid, for the Time being, or the major Part of

Election of Recorder.

them (of whom the Mayor for the Time being WE WILL to be one), to elect and prefer one other honest and discreet Man, learned in the Laws of England, to be Recorder of the Borough aforesaid, to continue in the same Office during the Pleasure of the Mayor, Aldermen, and Bailiffs of the same Borough aforesaid, for the Time being, first taking a corporal Oath in Form aforesaid; And so as often as the Case shall so happen. AND FURTHER WE WILL, and by these Presents, for us, our Heirs, and Successors, grant and confirm to the aforesaid Mayor, Bailiffs, and Burgesses of the Borough aforesaid, and their Successors, That the Mayor and Recorder of the

Mayor, Recorder, and late Mayor,

Borough aforesaid for the Time being, and the last Predecessor of every Mayor of to be taken, arrested, attached, or found in the aforesaid Borough of *Wicombe*, the Liberties or Precincts thereof, for the aforesaid Murders, Homicides, Robberies, or other Felonies, done or to be done, or for Suspicion of Felony, and so as aforesaid to be sent to the aforesaid common Gaol of the aforesaid County of *Buckingham*, and shall safely keep them, there to remain to be tried, and to answer before the Justices of us, and of our Heirs and Successors, of Oyer and Terminer, or the Justices assigned, and to be assigned, to deliver the Gaol of the County aforesaid, for the Time being; and these our Letters Patent, or the Inrolment thereof, shall be to the aforesaid Sheriff and Keeper of the common Gaol of the County of *Buckingham* aforesaid, for the Time being, sufficient Warrant and Exoneration for the same in that Behalf: AND MORE-OVER WE WILL, and for us, our Heirs and Successors, by these Presents grant and confirm to the aforesaid Mayor, Bailiffs, and Burgesses of the said Borough of *Wicombe*, and their Successors, That they and their Successors may and shall have full Power, Authority, and Faculty, whensoever it shall please them to assign, nominate, constitute, and appoint one fit Person to the Office of Bailiff of the aforesaid Borough, to serve in the Court aforesaid, for the executing and performing Proclamation, Arrest, Process, Execution, and other Things to the same Office incumbent, belonging or appertaining, to be had within the aforesaid Borough and Parish of *Wicombe*, and the Limits, Bounds, and Precincts thereof: AND ALSO WE WILL, and by these Presents for us, our Heirs and Successors, grant and confirm to the aforesaid Mayor, Bailiffs, and Burgesses of the Borough aforesaid, and declare by these Presents, that the Bounds and Limits, Metes, Circuit, and Precincts of the Borough aforesaid, shall extend and stretch themselves, as is hereunder limited and specified (that is to say) from a certain Bridge, called *Wynkles Bridge*, in *Frogmore*, situate at the West End of the same Borough or Town, unto a certain Meadow, called *Halywell Mead*, situate at the East End of a certain common Pasture, called *Rye Mead*, belonging to the said Mayor, Bailiffs, and Burgesses, and being Parcel of their Possessions; and from thence to a certain Ditch, situate on the North Part of a certain Curtilage, called *Bowrhayes*, and from the same Ditch unto a certain Bridge in the Street, called *Saint Marye Street*, contiguous to a certain House or Farm, called *Lokes*, which same Bridge leads to the Town of *Marlow*, on the South Part; and that all and singular Houses, Edifices, Lands, Tenements, void Grounds, and Soil whatsoever, within the Bounds, Metes, and Limits, of the same now are and from henceforth may be, shall be, and shall be reputed to be Parts and Parcel of the said Borough of *Wicombe*, now by these Presents incorporated and confirmed into a Body Politic as aforesaid: AND FURTHER WE WILL, and of our certain Knowledge and mere Motion, for us, our Heirs, and Successors, by these Presents grant and confirm to the aforesaid Mayor, Bailiffs, and Burgesses of the Borough of *Wicombe* aforesaid and their Successors, That they shall have and hold, and shall and may be able to have and hold a certain Court before the Mayor, Bailiffs, and Recorder of the Borough aforesaid, or their or any of their sufficient Deputy or Deputies, being Burgesses of the Borough aforesaid, in a certain Common Hall,

Bailiff.

Limits of the Borough.

Shall hold a Court.

called the Guildhall, or other Place in the same Borough most convenient, from three Weeks to three Weeks or oftener, to be holden at their Will for ever; and that the same Mayor, Bailiffs, and Recorder, or their or any of their sufficient Deputy or Deputies shall have full Power and Authority to hear and determine in the same Court by Plaints to be levied in the same Court all and singular Pleas, Plaints, and Actions concerning all and all Manner of Debts, Accounts, Covenants, Contracts, Trespasses by Force and Arms, or otherwise, in Contempt of Us, Our Heirs, or Successors, done, Covenant, Detinue, Contempt, Deceit, Withernam, and other Things and Actions, real, personal, and mixt, whatsoever, within the aforesaid Borough of *Wicombe*, and the Limits, Bounds and Limits, and Liberties thereof, in any wise arising or to arise, happening or to happen; Provided the same Debts, Accounts, Covenants, Contracts, and other Actions, personal or mixt, shall not exceed the Sum or Value of Forty Pounds: AND FURTHER WE WILL, and by these Presents, for us, our Heirs and Successors, grant and confirm to the aforesaid Mayor, Bailiffs, and Burgesses of the Borough aforesaid, and their Successors, that they and their Successors shall have, hold, and keep, and shall and may be able to have, hold, and keep, within the Borough aforesaid, in every Year for ever, four Fairs or Marts; the first of the same Fairs or Marts to begin on the Feast of *Saint John* the Baptist, and to continue for the whole of the same Feast; and the second Fair to begin on the Fourteenth Day of September and to be kept and continue for the whole of that Day; and the third Fair of the same four Fairs or Marts to begin on the Day of the Feast of *Saint Simon* and *Saint Jude*, the Apostles, and to be kept and continue for the whole of that Day of the Feast of *Saint Simon* and *Saint Jude;* and the fourth Fair of the same four Fairs or Marts to begin on Saturday next before the Feast of Lent, and to be kept and continue for the whole of that Saturday, together with a Court of Piepowder, to be holden there in the Time of the same Fairs or Marts, and with all Liberties and Free Customs, Tolls, Stallage, Piccage, Fines, Amerciaments, and all other Profits, Commodities, Advantages, and Emoluments whatsoever, to such Fairs, Marts, and Courts of Piepowder, appertaining, arising, accruing, or happening, or in any wise appertaining or belonging; so nevertheless that the aforesaid Fairs or Marts shall not be to the Prejudice or Damage of other neighbouring Fairs, near adjacent: AND FURTHER WE WILL, and by these Presents, for us, our Heirs and Successors, grant and confirm to the aforesaid Mayor, Bailiffs, and Burgesses of the Borough aforesaid, and their Successors, That they their Heirs and Successors shall have, hold, and keep, and shall and may be able to have, hold, and keep, within the Borough aforesaid, one Market in every Week in every Year for ever, on Friday, to be holden and kept within the same Borough; and that at the Time of the same Market all and every Person coming and resorting to the same Market, shall and may be able to sell, buy, and expose to Sale from henceforth for ever as well all and singular Wares, Merchandize, Grain, and Things whatsoever, as all and all Manner of Oxen, Sheep, Pigs, Horses, Mares, Geldings, and Colts, and all and all Manner other Animals and Cattle alive and dead

Its Powers.

Fairs.

Court of Piepowder.

Market.

whatsoever, at their Pleasure, according to the Laws, Customs, and Statutes of our Kingdom of *England*, paying the Tolls and Customs therefore due to the same Mayor, Aldermen, and Burgesses of the Borough aforesaid, for the Time being, to the proper Use and Behoof of the same Mayor, Bailiffs, and Burgesses and their Successors, towards the Support and Maintenance of the Charges and Expenses of the same Borough; together with a Court of Piepowder, there to be holden at the Time of the same Market, and with all and all Manner of Liberties and free Customs, Tolls, Stallage, Piccage, Fines, Amerciaments, and all other Profits, Commodities, Advantages, and Emoluments whatsoever, to such Market and Court of Piepowder appertaining, arising, accruing, or happening; so nevertheless that the same Market shall not be to the Damage or Prejudice of other neighbouring Markets there near adjacent; and that no Foreigner who shall dwell out of the Borough aforesaid, unless he shall be a Victualler or a Tanner, from henceforth shall make, take, and use any Stalls within the Borough aforesaid, at the Time of the Market there, without the Licence of the Mayor and Aldermen of the same Borough, or the major Part of them, of whom the Mayor for the Time being WE WILL to be one: AND FURTHER WE WILL, and by these Presents, for us, our Heirs and Successors, give, grant, and confirm to the aforesaid Mayor, Bailiffs, and Burgesses of the Borough aforesaid, and their Successors, all and all Manner of Liberties, Franchises, Immunities, Exemptions, Privileges, Acquittances, Jurisdictions, Lands, Tenements, Wastes, void Grounds, Commons, and Hereditaments whatsoever, which the Mayor, Bailiffs, and Burgesses of the Borough aforesaid now have, hold, use, and enjoy; and which any of them or their Predecessors, by whatsoever Names or Name, or by whatsoever Incorporation, or by Pretext of whatsoever Incorporation heretofore have had, held, used, or enjoyed, or ought to have, hold, use, or enjoy, of any hereditary Estate, by Reason or Pretext of any Charters or Letters Patent, by any of our Progenitors or Ancestors, late Kings or Queens of *England*, in any wise heretofore made, granted, or confirmed, or by whatsoever other lawful Manner, Right, or Title, Custom, Usage, or Prescription heretofore lawfully used, had, or accustomed; To HAVE, HOLD, AND ENJOY, to the aforesaid Mayor, Bailiffs, and Burgesses of the Borough aforesaid, and their Successors for ever; except always out of these our Letters Patent, and this our Grant and Confirmation wholly reserved, all and all Manner of Rents, Services, Sums of Money, and Demands whatsoever, which to us or to any of our Progenitors or Predecessors, or to any other Person or Persons for or in respect of the Premises, or of any or either of them have heretofore been accustomed to be rendered or paid, or ought to be rendered or paid: WHEREFORE WE WILL, and by these Presents, for us, our Heirs and Successors, firmly enjoining, command and order, that the aforesaid Mayor, Bailiffs, and Burgesses of the Borough aforesaid, and their Successors, shall have, hold, use, and enjoy, and shall and may be able fully and wholly to have, hold, use, and enjoy, for ever, all the Liberties, free Customs, Privileges, Authorities, Jurisdictions, and Acquittances aforesaid, according to the Tenor and Effect of these our Letters Patent, without the Hindrance or Impediment of us, our

---

Court of Pie-powder.

No Foreigner, to hold a Stall without a Licence, except &c.

Former Charters confirmed.

Heirs or Successors whomsoever; being unwilling that the same Mayor, Bailiffs, and Burgesses of the Borough aforesaid, and their Successors, or any or either of them, by Reason of the Premises, or of any of them, shall therefore be hindered, molested, vexed, or aggrieved, or in any wise disturbed, by us, or our Heirs or Successors, the Justices, Sheriffs, Escheators, or other Bailiffs or Ministers of us, our Heirs or Successors whomsoever : WILLING, and by these Presents ordering and commanding, as well the Treasurer, Chancellor, and Barons of our Exchequer at Westminster and other the Justices and Officers of us, and of our Heirs and Successors, as our Attorney and Solicitor General, for the Time being, and every of them, and all other our Officers and Ministers whomsoever, that neither they nor any or either of them shall prosecute, or continue, or make or cause to be prosecuted or continued any Writ or Summons of Quo Warranto or any other our Writ, Writs or Process whatsoever, against the aforesaid Mayor, Bailiffs, and Burgesses of the Borough aforesaid, or any or either of them, for any Titles, Things, Matters, Offences, Claim, or Usurpation, or any of them, by them or any of them duly claimed, used, attempted, had, or usurped, before the Day of the making of these Presents; WILLING ALSO, that the Mayor, Bailiffs, and Burgesses of the Borough aforesaid, or any of them, shall be in no wise molested or disturbed by any or either of the Justices, Officers, or Ministers aforesaid, in or for the due Use, Claim, or Abuse of any other Liberties, Franchises, or Jurisdictions, within the Borough aforesaid, the Limits and Precincts thereof, before the Day of the making of these our Letters Patent, or shall be compelled to answer for the same or any of them : AND WHEREAS the *Lady Elizabeth*, late Queen of *England*, by her Letters Patent, sealed with her great Seal of *England*, bearing Date the twenty-first Day of July, in the fourth Year of her Reign, DID give and grant to the Mayor, Bailiffs, and Burgesses of the Borough of *Wicombe* aforesaid, all the Scite, Bound, and Circuit of the late Hospital of *Saint John* the Baptist, in *Wicombe* aforesaid, and all the Hospital aforesaid; and all Messuages, Lands, Tenements, in *Wicombe* aforesaid, and in the Parishes of *Penne, Hichenden,* and *Great Marlow*, in the County of *Buckingham*, and elsewhere wheresoever in the same County, which to the said late Hospital did formerly belong; and all her Messuages, Lands, Tenements, and Hereditaments in *Wicombe* aforesaid, called by the Name of the Fraternity of the *Blessed Mary*, or by the Name of our *Lady Rents*, which same Lands, Tenements, and Hereditaments, so by the aforesaid late *Queen Elizabeth*, were given and granted to the same Mayor, Bailiffs, and Burgesses solely towards the perpetual Maintenance of one Grammar School in *Wicombe* aforesaid; and also towards the perpetual Maintenance and Relief of four poor Persons, to be relieved in the same Borough; as by the same Letters Patent among other Things doth more fully appear : AND WHEREAS WE are credibly informed by the Information of the now Mayor, Bailiffs, and Burgesses of the said Borough, that the Number of poor and needy Persons in the same Borough is much increased, and daily doth more and more increase, to the great Charge of the same Borough : AND ALSO WE are likewise informed, that the

Grant of Queen Elizabeth for Maintenance of a Grammar School, &c.

M M

said late Hospital of *Saint John* the Baptist, and the aforesaid Messuages, Lands, Tenements, and Hereditaments, by the said late *Queen Elizabeth*, as aforesaid given and granted, towards the perpetual Maintenance and Support of the Grammar School and four poor Persons, in *Wicombe* aforesaid, will well and competently suffice, as well for the Maintenance and Support of the aforesaid Grammar School, and four poor Persons, according to the Ordinances and Intent of the said late Queen in the said Borough ; as also for the Relief of many other poor and needy Persons in the same Borough : WE desiring to relieve the great Charges and Expenses of the same Borough, and also willing that the poor and needy People of the same Borough may be succoured by all good and convenient Ways and Means ; and nevertheless willing that the aforesaid Grammar School and the aforesaid four poor Persons by the aforesaid Letters Patent of the said late *Queen Elizabeth*, to be relieved in the same Borough, shall be perpetually supported and maintained, more especially and before all others, according to the Ordinances and Intent of the same late Queen, in the same Letters Patent mentioned, of our especial Grace and of our certain Knowledge **Confirmed.** and mere Motion, HAVE given, granted, and confirmed ; and by these Presents, for us, our Heirs and Successors, DO give, grant, and confirm Licence, Power, and Authority to the aforesaid Mayor, Aldermen, and Bailiffs of the Borough aforesaid, and their Successors, That they and their Successors, by the Discretion of them, or the major Part of them, from Time to Time, shall take, expend, and dispose of all and singular the Issues, Rents, Revenues, and yearly Profits whatsoever of all and singular the aforesaid Messuages, Lands, Tenements, and Hereditaments so by the aforesaid late Queen given and granted to the Maintenance of the aforesaid Grammar School and four poor Persons as aforesaid, as well to the perpetual Support and Relief of the aforesaid Grammar School and four poor Persons, according to the pious Intention of the said late Queen, in the same Borough to be supported and relieved, as also to the Relief and Support of other poor and needy Men in the same Borough, from Time to Time inhabiting and dwelling ; and also to the Support of the Charges and Expenses of the same Mayor, Bailiffs, and Burgesses, in and about the Defence of their Title in and to the aforesaid Hospital, Messuages, Lands, Tenements, Rents, and other the Premises to the same Mayor, Bailiffs, and Burgesses, by the aforesaid late *Queen Elizabeth*, so as aforesaid given and granted, and to no **Oaths to be** other Uses, Intents, or Purposes : AND FURTHER WE WILL, and by these Presents, **taken by** for us, our Heirs, and Successors, ordain, and firmly enjoining Command, That the **Officers of the** Mayor, Aldermen, Bailiffs, Recorder, and all other the Officers and Ministers of the **Borough.** Borough aforesaid, and their Deputies, and also all Justices of the Peace of us, our Heirs and Successors within the Borough aforesaid, in or by these our Letters Patent, now nominated, or by Virtue, or according to the Tenor of the same Letters Patent, or of any other Letters Patent heretofore made, hereafter to be nominated, elected, or constituted, before they shall be admitted to the Execution or Exercise of the Office or Offices, Place or Places to which they are now respectively nominated, appointed, or constituted, so as aforesaid, or hereafter in Form aforesaid, shall be nominated, elected, or constituted, or shall in any wise intermeddle in that Behalf, and every of them shall take, as well the corporal Oath, commonly called the Oath of Obedience, as the corporal Oath, commonly called the Oath of Supremacy, upon the Holy Gospel of God, before such Person or Persons, as and who are at present appointed and designated, or hereafter shall be appointed and designated by the Laws and Statutes of this Kingdom to give and take such Oath: AND FURTHER WE WILL, and declare our Royal Intent, That no Recorder, or Common Clerk of the Borough aforesaid, from henceforth to be elected or constituted, shall intermeddle in such Office or Offices, or any of them respectively before they and each of them respectively shall be approved by us, our Heirs, or Successors; any Thing in these Presents contained, or any other Thing, Cause, or Matter whatsoever to the contrary thereof in any wise notwithstanding, ALTHOUGH express Mention, &c. IN WITNESS whereof, &c. WITNESS, THE KING, at Westminster, the sixteenth Day of November.

Recorder and Common Clerk to be approved of by the King before entering upon Office.

By Command of the King.

CHARLES THE SECOND,

By the Grace of God of England Scotland France and Ireland King Defender of the Faith, &c.

TO all to whom these our present Letters shall come Greeting. We have beheld a certain Record remaining in our white Tower of London in these words an Antient Charter remaining in the white Tower of London. Henry by the grace of God King of England and of France and Lord of Ireland to all and Singular our Loving Subjects of England to whom our present Charter shall come Greeting. Know yea that we have given and by this our present Charter Confirmed to our beloved Subjects and Commoners which belong's to Holmere Heath in the County of Bucks; to wit, the Village of Penn and the Forrens of Amersham, Little Missenden and the Forrens of great Missenden, Hitchinden and the Forrens of *Chiping Wickham* and the Forrens of Wendover Eborat : with all Libertyes and Priviledges underwritten to wit the Metes and bounds are set forth as followeth, In the first place Hasselmere Widdemere and Niming Chase Watts hatch Holmers hatch Lerepynnes hatch Wildens hatch Samsons hatch with Witchmere hill, Gawdestakes and so as the way leadeth to Woodsheeves lyeing and being towards the Gate stakes of Pennbury the Mannor of St. Roger atte Penn Knight Rogmansham hatch Garret Green Colmorham, Devonseeles hatch Totteridge hatch Crendens hatch with Hasselmere with all the parsells and appurtenances whatsoever belonging to the Common with all Libertyes Freedom's and immunities of Commoning belonging to the said Towns and Villages as aforesaid that is to say the Town of Penn the Forrens of Amersham little Missenden and the Forrens of great Missenden Hitchinden and the Forrens of *Chiping Wickham* and the Forrens of Wendover Eborat : with all Liberties underwritten that is say Tollage in fornat-solve, Litood, vite fleed vite strefe Gelde, Hideage Stallage, Misdeming, Wardquint, Borr the boot to have and to hold all the aforesaid Common with all the Liberties and Priviledges above specified for ever : Now know yea that this our present Charter for us and our Heirs as much as in us lyeth we have warranted and Defended to the aforesaid men and their Heirs in the aforesaid Town's and Villages for ever. In Witness whereof &c. The King being Witness at Westminster in the day of St. Peter in Chaines. Now know yea that the Tenor of the aforesaid Record at the desire and request of Walter Cary and Stephen Young, Gentlemen, Edward Sparkes, Jeremy Sexton, Okenden Maid, Samuel Skidmore, John Sexton, Richard Freeze, Silvester Barkley, John Barkley, Frances Alnott, Wm Morton, Thomas Fellow, Wm Mead, Tho. Lane, Tho. Morton, Richard

Morton, Wm Russell, Robt Biscow, Francis Putnam, Wm Russell, Richd Terry, Wm Winter, Michael Cox, Joseph Bovingdon, Zacharia Alnott, Joseph Child, James Child, Anthony Ball, John Child, Thos Harwood, Edward Brown, Stephen Herne, Ralph Dennis, Wm Kemp and Jonas Humphry, We have Caused to be exemplified by these Presents In Witness whereof we have made these our Letters Pattents Witness myself at Westminster the 20.th Day of June in the 17.th year of our Raign.

GRIMSTON.

Conveint cum Recordo Gulielmust Ryley,
      June ye 20.th 1665.

Examined by { JOHN COELT and THOMAS ESTCOURT. } Clerks.

We whose names are Subscribed saw Mr Wm Ryley attest by his Hand Written that this Coppy agreeth with the Record.

JOHN PHILLIPS Clerk.
ROBERT PARKER.

1. Tolage, Signifieth a Tole or Tax and to be Tole free in Markets and Fairs.
2. Stallage, Signifies Money Paid for Pitching of Stalls in a Fair or Market.
3. Geld, Signifies Money or Tribute.
4. Hideage, is an extraordinary Tax to be paid for every Hide of Land.
5. Miss Deming, Chainging of Speech in Court.
6. Litwood, or litood Cutting of wood for the Tenants or Commoners.
7. Borr, the Boot Timber for Building and Fences.
8. Wardquint, Free from Wardshipp.

[OUR WYCOMBE ACTORS OF THE TIMES OF THE TUDORS.

IN a book of expenses of the reign of Henry VII., there is an entry of one hundred shillings, given as a reward to the King's players. In the household books of this Sovereign, from 1492 to 1509, several companies are mentioned, that of the King, of the Duke of Buckingham, the Earls of Oxford, and Northumberland; and according to the same authority, a company was attached to each of the following cities and towns : London, Coventry, *Wycombe*, Mile End, Wymborne Minster, and Kingston.

The first legislative enactment in which the profession of Actor is mentioned, is one of the reign of Edward IV., and in it, all players are exempt from the sumptuary laws. (See Statutum De Cibariis Utendis, 10th Edward III., A.D. 1336.) It may not be altogether uninteresting to add, that the object of this Statute was to restrain the expense of entertainments; it recites the great inconvenience to the more opulent, by expense in eating, and the ruin to those of less affluent fortunes, from an endeavour to imitate this extravagance. It therefore ordained, that no one should be allowed, either for his dinner or supper, above two courses, as also not above three dishes in each course; and it likewise expressly declared, that soused meat was to count as one of these dishes; certain feasts were however excepted, in which three courses were permitted. We need not look further than into a bill of fare for a great feast, or entertainment in those days, to see that the expense and gluttony were immoderate. (See Barrington on the more ancient Statutes, pa. 240.)]

APPENDIX II.

"A TRUE ACCOUNT

OF THE

WYCOMB ELECTION

IN A LETTER TO A MEMBER OF PARLIAMENT."

"SIR,—

Quis tulerit Graccos de seditione Querentes, is a reflection I made with myself, upon reading an account of the Wycomb Election, wrote, as I suppose, in favour of Mr. Waller; if anything that is full of falsehoods and inconsistencies can be said to be done in favour of a Gentleman; the notoriety of the fact is this,—that on the day of Election, a rabble procur'd from all adjacent parts, had, by the Chamberlain's permission, taken possession of the Town-Hall, and secur'd to themselves the advantageous posts, with a full purpose to obstruct the Honourable Mr. Collyer's voters; that as the Mayor was coming to open the Election, himself was insulted, beat and menac'd. That when he attempted to go up into the Town-Hall his Officers were overpower'd, and he, with the apparent risque of his life, forc'd to retreat; that seeing the violence so outragious, he had no other way to consult his own safety, and the freedom of Election, but by betaking himself to a place where the Rioters might be excluded. That, on this necessity, he thought the George-Inn not an improper place, being near at hand, and having rooms spacious enough to receive the Voters; That, being seated there, he sent for the two Candidates, to apprize them of the danger he conceiv'd himself in, by attempting to come to the Town-Hall, and desir'd them to bring their Electors thither; That, accordingly, he proceeded to take the Poll regularly, and if Mr. W—— thought not proper to let his Voters appear, it must be occasion'd from a consciousness of his minority, which he hoped to supply (when Bribery prov'd ineffectual) with force and violence; and now that he is defeated every way, makes calumny his refuge at last; for when he charges Mr. Smales with endeavouring to engross the Corporation, he forgets the attempt not long ago made of obtruding fourscore and more Honorary Members upon it, and 'tis to Mr. Smale's lasting honour and reputation, that he opposed so gross an invasion, and so justly defended the Corporation's rights.

This, Sir, in short, is the truth of the case; and I have only this short reflection to make from the whole, that the freedom of Elections is quite extinct and gone, when the dint of money, and the force of a prevailing riot shall pretend to postpone a manifest majority.

I am, Sir, &c."

"A TRUE STATE

OF

WYCOMB ELECTION.

" This Corporation in the year 1720 consisted of about 120 legal Voters ; but some short time before the election of Members for the present Parliament, a Relation of the present Petitioner did, with the assistance of the then Mr. Bedder, a Butcher and Ale-house keeper, procure 80 new Burgesses to be made at one time, contrary to law and the ancient usage of the said Borough.

For redressing that irregular practice, application was immediately made to the Court of King's Bench, and Informations in the nature of Quo Warrantos were exhibited against the said 80 new made Burgesses : And upon a fair and full trial had at the Assizes for the County of Buckingham, it was determined that they were illegally chosen ; and Judgment was given that they should be ousted and removed.

About 60 Burgesses have been since made at several times, according to the Charter and the constant usage of the Borough ; not by the contrivance of Mr. Smales, as has been suggested, but by the general consent and nomination of the then Mayor, Alder-men, and Bailiffs ; and not one of their Elections has been controverted. And to convince even Mr. Waller, the Petitioner, that those 60 new Burgesses were impartially made, there needs no more than to observe, that 25 of them have appeared in his interest, and signed their names to a Petition in his favour.   As to Mr. Richard Shrimpton and Smales, they were so far from having any view of being alternately chosen Mayors of the said Borough by means of those last made Burgesses, that in the year 1723, which was the very next year after the making of those Burgesses, Ferdinando Shrimpton (the Town Chamberlain, and Mr. Waller's principal Agent at the late Election) was chosen Mayor of the said Borough, and held the said Office for that year, the said Smales the ensuing year, and Mr. Richard Shrimpton this year.

Thus the Corporation stood, when the Mayor received the Precept for the last Election ; at which the Candidates were the Honourable Charles Collyer Esq. and Harry Waller Esq.

It is admitted that the Town-Hall was the place appointed for the Election, and it will appear by unquestionable evidence, that the present Mayor intended, and on the day of Election used his utmost endeavours, even with the hazard of his life to go into the Town Hall, in order to proceed on the Election with all fairness and im-partiality, but was industriously and tumultuously opposed and prevented from so doing by the Petitioner's Agents and followers : And there is good reason to believe that this opposition was made by the direction or privity of Mr. Waller, the Petitioner; for that the said Mayor having intimation given him some few days before the Election, that several Bargemen, and other persons from the adjacent Towns, who had no pretence of voting at the said Election, did intend to assemble there upon the day of Election in favour of Mr. Waller, in order to disturb the orderly proceeding at the said Election; and that Ferdinando Shrimpton, the present Chamberlain of the said Town, and a professed Agent for the said Mr. Waller, had clandestinely gotten the keys of the Town Hall into his possession; the said Mayor thought he had just reason from these unusual proceedings to suspect that some unfair designs were carrying on by the said Mr. Waller, or his Agent the Town Chamberlain. And therefore, to preserve the peace of the said Election, and prevent any disorders that might be intended, the said Mayor sent to the said Town Chamberlain the evening before the day of Election to deliver him the said keys, which he peremptorily refused.

Upon the morning of the Election the Mayor, observing that his former suspicions were just, and that the Town Chamberlain made use of his keys partially in letting in the Friends, Agents, and Voters of Mr. Waller, to the said Hall and excluding all other persons, sent again to him to demand the said keys, in order to prevent such irregular proceedings, but was again refused.

About one or two a clock on the day of Election, the Mayor proceeded towards the Town Hall in his usual formality, with his Constables and other Officers attending him, and as he came near the said Hall, found the whole area and the Stairs leading to the Town Hall crowded with Bargemen and other tumultuous persons riotously assembled, armed with Clubs, and obstructing his going into the said Hall, and crying out A Waller, A Waller.

The Mayor being surpriz'd at this tumultuous and unusual proceeding ordered his officers to make way for him, which they endeavoured by all possible means to do; but the said crowd the more opposed, shouting and crying A Waller, A Waller, holding up their clubs; and one of the Servants of a near Relation of Mr. Waller drawing his sword, and holding it up drawn in his hand, rendered it totally impossible for the said Mayor to enter the said Town Hall to proceed to an Election there, as he really intended and endeavoured to do.

The Mayor then called for the Proclamation to be read, in order to disperse the said Mob so riotously assembled, but could not procure any to be brought to him.

At length the said Mayor perceiving that he could not possibly make his way into the said Hall, notwithstanding his hearty endeavours so to do, but observing some of his officers knockt down and much bruis'd, and himself insulted and thrown against a post; and being a man of 70 years of age, unable to contend longer against so great a multitude, was forced to give over his attempt to get admittance to the said Hall and to consider in what other place he could best perform his duty in obedience to the precept delivered to him.

N N

The George Inn was the nearest, the largest, and most convenient Publick House, or Place to receive so great a company; and Mr. Waller, one of the Candidates, continuing up Stairs in the Town Hall, and not endeavouring to appease or disperse the riotous Assembly, so that the Mayor could not possibly converse with or consult him: He found himself under a necessity either to be guilty of a total breach of his duty in not proceeding to an Election, or else to adjourn to some other place to do it in. And accordingly he caused Publick Proclamation to be made in the place where he stood below the Hall, surrounded by the said Crowd, to adjourn the said Election or Poll to the said George Inn; and immediately caus'd notice to be given of this Adjournment to the said Mr. Waller and his Friends and Voters.

At the same time the said Mayor gave strict orders to his constables and other officers, to preserve the Entrance into the said Inn, and into a large Ground Room next the Street there, free and clear from all disturbances, that the Candidates, their Agents and Voters might have an entry and free access to come and Poll as they pleas'd: Which Orders were observ'd accordingly, and every Person had free liberty to come in and Vote or Poll as they had right and thought fit.

Before the Poll began, Mr. Waller, with several of his Friends and Agents, came into the said Room where the Poll was appointed to be taken, and had notice given them, that the said Mayor was forc'd to adjourn the Poll to that Place, and was ready to receive the Poll of such as pleas'd to offer it. And thereupon several Burgesses appear'd and poll'd for Mr. Collyer the sitting Member, and Mr. Ferdinando Shrimpton, the Town Chamberlain, and one of the principal agents for Mr. Waller, and one Bedder, another Burgess, appear'd and Poll'd for the said Mr. Waller, and some other Burgesses appear'd for him. But the said Mr. Waller, well knowing that a great majority of legal Burgesses were ready to vote for the sitting Member, and whom, by the scheme before concerted between him and the Town Chamberlain, in securing the Town Hall to themselves, they thought they should be able to exclude, withdrew himself, and gave up the Election, and refus'd to Poll any more of his Voters.

And now the said Mr. Waller, who by his Agents and Friends so violently and obstinately oppos'd the said Mayor, and prevented his coming into the said Town Hall to perform his duty in proceeding to the said Election in the usual Place of Election, and who put the said Mayor under an absolute necessity of adjourning to some other Place, or rendering himself liable to the censure of the Honourable House of Commons, by not proceeding to an Election at all, disengenuously makes use of this so necessary and legal an adjournment, as a pretence to conceal his own minority, and call in question your sitting Member's fair Election by an undoubted majority of legal votes.

It is hoped that the necessity the Mayor was under to adjourn the Poll, being occasion'd by the impossibility put upon him by the Petitioner and his Agents to proceed in the usual place, will prevent any imputation of irregularity in the said Mayor in that respect.

"On the whole matter, the adjournment was absolutely necessary and strictly "legal; for it will hardly be pretended, that the consent of the Candidates was "any ways requisite to such an adjournment; there being no law forbidding the "Chief Magistrate of a Borough, in such an exigence, or even on any occasion, "to adjourn an Election or Poll to a convenient Place within the same Borough; "And the Mayor having made the said Adjournment as near the Town Hall, as "he could possibly do with safety, and that in the hearing and sight of the Peti-"tioner and his Adherents, who obstructed the Mayor's going to the place first "appointed for the Election, it follows evidently that the adjournment was as law-"ful as if it had been made in the Town Hall.

"It hence follows, by necessary consequence, that the Election at the George "Inn was in every respect as legal as if it had been begun and carried on in "the Town Hall; and the rather for that the Voters had freer and safer access "to the George Inn, than they could possibly have had to the Town Hall; in "regard the Mayor and Constables (the proper Peace Officers of the Borough) "were ready at the George Inn, to admit all the Voters and to afford them the "protection of the Law; whereas the Town Hall was beset by a multitude of "disorderly and riotous Fellows raked up from all corners, by the Petitioner to "obstruct the Mayor in the execution of his Office: And so from first to last, "it seems plain that the Sitting Member was as duly elected and returned, as "if he had been chosen in the Town Hall by the unanimous voice of all the "legal Voters of the Borough."

WYCOMB ELECTION.

The unparalleled attempt at the George Alehouse at Wycomb having mis-carried, and the Election being declared void, a new Writ was issued out for electing a new Burgess in the room of the Honourable Mr. Collyer, and the Precept having been delivered to the Mayor, he, according to his usual manner, pocketed the same several days, before he proclaimed the Election.

The day of Election being come, the Mayor proceeded to the Poll, when a noble Lord, a Stranger of the Borough, to whom Smails had resigned his Minis-try, took upon him to direct the Mayor, and, in effect, presided at the Election. All the Votes, that stood upon the Town Books, being call'd over, and as many as were present on both sides being polled, it was expected that the Mayor wou'd have declared the majority upon the Poll, as is usual, and as was desired by the Candidate, Mr. Waller. But the Mayor refused to do so, and proceeded to call for three persons (and admitted them to poll for Mr. Collyer) who never pretended to any right to vote at any Election before, two whereof were made free, as they said, by the illegal Charter of King James II., and the other under strong suspicion of being qualified that morning by a Razure, and a little Forgery in the Town Books.

The Poll being thus concluded, the Mayor still declined to cast up the Books, and declare the majority; but Mr. Collyer, being conscious how it stood, demanded a scrutiny, which the Mayor, with the advice of his new Governor, readily complied with.

The Gentlemen met accordingly, and the Mayor having made a previous de-claration, that he wou'd return Mr. Collyer at all events, they proceeded to this pretended scrutiny. Some objection was made by the Mayor to one vote of Mr. Waller's; upon which the Mayor being desired to produce the Ledger Books that contain'd the entry of the names of the several Burgesses, in order to examine the right of that vote, he absolutely refused to do it, tho' 'tis well known, that the Books are the very foundation of all scrutinies in the like cases, and more particularly necessary in this, for the information of those Gentlemen on Mr. Collyer's side, that were Strangers to the Borough: But they having been so civil, as to compliment the Mayor that he knew better than them, and that he had no occasion for Books, but was the sole Judge, and might admit or disallow as he thought fit without inquiry;

the Gentlemen on the other side quietly withdrew, being unwilling to interrupt them in so fair and so impartial a proceeding. The way being thus made clear for him, the Mayor took care to strike as many votes from Mr. Waller's Poll as would leave Mr. Collyer a Majority of one single vote; so nicely scrupulous was he of taking more from Mr. Waller than wou'd just do his Business.

Thus ended the famous scrutiny of the Poll at Wycomb; a scrutiny carried on by persons, on one side, intirely ignorant of the rights and qualifications, as well as the very persons of the Electors; without evidence of any kind, or the very Ledger Books of the Corporation, which contain the names and qualifications of the Electors, and which are the proper evidence upon all Scrutinies of this nature, in all Corporations whatsoever; and before a determined Judge, who refused all information even from the Books in his own custody, and had bravely declared beforehand his firm resolution to return Mr. Collyer.

Thus prepared the Mayor proceeded to the Town Hall and there declared the numbers to be 80 and 81, and being ask'd who had the 80 he said Mr. Collyer. Notwithstanding which, Mr. Collyer produced an Indenture ready drawn, returning himself, and made the Mayor sign it, having his hand upon the Indenture all the time; which being taken notice of as an irregular proceeding by the other Candidate and his Friends, Mr. Collyer immediately called for Marshall the Post Master, that keeps the George Ale-house, and bid him read the Proclamation against Riots, which he accordingly did, whereupon most of the Gentlemen and Electors, whereof several were Justices of the Peace, dispers'd and left the Hall.

Thus ended this Election, which though extraordinary in every part of it, yet was concluded with the most amazing circumstance that ever was heard of. The Freemen and Electors of England, assembled by virtue of his Majesty's Writ, in the exercise of their just Rights and Privileges, according to the constitution of the Kingdom, dispersed by a Proclamation like so many Felons and Vagabonds; and this done by the order of a Gentleman that had no authority (though in the presence of the Mayor) and by a Person that was not an Officer of the Peace, is a specimen of a dangerous nature, to shew what may be done in future Elections, if not prevented by the Justice of Parliament; But it is to be hoped, that a Law, which was pass'd so lately, for preserving the Peace of the Kingdom, and for the security of his Majesty's Person and Government, shall not be made an Engine to terrify the Electors and the Freeborn subjects of the Kingdom, and to disperse them when legally assembled to choose their Representatives in Parliament.

WYCOMB ELECTION.

.

The Corporation of Chipping Wycomb, at the time of the Election of Members for this present Parliament, consisted of about one hundred voters; since which time, Richard Shrimpton, the present Mayor, who was likewise chosen to that office in the year 1722, by the contrivance of one Smales, an Alderman of that Town, has made above Seventy Honorary Freemen, scatter'd abroad in all parts of the Kingdom, by which means the said Shrimpton and Smales have been alternately chosen into the Office of Mayor of the said Borough, exclusive of the rest of the Corporation.

Thus it stood, when the present Mayor receiv'd the Precept for making the late Election, which was proclaimed by him to be made on the first of this instant February, at the Town Hall at Wycomb, the usual place of Election; at which time Henry Waller, Esq., a neighbouring Gentleman, and Capt. Collyer, stood Candidates.

The day of the Election being come, the Mayor sent to the Town-Chamberlain, to demand the keys of the Town Hall; but this Officer being appointed by the Common Council and Corporation, and entrusted by them with the custody of the said keys, suspecting some ill design in making that demand, which had never been made by any Mayor whatsoever at any Election before, returned a very civil answer; and acquainted him, That whenever he sent Notice that he was ready to proceed to the Election, he would wait upon him with the keys; and accordingly the Chamberlain did attend at the Town Hall for two or three hours for that purpose, and did, before the Mayor pretended to come to the Hall, open the Doors, and gave the keys to the Mayor's Officers who were left there to guard the same.

In the mean time, many of the Burgesses being admitted into the Hall by the said Officer as usual, and having waited there several hours, sent to the Mayor, to desire to know, when he would come to the Election; to which he sent for answer, That he would come when he thought fit. About half an hour after two, the Mayor proceeded to the Town Hall with mighty pomp, and a great number of Drums, Kettledrums, Trumpets, Hautboys, and other Warlike Musick, attended with the Candidate, Capt. Collyer, and a vast Retinue of Servants and others, which drew together a great crowd of people, as well out of curiosity as admiration of so unusual a sight. Thus they marched to the Foot of the Stairs leading up to the Hall, which were guarded by the Mayor's own Officers, with their Staffs in their Hands. Several of Capt. Collyer's Voters went up into the Hall before him with great ease, notwithstanding the press that was chiefly owing to his Cavalcade, and the resort of so many Strangers as is usual on such occasions. But as the Mayor seem'd to proceed to go up the stairs, Smales pull'd him by the Sleeve, and led him off to the George Ale-house, as had been before concerted, where they intended to proceed to the pretended Election.

What notice they gave to their friends upon this occasion to repair to the George, was not known to the other Candidate, Mr. Waller, and his Friends, who attended in the Hall, expecting the Mayor, till they heard he was at the George Inn. Then Mr. Waller, with about four or five Burgesses and Gentlemen, went to the said Inn, to desire him to come to the Hall, and proceed to the Election, assuring him there was no disorder nor disturbance; and this was before he had begun to proceed upon his pretended Election, which was in a little Room, that would not hold above 20 or 30 people. But the Mayor, in answer, bid them be gone for a pack of Rogues and Rascals, and ask'd them, What business they had there? and some persons in the Room desir'd the Mayor to read the Proclamation against Riots, and disperse those idle Fellows.

Soon after that, the two Bailiffs, with several of the Aldermen, and others, went likewise to the Mayor, to desire him to come to the Hall, to proceed to an Election, assuring him all was peaceable and quiet; and told him, if he apprehended any Mob, he might easily disperse them, and they would give him their utmost assistance; but he was determined to the contrary, and continued in the Alehouse, and made a sham Poll among their own Friends, whilst the major part of legal Voters were attending in the Town Hall, till after they had made this pretended Election.

Mr. Waller and his Friends, having attended till after five o'clock at the Town-Hall, and hearing what was done, drew up a Petition to the Honourable House of Commons, which was signed by 75 legal Voters; whereas the pretended Poll, consisted of but 49 against 2, whereof one indeed, a Creature of theirs, was order'd to vote for Mr. Waller, to give some pretence to call it a Poll.

This is what they call an Election, not begun at the Place appointed by Proclamation, nor adjourned by consent of parties; nor made in any Publick Place where the Voters cou'd have free access, or where they cou'd have the protection of the Magistrate; but huddled up in an Alehouse, where the Mayor had no authority, where the Inn-Keeper was sole Master, and might, without breach of any Law, admit, or exclude, whom he pleas'd; as was intended, if Mr. Waller's Friends had come to Poll; of which Design, Affidavits have been made by those that heard the orders given for that purpose. Thus was this Election made in an Alehouse, under the very Tap; in an Alehouse, kept by a principal Agent of Capt. Collyer, and, what is more extraordinary, a Post Master, who, by an express Law, is forbid, under the severest penalties, to meddle in Elections, in any manner whatsoever.

In short, if the facts above mention'd are compar'd with the Laws now in force for preserving the freedom of Elections, it will appear that there is not one clause in any one of them that has not been violated on this occasion, and that this single stratagem of making Elections in obscure, uncertain places, if allow'd of, is sufficient to evade all the Laws that ever were, or ever can be, made, to secure the very basis of our constitution which is a free and open choice of members to serve in Parliament.

APPENDIX III.

AN ACCOUNT

OF THE

MARQUIS OF WHARTON'S CANVASS

OF THE

BOROUGH OF WYCOMBE,

IN THE LIBERAL INTEREST, IN THE REIGN OF GEORGE I.

The Marquis of Wharton, who was an adept in electioneering tactics, "recommended," says his Biographer, "two Candidates to the Borough of Wycombe ; the Tories invited two of their own party, to oppose him, and money was spent on both sides. A gentleman, a friend of the Tory Candidates, was requested to go down to the Borough with them, to assist them in their canvass. When they came to Wycombe, they found my Lord Wharton was got there before them, and was going up and down the Town with his friends to secure votes. The gentleman with his two candidates, and a few followers, marched on one side of the Street, my Lord Wharton, his candidates, and a great company, on the other. The gentleman not being known to my Lord, or the townsmen, joined in with his Lordship's men to make discoveries, and was by, when my Lord, entering a shoemaker's shop, asked, " where Dick was ? " The good woman said, her husband was gone two or three miles off with some shoes, but his Lordship need not fear him, she would keep him tight ! " I know that," says my Lord, "but I want to see Dick, and have a glass with him ! " The wife was very sorry Dick was out of the way. " Well " says his Lordship, " how do all thy children ? Molly is a brave girl by this time, I warrant ! " " Yes I thank ye, my Lord," says the woman. And his Lordship continued " Is not Jimmy breeched yet ? " This sort of interference by a Peer of the realm rendered opposition hopeless. The " gentleman " slipped away to tell his friends, that no one had a chance against a Marquis with such a memory as this, and who had the happy address to make himself beloved by every rank. They therefore " immediately relinquished the contest."

Since the Author has sent the manuscript of his Early History and Antiquities of Wycombe to the Press, the Charity Commissioners have made a Scheme relating to Wycombe, Pelham's, and other Charities, already described in the preceding pages, and which Scheme has been approved by the Queen in Council. The Author has much pleasure in adding a copy of the Scheme with Her Majesty's approval of the same, to the Appendix, with a list of the Governors under the Scheme.

APPENDIX IV.

———

AT THE COURT AT WINDSOR,

THE 29TH DAY OF JUNE, 1878.

PRESENT:

THE QUEEN'S MOST EXCELLENT MAJESTY IN COUNCIL.

———

WHEREAS the Charity Commissioners for England and Wales have, in virtue of the powers conferred upon them by "The Endowed Schools Acts, 1869, 1873, 1874," and of every other power enabling them in that behalf, made a Scheme, relating to Wycombe, Pelham's, and other Charities:

AND WHEREAS all the conditions in regard to the said Scheme, which are required to be fulfilled by the said Acts, have been fulfilled:

Now, THEREFORE, Her Majesty, having taken the said Scheme (copy whereof numbered 501 is herewith annexed), into consideration, is pleased, by and with the advice of Her Privy Council, to declare, and doth hereby declare, Her approval of the same.

C. L. PEEL.

Preliminary meeting.

11. A preliminary meeting for the arrangement of the conduct of the business shall be held upon the summons of the Clerk to the Municipal Trustees of Wycombe upon some day to be fixed by him being within one calendar month after the time at which, under the provisions herein contained, the administration of the Foundation shall be assumed by the Governors in place of the present Governing Body.

Chairman.

12. The Governors shall, at the said preliminary meeting, and afterwards at their first meeting in each year, elect one of their number to be Chairman of their meetings for the current year, and they shall also make regulations for supplying his place in case of his death, resignation, or absence during his term of office. The Chairman shall always be re-eligible.

Quorum and voting.

13. A quorum shall be constituted when five Governors are present at a meeting. All matters and questions shall be determined by the majority of the Governors present at a duly constituted meeting ; and in case of equality of votes the Chairman shall have a second or casting vote. Whenever any decision is carried by the votes of less than a majority of the whole existing number of Governors, any two Governors may, within fifteen days from the day of the decision, require by a notice addressed to the Chairman of the meeting that the decision shall be once reconsidered at a special meeting, to be held not later than one calendar month next after such decision.

Special meetings.

14. The Chairman or any two Governors may at any time summon a special meeting for any cause that seems to him or them sufficient. All special meetings shall be convened by or under the direction of the person or persons summoning the meeting by notice in writing delivered or sent by post to each Governor, specifying the object of the meeting. And it shall be the duty of the clerk, if any, to give

CHARITY COMMISSION.

IN THE MATTER OF THE ENDOWED SCHOOLS ACTS, 1869, 1873, AND 1874.

SCHEME for the Administration of the Foundation known as the Grammar School and Almshouse Charity in the Borough of Chipping Wycombe, otherwise High Wycombe, otherwise Wycombe, in the County of Buckingham, originally established in pursuance of a charter or Letters Patent of Queen Elizabeth, dated on or about the 21st day of July 1562, and since regulated by a Scheme of the Court of Chancery, dated on or about the 26th day of July 1856, and of certain other Foundations and Endowments.

GENERAL ADMINISTRATION OF FOUNDATION.

Future administration of Foundation.

1. The Foundations and endowments above-mentioned or referred to shall henceforth be administered as one Foundation by the Governing Body herein-after constituted, in accordance with the provisions of this Scheme, under the name of the Wycombe Grammar School and Almshouse Foundation, herein-after called the Foundation.

Foundations comprised in Scheme.

2. The Foundations and endowments above-mentioned or referred to are the above-mentioned Grammar School and Almshouse

Charity, and also such or so much of certain other Foundations and endowments at Wycombe above-named as shall become part of the Foundation hereby established, and subject to the provisions of this Scheme under the provisions of any other Scheme or Schemes to be made under the Endowed Schools Acts, 1869, 1873, and 1874.

Almspeople. 3. Part of the Foundation, being the part now applicable for charitable purposes, not educational, namely, the land and buildings now occupied exclusively for the benefit of the fourteen existing Almspeople of the said Grammar School and Almshouse Foundation, and the yearly sum of £187 4s. out of the income of the Foundation shall be applied for the benefit of the Almspeople as herein-after provided. Subject as aforesaid the Foundation shall be applicable wholly to the educational purposes of this Scheme.

Governing Body. 4. The Governing Body, herein-after called the Governors, shall, when completely formed and full, consist of 15 persons, of whom nine shall be called Representative Governors, and six shall be called Coöptative Governors.

Representative Governors. 5. The Representative Governors shall be competent persons duly qualified to discharge the duties of the office, and shall be appointed by the following electing bodies respectively in the following proportions, that is to say,—

Two by the Town Council of the Borough of Chipping Wycombe.

Two by the Local Board of the Parish of Chipping Wycombe.

One by the School Board for the Borough of Chipping Wycombe;

One by the School Board for the Parish of Chipping Wycombe;

Two by the Justices of the Peace for the County of Buckingham, acting in and for the Petty Sessional division in which the parish of Chipping Wycombe is situate;

One by the Justices of the Peace for the Borough of Chipping Wycombe.

Such appointments shall be made as often as there may be occasion by the body entitled to appoint, at a meeting thereof which shall be convened, held, and conducted as nearly as may be in conformity with the ordinary rules or practice of such body, or failing such rules or practice, then in conformity with regulations to be made or approved by the Charity Commissioners for England and Wales. Every Representative Governor shall be appointed to office for the term of five years, reckoned from the date of the appointment. The first Representative Governors shall be appointed as soon as conveniently may be after the date of this Scheme. The Chairman or other presiding officer of each meeting at which the appointment of any Representative Governors or Governor shall be made, shall forthwith cause the names or name of the persons or person so appointed to be notified, in the case of the first such appointment to the clerk to the Municipal Trustees of the Borough of Wycombe, and in the case of every subsequent appointment to the Chairman of the Governors or their clerk, if any, or other acting officer. Any appointment of a Representative Governor not made as aforesaid, within six calendar months from the date of this Scheme, or of the notice herein-after prescribed of the occurrence of a vacancy, as the case may be, shall for that turn be made by the then existing Governors.

6. The Coöptative Governors shall at first be eight instead of six, namely :-- Coöptative Governors.

P P

     * Joseph Hunt,
      The Rev. Robert Chilton,
      James Thurlow,
      Randolph Henry Crewe,
      Charles Strange,
      Thomas John Reynolds,
      Herbert Simmonds, and
      William Rose,

being eight of the Municipal Trustees of Wycombe; and their appointment shall take effect from the date of this Scheme, and shall be for the term of their respective lives.

The future Coöptative Governors shall be competent persons duly qualified to discharge the duties of the office, and shall be appointed in every case by the general body of Governors at a special meeting, by a resolution to be forthwith notified by them, with all proper information to the Charity Commissioners, at their office in London; but no such appointment shall be valid until it has been approved by the said Commissioners, and their approval certified under their official seal. The future Coöptative Governors shall be appointed to office for the term of eight years, reckoned from the date of the approval.

Vacancies.   7. Any Representative or Coöptative Governor who, during his term of office, shall become bankrupt or incapacitated to act, or express in writing his wish to resign, or omit for the space of two consecutive years to attend any meeting, shall thereupon forthwith vacate the office of Governor; and the Governors shall cause an entry to be made in their minute book of every vacancy occasioned by any of

---

* Deceased.

Preliminary meeting.

11. A preliminary meeting for the arrangement of the conduct of the business shall be held upon the summons of the Clerk to the Municipal Trustees of Wycombe upon some day to be fixed by him being within one calendar month after the time at which, under the provisions herein contained, the administration of the Foundation shall be assumed by the Governors in place of the present Governing Body.

Chairman.

12. The Governors shall, at the said preliminary meeting, and afterwards at their first meeting in each year, elect one of their number to be Chairman of their meetings for the current year, and they shall also make regulations for supplying his place in case of his death, resignation, or absence during his term of office. The Chairman shall always be re-eligible.

Quorum and voting.

13. A quorum shall be constituted when five Governors are present at a meeting. All matters and questions shall be determined by the majority of the Governors present at a duly constituted meeting; and in case of equality of votes the Chairman shall have a second or casting vote. Whenever any decision is carried by the votes of less than a majority of the whole existing number of Governors, any two Governors may, within fifteen days from the day of the decision, require by a notice addressed to the Chairman of the meeting that the decision shall be once reconsidered at a special meeting, to be held not later than one calendar month next after such decision.

Special meetings.

14. The Chairman or any two Governors may at any time summon a special meeting for any cause that seems to him or them sufficient. All special meetings shall be convened by or under the direction of the person or persons summoning the meeting by notice in writing delivered or sent by post to each Governor, specifying the object of the meeting. And it shall be the duty of the clerk, if any, to give

such notice when required by the Chairman or by any Governors having a right to summon such meeting.

15. If a sufficient number of Governors to form a quorum are not present at any meeting, or if the business at any meeting is not fully completed, those present may adjourn the meeting to a subsequent day and time, of which notice shall be given in manner aforesaid to each Governor.

Adjournme of meetings

16. A minute book and proper books of account shall be provided by the Governors, and kept in some convenient and secure place of deposit to be provided or appointed by them for that purpose, and minutes of the entry into office of every new Governor, and of all proceedings of the Governors, shall be entered in such minute book.

Minutes.

17. The Governors shall cause full accounts to be kept of the receipts and expenditure in respect of the Foundation; and such accounts shall be stated for each year, and examined and passed annually by the Governors at the first or second meeting in the ensuing year, unless some other meeting shall be appointed for the purpose with the approval of the Charity Commissioners, and every such account shall be signed by the Governors present at the meeting at which it shall be passed.

Accounts.

The Governors shall cause sufficient abstracts of the accounts to be published annually for general information. Such abstracts may be in the form given in the schedule hereto, unless some other form is prescribed by the Charity Commissioners, in which case the form so prescribed shall be followed.

18. The Governors may from time to time make such arrangements as they may find most fitting for the custody of all deeds and

B a

other documents belonging to the Foundation, for deposit of money, for the drawing of cheques, and also for the appointment of a clerk or of any necessary agents or other proper officers for their assistance in the conduct of the business of the Foundation, at such reasonable salaries or scale of remuneration as shall be approved by the Charity Commissioners, but no Governor acting as such clerk or officer shall be entitled to any salary or remuneration.

Vesting property.   19. From and after the date of this Scheme all lands and hereditaments, not being copyhold, belonging to the Foundation, and all terms, estates, and interests therein, shall be vested in the Official Trustee of Charity Lands, and his successors, in trust for the Foundation; and all copyhold hereditaments belonging to the Foundation, and all terms, estates, and interests therein, shall be vested in like manner, upon such terms and conditions as shall be agreed upon between the Governors and the lord of the manor. And all stock in the public funds and other securities belonging to the Foundation, and not hereby required or directed to be otherwise applied or disposed of, shall be transferred to the Official Trustees of Charitable Funds, in trust for the Foundation.

Management and letting of estates.   20. All the estates and property of the Foundation not required to be retained or occupied for the purposes thereof, shall, subject as herein-after provided with regard to the part thereof known as the Rye Mead otherwise the Rye, be let or otherwise managed by the Governors, or by their officers acting under their orders, according to the general law applicable to the management of property by trustees of charitable foundations.

Timber and minerals.   21. Any money arising from the sale of timber or from any mines or minerals on the estates of the Foundation shall be treated as capital, and shall be invested in the name of the Official Trustees of Charitable Funds, under the direction of the Charity Commissioners, except in any special cases in which the Governors may be authorised by such Commissioners to deal otherwise with such money or any part thereof.

22. So soon as the full number of Governors shall have been completed according to the provisions of this Scheme, or upon the expiration of the first three calendar months after the date of this Scheme, if the full number of Governors shall not then have been completed, the administration of the Foundation shall pass to the said Governors in place of the present Governing Body, and such Governing Body shall thereupon become ipso facto removed and discharged from their office, and shall cause all deeds, minute and account books, and other papers and documents belonging or relating to the Foundation, and all cash balances and personal effects belonging thereto, and not herein required to be transferred to or vested in the Official Trustees of Charitable Funds, to be delivered or transferred unto the said Governors or as they shall direct. In the meantime the Foundation shall continue to be administered and managed so far as may be necessary by the present Governing Body as nearly as may be in conformity with the provisions of this Scheme. The aforesaid time of three calendar months may be extended, if necessary, by an order of the Charity Commissioners, made upon the application of any one or more of the present Governing Body, or of the Governors, if any.

Transfer of administration of Foundation to Governors.

23. After the administration of the Foundation has passed to the Governors as aforesaid, the Governors for the time being, if a quorum is constituted, may act for all the purposes of this Scheme although the Governing Body as herein-before constituted is not full.

Governors may act although body not full.

Temporary continuance

24. So far as may be practicable and convenient. the School may be carried on as heretofore until the end of the school term which may be current at the date of this Scheme. or which according to the previously established practice would begin next after that date, or until such other time as may with the approval of the Charity Commissioners be fixed by the body for the time being having the administration of the Foundation under this Scheme.

Provision as to present Master.

25. The Rev. James Poulter, the present Master, shall have the option on declaring the same to the Governors in writing of being retained as the first Head Master under this Scheme, and if he exercises such option. so as to become the first Head Master under this Scheme, shall not be liable to be removed, except for a cause for which he might have been dismissed from his present office, if this Scheme had not taken effect: but if he fail to exercise such option as aforesaid within six calendar months from the date of this Scheme the Governors may forthwith remove him from his present office; and the question of compensation to be assigned to him on such removal shall be determined by the Charity Commissioners. If the said James Poulter exercises such option as aforesaid the Governors may, on his ceasing to be Head Master, grant to him such pension, if any, as may be approved by the Charity Comissioners.

Scheme to be brought into operation as soon as practicable.

26. The Governors shall take all requisite measures for bringing the provisions of this Scheme into active operation for the regulation of the School as soon as practicable, and they shall have power to make all suitable and proper arrangements for that purpose.

Saving of interests of scholars.

27. Any payment, or exemption from payment, Scholarship, Exhibition, or other benefit to which any free scholar or other boy who was on the Foundation on the 1st day of June 1875 is legally entitled thereunder shall be continued to him.

The School and its Management.

28. As soon as conveniently may be the Governors, either by altering or adding to the present school buildings, shall provide proper school buildings and a residence for the Head Master suitable for not less than 100 day scholars and 20 boarders, and planned with a view to convenient extension, and may apply for the purpose a sum not exceeding £5,000 to be provided or raised, if needful, out of the capital endowment or property of the Foundation by sale or otherwise, but for all the purposes of this clause they shall act subject to the consent and approval of the Charity Commissioners.

School site and buildings.

29. No person shall be disqualified for being a Master in the School by reason only of his not being, or not intending to be, in Holy Orders.

Masters not to be required to be in Holy Orders.

30. There shall be a Head Master of the School. He shall be a graduate of some University in the United Kingdom. Every future Head Master shall be appointed by the Governors at some meeting to be called for that purpose, as soon as conveniently may be after the occurrence of a vacancy, or after notice of an intended vacancy. In order to obtain the best candidates, the Governors shall, for a sufficient time before making any appointment, give public notice of the vacancy and invite applicants for the office by advertisements in newspapers, or by such other methods as they may judge best calculated to secure the object.

Head Master.

Appointment.

31. The Governors may dismiss the Head Master without assigning cause, after six calendar months, written notice, given to him

Dismissal.

Q Q

in pursuance of a resolution passed at two consecutive meetings held at an interval of at least fourteen days, and convened for that purpose, such resolution being affirmed at each meeting by not less than two thirds of the Governors present.

32. The Governors for what in their opinion is urgent cause may, by resolution passed at a special meeting convened for that purpose, and affirmed by not less than two thirds of the whole number of Governors for the time being, declare that the Head Master ought to be dismissed from his office without the aforesaid notice, and in that case they may appoint another special meeting to be held not less than a week after the former one, and may then by a similar resolution, affirmed by as large a proportion of Governors, absolutely and finally dismiss him. And if the Governors assembled at the first of such meetings think fit at once to suspend the Head Master from his office until the next meeting, they may do so by resolution affirmed by as large a proportion of Governors. Full notice and opportunity of defence at both meetings shall be given to the Head Master.

Declaration to be signed by Head Master.

33. Every future Head Master, previously to entering into office, shall be required to sign a declaration, to be entered in the minute book of the Governors, to the following effect :—

" I   declare that I will always, to the best of " my ability discharge the duties of Head Master of the Wycombe " Grammar School during my tenure of the office, and that if I am " removed by the Governors I will acquiesce in such removal, and " will thereupon relinquish all claim to the mastership and its future " emoluments, and will deliver up to the Governors, or as they direct, " possession of all the property of the School then in my possession " or occupation."

34. The Head Master shall dwell in the residence assigned for him. He shall have the occupation and use of such residence and of any other property of the School of which he becomes the occupant as such Head Master, in respect of his official character and duties, and not as tenant, and shall, if removed from his office, deliver up possession of such residence and other property to the Governors, or as they direct. He shall not, except with the permission of the Governors, permit any person not being a member of his family to occupy such residence or any part thereof.

Head Master's official residence.

35. The Head Master shall give his personal attention to the duties of the School, and during his tenure of office he shall not accept or hold any benefice having the cure of souls, or any office or appointment which, in the opinion of the Governors, may interfere with the proper performance of his duties as Head Master.

Head Master not to have other employment.

36. No Head or Assistant Master of the School shall be a Governor.

Masters not to be Governors.

37. Neither the Head Master nor any Assistant Master shall receive or demand from any boy in the School, or from any person whomsoever on behalf of any such boy, any gratuity, fee, or payment except such as are prescribed or authorised by this Scheme.

Masters not to receive other than authorised fees.

38. Within the limits fixed by this Scheme the Governors shall prescribe the general subjects of instruction, the relative prominence and value to be assigned to each group of subjects, the arrangements respecting the school terms, vacations, and holidays, the payments of day scholars, and the number and payments of boarders. They shall take general supervision of the sanitary condition of the school buildings and arrangements. They shall determine what number of Assistant Masters shall be employed. They shall every

Jurisdiction of Governors over school arrangements.

year assign the amount which they think proper to be contributed out of the income of the School Foundation for the purpose of mnintairing Assistant Masters and providing and maintaining a proper school plant or apparatus and otherwise furthering the current objects and the efficiency of the School.

Governors to consider views and proposals of the Head Master.

39. Before making any regulations under the last foregoing clause, the Governors shall consult the Head Master, in such a manner as to give him full opportunity for the expression of his views. The Head Master may also from time to time submit proposals to the Governors for making or altering regulations concerning any matter within the province of the Governors. The Governors shall fully consider any such expression of views or proposals, and shall decide upon them.

Jurisdiction of Head Master over school arrangements.

40. Subject to the rules prescribed by or under the authority of this Scheme the Head Master shall have under his control the choice of books, the method of teaching, the arrangement of classes and school hours, and generally the whole internal organisation, management, and discipline of the School, including the power of expelling boys from the School or suspending them from attendance thereat for any adequate cause to be judged of by him : Provided that, upon expelling or suspending any boy he shall forthwith report the case to the Governors.

Appointment, dismissal, and payment of Assistant Masters.

41. The Head Master shall have the sole power of appointing and of dismissing all Assistant Masters, and shall determine, subject to the approval of the Governors, in what proportions the sum assigned by the Governors for the maintenance of Assistant Masters, or the other current objects of the School, shall be divided among the various persons and objects for which it is assigned in the aggregate. And

the Governors shall pay the same accordingly, either through the hands of the Head Master or directly, as they think best.

42. The Head Master shall receive a fixed yearly stipend of £150. He shall also be entitled to receive a further or capitation payment calculated on such a scale, uniform or graduated, as may be fixed from time to time by the Governors, at the rate of not less than £1 10s. a year for each boy attending the School. The amount of this further or capitation payment shall be ascertained and paid to the Head Master by the Governors, together with the proper proportion of his fixed stipend, at such convenient intervals or times as the Governors may think fit. So long as the said Rev. James Poulter holds the office of Head Master he shall receive out of the income of the Foundation such a further yearly payment, if any, as may be needed to make up his income under this clause to £220 yearly.

Income of Head Master.

43. The Governors may make such regulations and arrangements as they may think right for the reception of boarders either in the house of any Master, or in a hostel or hostels conducted under the management of the Governors, or, if they think fit, in both of those ways.

Boarders.

44. All boys, including boarders, except as herein-after provided, shall pay tuition fees, to be fixed from time to time by the Governors, at the rate of not less than £4 nor more than £8 a year for any boy. No difference in respect of these fees shall be made between any scholars on account of place of birth or residence or of their being or nor being boarders. The payments to be required from a boarder exclusive of the tuition fees shall not exceed the annual rate of £40 for each boy. No extra or additional payment of any kind shall be allowed without the sanction of the Governors

Payments for tuition and boarding.

and the written consent of the parent, or person occupying the place of parent, of the scholar concerned.

45. All payments for tuition fees shall be made in advance to the Head Master, or to such other person as the Governors shall from time to time determine, and shall be accounted for by the person receiving them to the Governors, and treated by them as part of the general income of the Foundation.

Ages for the School.

46. No boy shall be admitted into the School under the age of seven years. No boy shall remain in the School after the age of 17 years, or if he attains that age during a school term then after the end of such term, except with the permission of the Governors, which in special cases may be given upon the recommendation of the Head Master.

To whom School is open.

47. Subject to the provisions established by or under the authority of this Scheme, the School and all its advantages shall be open to all boys of good character and sufficient health who are residing with their parents, guardians or near relations within degrees to be determined by the Governors, or in some boarding house established under the sanction of the Governors. No boy not so residing shall be admitted to the School without the special permission of the Governors.

Applications for admission.

48. Applications for admission to the School shall be made to the Head Master, or to some other person appointed by the Governors, according to a form to be approved of by them, and delivered to all applicants.

Register of applications.

49. The Head Master or some other person appointed by the Governors shall keep a register of applications for admission show-

ing the date of every application and of the admission, withdrawal, or rejection of the applicant, and the cause of any rejection and the age of each applicant. Provided that every person requiring an application to be registered shall pay such fee as the Governors may fix, not exceeding 5s. for each applicant.

50. Every applicant for admission shall be examined by or under the direction of the Head Master, who shall appoint convenient times for that purpose and give reasonable notice to the parents or next friends of the boy to be so examined. No boy shall be admitted to the School except after undergoing such examination and being found fit for admission. Those who are so found fit shall, if there is room for them, be admitted in order according to the dates of their application. *Entrance examination.*

51. The examination for admission shall be graduated according to the age of the boy, and shall be regulated in other particulars from time to time by or under the direction of the Governors, but it shall never for any boy fall below the following standard, that is to say :—

> Reading.
> Writing from dictation.
> Sums in the first four simple rules of arithmetic, and the multi-
> plication table.

52. The parent or guardian of or person liable to maintain or having the actual custody of any day scholar may claim, by notice in writing addressed to the Head Master, the exemption of such scholar from attending prayer or religious worship, or from any lesson or series of lessons on a religious subject, and such scholar shall be exempted accordingly, and a scholar shall not by reason of any *Special exemptions from religious instruction and worship.*

exemption from attending prayer or religious worship or from any lesson or series of lessons on a religious subject, be deprived of any advantage or emolument in the School to which he would otherwise have been entitled. If the parent or guardian of, or person liable to maintain or having the actual custody of any scholar who is about to attend the School, and who but for this clause could only be admittted as a boarder, desires the exemption of such scholar from attending prayer or religious worship, or from any lesson or series of lessons on a religious subject, but the persons in charge of the boarding houses of the School are not willing to allow such exemption, then it shall be the duty of the Governors to make provisions for enabling the scholar to attend the School, and have such exemption, as a day scholar, without being deprived of any advantage or emolument to which he would otherwise have been entitled. If any teacher in the course of other lessons at which any scholar exempted under this clause is in accordance with the ordinary rules of the School present, shall teach systematically and persistently any particular religious doctrine, from the teaching of which any exemption has been claimed, as in this clause before provided, the Governors shall, on complaint made in writing to them by the parent, guardian, or person liable to maintain or having the actual custody of such scholar, hear the complainant, and inquire into the circumstances, and if the complaint is judged to be reasonable, make all proper provisions for remedying the matter complained of.

Instruction.

53. Subject to the foregoing provision, religious instruction shall be given in the School under such regulations as shall be made from time to time by the Governors. Such instruction shall be in accordance with the principles of the Christian Faith. No alteration in any such regulations shall take effect until the expiration of not less than one year after notice of the making of the alteration shall have

been given by the Governors in such manner as they shall think best calculated to bring the matter within the knowledge of persons interested in the School.

54. Instruction shall also be given in the School in the following subjects :—

> Reading, Writing, and Arithmetic.
> Geography and History.
> English Grammar, Composition, and Literature.
> Mathematics.
> Latin.
> At least one Foreign European Language.
> Natural Science.
> Drawing and Vocal Music.

Subject to the above provisions, the course of instruction shall proceed according to the classification and arrangements made by the Head Master.

55. There shall be once in every year an examination of the scholars by an Examiner or Examiners appointed for that purpose by the Governors, and paid by them, but otherwise unconnected with the School. The day of examination shall be fixed by the Governors after consulting with the Head Master. The Examiners shall report to the Governors on the proficiency of the scholars and on the position of the School, as regards instruction and discipline, as shown by the result of the examination. The Governors shall communicate the report to the Head Master. **Annual examination.**

56. The Head Master shall make a report in writing to the Governors annually at such time as they shall direct on the general **Head Master's annual report.**

R R

condition and progress of the School, and on any special occurrences during the year. He may also mention the names of any boys who, in his judgment, are worthy of reward or distinction, having regard both to proficiency and conduct.

Scholarships.

57. Scholarships shall be maintained in the School, in the form of exemptions, total or partial, from the payment of tuition fees representing an aggregate yearly value of not less than £40 for such periods, and granted, subject to the provisions of this Scheme, on such conditions as the Governors think fit. Boys to whom such exemptions shall be granted shall be called Foundation Scholars. The exemptions may be awarded in favour of candidates for admission to the School, on the result of the examination for admission, and in favour of boys already attending the School, upon the reports of the Examiners made on the result of the annual examination, but no exemption shall be granted to any such last-mentioned boy unless the Head Master shall report that he is deserving of it by reason of his character and good conduct. No more than 10 per cent. shall be wholly free, and no partial exemption shall be granted so as to extend the number of Foundation Scholars to more than 20 per cent. of the boys actually attending the School. In awarding such Scholarships preference shall be given to the extent of one half of the total number of Foundation Scholars to boys who shall during at least two years have attended some Public Elementary School within the Parliamentary borough of Wycombe.

Pupil Teachers.

58. In the case of any scholar of special promise and aptitude for teaching, the Governors may prolong the period during which he may remain at the School beyond the time otherwise prescribed; and otherwise make arrangements whereby he shall receive instruction in the art of teaching, and shall give such assistance in the

ordinary work of instruction in the School as may be deemed
desirable. They may award any reasonable sum by way of
remuneration for services so rendered to the School by any scholar
so retained as a teacher.

59. Subject to such reasonable regulations, not inconsistent with the **Exhibitions.**
provisions of this Scheme, as the Governors may from time to time
prescribe, the Governors shall establish Exhibitions tenable at any
place of higher education approved by them, and to be awarded
to boys who are being and have for not less than three years been
educated at the School. Two such Exhibitions, each of a yearly
value of not less than £30 tenable for four years, shall be established.
The yearly amount applicable under this clause may be reduced
or suspended, if necessary, owing to insufficiency of income.

60. Every Scholarship and Exhibition established under this **Conditions as to Scholarship and Exhibitions.**
Scheme shall be given as the reward of merit, and shall, except so
far as any restriction as aforesaid extends, be freely and openly com-
peted for, and shall be tenable only for the purposes of education.
If the holder shall, in the judgment of the Governors, be guilty of
serious misconduct or idleness, or fail to maintain a reasonable
standard of proficiency, or wilfully cease to pursue his education,
the Governors may at once determine the Scholarship or Exhibition,
and for this purpose, in the case of an Exhibition held away from
the School, may act on the report of the proper authorities of
the School or place of education at which the Exhibition is held,
or on such other evidence as the Governors think sufficient. For
the purposes of this clause the decision of the Governors shall
be final in every case.

THE ALMSPEOPLE.

Land and buildings, and number of Almspeople.
61. The said land and buildings applicable as aforesaid for the benefit of the Almspeople shall continue to be applied for this purpose. The number of Almspeople shall henceforth be fourteen, and they shall, as vacancies in this number occur, be appointed by the Governors as herein-after provided.

Qualification of Almspeople.
62. The Almspeople shall be appointed from amongst those duly qualified, as follows, that is to say :—the candidates for admission shall be of the age of fifty years and upwards, and shall have resided in the borough of Chipping Wycombe for the space of five years next preceding the time of their election, and shall be such as by some unforeseen misfortune not happening by their own default shall have become reduced in circumstances and be in greatest want, and shall not have been in the receipt of parochial relief within a period of one year next preceding the time of their election.

Stipends of Almspeople.
63. The stipends for the Almspeople shall be as follows; that is to say, for four of them 8s. each, weekly, and for the others 4s. each, weekly. The four almspeople now in receipt of 8s. each, weekly, shall be the first four entitled, subject as herein-after provided, to the receipt of the sum of 8s. weekly.

Appointment of Almspeople.
64. The Almspeople shall be appointed by the Governors from amongst proper objects on the occasion of every vacancy, but no election shall take place until the expiration of one month after the notice of the vacancy signed by the clerk or other proper officer shall have been fixed on the door of the vacant Almshouse and on the Town Hall. The Governors shall not in rotation elect a person to fill the vacancy, but shall elect only such persons as shall, after a careful con-

sideration of the claims of the several candidates, appear best to answer the qualifications aforesaid and to be most deserving.

65. The Governors shall provide a minute book for the Almshouses in which the clerk or other proper officer shall enter the name and age of every person elected thereto, together with the date of the admission and the state of health, station, and condition in life of every such person previous to the election, and the date and cause of death or removal. The particulars required by the next following clause to be given shall also be entered in such minute book.

Minute book for Alms-people.

66. All applications for admission to the Almshouses shall be made in writing through the clerk or other proper officer, and shall be taken into consideration by the Governors at their next meeting. Such applications shall contain the name, age, and places of residence during the preceding five years of the applicant, together with his or her state or condition in life.

Application for admission.

67. None of the Almspeople shall at any time absent themselves from the Almshouses for a period exceeding twenty-four hours, without the special consent in writing of one of the Governors or of the clerk or other proper officer, and then only for such time as shall be then authorised.

Almspeople not to absent themselves.

68. If at any time it shall appear that any of the Almspeople shall be given to insobriety or immoral or unbecoming conduct, the Governors, on proof thereof to their satisfaction, may, if they shall think fit, displace such person so misbehaving, and proceed to place another or others in his or her place. The provisions of this clause shall be made known to every person at the time of his or her entering the Almshouses.

Power to remove inmates.

Almshouses
not to be
underlet.

69. None of the Almspeople shall be permitted to underlet the Almshouse premises allotted to him or her, or to suffer any stranger to occupy the same or any part thereof.

APPLICATION OF INCOME.

Repairs and
improvements
fund.

70. As soon as the state of the School funds will admit, the Governors shall transfer the sum of £1,333 6s. 8d. Government stock into the name of the Official Trustees of Charitable Funds, and shall place the same in their books to a separate account, entitled " Repairs and Improvements Fund." The income of such Fund shall be paid to the Governors, and applied by them in ordinary repairs or improvements of property used for the purposes of the School and of the Almspeople, and if not wanted for that purpose shall be accumulated by them for the like purpose in any future year or years. Until the Repairs and Improvements Fund is provided, the Governors shall treat the sum of £40 yearly as applicable to the same purposes as the income of the Repairs and Improvements Fund, as to £30 thereof for the purposes of the School, and as to the remaining £10 for the purposes of the buildings occupied for the benefit of the Almspeople.

Other ex-
penses.

71. After defraying the expenses of management, and of any ordinary repairs or improvements which the income of the Repairs and Improvements Fund or the yearly sum payable in lieu thereof may be insufficient to answer, and providing for the Alms branch as aforesaid, the Governors shall employ the income of the Foundation in paying the Head Master, and in making the several payments herein-before directed or authorised for the purposes of the School.

Pensions.

72. The Governors may, if they think fit and the income at their disposal suffice for the purpose, agree with the Head Master for the formation of a fund in the nature of a Pension or Superannuation

Fund, the main principles of such agreement being that the Head Master and the Governors respectively shall contribute annually for a period of 20 years such sums as may be fixed on; that these contributions shall accumulate at compound interest; that in case the Head Master serves his office for 20 years he shall on his retirement be entitled to the whole accumulated fund; that in case he retires earlier on account of permanent disability from illness he shall also be entitled to the whole of the same fund; that in all other cases he shall, on his ceasing to be Master, be entitled to the amount produced by his own contributions. If any question shall arise upon the construction or working of this provision, the same shall be referred by the Governors to the Charity Commissioners, whose decision thereon shall be final and conclusive.

73. The residue of income of the Foundation, if any, may be employed in improving the accommodation or convenience of the school buildings, or premises, or generally in extending or otherwise promoting the objects and efficiency of the School. Whatever shall not be so employed shall, on passing the yearly accounts be treated as Unapplied Surplus, and shall be deposited in a bank for the account of the Governors, to the intent that the same, so soon as it shall amount to a suitable sum, shall be invested in the name of the Official Trustees of Charitable Funds in trust for the Foundation in augmentation of its general endowment. *Residue.* *Unapplied surplus.*

GENERAL.

74. The said Rye Mead, subject to any existing rights of the inhabitants of the borough of Chipping Wycombe in or over the same, may be retained by the Governors for the purpose of a recreation ground for the scholars and Almspeople of the Foundation and of such inha- *Maintenance of Rye Mead.*

bitants. For the expenses of management and of any improvements of the said Rye Mead, the Governors may apply all fees or payments received from such inhabitants in respect of the exercise of their rights in or over the same, and may also apply any further yearly sum not being in any year more than £12 14s.

Payment in respect of Littleboy's Charity.
75. If and so soon as the Foundation, known as Littleboy's Charity, at Wycombe aforesaid, becomes subject to the provisions of this Scheme, the Governors shall in respect thereof apply the sum of £8 10s. yearly in the distribution of bread according to the directions of the will of William Littleboy the Founder of that Charity.

Further endowments.
76. The Governors may receive any additional donations or endowments for the general purposes of the Foundation. They may also receive donations or endowments for any special objects connected with the School, which shall not be inconsistent with or calculated to impede the due working of the provisions of this Scheme. Any question arising upon this last point shall be referred to the Charity Commissioners for decision.

General power of Governors to make regulations.
77. Within the limits prescribed by this Scheme the Governors shall have full power from time to time to make regulations for the conduct of their business and for the management of the Foundation, and such regulations shall be binding on all persons affected thereby.

Question of proceedings under Scheme.
78. Any question affecting the regularity or the validity of any proceeding under this Scheme, shall be determined conclusively by the Charity Commissioners upon such application made to them for the purpose as they think sufficient.

Construction of Scheme.
79. If any doubt or question arises among the Governors as to the proper construction or application of any of the provisions of this

Scheme, the Governors shall apply to the Charity Commissioners for their opinion and advice thereon, which opinion and advice when given shall be binding on the Governors and all persons claiming under the Trust who shall be affected by the question so decided.

80. From the date of this Scheme all jurisdiction of the Ordinary relating to or arising from the licensing of any Master in the School shall be abolished.

Jurisdiction of Ordinary abolished.

81. From the date of this Scheme all rights and powers reserved to, belonging to, claimed by, or capable of being exercised by, Her Majesty, as Visitor of this Foundation, and vested in Her on the 2nd day of August, 1869, shall be exercised only through and by the Charity Commissioners for England and Wales.

Jurisdiction of Crown as Visitor.

82. The Charity Commissioners may from time to time, in the exercise of their ordinary jurisdiction, frame Schemes for the alteration of any portions of this Scheme, provided that such Schemes be not inconsistent with anything contained in the Endowed Schools Acts, 1869, 1873, and 1874.

Charity Commissioners to make new Schemes.

83. From and after the date of this Scheme the Foundation shall for every purpose, except as herein provided, be administered and governed wholly and exclusively in accordance with the provisions of this Scheme, notwithstanding any former or other Scheme, Act of Parliament, Charter, or Letters Patent, statute, or instrument relating to the subject matter of this Scheme.

Foundation to be governed exclusively by this Scheme.

84. The Governors shall cause this Scheme to be printed and a copy to be given to every Governor, Master, and Assistant Master

Scheme to be printed and sold.

S S

upon their respective appointments, and copies may be sold at a reasonable price to all persons applying for the same.

Date of
Scheme.

85. The date of this Scheme shall be the day on which Her Majesty by Order in Council declares Her approbation of it.

SCHEME for the Administration of the Foundation known as Bowden's Gift, in the Borough of Wycombe, originally established by the will of Mary Bowden, dated on or about the 30th day of October, 1790.

1. From and after the date of this Scheme the above-mentioned Foundation and its endowment shall be part of the Foundation established by a Scheme made under the Endowed Schools Acts, 1869, 1873, and 1874, under the name of the Wycombe Grammar School and Almshouse Foundation, and shall be administered according to the provisions of the said other Scheme.

Union with Wycombe Grammar School.

2. From and after the date of this Scheme all lands and hereditaments, not being copyhold, belonging to this Foundation, and all terms, estates, and interests therein, shall vest in the Official Trustee of Charity Lands and his successors in trust for the said Wycombe Grammar School and Almshouse Foundation; and all copyhold hereditaments belonging to this Foundation, and all terms, estates, and interests therein, shall be vested in like manner upon such terms and conditions as shall be agreed upon between the Governors and the lord of the manor; and all stock in the public funds and other

Vesting property.

securities belonging to this Foundation shall be transferred to the Official Trustees of Charitable Funds, in trust for the said Wycombe Grammar School and Almshouse Foundation.

Charity Commissioners may make new Scheme.

3. The Charity Commissioners may from time to time in the exercise of their ordinary jurisdiction frame Schemes for the alteration of any portions of this Scheme, provided that such Schemes be not inconsistent with anything contained in the Endowed Schools Acts, 1869, 1873, and 1874.

Date of Scheme.

4. The date of this Scheme shall be the day on which, under the provisions of the said other Scheme, the administration of the said Wycombe Grammar School and Almshouse Foundation passes to the Governors constituted under that Scheme.

Charity Commission,

31 July 1877.

AT a Meeting of the Board held this day, at which there were present five Commissioners, of whom one was the Chief Commissioner, this Scheme was approved and directed to be submitted to the Committee of Council on Education.

(Signed)   D. C. RICHMOND,

Secretary.

SCHEME for applying for the advancement of Education the Endowment of the Foundation known as Littleboy's Charity, in the Borough of Wycombe, in the County of Buckingham, originally established by or under the will of William Littleboy in or before the year 1633, subject nevertheless as in this Scheme is referred to, and for the administration of the same Foundation and its endowment.

1. It is hereby declared, with the consent of the Governing Body, that it is desirable to apply for the advancement of education the endowment of the above-mentioned Foundation, subject as hereinafter referred to. Declaration.

2. From and after the date of this Scheme this Foundation and its endowment shall be part of the Foundation established by a Scheme made under the Endowed Schools Acts, 1869, 1873, and 1874, under the name of the Wycombe Grammar School and Almshouse Foundation, and shall be administered according to the provisions of the said other Scheme. Union with Wycombe Grammar School.

3. From and after the date of this Scheme all lands and hereditaments, not being copyhold, belonging to this Foundation, and all Vesting property.

terms, estates, and interests therein, shall vest in the Official Trustee of Charity Lands and his successors in trust for the said Wycombe Grammar School and Almshouse Foundation, and all copyhold hereditaments belonging to this Foundation, and all terms, estate, and interests therein, shall be vested in like manner upon such terms and conditions as shall be agreed upon between the lord of the manor; and all stock in the public funds and other securities belonging to this Foundation shall be transferred to the Official Trustees of Charitable Funds, in trust to the said Wycombe Grammar School and Almshouse Foundation.

Payment in respect of Littleboy's Charity.

4. It is intended that in respect of this Foundation the sum of £8 10s. yearly shall, subject to any alteration of this Scheme or of the said other Scheme, be applied according to the provisions expressed in the said other Scheme in respect of this Foundation.

Charity Commissioners to make new Schemes.

5. The Charity Commissioners may from time to time in the exercise of their ordinary jurisdiction frame Schemes for the alteration of any portions of this Scheme, provided that such Schemes be not inconsistent with anything contained in the Endowed Schools Acts, 1869, 1873, 1874.

Date of Scheme.

6. The date of this Scheme shall be the day on which, under the provisions of the said other Scheme, the administration of the said Wycombe Grammar School and Almshouse Foundation passes to the Governors constituted under that Scheme.

CHARITY COMMISSION.

In the Matter of the Foundations respectively known as PEL-HAM'S CHARITY, CONWAY'S CHARITY, DORMER'S CHARITY, CHURCH'S CHARITY, WAINWRIGHT'S CHARITY, THE SAW PIT HOUSE CHARITY, FREER'S GRANT, and THE KING'S HILL FARM CHARITY, in the Borough of WYCOMBE, in the County of BUCKINGHAM ; and

In the Matter of the Endowed Schools Acts, 1869, 1873, and 1874.

SCHEME FOR APPLYING FOR THE ADVANCEMENT OF EDUCATION THE ENDOWMENTS OF THE ABOVE-MENTIONED FOUNDATIONS.

1. It is hereby declared, with the consent of the Governing Body, that it is desirable to apply for the advancement of education the Endowments of these Foundations so far as not already so applicable.

Advanceme of educatio

2. From and after the date of this Scheme, these Foundations and their Endowments shall be part of the Foundation regulated by a Scheme made under the Endowed Schools Acts, 1869, 1873, and

Union with another Foundation

1874, under the name of the Wycombe Grammar School and Almshouse Foundation, and shall be administered according to the provisions of the said other Scheme.

Vesting property.

3. From and after the date of this Scheme, all lands and hereditaments, not being copyhold, belonging to these Foundations, and all terms, estates, and interests therein, shall vest in the Official Trustee of Charity Lands and his successors in trust for the said Wycombe Grammar School and Almshouse Foundation; and all copyhold hereditaments belonging to these Foundations, and all terms, estates, and interests therein, shall be vested in like manner upon such terms and conditions as shall be agreed upon between the lord of the manor; and all stock in the public funds and other securities belonging to these Foundations shall be transferred to and vest in the Official Trustees of Charitable Funds in trust for the said Wycombe Grammar School and Almshouse Foundation.

Charity Commissioners to make new Scheme.

4. The Charity Commissioners may from time to time in the exercise of their ordinary jurisdiction frame Schemes for the alteration of any portions of this Scheme, provided that such Schemes be not inconsistent with anything contained in the Endowed Schools Acts, 1869, 1873, and 1874.

Date of Scheme.

5. The date of this Scheme shall be the day on which, under the provisions of the said other Scheme, the administration of the said Wycombe Grammar School and Almshouse Foundation passes to the Governors constituted under that Scheme.

WYCOMBE GRAMMAR SCHOOL AND ALMSHOUSE FOUNDATION.

LIST OF GOVERNORS, 1878.

Coöptative Governors mentioned in the Scheme.

THE REV. ROBERT CHILTON.
JAMES THURLOW.
RANDOLPH HENRY CREWE.
CHARLES STRANGE.
THOMAS JOHN REYNOLDS.
HERBERT SIMMONDS, AND
WILLIAM ROSE.

Representative Governors.

WILLIAM PHILLIPS and GEORGE WHEELER	Appointed by the Town Council of the Borough of Chepping Wycombe.
GEORGE LONG and ALFRED STONE	Appointed by the Local Board for the Parish of Chepping Wycombe.
THOMAS MARSHALL	Appointed by the School Board for the Borough of Chepping Wycombe.
DANIEL CLARKE	Appointed by the School Board for the Parish of Chepping Wycombe.
The Rev. GEORGE PHILLIMORE Sir PHILIP ROSE, Bart.	Appointed by the Justices of the Peace of the County of Buckingham, acting for the Petty Sessional Division in which the Parish of Chepping Wycombe is situate.
ALFRED GILBEY	Appointed by the Justices of the Peace for the Borough of Chepping Wycombe.

T T

Ingram Content Group UK Ltd.
Milton Keynes UK
UKHW050739190623
423681UK00014B/564